Rochester and the pursuit of pleasure

Manchester University Press

John Wilmot, 2nd Earl of Rochester by Sir Peter Lely. Collection of Charles Malet, Somerset County Council, Dillington House.

Rochester and the pursuit of pleasure

Larry Carver

MANCHESTER UNIVERSITY PRESS

Copyright © Larry Carver 2024

The right of Larry Carver to be identified as the author of this work has been asserted in accordance with the Copyright, Designs and Patents Act 1988.

Published by Manchester University Press
Oxford Road, Manchester, M13 9PL

www.manchesteruniversitypress.co.uk

British Library Cataloguing-in-Publication Data
A catalogue record for this book is available from the British Library

ISBN 978 1 5261 7367 6 hardback
ISBN 978 1 5261 9547 0 paperback

First published 2024
Paperback published 2026

The publisher has no responsibility for the persistence or accuracy of URLs for any external or third-party internet websites referred to in this book, and does not guarantee that any content on such websites is, or will remain, accurate or appropriate.

EU authorised representative for GPSR:
Easy Access System Europe – Mustamäe tee 50, 10621 Tallinn, Estonia
gpsr.requests@easproject.com

Typeset
by Cheshire Typesetting Ltd, Cuddington, Cheshire

For Jill, her love, courage, and creativity

Contents

List of illustrations	*page* viii
Acknowledgements	ix
List of abbreviations	x
Introduction	1
1 Interpreting Rochester	7
2 '*A Ramble in St.* James's Park': The fall of the well-bred man	49
3 Development of the satirist	76
4 'Cripples in their Art': The major satires	107
5 'Wise about my owne follyes': *Lucina's Rape Or The Tragedy of Vallentinian*	157
6 'The principal Disputant against God and Piety'	184
Appendix: Authorship of *Sodom*	235
Bibliography	245
Index	256

Illustrations

Frontispiece:	John Wilmot, 2nd Earl of Rochester by Sir Peter Lely. Collection of Charles Malet, Somerset County Council, Dillington House.	*page* ii
2.1	John Wilmot, 2nd Earl of Rochester after Sir Peter Lely. National Trust Images/National Portrait Gallery London.	50
4.1	John Wilmot, 2nd Earl of Rochester by unknown artist. National Portrait Gallery London.	108
6.1	John Wilmot, 2nd Earl of Rochester, artist unknown. Collection of the Earl Bathurst, Cirencester Park.	185

Acknowledgements

Many friends and colleagues have given me help with research, advice, and support in the writing of this book. I am particularly indebted to Professor James William Johnson and Dr Nicholas Fisher. My intention in going to graduate school was to focus on American literature, to write a dissertation on the work of William Faulkner. Bill Johnson, his electrifying graduate seminars and cherished mentorship, changed all that. It was Bill who introduced me to the literature of English Restoration and the eighteenth century, and during those graduate school years, we began a friendship and conversation about Rochester that would last until Bill's death on 9 May 2022, a conversation that in some mystical way continues. Around 2010, Nick Fisher read several of my articles on Rochester and asked if there was more. I sent him a manuscript of the book and he encouraged me, while providing abundant guidance, to dust it off and get back to writing. In his knowledge of and love for all things Rochester Nick is without peer, his energy and good humour infectious. I cannot thank Nick and his wife, Pam, enough for all that they have done for me. Heartfelt thanks goes as well to two leading scholars of the English Restoration, Paul Hammond and Warren Chernaik. Both commented extensively on the manuscript, making it much better. And I am grateful for and owe ever so much to my many colleagues at the University of Texas at Austin and want to thank professors Janine Barchas, Lance Bertelsen, Douglas Bruster, John Farrell, James Garrison, the late Wayne Lesser, the late William Livingston, John Rumrich, and particularly Warwick Wadlington, for introducing me to the work of Kenneth Burke. I love them all. I would be remiss in not thanking Virginia Chilton, the personal assistant to the Countess Bathurst, for photographing and securing permission to use a photograph of the portrait of the Earl of Rochester in the collection of the Earl Bathurst to illustrate this book. Last, but certainly not least, it has been a privilege and joy to work with those at Manchester University Press, my gratitude and special thanks to Matthew Frost, Paul Clarke, Humairaa Dudhwala, and Kate Hawkins.

Abbreviations

Burnet	Gilbert Burnet, *Some Passages of the Life and Death of Rochester*. In *Rochester: The Critical Heritage*, ed. David Farley-Hills (New York: Barnes & Noble, 1972).
Colie	Rosalie L. Colie, *Paradoxia Epidemica: The Renaissance Tradition of Paradox* (Hamden, CT: Archon Books, 1976).
Dryden	John Dryden, *The Works of John Dryden*, ed. H.T. Swedenberg, Jr et al. (Berkeley: University of California Press, 1956–1984).
ECS	*Eighteenth-Century Studies*
ELH	*English Literary History*
Greer	Germaine Greer, *John Wilmot, Earl of Rochester* (Devon: Northcote House Publishers, 2000).
Griffin	Dustin H. Griffin, *Satires Against Man: The Poems of Rochester* (Berkeley: University of California Press, 1973).
HLQ	*Huntington Library Quarterly*
Johnson, *Dictionary*	Samuel Johnson, *A Dictionary of the English Language* (London: W. Strahan, 1755; facsimile edition, New York: Arno Press, 1979).
Johnson	James William Johnson, *A Very Profane Wit: The Life of John Wilmot, Earl of Rochester* (Rochester, NY: University of Rochester Press, 2004).
N&Q	*Notes and Queries*
Love	Harold Love, ed. *The Complete Works of John Wilmot Earl of Rochester* (Oxford: Oxford University Press, 1999).
OED	*Oxford English Dictionary*
Parsons	Robert Parsons, *A Sermon Preached At the Funeral of the Rt Honorable John Earl of Rochester, Who died at Woodstock-Park, July 26. 1680, and was buried at Spilsbury in Oxford-shire, Aug. 9* (Oxford: Printed at the Theater for *Richard Davis* and *Tho: Bowman*. 1680).
PBSA	*The Papers of the Bibliographical Society of America*

Pepys	Samuel Pepys, *The Diary of Samuel Pepys*, ed. Robert Latham and William Matthews (Berkeley: University of California Press, 1979).
Pinto, *Enthusiast*	Vivian de Sola Pinto, *Enthusiast in Wit* (Lincoln, NE: University of Nebraska Press, 1962).
Pinto, *Poems*	Vivian de Sola Pinto ed. *Poems by John Wilmot Earl of Rochester* (London: Routledge & Kegan Paul, 1953).
PLL	*Papers on Language and Literature*
POAS	George deF. Lord, ed. *Poems on Affairs of State: Augustan Satirical Verse, 1660–1714* (New Haven, CT: Yale University Press, 1963, vol. 1).
Thormählen	Marianne Thormählen, *Rochester: The Poems in Context* (Cambridge: Cambridge University Press, 1993).
Tilmouth	Christopher Tilmouth, *Passion's Triumph Over Reason: A History of the Moral Imagination From Spenser to Rochester* (Oxford: Oxford University Press, 2007; paperback 2010).
Treglown	Jeremy Treglown, ed. *The Letters of John Wilmot Earl of Rochester* (Chicago: University of Chicago Press, 1980).
Vieth, *Attribution*	David M. Vieth, *Attribution in Restoration Poetry: A Study of Rochester's 'Poems' of 1680* (Yale Studies in English 153. New Haven, CT: Yale University Press, 1963).
Vieth, *Poems*	David M. Vieth, ed. *The Complete Poems of John Wilmot, Earl of Rochester* (New Haven, CT: Yale University Press, 1968).
Walker	Keith Walker, ed. *The Complete Poems of John Wilmot Earl of Rochester* (Oxford: Basil Blackwell, 1984).
Walker and Fisher	Keith Walker and Nicholas Fisher, eds *John Wilmot, Earl of Rochester: The Poems and Lucina's Rape* (Oxford: Wiley-Blackwell, 2010).

Introduction

John Evelyn and Francis Fane sketched him in miniature, the one finding him 'a very profane Wit'[1] and the other, 'an Enthusiast in Wit'.[2] Nathaniel Lee cast him as Count Rosidore, 'the Life, the Soul of Pleasure',[3] while Aphra Behn and John Oldham, working in a more emblematic mode, mourned him as 'Strephon'[4] and 'Bion'.[5] These and a host of other verbal portraits of John Wilmot, 2nd Earl of Rochester, have come down to us but with what truth to likeness it is not easy to tell. For Rochester was no passive sitter. He took an active part in shaping the ways in which he would be portrayed: playing the footman to spy on Miss Price, donning a tinker's outfit and tools to trick the good people of Burford, and disguising himself as the quack, Alexander Bendo, to dispense medical lore and seduce citizens' wives. Diarists, playwrights, biographers, and the poet himself in turn captured these poses and roles, a process that culminated in such poems as 'To the Postboy', in George Etherege's play, *The Man of Mode*, in which Rochester became Dorimant and Dorimant became him, and in Gilbert Burnet's twilight portrait of the death of a prodigal son. Burnet in sketching Rochester during his last days drew on metaphors from the sister art of painting, confessing that he had seen Rochester 'only in one light' and therefore could not 'give his picture with that life and advantage that others may who knew him when his parts were more bright and lively'.[6]

We will never know how often and to whom Rochester sat to have his portrait done. Nor will we ever know how often a given portrait was copied or by whom. William Wimsatt, in his magisterial account of the portraits of Pope, points to various commonplaces governing the practice of portraiture in Pope's – and Rochester's – time, two of them being 'the extensive multiplication of portrait replicas, even by the original artists or in their studios, and of engravings, especially mezzotints, after oil portraits ... [and] the frequency, nevertheless, with which during a few generations both artists' and subjects' names came to be detached from portraits and wrong names substituted'.[7] Further blurring our vision into the past is that contemporary descriptions of what Rochester looked like are few. According to Burnet, when Rochester 'came from his Travels in the 18th Year of his Age, and appeared at Court ... He was a Graceful and well-shaped Person, tall, and well made, if not a little too slender' (Burnet, p. 49). Other contemporary descriptions are equally vague,[8] and therefore it is difficult to say what likeness to truth portraits of Rochester bear or whether the sitter is indeed John Wilmot.

The portrait that serves as the frontispiece to this book almost surely captures Burnet's 'more bright and lively' Rochester. Its provenance is well documented, the portrait being from the collection of Charles Malet.[9] Still, questions abound. Long thought to be the work of Sir Peter Lely, no less an authority than Malcolm Rogers attributes it to Godfrey Kneller. In its grand manner, this portrait fits into the category of what Andrew Wilton has identified as 'The Swagger Portrait', displaying as it does 'a degree of self-consciousness' on the part of sitter and artist, 'which causes the portrait to transcend the private statement (in which the sitter communes with a single viewer), and addresses itself to the public at large'.[10] Here the mimetic and emblematic come together, the latter serving to intensify or perhaps undermine the former. While almost certainly the Earl of Rochester in a plausibly realistic setting, the portrait so brims with youth and power, sensuality and sexuality, that it becomes a display, a performance, of something beyond the historical figure. For Graham Greene this is Wilmot as Dorimant, the theatrical setting supporting such a reading.[11] For students to whom I have shown the portrait, the sitter comes across as a seventeenth-century rock star, the black wig, gorgeous russet-red robe, the silk, the sensuous extended left hand, knowing smile, self-conscious demeanour and stance all indicative of qualities that transcend the person. If this emblematic reading has any truth, the painting intentionally makes one question the sitter (Who is this man? Who sits for such a portrait? And why?); the artist (Is he depicting a person, providing entertainment, fabricating a cultural icon?); and the audience (Who are we to be in attendance at the morning levee of this powerful, sexual nobleman?).

I once thought there might be as many as eight authentic portraits in oil of Rochester, but that number may be as few as five.[12] A painting supposedly of Rochester in Barbados attributed to Lely turns out neither to be of Rochester nor by Lely.[13] It is doubtful that the three-quarter-length portrait in Lord Sackville's private collection at Knole long thought to be Rochester depicts John Wilmot. And the portrait in the collection of the Harry Ransom Humanities Research Center at The University of Texas at Austin attributed to Mary Beale, which I once believed to be Rochester by Beale, is probably by William Wissing, the sitter probably not Rochester.[14] All agree that the portrait of the man crowning a monkey with the bays is Rochester but the artist remains elusive. Jacob Huysmans? Godfrey Kneller? We do not know.

As with the portraits so with John Wilmot's poetry, dramatic works, and letters. There is so much we do not know. Half of Rochester's poems and letters remain undated; the authorship of key works – *Timon*, 'TO *The Honourable***In the Pall-Mall*' ('*Fling this* useless *Book away*'), '*Signior Dildo*', and the notorious play, *Sodom* – is in dispute. The historical evidence, such as it is, must be disentangled from the biased accounts, past and present, of biographers and critics who have mistaken the legend for the life. In the poems, moreover, Rochester assumes a multiplicity of identities, and the real-life Rochester often donned disguises 'so that his nearest Friends could not have known him' (Burnet, p. 54). As Harold Love points out, 'Rochester studies is not and has never been a field of safety-first scholarship.'[15]

That said, thanks to David Vieth's *Attribution in Restoration Poetry: A Study of Rochester's 'Poems' of 1680* (1963) and his edition of Rochester's poetry (1968), Keith Walker's old-spelling edition of the poems (1984),[16] Harold Love's edition of Rochester's *Works* (1999), James William Johnson's biography, *A Profane Wit: The Life of John Wilmot Earl of Rochester* (2004), the three full-length studies of Rochester's work by Dustin Griffin (1973), David Farley-Hills (1978), Marianne Thormählen (1993),[17] and to the work of many gifted scholars to which this book is indebted, we know a good deal more than we did sixty years ago about John Wilmot, his life and work. In an attempt to contribute to the ongoing conversation that we who care about Rochester have been having since the pioneering work of Charles Whibley, John Hayward, Johannes Prinz, and Vivian de Sola Pinto,[18] this book makes three claims. The first is that Rochester's work, despite well-grounded arguments to the contrary, should be read in a biographical context, the works in many cases crafted to be read that way. Interpretations and editions of Rochester's work, sometimes tacitly, sometimes not, are inextricably tied to assumptions about the historical John Wilmot. This book is no exception; it simply attempts to realize the implications more fully than have past studies, trying to avoid the many pitfalls of biographical criticism while suspecting, and in many cases knowing, that Rochester in his work drew upon his experience, his emotional, religious, and intellectual life. It assumes that Rochester wrote about what engrossed him, that his writings are in Kenneth Burke's words, 'answers to questions posed by the situations in which they arose'.[19]

The second claim is that reading the works as doing something for the poet and for his audience reveals that Rochester's work clusters about a central theme, the pursuit of pleasure.[20] This phrase is shorthand for a complex process in which so many of Rochester's mid-seventeenth-century contemporaries were engaged. No longer sure under the old dispensation of their duties – familial, political, religious, or artistic – they sought new grounds for their motivations. For Rochester and perhaps for a number of his libertine companions this pursuit of pleasure was motivated by a courtship of purity that probably grew out of a religious neurosis, the book's third claim being that Rochester's work everywhere reflects his Christian and God-fearing upbringing and provides evidence of an excessive preoccupation with and, at the end of his life, acceptance of Christianity. As the various speakers, and the man himself, pursue pleasure by courting king, wife, mistresses, and the craft of writing, they also often in perverse, even criminal, ways court God.

Chapter 1 explores some of the long-standing problems of biographical criticism. It focuses on two poems – 'A very heroical epistle in answer to Ephelia' and 'An Epistolary Essay, from M.G. to O.B. upon their mutuall Poems' – and argues that they reveal an awareness of the epistemological problem modern critics face when taking a biographical approach. As we come to understand how the poems play with and make thematic the paradox of self-reference, we are better able to understand our own approach to Rochester and his work. Chapter 2 outlines briefly what I see as the major orientations in Rochester's life and goes on to provide a biographical reading of an early but central work in the Rochester canon, 'A Ramble in St. James's Park'. Chapter 3, perhaps the most controversial in the book, attempts to show that reading *Sodom* in the context of Rochester's apprentice work provides corroborative evidence that Rochester may have had a hand in writing this notorious farce. I am not arguing that *Sodom* should be attributed to John Wilmot, rather that it is has been, is, and probably will be for some time to come *associated* with Rochester because of how closely *Sodom* fits in – artistically, thematically, ideologically – with Rochester's early work.

Chapter 4 goes on to examine the half dozen poems written by Rochester that will continue to be read so long as the English language endures. The corrosive ironies of these major poems in which the speakers attempt to unite grace with nature are, or so I argue, addressed by Rochester in his adaptation of John Fletcher's *Valentinian*, the subject of Chapter 5. Chapter 6, the last chapter and the one most heterodox in content and method, explores the rhetoric of the letters, the conversations with Burnet, and the songs. In this, what I call after Kenneth Burke the rhetoric of courtship, we can see the unity of Rochester's work as the courtier and his various *personae* try to persuade his audiences, secular and divine, of his worth.

Notes

1 John Evelyn, *The Diary of John Evelyn*, ed. E.S. de Beer (London: Oxford University Press, 1959), p. 547.
2 'Dedication' to *Love in the Dark* (London: 1675), Sig. A 2^r.
3 *The Princess of Cleves*, I. ii., in *Rochester: The Critical Heritage*, ed. David Farley-Hills (New York: Barnes & Noble, 1972), p. 28.
4 'On the Death of the late Earl of Rochester', in *Rochester: The Critical Heritage*, ed. David Farley-Hills (New York: Barnes & Noble, 1972), pp. 101–4.
5 *Bion, A Pastoral, in Imitation of the Greek of Moschus, Bewailing the Death of the Earl of Rochester*, in *Rochester: The Critical Heritage*, ed. David Farley-Hills (New York: Barnes & Noble, 1972), pp. 94–101.
6 Gilbert Burnet, *Some Passages of the Life and Death of John Earl of Rochester*, in *Rochester: The Critical Heritage*, ed. David Farley-Hills (New York: Barnes & Noble, 1972), p. 47. Hereafter cited in the text as Burnet.
7 William Wimsatt, *The Portraits of Alexander Pope* (New Haven, CT: Yale University Press, 1965), p. xv.
8 Vague, few, and from unreliable sources. Graham Greene quotes St Evremond: '"His person was graceful tho' tall and slender, his mien and shape have something extremely engaging"' (*Lord Rochester's Monkey being the Life of John Wilmot, Second Earl of Rochester* (New York: Viking Press, 1974), p. 36). James William Johnson writes that 'His complexion was fair, and of a rosy hue' and cites his source as Aubrey's *Brief Lives*, a citation I have been unable to confirm (*A Profane Wit: The Life of John Wilmot Earl of Rochester* (Rochester, NY: University of Rochester Press, 1974), p. 62).
9 Collection of Charles Malet, Somerset County Council, Dillington House.
10 Andrew Wilton, *The Swagger Portrait: Grand Manner Portraiture-Painting in Stuart and Georgian England* (Oxford: Clarendon Press, 1990), p. 130.
11 Greene, *Lord Rochester's Monkey*, p. 182.
12 It is commonly agreed that these five portraits are of John Wilmot: (1) Three-quarter-length crimson robe over a cuirass, right hand on hip, left arm resting on a table, the index finger extended down (49 × 37"). Artist: Peter Lely, c.1666–67. Victoria and Albert Museum, London. After Peter Lely copies of this portrait are in the collections at Lydiard House, Lydiard Tregoze, Swindon and Attingham Park, Shropshire, and in the collection of the Earl of Lisburne, this latter portrait being remarkable in that upon the table at Rochester's elbow rests a crown. (2) Three-quarter length in armour, holding a truncheon in right arm (49 × 39"). Artist: William Wissing. From the Collection of Viscount Hinchingbrooke; bought by Alvin C. Detweiler in 1957; current location unknown. (3) Three-quarter length in a russet-red robe (50 × 40"). Artist: thought to be by Peter Lely. Malcolm Rogers attributes it to Godfrey Kneller. Collection of Charles Malet, Somerset County Council, Dillington House. (4) Full length in a red cloak (49 × 39½"). Artist unknown. Collection of the Earl Bathurst, Cirencester Park. (5) Rochester crowning a monkey with the laurels (49⅝ × 40⅜"). Artist unknown. Once thought to be by Jacob Huysmans

or Godfrey Kneller. Original from the Collection of the Earl Warwick, sold by Sotheby's to a private collector, 9 July 2014; copy in the National Portrait Gallery.

13 A finding confirmed by Jeremy Treglown. See *The Letters of John Wilmot Earl of Rochester*, ed. Jeremy Treglown (Chicago: University of Chicago Press, 1980), p. xi.

14 'A Painter, Man of Letters, Novelist, and a Poet: Mary Beale, J. Frank Dobie, and Graham Greene Encounter the Earl of Rochester', *The Library Chronicle of The University of Texas*, 23 (1993), pp. 118–29.

15 *The Works of John Wilmot Earl of Rochester*, ed. Harold Love (Oxford: Oxford University Press), p. viii.

16 Revised and updated by Nicholas Fisher in 2010, an edition that includes *Lucina's Rape Or The Tragedy of Vallentinian*.

17 Dustin H. Griffin, *Satires Against Man: The Poem of Rochester* (Berkeley: University of California Press, 1973); David Farley-Hills, *Rochester's Poetry* (London: 1978); and Marianne Thormählen, *Rochester: The Poems in Context* (Cambridge University Press, 1993).

18 Charles Whibley, 'The Court Poets', *The Cambridge History of English Literature*, 8: *The Age of Dryden* (New York: G.P. Putnam's Sons, 1912), pp. 224–52; John Hayward, ed., *Collected Works of John Wilmot, Earl of Rochester* (London: Nonesuch Press, 1926); Johannes Prinz, *John Wilmot Earl of Rochester: His Life and Writings* (Leipzig: Mayer & Muller, 1927); Vivian de Sola Pinto, *Rochester: Portrait of a Restoration Poet* (London: The Bodley Head, 1935; rpt. as *Enthusiast in Wit*, Lincoln, NE: University of Nebraska Press, 1962).

19 Kenneth Burke, *The Philosophy of Literary Form: Studies in Symbolic Action* (Louisiana State University Press, 1941; rpt. Berkeley: University of California Press, 1973), p. 1. Burke goes on to write: 'They are not merely answers, they are *strategic* answers, *stylized* answers ... There strategies size up the situations, name their structure and outstanding ingredients, and name them in a way that contains an attitude toward them. The situations are real; the strategies for handling them have public content; and in so far as situations overlap from individual to individual, or from one historical period to another, the strategies possess universal relevance.'

20 As Thormählen astutely notes in a comment that sums up in small the argument of this book, 'It seems to me that Reba Wilcoxon is quite right when maintaining that Rochester's ethic is based on sensual pleasure as the highest good. The trouble is that it is not good enough' (*Poems in Context*, p. 1, quoting Wilcoxon, 'Rochester's Philosophical Premises: A Case for Consistency', *Eighteenth-Century Studies* 8 (Winter 1974–75), p. 198).

1

Interpreting Rochester

Poetics bears, as Barthes says, not so much on the work itself as on its intelligibility ... therefore problematic cases – the work which some find intelligible and others incoherent, or the work which is read differently in two different periods – furnish the most decisive evidence about the system of operative conventions.

Jonathan Culler

But dealing with irony shows us the sense in which our court of final appeal is still a conception of the author: when we are pushed about any 'obvious interpretation' we finally want to be able to say, 'It is inconceivable that the author could have put these words together in this order without having intended this precise ironic stroke.'

Wayne Booth

'Madam,
   If you're deceived, it is not by my cheat.'
            ('A very heroical epistle in answer to Ephelia', line 1)

The orthodox position in any body of criticism is indispensable yet suspect, indispensable because like that point where the optic nerve joins the retina it affords the necessary blind spot that allows us to see; suspect because in allowing us to see some things it blinds us to others. The orthodoxy that pervades Rochester criticism – that the poems reflect the life – has proven no less indispensable, but no less suspect than this critical dictum would lead us to expect. First, while the pioneering works of Vivian de Sola Pinto, Graham Greene, and more recently of James William Johnson explore the life of John Wilmot, 2nd Earl of Rochester, with increasing knowledge and expertise, tantalizing gaps remain, these gaps leading critics into that seductive tautology of extrapolating the life of the man from the work and then of reading the work as confirmation of the life. Moreover, this pragmatic difficulty hides a troublesome theoretical conundrum. Any biographical statement ultimately refers to the man himself; because this information refers only to itself, it is unverifiable. As Rosalie Colie cleverly points out:

> No one nowadays takes biography seriously as the sole, or even the major, clue to literary imagination: the poet writing lyric verse has license to present himself however he will, to distort this own personality and feelings however he wishes to make his poetic point. For even supposing the poet were totally 'sincere', his sincerity is, to other men, unverifiable.
>
> The Liar paradox is the classical paradox of self-reference, as well as the classical paradox of infinite regress. It cannot be verified internally, since there is no measuring rod for its accuracy; it cannot be confirmed externally, since it refers only to itself. So is it also with self-portraits: the more faithful the likeness, the greater the falsity of the picture, the greater its isolation from any reference point outside of the creating, re-creating self.[1]

Colie stakes out the extreme position; all Cretans, as Clifford Gertz reminds us, are not liars. Nevertheless, puzzling out reliable information from biographical sources requires intellectual tact, 'guessing at meanings, assessing the guesses, and drawing explanatory conclusions from the better guesses'.[2]

This chapter examines why, in the face of these formidable difficulties, the biographical approach has dominated Rochester criticism and why, despite the problems, it should continue to do so. As critics ponder the relationship of poet to poetry, they recapitulate the interpretative paradoxes that the poems, with their focus on the self, often explore. Like art critics gazing at Velázquez's *The Maids of Honour*, we look into a mirror of a man looking into a mirror. We need to understand the man in order to know the poetry that reflects him – a seemingly impossible task. Not only does his image but our own also intrudes. We along with the poet encounter the paradox of self-reference. This chapter examines two poems: 'A very heroical epistle in answer to Ephelia' and 'An Epistolary Essay, from M.G. to O.B. upon their mutuall Poems'.[3] Because they address this epistemological paradox and have been the focus of a spirited critical debate, they allow us to understand the relationship between Rochester and his poetic persona and to scrutinize the conventions by which we have interpreted the poems.

'Rochester's relationship with his speakers', Dustin Griffin writes, is 'a central problem in interpretation of his poems'.[4] Earlier commentators had not found it so. For them, the persona in the poems was the historical Rochester – and understandably so. Anyone who has read a poem by the 'Mad Earl' knows the temptation of moving from work to world. The poetry traffics in the quotidian; we recognize places, St James's Park, and know that the various characters – Charles II, Barbara Villiers, and the Duke of Monmouth – once walked the boisterous, smelly streets of Restoration London. Like so many Restoration authors, Rochester, moreover, delights in blurring the real and fictive. Rochester bore the name Strephon, Aphra Behn was Astrea, and they inhabited the world of David, Orinda, Zimri, and Adriel. To distinguish the fictive from the historical selves remains no easy task. Rochester also writes in the genres that lie closest, or pretend to lie closest, to the world we experience – satire and parody. Writing in these genres, Rochester seemingly composes with a scientific rather than poetic eye. Sir Carr Scroope penned a graceful lyric beginning, '*Madam.*/ I cannott chang as others doe'; Rochester responded with an obscene parody, 'I *Fuck* no more then others doe' (*Answer*, line 1). Rochester reduces Scroope's idealistic address to his mistress, which admittedly makes a coy, muted appeal to the body, to mere physical appetite. The nobility of the baronet's claims to fidelity is exposed as nothing more than the plaintive plea of a young man begging favours of a whore. The motivations of the mistress, probably Cary Frazier, arise not from some concept of honour but are purely a function of bodily needs. As she puts it: 'Can I said she with Nature strive?/ Alas I am, alas I am, a Whore' (lines 7–8). Scroope writes within artistic convention; one would hardly judge his poem by its verifiability, its adherence to the world we know. It makes us think not of real people but of genre, of the poet's craft, of how well he has employed that craft to serve generic demands. Rochester's poem, however, creates the impression of pursuing truth, things as they really are. It searches out the biographical and makes the claim that if you really knew Cary Frazier, she would speak like this and her motives would be explicitly physical. In Wallace Stevens's phrase, Rochester invites his readers 'to step barefoot into reality'.[5]

Many of us readily accept this invitation for yet another reason. When confronted with the 'I' of any poem, we tell ourselves a story in order to make sense of the character speaking. Rochester's speakers – candid, clever, and splendidly wicked – quicken this narrative instinct. This way of understanding coupled with the Rochester legend – the quintessential rake, handsome, witty, and utterly debauched – tempts us to think that we are not just trying to understand a poem but are discovering intimacies of a spectacular life. As David Vieth has observed, Rochester's poems are 'part of a life-story so compelling that it constantly threatens to overwhelm his poetry'.[6]

Many critics have taken the 'story' to be the 'life' and have allowed it to overwhelm the poetry. Vieth deftly makes the distinction. He is keenly aware that even when there are no good grounds for doing so Rochester's poems all but seduce the critic to read them as biographical documents. 'Rochester's poems to the extent that they are a coherent body of expression, acquire a corporate unity as projections of *what we imagine* to have been his real-life personality. To a greater or lesser degree the "I" of each poem is always Rochester, even when the speaker is a woman' (Vieth, *Poems*, p. xli; italics mine). In his edition of the poems Vieth prefaces the song, 'Leave this gaudy gilded stage', with the remark that 'It is tempting to imagine that this lyric, which survives in Rochester's own handwriting, was addressed to some actress who was his mistress, perhaps Elizabeth Barry' (Vieth, *Poems*, p. 85). He acknowledges the biographical pull yet realizes that in fabricating this story he is interpreting, not discovering a biographical truth.

While admiring Vieth's intellectual acumen, one nevertheless wonders whether for critics of Rochester's poetry this distinction is important. The various commentators, whatever their awareness of interpretative niceties, have been in remarkable agreement on the identity of the Rochester in the poems, and we know enough of the life to find it plausible that Rochester really was Dorimant, 'a Devil' who 'has something of the Angel yet undefac'd in him'.[7] So long as the critics are engaged in interpreting poems and not in confirming biographical occurrences, their failure to distinguish between life and story would seem not to matter. In this view – and I think it is the one that prevails today – biographical criticism allows interpretation to take place. As a necessary fiction, it enables critics to escape in practice if not in theory from relativism. In bodies of criticism where the fiction is long-standing, critics rarely mention it openly, and they conduct their inquiries within clearly discernible but tacitly acknowledged boundaries. Should a critic, for example, make a persuasive case that Donne were homosexual, we would no doubt be greeted with a spate of new readings followed by a great number of sardonic rejoinders reasserting the orthodox view of Donne as the self-critical libertine who became religious. Attempts to synthesize these two views would probably follow, and in time this process would lead to a new orthodoxy or to a reaffirmation of the old.

Similarly, should someone suggest a different view of Rochester, one that did not fit readily into the critical model of the man as rake speaking in the poems in his own voice, we could expect critical disagreements. The anomaly would threaten critical relevance and coherence established through the accepted and long-tested *persona*. Such a shaking of the foundations actually occurred in Rochester criticism when Vieth, following and fully realizing the lead of John Harold Wilson, presented a new reading of 'A very heroical epistle' and 'An Epistolary Essay'.[8] The poems had been taken as personal revelations that, depending upon the interpretation, either defended or explored various facets of the libertine's code. Pinto, for example, took the first, in which Bajazet defends amorous inconstancy to a cast mistress, as evidence that Rochester 'had accepted the materialism of Hobbes and had applied it to the act of living'.[9] The second had been viewed as Rochester's bold explication of his own self-centred literary principles. Vieth, after considerable scholarly digging, was able to show, however, that the poems satirize one of Rochester's inveterate enemies, John Sheffield, Earl of Mulgrave, and that the speaker in both is Mulgrave, not Rochester. In coming to this conclusion Vieth ostensibly did what other critics claimed to have done: he had read the poems by employing biography. But Vieth had actual details of the life, not pieces of the legend.

The anomalous finding in criticism promises and threatens. It promises that if we pursue the method providing the anomalous reading further it will yield other, more satisfying readings, a process that will lead to a new critical framework capable, as the old was not, of providing the most interesting and comprehensive readings. The threat is that we will have to abandon cherished readings. Rather than do that, we are often tempted to explain away or to ignore the anomalous and return to an elaboration of established readings. Because so much of what we would like to know about Rochester's life remains incomplete, no one has been able to test whether the promise of his anomalous finding is chimera or not. Predictably, critics have continued to sense that the significance of Rochester's poetry lies in seeing it in context of the life, but they have continued to ignore the problems raised by biographical criticism. Orthodoxy has prevailed. In writing *Satires Against Mankind* (1973), Dustin Griffin, however, saw clearly what is at stake in Vieth's readings, and in his account of the two poems he clearly registered the threat. Though this shaking of the foundations occurred over a half century ago, an understanding of Vieth's and Griffin's position remains essential for an appreciation of Rochester, the after-shocks being felt to this very day.

While claiming that 'Rochester's relationship with his speakers' is 'a central problem in interpretation of his poems', and therefore assuming the significance of biography, Griffin curiously shifts grounds when he comes to interpret 'A very heroical epistle' and 'An Epistolary Essay'. He first attempts to show that Vieth's evidence for equating the speakers and Mulgrave is problematic; he then goes on to interpret the poems by employing three other contexts: literary tradition, Rochester's work as a whole, and the intellectual tradition of libertinism. As he puts it:

> In sum, whether or not Mulgrave is involved, the 'Heroical Epistle' is more than a simple confession or piece of ironic inversion. It displays many conventional characteristics – of the Ovidian heroical epistle, or the libertine defense of inconstancy – and some affinities with Rochester's love songs. (Griffin, p. 67)

'An Epistolary Essay', he writes,

> can be read as a knowing and playful celebration of an egoistic theory of writing, a theory consisting of a number of principles, most of them reasonable in themselves, but here pushed to and beyond their usual logical limits. Such an interpretation shifts our attention, as in the reading of the 'Heroical Epistle', from the identity of the speaker and his correspondent to the poem's ideas, allowing us to judge more disinterestedly their reasonableness. (Griffin, p. 68)

There is no limit to the number of contexts into which the poems can be placed, no limit to the ways they can be made to mean. Griffin might have gone on to cite, for example, the psychological or the providential. As an Ovidian epistle, 'A very heroical epistle' could be used as evidence in a history of that genre, or we could recuperate meaning on the level of everyday human experience by pointing out, as Vieth does, that both 'Bajazet and M.G. pose the eternal problem of individual freedom in conflict with social and universal laws' (Vieth, *Attribution*, p. 128). Valid as each of these interpretative contexts may be, they do not tell us what it is we need and want to know if our focus is to be on the poems and not on the poems as evidence to confirm some larger thesis. And that is, what is their tone? What attitude are we to take toward the speakers?

Griffin senses this and consequently makes another critical swerve. While claiming that the 'biographical context' of both poems is 'problematic', he nevertheless draws conclusions from the other contexts of meaning – genre, author's other works, and intellectual history – to make a biographical assessment. 'A very heroical epistle' 'furthers Rochester's exploration of man's painful, anxious state' (Griffin, p. 67), and in 'An Epistolary Essay' 'Rochester argues cogently for a conception of the poet's role that is both daringly self-centered and based on soundly considered principles' (Griffin, p. 72). But if Vieth is right and Mulgrave is the spokesman in both poems, then Griffin's conclusions are suspect.

Griffin is a sensitive, highly capable critic. It is probable though not certain that the speakers are Mulgrave. But that makes little difference because we should focus on the ideas in the poems in which, by the way, Rochester explores his ethical and aesthetic stances. Thus his tortuous reasoning gives us pause. Why would he find it necessary to engage in such critical prestidigitation? Because the issue is one in being right about irony, no doubt all sorts and levels of motives are at work. As Wayne Booth reminds us,

> Our pride is more engaged in being right about irony than about many matters that might seem more important – being logical or consistent, for example. If I am wrong about irony, I am wrong at deeper levels than I like to have exposed. When I am 'taken in', my profoundest beliefs and my most deeply rooted intellectual habits are under judgment.[10]

But deeply rooted intellectual habits aside, I would guess that if Griffin is like me, or like generations of Rochester's critics, what goads him on here is another person's conception of the poet behind the poem. Griffin simply cannot believe that Vieth's Rochester is the right Rochester.

Vieth's Rochester, at least in these two poems, is a spokesman for the 'official' values of Restoration culture. 'The satire of the "Heroical

Epistle"', he tells us, 'works through Bajazet's (Mulgrave's) unconscious violation of implicit norms, the poem's thematic center being an ironic inversion of that aggregate of traditional ideas well known to literary scholars under the term of "degree"' (Vieth, *Attribution*, p. 109). He goes on to contend that 'Bajazet's behavior represents a self-centered materialism' (Vieth, *Attribution*, p. 112) and that he reduces humanistic and Christian values to an amoral materialism. His interpretation of the 'An Epistolary Essay' is similarly 'official'. The poem satirizes

> M.G.'s methods of writing by presenting them as ironic inversions of traditional standards which almost any Augustan would have considered essential to good poetry. Instead of submitting his verses to the collective good taste and judgment of educated readers, as an Augustan poet was expected to do, M.G. disavows any ambition 'to be admir'd', despises '*Fame*', and cares nothing for the 'cens'ring critic'. (Vieth, *Attribution*, p. 122)

It is Rochester as official Augustan that has shaped Griffin's critical response. 'Not only does Vieth', he writes, 'wish us to read the poem ['A very heroical epistle'] as an expression of views antithetical to Rochester's, but he also wishes us to see in Bajazet an unconscious violation of traditional values' (Griffin, p. 57). Of 'An Epistolary Essay' he writes:

> Setting aside the very doubtful assumption that Rochester is a doctrinaire Augustan ... The principles of composition set forth here (that even fools can think themselves inspired, that writing for admiration and fame is contemptible, that a poet ought to reverence his own genius, that critics are splenetic and their judgments worthless) might well be held, in suitably moderated and qualified form, by any Augustan. What M.G. does is to present them without qualification, as part of a calmly considered and self-consciously egoistic theory that might well appeal to aristocratic, amateur, libertine poets such as Rochester and his friends. (Griffin, p. 70)

Clearly, Griffin thinks he knows what Rochester's values are, what would appeal to him and his friends, and they are not those of the humanistic, Christian culture Vieth evokes.

As I read the poems, he has a point. If Bajazet is not a spokesman for Rochester's libertinage, he certainly sounds like one. His voice is that of the speaker in the song, 'Love and Life'. Bajazet too would wittily reduce love to physical appetite to rid himself of a mistress. He demonstrates the manners and attitudes we might well associate with the aristocratic libertine and might in another context (i.e., 'Love and Life'), judge as appropriate if not admirable. Moreover, the attitude toward the poet and poetry in 'An Epistolary Essay' is similar to the one expressed by Timon who confesses: 'A Song to Phyllis, I perhaps might make/ But never Rhym'd but for my Pintles sake' ('*Satyr.* [Timon]', lines 21–22).[11] In 'An Allusion to

Horace' the speaker, without ironic qualification, advises poets to 'Scorn all applause the Vile Rout can bestow/ And be content to pleas those few who know' (lines 102–103). Speakers in Rochester's poetry after 1671 voice in many guises the theme that language lies, that the vocabulary of poetry, religion, and ethics has its origins in physical appetites and serves as a mask for them. Such contextual arguments do not stand in lieu of interpretation, but when our reading of a poem goes directly against the attitudes found in other poems it does or should make us question our findings.

Reading Vieth and Griffin side by side on these two poems raises a quandary. Vieth has the biographical data and the better argued interpretation, yet his conclusion does not match the experience that generations of Rochester's critics have had in reading the poems. What Griffin takes to be biographical data demonstrably derives from legend and from the poems themselves. Furthermore, his argument contains contradictions. Nevertheless, his conclusion that the values in the poems are libertine though expressed by a sensibility that is self-critically libertine seems right. Yet Vieth's evidence makes such a conclusion appear untenable.

This quandary can be resolved, but we first need to understand why it came about. Griffin draws conclusions about Rochester's beliefs from the poet's use of genre, from the attitudes and opinions expressed in the poems, and from the ideas the poems employ. He assumes that genre has an inherent meaning and that one using it will have particular meanings in mind. Similarly, he believes that if we find opinions in one poem and those same opinions in another, then they can often be taken to mean much the same thing. He brings a deductive approach to the poems, one based on the assumption that certain signs have semantic stability not only over a writer's career but through literary history.

Vieth's interpretation appears so convincing because he seems to work in a completely opposite way, not rationalistically but empirically. Behind the appearance, however, lies clever juggling. Vieth places his critical interpretations of these poems (Vieth, *Attribution*, pp. 107–29) before his scholarly findings that link the speaker to Mulgrave (Vieth, *Attribution*, pp. 129–36). In moving from criticism to scholarship, he writes: 'Once the critic's concern with the "Epistolary Essay" has received minimal attention, the scholar's task is vastly simplified. The similar satiric accusations in the "Epistolary Essay" and the "Heroical Epistle" should lead even a casual reader to suspect that M.G., like Bajazet, represents Mulgrave' (Vieth, *Attribution*, p. 129). This is more rhetorical than true. The 'minimal attention' had been twenty-two pages of detailed, rigorous argumentation, and the expert, let alone the casual, reader had not, until the discoveries of John Harold Wilson, suspected any such thing.[12] Vieth wants us to believe that both poems provide sufficient internal clues to guide the reader, through their ironies, to the conclusion that Mulgrave is being satirized for violating traditional canons of ethics and aesthetics. He finds that the speakers in both poems betray ignorance and foolishness that is 'simply incredible', and that both violate conventional judgments.[13] Of M.G.'s comparison of poetry and excrement, Vieth writes: 'It is difficult to understand why the irony of this passage has gone undetected, since M.G.'s comparison should appear ridiculous even to readers who lack a knowledge of Augustan literary criteria' (Vieth, *Attribution*, p. 123). He goes on to tell us that by 'Asserting his self-sufficiency in opposition to the concept of degree, Bajazet dismisses as "Names by dull *Fools*, to plague Mankind found out" those values of individual and social conduct – courtesy, honesty, generosity, courage, and the like – which were traditionally thought necessary to bind together the corporate structure of society' (Vieth, *Attribution*, p. 111).

Clearly, Rochester intends us to see a conflict between the beliefs expressed in these poems and the ones we hold and have good reason to suspect that he holds. But Vieth has provided no corroborating evidence that Rochester as a satirist would adhere to traditional norms. What we do know of the life leads us to suspect, along with Griffin, that such violations of conventional beliefs for Rochester would be staple fare. We suspect further that Vieth has been able to read the poems as ironic because he had been able first to establish, not critically, but biographically, the initial bits of knowledge that showed the poems to be satires on Mulgrave. That is, his 'official' Rochester is a construction after the fact. Vieth has fabricated a Rochester to fit what he knows to be the historically verifiable intention of the poems. Because his interpretation of the poems is comprehensive and cogent, the view of Rochester as Augustan is persuasive. But we should not confuse that view with the historical Rochester; it is an interpretative device; there are a number of Rochesters that could be constructed to account for these poems as satires upon Mulgrave.

Griffin's deductive reasoning has its obvious difficulties, but can we fault Vieth's method of proceeding? Because he has taken external evidence – information about Mulgrave and Rochester – treated it as internal evidence, and then used that external evidence to corroborate his findings, he is guilty of a sleight of hand. But that piece of juggling aside, he argues in an exemplary fashion, carefully gathering his evidence, formulating a hypothesis to account for that evidence, and in turn using that hypothesis to gather more evidence for testing. As we trace the skilful movements of this gifted mind at work, we are reminded, however, that there is no purely inductive method. Any critic, any thinker, inevitably begins with a construct in the mind that has no necessary congruence to reality – and Vieth is no exception. The idea of Rochester as Augustan guides Vieth's choice of data and his interpretation of them, though it is not until page 221 of *Attribution* that he explicitly states what is implicit throughout his study: 'Outwardly rebellious he may have been, but his innermost values were as conservative as Pope's and more conservative, perhaps, than Dryden's.' This is a hypothesis about reality, not reality itself. It is precisely the validity of such categorical thinking, crude or sophisticated, that the poems question.

Both poems are paradoxes of self-reference, paradox being a mode designed to show that our conceptions of the world and our experience of it often do not match. In both poems a man speaks, in one as a court rake and in the other as an insouciant amateur poet. How are we to know whether he is a legitimate rake or poet? How are we to know that he is to be judged harshly? The conundrum the poems present resembles that with which Rochester confronted his audience in that dashingly ingenious piece of prose he fashioned while masquerading as the mountebank Alexander Bendo on Tower Hill. How, Bendo asks, can one know the real physician from the counterfeit, the politician from the fool

> in a world like this (where Virtue is so exactly counterfeited, and Hypocrisie so generally taken notice of, that every one arm'd with Suspicion, stands upon his Guard against it) 'twill be very hard for a Stranger especially to escape censure: All I shall say for my self on this score is this, if I appear to any one like a Counterfeit, even for the sake of that chiefly ought I to be construed a true man, who is the Counterfeits example, his original, and that which he imploys his industry and pains to imitate and copy; is it therefore my fault if the Cheat by his Wits and Endeavours makes himself so like me, that consequently I cannot avoid resembling of him?
> [...]
> Now for the Politician, he is a grave, deliberating, close, prying Man: Pray are there not grave, deliberating, close, prying Fools? If then the difference betwixt all these (though infinite in effect) be so nice in all apparance, will you expect it should be otherwise betwixt the false Physician, Astrologer, &c. and the true? the first calls himself Learned Doctor, sends forth his Bills, give Physick, and Councel, tells and foretells; the other is bound to do just as much, 'tis only your experience must distinguish betwixt them. (*Alexander Bendo's brochure*, Love, pp. 113–14)

Similarly, the speaker in these two poems may well be a legitimate courtier-libertine and poet, in short, a Rochester. On the other hand, he may be a fraud, a Mulgrave. Ironically, the impersonator would be more faithful to the real Mulgrave than would the real Mulgrave who is by definition false. The point is that one cannot know who or what the speaker is without experience. As Ephelia learned, the speaker is deceptive, but she could only know this after the fact, after having experienced what she did. No a priori systems of thought could have told her; ''tis only your experience must distinguish betwixt them'. Rochester had such experience, and so did at least some of the audience for whom he wrote the poems.

The critic bears a relationship to the poems analogous to Ephelia's position vis-à-vis Bajazet–Mulgrave. He can only make sense of the poems in the way intended by experiencing as closely as possible the biographical context out of which they were written. The poems are not composed of stable ironies with readily accessible cues for reading. The key words can mean and mean significantly in a number of different and overlapping frames of reference – libertine, heroic, classical, humanistic, and Christian – and the precise meaning can be assessed only in the contexts of the poems' making and their intended audience. The values and norms of the poems, I am arguing, are highly private and deliberately so. If one is to understand the precise meaning of 'nature', or 'deceived', or 'star' or any number of words in the poems, one needs to know, among other things, that Mulgrave was goggle-eyed, uncommonly ugly, and extraordinarily fickle. One needs to know about the prickly pride he placed in wearing his star of the Order of the Garter, about his lust and avarice, about his affair with Mall Kirke, and his subsequent duel with her brother. In gathering this information Vieth, wittingly or no, recapitulated the epistemological situation upon which the poems depend. That epistemology is aristocratic and sceptical, aristocratic in that it is not the event that is important but the attitude towards it, and sceptical in that this proper attitude arises from experience. For Rochester and the audience for whom he wrote, such experiential knowledge allowed them to make sense of these poems as satires on Mulgrave. He and they depended on shared experience to bracket the words and give them their intended meanings. We are aware, as I think Rochester was too, that such shared experience itself is subject to interpretation and provides no stay against linguistic ambiguity and deception. We could have all the requisite biographical information and still not come to the interpretation of the poems Rochester intended; indeed, the fate of the poems over the years suggests the fragility of knowledge built up through personal experience and testimony. But if we are to approach in any significant way the intended meanings of the poems and understand, though perforce in limited ways, the reasons Rochester wrote poems that deliberately challenge our attempts to make sense of them, then we have little choice but to explore as far as possible the biographical context, particularly the relationship between John Wilmot and John Sheffield.

Most accounts note that Mulgrave was Rochester's enemy and that being incredibly proud and arrogant he was fully deserving of the abuse Rochester heaped upon him. The following attempt to create a plausible psychological understanding of the two suggests that their relationship was more interesting and more complex. The animosity between the two began in an intimacy perhaps only 17-year-old males can know, one in which friendship is mingled with competition, love with hatred. As alter egos, each seemed compelled to seek in the other a reading of his own identity. It was perhaps inevitable that they should enter into a lifelong duel involving verbal swords and real.

Fate cast the two in remarkably similar roles. They were born in April, a year apart, Wilmot on 1 April 1647, and Mulgrave on 7 April 1648; both were christened John, were aristocrats, and raised in the country. Though Mulgrave, unlike Rochester, most certainly saw his father, that father died when the boy was ten. Mulgrave too was an only son, educated by his mother and tutors, and like Rochester, he was a graduate of the grand tour, having travelled on the Continent at the same time as Rochester. When Rochester appeared at Court on Christmas Day 1664, Mulgrave was either there or soon would be. Shortly afterwards, Rochester along with Mulgrave, Etherege, and Savile founded the notorious Ballers Club. Though fashionably rakish, both, unlike many of their peers, were also bookish, sharing what seems to have been in both a genuine love for the classics. They also experienced war; Rochester had volunteered for the fleet in 1665, and Mulgrave joined him a year later.

Returning from the Second Dutch War, the two embarked on much the same career: the calculated pursuit of riches and preferment through service, be what it may, to the King. Both became Gentlemen of His Majesty's Bedchamber. Friction was bound to arise between two young, ambitious, proud courtiers, only sons vying for the favour of their surrogate father. In November 1669 the friction led to fire. Rochester left no account of the duel; Mulgrave did, and though laced with pomposities, it has the ring of authenticity.

According to Mulgrave, 'the Earl of *Rochester* had said something of me, which, according to his custom, was very malicious; I therefore sent Colonel *Aston* ... to call him to account for it'. Rochester, however, denied he had uttered the venomous words, and Mulgrave was 'convinced he had never said them'. Nevertheless, Mulgrave, ever proud, felt compelled because of the 'meer report, tho' I found it to be false, obliged ... (as I then foolish thought) to go on with the quarrel'. The combatants met at Knightsbridge, but Rochester, 'so weak with a certain distemper', could not fight. Mulgrave, concerned with his reputation, 'took the liberty of representing what a ridiculous story it would make, if we returned without fighting ... advised him for both our sakes, especially for his own, to consider better of it'. But Rochester was truly ill. Mulgrave had the seconds in to witness what he took to be his enemy's ignominious withdrawal, and his second, Aston, wrote up an account to spread 'every where'. The report, Mulgrave noted with a self-aggrandizing solicitude, intirely ruined his reputation as to courage (of which I was really sorry to be the occasion) tho' no body had still a greater as to Wit; which supported him pretty well in the world notwithstanding some more accidents of the same kind, that never fail to succeed one another when once people know a man's weakness.[14]

Mulgrave's account of this truncated fiasco, fascinating in so many ways, unwittingly reveals a great deal about the verbal war that ensued. It everywhere bears the stamp of Mulgrave's pride, concern for reputation, and over-weaning masculinity.[15] Reading between the lines, we glimpse a lack of self-awareness and an inability to catch ironies or to laugh at oneself. Rochester, rightly famous for his impudent wit, could sting a man while leaving him uncertain as to whether he should laugh or draw his sword. As Burnet incisively put it: 'he had a peculiar Talent of mixing his Wit and his Malice, and fitting both with such apt words, that Men were tempted to be pleased with them' (Burnet, p. 51). Mulgrave never really knew whether he had been put on, whether Rochester's insults were real or the apology feigned. Rochester, sick as he was, nevertheless saw the humour in Mulgrave's demand that they fight for form's sake. If they could not fight, then a report would have to be made so all the world would know that it was not Mulgrave who had lacked courage. Throughout the 1670s Rochester would attack the pride, the boastful masculinity, and narcissism of his once close friend and gleefully play upon his obtuseness. In turn Mulgrave would lash out at Rochester's 'reputation' for courage and wit.

In lampooning each other, both engaged in self-laceration. Rochester hardly lacked humour, and few men were ever more self-aware. In addition, his wit and superior poetic talents gave him an indisputable edge in this verbal conflict. But he was ambitious and preoccupied with money. As a boy and a man, he was pale and physically delicate, and doubts about certain aspects of masculinity are articulated through a variety of personae in his work. Mulgrave's attacks on Rochester manifest perhaps an even clearer concern for self. The courage he persistently vaunted he also deeply suspected, and even he probably knew at some level that he did not possess the wit he admired and accused Rochester of lacking. His arrogance about his wit and courage perhaps testify to his insecurity about them.

Throughout the 1670s the two were locked in psychological warfare, their satires on each being a measure of the intensity of the battles. *Sodom* sports a crude caricature of someone whom I take to be Mulgrave, the poxed courtier, Pockanello. Rochester may have had a hand in this attack on Mulgrave's mean ambitions and his unctuous manner of fulfilling them. This puppet, this 'Punchinello', can be manipulated to do anything for advancement – anything. The sexually crazed king, Bolloxinian, announces:

> And Pock^{llo} for my mate I choose
> His Arse for a minute shall be my Spowse.
> (lines 53–54)

Pockanello replies:

> That Spows shall, mighty S^r, atho' itts blind,
> Proue to my Lord both dutyfull & kind.
> Its all I wish that Pock^{os} arse
> May still find fauo^r from yor Royall Tarse.
> (lines 55–58)[16]

Pockanello further ingratiates himself with his monarch by informing on others, and in what may be the early version of *Sodom* he makes a mock-heroic progression, via intrigue and sexual favours, from catamite to 'King John', the pun holding then as it does now. That Pockanello–Mulgrave, like Rochester himself, flirts with conversion to Catholicism and panders to his king in an unceasing quest for preferment is psychologically telling and a point to keep in mind when we turn to a scrutiny of 'A very heroical epistle' and 'An Epistolary Essay'.[17] Pockanello arguably marks a crude, preliminary study for these later deft portraits. In '*My Lord* All-pride' Rochester would again resort to invective and lampoon, though his attack on 'Punchinello' brings as much subtlety and art to the lampoon as the form allows. Ironically but unsurprisingly, the amusing praise of Rochester follows immediately the satire on Mulgrave in the 'Advice to Apollo', possibly the work of Rochester and his fellow wits:

> But Mulgrave strike with many angry darts;
> He who profanes thy name, offends thy arts,
> Ne'er saw thy light, yet would usurp thy pow'r,
> Would govern wit, and be its emperor,
>
> In fee with Dryden to be counted wise,
> Who tells the world he has both wit and eyes.[18]

Throughout his career, Rochester, if not Apollo, struck Mulgrave with many an angry dart.

Mulgrave was equally preoccupied with Rochester, if not more so. The lines just quoted refer to 'An essay on satyr', which Mulgrave wrote perhaps in collaboration with Dryden.[19] The poem, an early version of which may have been in circulation by 1676, contains the most vicious satire on Rochester not penned by Rochester himself. Not surprisingly, the satire lashes Rochester for his lack of courage and wit.

> *Rochester* I despise for his meere want of Witt,
> Though thought, to have a Tayle, and cloven Feete.

> For while he mischeife meanes to all Mankind,
> Himselfe alone the ill effect does fynd,
> And soe, like Witches, justly suffers Shame,
> Whose harmless Malice is so much the same.
> False are his Words affected, as his Witt,
> Soe often he does ayme, soe seldom hitt.
> To ev'ry Face he cringes, whilst he speakes,
> But when the Back is turn'd, the head he breakes.
> Meane in each Motion, Lewd in ev'ry Limbe;
> Manners themselves are mischeavous in him;
> A proofe that Chance alone makes ev'ry Creature,
> A very *Killegrew* without good nature;
> For what a *Bessus* hath hee alwayes liv'd?
> And his owne kicking notably contriv'd.
> For there's the Folly, that's still mixt with Feare,
> Cowards more blows, then any Heroe beare:
> Of fighting Sparkes some may their pleasure say
> But 'tis a bolder thing, to runn away.
> The World may well forgive him all his ill,
> For every fault does prove his penance still.
> Falsely he falls into some dangerous noose,
> And then as meanly labours, to get loose.
> A life soe infamous, it's better quitting,
> Spent in base injuring, and low submitting.
> I'de like, to have left out his Poetry,
> Forgott allmost by all, as well as mee:
> Sometymes he hath some humor, never Witt,
> And if it ever (very rarely) hitt,
> 'Tis under soe much nasty rubbish layd,
> To find it out,'s the Cynderwomans trade,
> Who for the Wretched Remnants of a Fire
> Must toyle all day in Ashes, and in Mire.
> So leudly dull his idle workes appeare,
> The wretched Text deserves noe comment here,
> Where one poore thought's sometymes left all alone
> For a whole page of dulness to atone.
> 'Mongst forty bad's one tolerable Line
> Without expression, fancy, or designe.
> (Love, lines 230–69)

Mulgrave and Dryden strategically placed this satire just before the poem's coda; only a portrait of Charles Sedley comes between it and the poem's panegyric on Mulgrave. Mulgrave's close identification with Rochester is further evidenced by the attention he devoted to his nemesis even after Rochester's death in 1680. In '*An Essay Upon Poetry*' (1682) Mulgrave sneered at Rochester's deathbed conversion before going on to denigrate his 'pretence to wit'.

> Here, as in all things else, is most unfit
> Bawdry barefac'd, that poor pretence to Wit;
> Such nauseous Songs as the late Convert made,
> Which justly call this censure on his Shade;
> Not that warm thoughts of the transporting joy,
> Can shock the Chastest, or the Nicest cloy;
> But obscene words, too gross to move desire,
> Like heaps of Fuel do but choke the Fire.
> That Author's Name has undeserved praise,
> Who pall'd the appetite he meant to raise.[20]

Nearly twenty-five years later, we find Mulgrave in what is almost surely a reference to Rochester and his famous 'Satyr' writing in his notes on the 'Ode to Brutus' the following gloss on 'reason':

> But the Sceptics evade this [i.e. that reason is 'a particular Talent' and 'Blessing bestowed on Mankind alone'] again, first, by denying that 'tis a Talent peculiar to Man, since other Animals appear manifestly endued with it, at least to some degree; and, if that degree be found inferior, yet the Difference seems as great sometimes between one Man and another, and (perhaps they may say merrily) even between themselves and their Adversaries.[21]

The sceptic is Rochester, the reference to a famous line he adapted from Montaigne ('Man differs more from Man, than man from Beast'), which Rochester may well have merrily applied to his adversary, Mulgrave. As a final piece of evidence that Rochester haunted Mulgrave, we note that his account of the Knightsbridge duel marks the most vivid, spirited piece of writing in the *Memoirs*.

They could not leave each other alone. Even had they wanted to do so, their similar pursuits often led them into each other's company. After reading their attacks on one another it comes as a shock to learn that 'the guests who used to attend the suppers of Charles II in the apartments of the duchess of Portsmouth, William Chiffinch and Nell Gwyn in 1676 and 1677 included Thomas Killigrew, Henry Savile, Henry Guy, Baptist May, and the earls of Dorset, Rochester, and Mulgrave'.[22] In this fashionable world that prized witty conversation, Rochester doubtlessly had opportunities to smile at his adversary while simultaneously opening a vein, and Mulgrave, suspended between laughter and anger, must have suffered many a moment of quizzical doubt. Coteries grew up around their animosities, and without an understanding of their relationship it is impossible to understand fully the literary history of the 1670s.

Out of this rivalry came 'A very heroical epistle' and 'An Epistolary Essay'. If we are going to understand the poems properly, however, we need in so far as is possible to know the specific events that led to each. As critics have noted, Rochester wrote 'A very heroical epistle' in part to respond to Dryden's dedication of *Aureng-Zebe* to Mulgrave in late 1675. Three years before, Dryden had dedicated *Marriage à La Mode* to Rochester. There Dryden had praised Rochester. Though a courtier and living at Court where 'Few men ... have that assurance of a Friend, as not to be made ridiculous by him, when they are absent', Rochester has not 'forgot either the ties of Friendship, or the practice of Generosity'. He goes on to laud Rochester for the 'charmes of your Conversation, the Grace of your Behaviour, your knowledge of Greatness ...'. He thanked him for commending the play 'to the view of His Majesty' and for being not only 'careful of my Reputation, but of my Fortune'. In passing he noted Rochester's 'accustomed goodness' and the 'Nobleness of your Nature'.[23] In a letter that no longer exists, Rochester thanked the laureate. Dryden replied in a calculatingly chatty and fulsomely thankful letter, telling Rochester among other things that 'You are that Rerum Natura of your own Lucretius, Ipsa suis pollen opibus, nihil indiga nostri ...'.[24] Evidently, Dryden had found, among 'some papers of your verses', Rochester's translation of Lucretius lines 44–49. The entire letter attempts to be as ingratiating as possible, Dryden the commoner even being so bold as to gossip about Rochester's friend Buckingham.

Shortly afterwards, for reasons not entirely clear, whatever friendship they shared turned sour. Either as a cause or as a symptom of this enmity, Dryden entered into Mulgrave's patronage. The disaffection between Rochester and Dryden smoldered throughout 1674 and into 1675. Then Dryden tossed a bomb. *Aureng-Zebe*, first acted 17 November 1675, was published shortly afterwards with a dedication that perfectly exemplified Dryden's critical dictum that turning over panegyric one finds satire. In this case, predictably enough, Rochester received the satire, Mulgrave the panegyric.

In a long opening paragraph Dryden presents 'the Character of a Courtier without Wit'. He is a man 'whose Ambition, Lust, or private Interest, seem to be the onely end of their Creation'. Because 'Specious', he can insinuate himself into his Prince's life. Of such men 'diligence in waiting, is their gilding of the Pill; for that looks like Love, though it 'tis onely Interest'. Growing harsher, Dryden observes that 'the nauseousness of such Company is enough to disgust a reasonable Man; when he sees, he can hardly approach Greatness, but as a Moated Castle; he must first pass through the Mud and Filth with which it is encompass'd'. He concludes his character sketch by noting:

> These are they, who, wanting Wit, affect Gravity, and go by the name of Solid men: and a solid man is, in plain *English*, a solid, solemn fool. Another disguise they have (for Fools as well as Knaves, take other names, and pass by an *Alias*) and that is the Title of honest Fellows. But this honesty of theirs ought to have many Grains for its Allowance; for certainly they are no further honest, than they are silly: They are naturally mischievous to their power; and if they speak not maliciously, or sharply, of witty men, 'tis only because God has not bestow'd on them the gift of utterance. They fawn and crouch to men of parts, whom they cannot ruine: quote their Wit when they are present, and when they are absent, steal their Jests: But to those who are under 'em, and whom they can crush with ease, they show themselves in their natural Antipathy; there they treat Wit like the common Enemy, and give it no more quarter, than a *Dutch*-man would to an *English* Vessel in the *Indies;* they strike Sail where they know they shall be master'd, and murder where they can with safety. (Dryden, vol. 12, pp. 149–50)

'Ambition, Lust, or private interest', 'nauseousness', 'Mud and Filth', 'disguise', and 'honesty' leave little doubt that Dryden has his former patron in mind. His present one must have been gratified with the attack on Rochester's wit and courage, these being along with 'nauseousness' and 'Filth' the focus of Mulgrave's own satire on Rochester. Dryden gives us a prose version of the portrait of Rochester that he and Mulgrave would use in *An Essay Upon Satire*. Rochester would, in turn, make parodic use of it in fashioning Bajazet. Dryden evidently knew how to ingratiate himself with Mulgrave, but even the Earl's gigantic ego must have been satiated by the flattery that followed.

Rochester and Mulgrave each considered the other to be the inverted and perverted version of himself. Taking Mulgrave's side, Dryden frankly said just that. 'This, my Lord, is the Character of a Courtier without Wit; and therefore that which is a Satyre to other men, must be a Panegyrick to your Lordship, who are Master of it [i.e. wit]' (Dryden, vol. 12, p. 150). For three pages Dryden goes on in the same vein. Mulgrave neither 'seeks a Commendation, or wants it. Your mind has always been above the wretched affectation of Popularity. A popular man is, in truth, no better than a Prostitute to common Fame, and to the People ... his Humility is onely disguis'd Ambition.' Unlike Cicero, who made himself ridiculous in 'his insatiable thirst of Fame', Mulgrave is not 'over-set with vanity'. Cicero begged historians 'to recommend himself to posterity ... to remember his consulship'. But, Dryden observes,

> all their Histories are lost, and the vanity of his request stands yet recorded in his own Writings. How much more great and manly in your Lordship, is your contempt of popular applause, and your retired Virtue, which shines only to a few. (Dryden, vol. 12, p. 151)

Dryden praises Mulgrave's 'Conversation', cites his 'good Nature and Generosity', his 'Resolution and Courage', his 'firmness in all your Actions', this latter trait being illustrated by a quotation from *Aeneid*:

Ille meos, primus qui me sibi junxit, amores
Abstulit; ille habeat secum, servetque sepulcro.

('No! He who had my vows, shall ever have;/ For whom I loved on earth, I worship in the grave' [trans. Dryden]).

(Dryden, vol. 12, p. 152)

The implicit criticism of Rochester in this panegyric becomes explicit when Dryden cites Lucretius. 'Methinks', he writes, 'there's something of a malignant joy in that excellent description of *Lucretius*',

Suave, mari magno turbantibus aequora ventis
e terra magnum alterius spectare laborem;
non quia vexari quenquam est jucunda volputas,
sed, quibus ipse malis careas, quia cernere suave est.

(How sweet it is, when winds are whipping the waters on the great sea, to watch from the shore the distress of someone else, not because it is delightful that anyone be troubled, but because it is sweet to realize from what ills you yourself are free [trans. Frederick Link]). (Dryden, vol. 12, p. 153)

Rochester's admiration for Lucretius was well known, and Dryden quotes his own text against him. The poet laureate had felt the sting of the aristocrat's rejection, the severity of which we have an accurate measure in the amused, detached, rapier criticism in 'An Allusion to Horace' and in Rochester's condescending appraisal of Dryden in a letter to Savile probably in the summer of 1676:

You write me word that I'm out of favour with a certain poet whom I have ever admired for the disproportion of him and his attributes. He is a rarity which I cannot but be fond of, as one would be of a hog that could fiddle, or a singing owl. (Treglown, pp. 119–20)

In his letter to Rochester in 1673 Dryden had assured the Earl that: 'You are that Rerum Natura of your own Lucretius, Ipsa suis pollens opibus, nihil indiga nostri: You are above any Incense I can give you; and have all the happinesse of an idle life, joined with the good Nature of an Active' (Treglown, pp. 87–88). Rochester reigns god-like in the Lucretian sense, beyond any tribute that a mere mortal like Dryden could give. Three years later the application of text to reality had changed. No longer does 'True greatness' consist of such exalted detachment; rather 'if it be anywhere on Earth, is in a private Virtue; remov'd from the notion of Pomp and Vanity, confin'd to a contemplation of itself, and centring on it self'. Dryden then quotes, with notable lacunae, the same passage from Lucretius:[25]

> *Omnis enim per se Divum natura, necesse est*
> *Immortali aevo summa cum pace frautur;*
> *– – – – – – – – – – – – Cura semota, metuque,*
> *Ipsa suis pollens opibus – – – – – – –*
> (Dryden, vol. 12, pp. 153–54)

Mulgrave, like Rochester, is '*ipsa suis pollens opibus*', mighty in his own resources, but unlike Rochester, he is not '*semota ab nostris rebus seiunctaque longe/ nam privata dolore omni, privata periclis*', far removed and separated from our troubles. Moreover, he is not in the condition of '*nil indigna nostri*', of needing us not at all. True greatness resides not in the 'malignant joy', in the detachment of a Rochester, but in the humility and friendship of a Mulgrave.

Dryden goes on to thank Mugrave just as he had Rochester three years earlier for recommending his play 'to the King's perusal' (Dryden, vol. 12, p. 155). Having solicited support for a proposed epic and answered a few critical objections to *Aureng-Zebe*, Dryden closes with this remarkable passage from Cicero

> which he sent with his Books *De finibus* to his Friend Brutus, *de ipsis rebus autem, saepenumero Brute vereor ne reprehendar, cum haec ad te scribam, qui tum in poesi (I change it from philosophia) tum in optimo genere poeseos tantum processeris. Quod si facerem quasi te erudiens, jure reprehenderer. Sed ab eo plurimum absum: nec, ut ea cognoscas quae tibi notissima sunt ad te mitto: sed quia facillime in nomine tuo acquiesco, & quia te habeo aequissimum eorum studiorum, quae mihi communia tecum sunt, aestimatorem & jedicem.* Which you may please, my Lord, to apply to yourself ....
>
> (As regards my subject, I often fear, Brutus, that I shall meet with censure for writing upon this topic to you, who are yourself so great an adept in [poetry], and in the highest branch of [poetry]. Did I assume the attitude of an instructor, such censure would be deserved. But nothing could be farther from me. I dedicate my work to you, not to teach you what you know extremely well already, but because your name gives me a very comforting sense of support, and because I find in you a most impartial sense of support, and because I find in you a most impartial judge and critic of the studies which I share with yourself [trans. Harris Rackham]). (Dryden, vol. 12, p. 158)

I have dwelt at length on this dedication because it provided both the impetus for and the subject matter of 'A very heroical epistle' and 'An Epistolary Essay'. Dryden praised Mulgrave as both courtier and poet. In doing so he had, Rochester knew, inverted Mulgrave's true character and sentiments as well as Dryden's own words and earlier loyalties. Rochester reacted not with blunt and cudgel but amused detachment. He did not answer Dryden directly. Instead he drew portraits of a man who, having the traits Rochester knew Mulgrave to have, could still accept such fulsome flattery as genuine. He sketched a sham courtier and poet but one too obtuse to know it, his intention being to reveal the distance between Dryden's portrait and Mulgrave and to reveal as well the stupidity and hypocrisy of this writer of dedications. Such a man might well pass for a genuine courtier and poet to Dryden, but among the knowing Mulgrave is clearly a fool.

In 'A very heroical epistle' Bajazet promotes himself as a true courtier, but he has the opposite traits Dryden attributed to him. A mirror image of the Rochester Dryden had portrayed, 'Ambition, Lust, or private interest' are 'the only end of [his] Creation'. He seeks not the retired humble greatness of which Dryden had written, but aspires to be a Sultan, to be 'like some God, the trembling crowd adore' and to live so that 'Each man's thy slave, and Woman-kind thy Whore' (lines 35–36). And all this for the sake of 'my dear self' (line 7). In the spring of 1676 Mulgrave's 'mean Ambition' was again galling Rochester. Mulgrave was assiduously courting the Duke of York and promoting his own cause by fuelling a contretemps between York and Monmouth. In a letter to Savile that spring Rochester defensively noted that 'I am not at all stung with my Lord M____'s mean ambition' (Treglown, p. 119). But he was, as he had been. In the 'A very heroical epistle', Rochester would strike back at his old enemy by portraying him as 'godlike', though not quite in the way Dryden had in mind (Dryden, vol. 12, p. 154).

The poem opens with Bajazet telling Ephelia: 'Madam/ If you're deceived, it is not by my cheat/ For all disguises are below the great' (lines 1–2). The lines satirize Dryden as well as Mulgrave, because in one respect Bazajet is being most honest. If one is deceived by such as Mulgrave, it is not due to the man, for those who have any experience of him would know better. Rather, the blame lies with the fawning, lying poets who deceive through their manipulation of language. In the hands of the likes of Dryden, words cheat. Dryden in his dedication to *Aureng-Zebe* had praised Mulgrave's 'firmness in all your Actions'; he had declared that in Mulgrave one could 'repose a confidence on him, whom no Adversity, no change of Courts, no Bribery of Interests, or Cabals of Faction, or Advantages of Fortune, can remove from the solid foundations of Honour and Fidelity' (Dryden, vol. 12, p. 152). This description hardly matched the Mulgrave who had just had a ridiculous affair with Mall Kirke; who was scheming to ruin Monmouth, one of his rivals for Mall, by setting York against him; and who was wooing York by contemplating a conversion to Catholicism. The true Mulgrave resembles Bajazet, who rhetorically asks Ephelia:

> What Man or Woman upon earth can say
> I ever us'd 'em well above a day?
> How is it then that I inconstant am?
> He changes not, who always is the same.
>   (lines 3–6)

Dryden portrayed a Mulgrave whose integrity was such that 'No! He who had my vows, shall ever have/ For whom I loved on earth, I worship in the grave.' The true Mulgrave, like the Dido whose words had been applied to him, is fickle, telling Ephelia:

> For 'tis as natural to change as Love.
> You may as justly at the Sun repine
> Because alike it does not alwayes shine.
> No glorious thing was ever made to stay,
> My Blazing Star but visits and away.
> (lines 17–21)

So much for 'constancy to your friends', and for Mulgrave's 'retir'd Virtue, which shines onely to a few; with whom you live so easily and freely, that you make it evident, you have a Soul which is capable of all the tenderness of Friendship' (Dryden, vol. 12, p. 151). Given the Mulgrave Rochester portrays, Dryden's claim that his 'Kindness, where you have once placed it, is inviolable', is questionable (Dryden, vol. 12, p. 151). 'A very heroical epistle' also exposes what Dryden took to be Mulgrave's 'good Nature and Generosity'. Bajazet, with Mulgravian condescension and feigned insouciance, tells Ephelia:

> The boasted favor you so precious hold
> To me's no more than changing of my gold.
> What e're you gave, I paid you back in bliss,
> Then where's the obligation, pray, of this?
> If heretofore you found grace in my eyes,
> Be thankful for it, and let that suffice.
> But Women Beggarlike, still haunt the door
> Where they've receiv'd a Charity before.
> (lines 24–31)

Moreover, this man of supposed 'Resolution and Courage' (Dryden, vol. 12, p. 152) fervently dreams of being where he need 'fear'st no injur'd Kinsman's threatning blade/ Nor Midnight ambushes by Rivals laid', where he need not be 'Disturb'd by Swords' (lines 53–54 and 56). Dryden had defined 'True greatness' as existing 'in a private Virtue; remov'd from the notion of Pomp and Vanity, confin'd to a contemplation of itself, and centring on itself'. Rochester ironically agreed. Given this definition, Bajazet-Mulgrave is a 'great man', one who 'In my dear self, I center every thing' (line 7).

With this one exception, the Mulgrave Rochester knew matched Dryden's portrait not at all; Rochester's Mulgrave instead is an imitation of Dryden's portrait of Rochester. 'Wanting wit', he 'affect[s] Gravity, and go[es] by the name of Solid men; and a solid man is, in plain *English*, a solid, solemn

Fool' (Dryden, vol. 12, p. 150). Mulgrave's affected gravity was notorious; his account of the Knightsbridge duel is but one of numerous examples of the pomposities larding his *Memoirs*. The man who penned the *Memoirs* differs little from the Bajazet who smugly classifies himself among 'the great' (line 2).

Another disguise these 'Courtiers without Wit' habitually don is the 'Title of honest Fellows'. Bajazet accordingly affects great honesty to carry out a dishonest end, that is, his deception of Ephelia. As the poem progresses and Bajazet moves from complacency to fear, we see that such men, as Dryden pointed out, are 'no further honest, than they are silly'. Such men also 'fawn and crouch to men of parts, whom they cannot ruine' (Dryden, vol. 12, p. 150). Bajazet's fear becomes fully manifest at the end of the poem. Apparently, Mulgrave had fawned and crouched to men of parts when Monmouth in September of 1674 had him picked up by the guard as he crept out of Mall Kirke's apartment in Whitehall and locked away for the rest of the night. In Rochester's portraits of Mulgrave, extreme pride always verges on spineless obsequiousness. Mulgrave is a man 'naturally mischievous to [his] power' (Dryden, vol. 12, p. 150). Bajazet–Mulgrave, like Damocles, becomes at the end of the poem the overly successful courtier, attending a feast he cannot enjoy. His success has undone him.

More than any other trait, 'A very heroical epistle' illustrates the penchant of 'Courtier without Wit' to steal the jests from men of parts. Bajazet mouths all the libertine clichés, but his words no more make him an authentic libertine than an honest man. Rochester persistently criticized Mulgrave as a bad actor. He is a 'Pockanello', but also a '*Punchinello*' who

> set's up for a Spark.
> With equal self-conceit too, he bears arms,
> But with that vile success his part perform's,
> That he burlesque's his trade, and what is best
> In others, turn's like *Harlequin* to jest.
> So have I seen at *Smithfield's* wondrous fair,
> (When all his Brother Monsters flourish there)
> A lubbard *Elephant* divert the Town
> With making legs and shooting off a gun.
> Go where he will he never find's a Friend,
> Shame and derision all his steps attend,
> Alike abroad, at home, ith Camp and Court,
> This Knight o' th' burning pestle makes us sport.
> ('*My Lord* All-Pride', lines 18–30)

An Essay Upon Satire tagged Rochester a 'Bessus', after a cowardly braggadocio character in *King and No King*. Mulgrave and Dryden were again attacking Rochester's courage. Rochester, in turn, cast Mulgrave as a 'Knight o' th' Burning Pestle', a hit at Mulgrave's pride in his womanizing, but a more fundamental criticism of the man's inability as soldier, courtier, or libertine to understand his place in the plot, indeed to distinguish between fiction and reality. Bajazet is a courtier-libertine who 'burlesque's his trade, and what is best/ In others, turn's like *Harlequin* to jest'.

Dryden concluded his account of the 'Courtier without Wit' by observing that such men

> to those who are under 'em, and whom they can crush with ease, they show themselves in their natural Antipathy; there they treat Wit like the common Enemy, and give it no more quarter, than a *Dutch*-man would to an *English* vessel in the *Indies*; they strike Sail where they know they shall be master'd, and murder where they can with safety. (Dryden, vol. 12, p. 150)

This account proved prophetic, the intended metaphor shortly becoming reality. On 17 June 1676 occurred the Epsom brawl in which Rochester's truly despicable behaviour led to the death of his friend, Edward Downes. When Dryden and Mulgrave turned this prose portrait into the verse of *An Essay Upon Satire*, they made the charge of 'murder where they can with safety' into a specific reference to Epsom:

> To ev'ry face he cringes, whilst he speaks,
> But when the back is turn'd the head he breaks.
> ...
> Of fighting sparks some may their pleasure say,
> But 'tis a bolder thing to run away.
>   (lines 238–39 and 248–49)

Interpreting 'those who are under 'em' with a witty literalness, Rochester applied the passage to Mulgrave. Bajazet fantasizes:

> Methinks I see thee underneath the shade
> Of golden Canopies supinely laid;
>
> Thy crowching slaves all silent as the night,
> But at thy nod all active as the light.
> Secure in solid Sloath thou there dost raign,
> And feel'st the joys of love without the pain.
> Each Female courts thee with a wishing eye,
> Whilst thou with awful pride walk'st careless by,
> Till thy kind pledge at last mark's out the Dame
> Thou fanciest most to quench thy present flame.
> Then from thy bed submissive she retires,
> And thankful for the grace no more requires.
> No loud reproach, nor fond unwelcome sound
> Of Womens tongues thy sacred ear dares wound.

> If any do, a nimble Mute straight tye's
> The true love knot, and stops her foolish cries.
> (lines 37–52)

It is Mulgrave who would 'crush with ease', 'murder ... with safety'.

'An Epistolary Essay' follows the same strategy as its companion piece. In response to Dryden's slashing criticisms, Rochester wrote an imaginary letter in reply to Dryden's epistolary dedication, aping the attitudes of the original as they would be expressed by the Bajazet-persona created in 'A very heroical epistle'. The poem spoofs Mulgrave by showing how false the noble sentences of the dedication were to his nature, and it simultaneously shows indirectly the lying nature of the fawning dedicator. Rochester portrayed an M.G. attempting to act the role of the accomplished poet Dryden said he was while outdoing Dryden's ingratiating flattery.

In his dedication Dryden had compared himself to Virgil, Mulgrave serving as his Maecenas: 'The times of Virgil please me better, because he had an *Augustus* for his Patron. And to draw the Allegory nearer to you, I am sure I shall not want a *Maecenas* with him' (Dryden, vol. 12, p. 155). With matching vanity parading as self-deprecation, M.G. replies:

> But, howsoever Envy, their [the censurers'] spleen may
>   raise
> To rob my Browes of the deserved Bayes
> Their thanks at least I merit, since thro' me,
> They are partakers of your Poetry.
> (lines 5–8)

Similarly, Dryden had praised Mulgrave as 'so great an adept in [poetry];' M.G. makes himself equally oleaginous, responding: 'T'obtain one line of your well worded sence/ I'de be content t'have writ the British Prince' (lines 10–11). Given Rochester's evaluation of Dryden's sense and the reputation of *The British Prince*, M.G. unwittingly bargains naught for nothing.

Dryden claimed that Mulgrave neither seeks 'Commendation, or wants it. Your mind has always been above the affectation of Popularity.' He went on to observe: 'How much more great and manly in your Lordship, is your contempt of popular applause, and your retir'd Virtue, which shines onely to a few' (Dryden, vol. 12, pp. 150–51). Aping the poet laureate's praise, M.G. admits:

> I'm none of those who think themselves inspird
> Nor write with the vain hope to be admir'd:
> But from a Rule I have (upon long Triall)
> T'avoid with care all sort of self deniall;
> Which way so er'e desire and fancy lead,
> (Contemning Fame) that path I boldly tread.

> And if exposing what I take for wit,
> To my dear self a Pleasure I beget
> No matter tho the cens'ring Criticks fret.
> Those, whom my Muse displeases are at strife,
> With equall spleen against my course of life,
> The least delight of which Il'e not forgoe,
> For all the flattring praise Man can bestow:
> (lines 12–24)

The rest of the poem mocks Dryden's evaluation of Mulgrave as embodying 'True greatness' and of being 'so great an adept in [poetry], and in the highest branch of [poetry]'. If 'True greatness' is 'confin'd to a contemplation of it self, and centring on it self', what sort of poetry would such a 'godlike life' produce? It would, according to the jesting Rochester, be poetry of the 'highest branch', that is, 'sublime' but not exactly in the sense intended by Longinus. M.G. confesses:

> In all I write shoud sence and wit and Rhyme
> Fail me at once, yet something so sublime
> Shall stamp my Poem, that the world may see
> It coud have been produc'd by none but me;
> And that's my end, for man can wish no more
> Then so to write as none 'ere writ before.
> (lines 44–49)

Despite Dryden's flattery, M.G. remains bemused about his status as poet.

> Yet why am I no Poet of the times?
> I have Allusion's, Similei's and Rhymes,
> And wit, or else 'tis hard that I alone,
> Of the whole Race of Mankind shoud have none.
> (lines 50–53)

The afterthought – 'And wit' – is telling. A feeling that he lacked wit haunted Mulgrave, and seemingly no praise could dispel it. He and Dryden could cast Rochester in the role of a 'Courtier without Wit', but Mulgrave sensed that the role was his. In lines 54–70, M.G. attempts in a clumsy bit of casuistry to convince himself that Dryden had written the truth about him, that he really sported a courtier's wit.

> Unequally the partiall hand of heav'n,
> Ha's all but this one onely Blessing [wit] giv'n.
> The World appear's like a great Familie
> Whose Lord opprest with pride and povertie
> That to a few great Plentie he may show
> Is fain to starve the numerous train below;
> Just so seem's providence, as poor and vain,

> Keeping more Creatures then it can maintain,
> Here 'tis profuse, and there it meanly saves,
> And for one Prince it makes Ten Thousand Slaves.
> In wit alone 't ha's been magnificent
> Of which so just a share to each is sent
> That the most avaritious are content.
> For none er'e thought (the due Division's such)
> His own too litle, or his Freind's too much:
> Yet most men shew, or find great want of wit,
> Writing themselves, or judging what is writ.
> (lines 54–70)

In Rochester's estimation M.G. epitomizes the 'Courtier without Wit', one of whose defining characteristics, according to Dryden, being that 'God has not bestow'd on [him] the gift of utterance' (Dryden, vol. 12, p. 150). In his case, Providence has 'meanly' saved; though being among the 'most avaritious', M.G. is 'content' and shows 'great want of wit' in writing of himself.

M.G. concludes his poem with a hyperbolic imitation of critical attitudes Dryden has expressed in the dedication. In defending *Aureng-Zebe*, Dryden argued:

> But, it may be, I am partial to my own Writings: yet I have labor'd as much as any man, to divest myself of the self-opinion of an Author; and am too well satisfi'd of my own weakness to be pleas'd with any thing I have written. But on the other side, my reason tells me, that, in probability, what I have seriously and long consider'd may be as likely to be just and natural, as what an ordinary Judge ... will think fit, in a transient Presentation, to be plac'd in the room of that which they condemn. The most judicious Writer is sometimes mistaken, after all his care: but the hasty Critick, who judges on a view, is full as liable to be deceiv'd. Let him first consider all the Arguments, which the Author had, to write this, or to design the other, before he arraigns him of a fault: and then, perhaps, on second thoughts, he will find his Reason oblige him to revoke his Censure. (Dryden, vol. 12, pp. 156–57)

In his obtuseness M.G. latches on to Dryden's argument without comprehending any of the subtle qualifications; consequently, he turns a reasonable assessment of the balance that ought to exist between author and critic into a purely egotistical theory of writing.

> Born to myself, myself I like alone
> And must conclude my Judgment good or none.
> For should my Sence be naught, how coud I know,
> Whether another man's were good or no?
> Thus I resolve of my own poetry
> That 'tis the best, and there's a Fame for me.
> If then I'm happie, what does it advance

> Whether to merit due, or Arrogance!
> Oh! but the world will take offence, thereby,
> Why then the world will suffer for 't, not I.
> Did er'e this sawcy world and I agree
> To let it have it's beastlie will on me?
> Why shoud my prostituted sence be drawn
> To ev'ry Rule their mustie Customes spawn?
> But men will censure you 'tis two to One,
> When er'e they censure, they'l be in the wrong.
> There's not a thing on Earth that I can name,
> So Foolish and so false as common Fame.
> (lines 73–90)

Nothing could be further from the truth about the man who had Colonel Aston spread abroad the report of the Knightsbridge duel. Mulgrave courted 'common Fame'. Whatever truth his propositions may have in the abstract, they become tainted in this context, because he, like his fawning dedicator, is a liar. In his dedication, Dryden had solemnly vowed that 'As a Poet ... The lowness of my Fortune has not yet brought me to flatter Vice; and 'tis my duty to give testimony to Virtue' (Dryden, vol. 12, p. 150). Rochester saw the truth differently. Dryden had not testified to virtue; he had flattered vice. Dryden confessed:

> The truth is, the consideration of so vain a Creature as man, is not worth our pains. I have fool enough at home without looking for it abroad: and am a sufficient Theater to my self of ridiculous actions, without expecting company, either in a Court, a Town, or Play-house. (Dryden, vol. 12, p. 154)

Rochester could only agree. Thus he has M.G. close his poem with a similar self-incriminating statement of Dryden's sentiment: 'These things considerd, make me in despight/ Of idle Rumour keep at home and write.'

'A very heroical epistle' and 'An Epistolary Essay' do reflect Rochester's beliefs and attitudes, and are self-critically libertine, but not in the way Griffin has taken them to be. They also satirize the Earl of Mulgrave, but Rochester's judgments are probably not so Christian and Augustan as Vieth would have us believe. The poems grew out of the context of Rochester's nearly lifelong, bitter antagonism with Mulgrave, their immediate impetus being Mulgrave's patronage of Dryden and Dryden's subsequent panegyric on Mulgrave and his barbed assessment of his former patron, Lord Rochester. Rochester constructed deliberately ambiguous poems in large part because from his perspective the quarrel was a matter of honesty and authenticity. To Rochester, Dryden and Mulgrave were liars; both were frauds parading as legitimate. To reveal the sham, he simply had Mulgrave in 'A very heroical epistle' speak in his own voice. Is such a man truly great? In 'An Epistolary Essay' he had him speak in the character that Dryden had created for him. Is such a man truly adept in poetry? Those who had not the experience of Mulgrave might well answer yes to both questions, but they would have been, like Ephelia and generations of Rochester's critics, deceived.

It is easy to see, however, why Griffin takes the poems to be Rochester's critical examination of himself and why Vieth maintains that 'To a greater or lesser degree the "I" of each poem is always Rochester' and that 'Bajazet and M.G. ... cannot be wholly detached from Rochester's personality despite their primary functions, as satirical portraits of Mulgrave' (Vieth, *Poems*, pp. xli–xlii). In attacking Mulgrave Rochester lacerated himself. So much of what he loathed, he himself embodied. Like Mulgrave, he was proud, self-centred, and ambitious – often meanly so. He pandered to his King, betrayed friends, and chased after women. Mulgrave embodied much that he hated in himself. That these two satires on Mulgrave should have turned out ironic, the norms of judgment being equivocal, is, given the biographical context, not surprising. As Kenneth Burke has pointed out, 'True irony, humble irony, is based upon a sense of fundamental kinship with the enemy, as one *needs* him, is *indebted* to him, is not merely outside him as an observer but contains him within, being consubstantial with him.'[26] As we have seen, these two men were in many senses consubstantial. Rochester needed Mulgrave and was, in a sense, indebted to him. Mulgrave allowed him to gain distance on himself and to escape, however briefly, from the self-hatred that finally consumed him. In part because of Mulgrave, Rochester managed to shape hatred into artefact. Mulgrave allowed him psychologically to escape momentarily from the solipsism to which his libertine epistemology condemned him; artistically, the imitative aesthetic of neo-classicism served much the same function.

Vieth's view of Rochester as Christian humanist and Augustan is, within the biographical context, also understandable. As Johnson has argued, following his vigorously Christian upbringing Rochester went on to pass through three stages of intellectual predisposition: Cyreniac or egotistical hedonism, a modified version of the pleasure principle as found in Epicurus, and finally during 1678 a return to Christianity. Apparently, a crucial transition occurred during the early 1670s as Rochester, confronted with personal experience of the failure of egotistical hedonism, attempted to place some ethical boundaries on the life lived according to pleasure.[27] For all his efforts to replace Christianity with pagan models, Rochester never succeeded. His search for such a model whether in Aristippus, Lucretius, or the contemporary French libertines he apparently read was always conducted in a dialectical relationship with Christianity. Christianity informs even the obscene and seemingly agnostic of his poems, the libertine and the Christian never being far apart in Rochester's work or life, the one, as Rochester later discovered, really demanding the presence of the other. In times of crisis the Christianity that he thought he had escaped always seemed to come forth to make its claim.

Both 'A very heroical epistle' and the 'An Epistolary Essay' are best read as Epicurean critiques of a purely egotistical hedonism. Mulgrave is a libertine, someone Rochester understood quite well because he himself had been just that. It is not that Mulgrave's search for pleasure is wrong, but that his methods, completely egotistical, defeat his goal. He lacks restraint, both as courtier and as poet. The implicit norms underlying both poems have to do with curbing the appetites, with upholding degree and moderation, but these values, at least at this stage in Rochester's life, derive less from the Christian-humanist tradition than from Epicureanism, though it is easy to confuse the two. The true epicure as opposed to sham one like Mulgrave upholds degree and good form in order to maximize pleasure. Epicurean and Christian values, so close in many respects, are interwoven in Rochester's thought. Rejection of the latter at an early age led to the dominance of the former during most of the 1670s. At the end of the decade, the latter again prevailed, understandably so. Both the orthodox Christian humanist and the Epicurean were, as Dale Underwood has pointed out, interested in 'reuniting "nature" and "grace", the physical and the spiritual man, by the proper relations of reason and the passions'.[28] Both stressed degree and moderation, though their ultimate goals differed, the one with its eye on eternal salvation and the other with its aim on earthly pleasure. As earthly felicity continued to elude Rochester, it was inevitable that he would look to eternity. These two poems, however, condemn not Mulgrave the violator of traditional norms and Christian precepts, but Mulgrave the bumbler whose megalomania prevents him from reaching the pleasure he so desires. A reformed Cyprian is condemning one of his former brothers.

Perhaps one example juxtaposing Vieth's, Griffin's, and my way of making sense of these two poems is in order. Bajazet mockingly protests:

> What Man or Woman upon earth can say
> I ever us'd 'em well above a day?
> How is it then that I inconstant am?
> He changes not, who always is the same.
> (lines 3–6)

Vieth writes of this passage that

> The notion that perpetual inconstancy constitutes a kind of constancy is a weary cliché of seventeenth-century love poetry. In the context of Rochester's satire, however, the cliché is revitalized, for the alleged absence of any consistency in Bajazet's behavior suggests the absolute Chaos antithetical to the

divine Logos. Bajazet's life is, by implication, a succession of small acts of Uncreation. (Vieth, *Attribution*, p. 111)

This is eloquent, but these suggestions and implications are generated by the critic's assumption that Rochester is a proto-Pope and here intends 'inconstancy' to draw meaning from the context of Christianity. Of the same passage, Griffin writes:

> In light of libertine conventions, Bajazet does not unconsciously violate standards (as Vieth would have it) or daringly confess egotism (in Pinto's terms), but strikes a traditional pose. Yet the poem is far more than a series of libertine clichés. Bajazet's answers restate the standard arguments with great flair, and pretend plain-dealing. (Griffin, p. 61)

Griffin is right. Mulgrave here speaks as a libertine, but if he is the target of satire – and he is – then we should not take his words as being dashingly wicked.

Read within the biographical context, these lines first of all ironically refer to Dryden's praise of Mulgrave's 'constancy to your Friends', to his 'good Nature and Generosity', and to his 'firmness in all your Actions'. Mulgrave is just the opposite of Dryden's portrayal in the dedication to *Aureng-Zebe*. He is not the true courtier but the 'Courtier without Wit' who 'steal[s] ... jests' from his betters, in this case, Rochester. Trying to sound like a true courtier, he merely repeats the dullest of truisms. But the target here is larger than Mulgrave. It is revealing that both Vieth and Griffin use 'cliché', for though their interpretations differ, they both hit upon what Rochester is doing. He has loaded both poems with libertine clichés. But how are we to know this? It would appear that Rochester simply does not have control of his poems. As Irving Ehrenpreis has observed:

> The art of the employer of the ironical mask springs from his power to combine ambiguous moral sentiments with an ambiguous attitude toward what he is saying. The reader must assume that the doctrines to be expounded are proper, decent things. He must also assume that the author is serious in proposing them. The skill of the writer appears in his disclosing the wickedness of the doctrines before disclosing the irony of his manner.[29]

Rochester, at least in these poems, lacks the necessary skill to maintain his ironic mask while disclosing why we should disapprove of the doctrines Mulgrave expounds. This criticism, however, misses the point. Rochester wished to expose not just Mulgrave's false character but Dryden's frightening power to change reality through language. In the hands of a Dryden, words can make even a Mulgrave appear great. How are we to know that he is not? Rochester's answer was experience. Any would-be rake could mouth libertine lines, but to know whether his words had the ring of authenticity would be to experience the person. Meaning is not absolute, but relative, dependent on context, something the poems were written to show, something that contemporary criticism, knowingly or not, has confirmed.

Vieth published his findings about 'The true character of the "Heroical Epistle" as a satire on Mulgrave' in 1963. Griffin's response came ten years later in 1973. Vieth presciently labelled Rochester's 'Epistolary Essay' 'A Crux for Critics and Scholars' (Vieth, *Attribution*, p. 103), and it has remained just that – a spirited critical conversation surrounding this poem and 'A very heroical epistle' continuing to this very day. For the most part, Vieth has prevailed. George deF. Lord in *Poems on Affairs of State: Augustan Satirical Verse, 1660–1714* included both poems, writing:

> In a recently-published study, *Attribution in Restoration Poetry*, David Vieth shows that the *Epistolary Essay* purports to be written by the Earl of Mulgrave to his poetic collaborator, Dryden (Old Bays). The identification had eluded previous critics of Rochester and the *Essay*, like the *Very Heroical Epistle in Answer to Ephelia*, had been regarded as Rochester's personal declaration. Like the *Heroical Epistle*, however, this satire employs a satirical persona to castigate Mulgrave for his arrogant disregard of rational human standards. The earlier poem devotes itself to Mulgrave's moral egotism, and this one exposes the false literary standards that grow out of such moral egotism.

Lord sees both poems, as I do, as 'attacks' on 'Dryden with a pervasive parody of his preface to *Aureng-Zebe* (1676)' and goes on intriguingly to suggest: 'The only known "mutual poem" of Mulgrave and Dryden is *An Essay upon Satire*. I assume that a draft of this poem was known by Rochester to be in existence as early as 1675.'[30] Given that one of the unsolved problems surrounding the 'Epistolary Essay' is its date, all Rochester critics would love to be able to find evidence for Lord's assumption.

In *Rochester: The Critical Heritage* (1972) David Farley-Hills follows Vieth: 'What were earlier taken to be autobiographical poems are shown to be mock heroic, in which the absurd boasting of the hero is the subject of satire.'[31] He goes on in *Rochester's Poetry* to argue that what has led to critics interpreting the poem '["An Epistolary Essay"] in opposite directions' is that 'the poem lacks clarity'.[32] In his gloss on 'The Epistolary Essay' Keith Walker notes that the poem

> was long thought to be ... written from Rochester to Mulgrave expressing in V. de Sola Pinto's words, 'naked self-worship' ... David Vieth decisively reoriented interpretation by arguing ... 'Rochester in "An Epistolary Essay" satirizes John Sheffield, Earl of Mulgrave, by depicting him as a persona ... the self-centered speaker renders himself ridiculous by unconsciously violating conceptions of good writing.'[33]

Frank Ellis has no doubt about the poem's speaker or its irony: 'As he did in *A Very Heroical Epistle from My Lord All-Pride* ... Rochester again takes the persona of Mulgrave ("M.G."), this time to reply to the attack on himself in lines 230–69 of *An Essay upon Satire*, of which Rochester read a MS copy on 21 November 1679.'[34] In the now standard edition of Rochester's works published in 1999, the pre-eminent scholar of Restoration poetry, Harold Love, set down what has become the orthodox critical assessment of 'An Epistolary Essay, from M.G. to O.B. upon their mutuall Poems', writing:

> Vieth ... was the first scholar to explain that this puzzling poem (at one time read as a personal manifesto) was a satirical monologue put into the mouth of Rochester's literary and political enemy, John Sheffield, third Earl of Mulgrave. While objections ... have been made to this hypothesis, it seems to the present editor to be the only one that makes coherent sense both of the poem and of its place in the broader controversy from which it arises between proto-Whig and proto-Tory factions at court. (Love, p. 429)

In *A Profane Wit: The Life of John Wilmot, Earl of Rochester*, James William Johnson agrees. While noting that 'An Epistolary Essay' 'has always been one of the most controversial in Rochester's canon' – its authorship, date, narrator, and point of view 'widely disputed' – Johnson concludes: 'Vieth has shown conclusively that the narrator (M.G.) is a satiric Mulgrave-persona and O.B. is Dryden his protégé-collaborator' (Johnson, pp. 238–39).

Keith Walker and Nicholas Fisher, echoing Love, note, however, that 'Vieth's persuasive arguments have not met with universal assent'.[35] And given that neither Vieth nor anyone else has been able definitively to date 'An Epistolary Essay' or to identify M.G. and O.B., David Brooks thought Vieth had argued 'mistakenly, that the *Epistolary essay* also depicts Mulgrave for the purpose of satirising him'.[36]

D.K. Alsop perceptively put his finger on what is a stake in this ongoing critical conversation about the poem: the identity of Rochester. 'There have been three main positions adopted with respect to Rochester's "Epistolary Essay" in the last sixty years', Alsop writes, 'making the poem paradigmatic of the problem of the persona in Rochester's writing'. He goes on to rehearse those positions, citing 'among others, Johannes Prinz, J.H. Wilson, and Vivian de Sola Pinto' who 'identified the speaker of the poem with Rochester himself' and examining the arguments of Griffin and Vieth, 'the two major spokesmen for revised readings of the "Epistolary Essay"'. Alsop rejects both, both relying as they do on conceptions of 'the historical Rochester'. In Alsop's view 'We have no access to the "real" Rochester, and in that he so manifestly enjoys adopting different roles it is always questionable that he speaks, in his poems, with "his" own voice.' Nevertheless, Alsop knows enough about 'the historical Rochester' to agree with Vieth, but not with his argument, that 'in "An Epistolary Essay from M.G. to O.B.", where Rochester so explicitly indicates that he is using an assumed voice, any identification of author and speaker is particularly open to question'.[37]

Time and time again a critic's assessment of 'An Epistolary Essay' is guided by an understanding, sometimes stated, sometimes not, of who Rochester was. In her hugely informative and useful study, *Rochester: The Poems in Context* (1993) Marianne Thormählen writes: 'It is true that Vieth's argumentation is speculative, but speculation can be more or less persuasive. The last word remains to be said on the subject, but one thing seems irrefutable to me: by no means can it be convincingly argued that the *Epistolary Essay* expresses Rochester's personal views.' The reason? The speaker of the 'Epistolary Essay' cannot be the same as the one in Rochester's 'Allusion to Horace'. 'My assumption that the speaker of that poem is Rochester himself', Thormählen admits, 'is not one for which hard evidence could be adduced'.[38] Nevertheless, that is her Rochester, and therefore the speaker of 'The Epistolary Essay' must be the butt of satire, a Mulgrave. Christopher Tilmouth also reads the 'The Epistolary Essay' in the context of 'An Allusion to Horace' and concludes that the 'crass tone' of the former is not one 'Rochester himself would adopt, and Wilmot clearly prefers the affirmation of his coterie ('Sydley, Shadwell' *et al.*) to Mulgrave's isolationism'. While pointing out that there are reasons why 'generations of readers have seen in Mulgrave's egoism an affinity with Rochester's', Tilmouth goes on to argue that

> the important point to emphasize is not that the *Epistolary Essay* portrays one Earl or the other but rather that it blurs the boundary between them, highlighting how tenuous Rochester's aesthetic distinctions are and how close to his position comes to Mulgrave's bald subjectivism. A skeptical void again opens up at the edges of his writing.[39]

Tilmouth's Rochester is a sceptic, one whose aesthetic distinctions are tenuous.

Recently Steven Zwicker succinctly and elegantly summed up some of the 'puzzles and uncertainties' raised by '*An Epistolary Essay from M. G to O.B. upon their mutuall Poems*' – from the dating of the poem, to its authorship, to its intention, to its occasion:

> In 1669, or was it 1679, or perhaps 1676, Rochester wrote, or may have written, what may be a send up of John Sheffield, Earl of Mulgrave, intent on mimicking Mulgrave's egotism and self-pride, or may be Rochester's personal manifesto or a piece of self-irony that uses satire's cold light to reveal the poet's

own character; or perhaps – as has long been thought, and by Rochester's contemporaries – a verse epistle from Rochester to Mulgrave. The poem may have been an answer to Mulgrave's attack on Rochester in *An Essay on Satire*, and if so would likely have been written late in 1679 for Mulgrave's *Essay on Satire* (if it were his) was circulating in November of 1679 when Rochester mentions the 'libel' in a letter to Henry Savile ... Or perhaps Rochester's *Epistolary Essay* is at once a savage burlesque of Mulgrave and a piece of ironic self-exposure that limns the uncomfortable proximity of Rochester and Mulgrave. Nor have we exhausted the difficulties and uncertainties of the poem, not least its intent and its attitude.

For Zwicker the poem's contradictions and perplexities are not a sign of critical inadequacy or of 'Rochester's ironies or his satiric brilliance (though the poem has enough of both)' but rather arise from 'the instabilities of satiric texts written within and into a field of gossip, innuendo, and hearsay'. Zwicker goes on brilliantly, placing the poem in context of the Restoration world of 'gossip, innuendo, and hearsay' Rochester would have known, only to conclude 'that we simply do not know enough to answer all the questions that the poem raises about origins and ends – that is about dating and identity, or stance, tone and intent'. Zwicker's conclusion about the poem being one of 'instabilities and uncertainties' arises in part because of his assessment of who Rochester was. Zwicker's Rochester had 'no peer in writing poetry from drunkenness and outrage; at times the life, the scandals and the poetry seem together one long collaborative project. Reckless of that life and careless in scattering his verse, Rochester was a poet without a stable literary identity and surely without a sense of literary immortality.'[40] Nowhere to be found in Zwicker's account is the Rochester who had a 'Christian Upbringing' and received a 'Classical Education', who had a happy, though often contentious, marriage and loved being a father. This Rochester was Keeper of Woodstock Park. He had game, timber, and a crew of woodsmen to oversee. He supervised estates, bred and raced horses, examined accounts, talked with agents and tenants, bought and sold livestock. This Rochester attended the House of Lords and delighted in arranging and presiding over the marriage between 'The King's favorite bastard-daughter, the Lady Charlotte Fitzroy' and his half-nephew, Edward Henry Lee, a marriage that healed a rift among the Wilmots and Lees and assuaged Charles II's anger over the disastrous marriage of Anne Lee to Thomas Wharton (Johnson, pp. 6–20, 21–27, and 184).

As Paul Hammond has pointed out, 'twentieth-century editions have also presented readers with a variety of Rochesters, in terms of text, canon, and authorial persona'.[41] Paddy Lyons, for example, finds the critical stance of Prinz and Pinto, one 'assuming the first-person stance to correspond to that held by the poet', as well as Vieth's 'More ingeniously ... argued' stance that the poem's speaker is 'a *persona* ... representing John Sheffield, Earl of Mulgrave, whose conceit and self-sufficiency are satirised', to be wanting. Why? Neither allows for the 'compelling and a very hilarious poet' Rochester was, one whose 'procedures of radical doubt ... destabilize distance, leaving the speaker's stance unfixed'.[42]

Harold Love has given us an amusing, important, and now famous example of how an editor's assumptions about the 'real' Rochester informs his critical choices, noting that Walker, 'when given a choice between an obscene word and a euphemism, seems nearly always to use the obscene word'. Love goes on to write: 'This is not done from what Greg called "a superfluity of naughtiness" but from an honest conviction that the direct colloquial terms is the one Rochester would have preferred; and yet it may be that this judgment has led to some coarsening of the poet's effects.'[43] As he readily admits, Love has his own conception of Rochester,[44] one that informs his editorial choices, a good example being his argument for including in his edition, 'Say *Heave'n-born Muse*, for only thou canst tell', a poem rejected by all other editors of Rochester's work:

> Rochester's inclusion as a character in his own lampoon (Vieth's main objection) is a predictable strategy to disguise authorship – the trick used in Mulgrave's "An essay upon satire", lines 194–209 ... That stylistic tests by John Burrows find the poem uncharacteristic of Rochester is easily explained by the fact that it performs a skilful parody of Virgilian syntax as well as heroic diction. There are verbal parallels to other Rochester texts at lines A4, 37, 46, 117. (Love, p. 415)

In short the Rochester Love knows would have written this poem.

Interpretations and editions of Rochester's work, sometimes tacitly, sometimes not, are inextricably tied to assumptions about the historical John Wilmot. This book is no exception. It attempts to realize the implications more fully than have past studies by trying to avoid the many pitfalls of biographical criticism while suspecting and in many cases knowing that Rochester in his work drew upon his experience, his emotional, religious, and intellectual life. We evaluate a critical work by its accuracy, consistency, scope, simplicity, and fruitfulness. This study attempts to be more accurate because it has the advantage of drawing upon the new information we have learned about Rochester since the 1960s, which is considerable. Vieth's 'grand desideratum ... a definitive biography of the Earl'[45] has not been forthcoming, and I suspect given the historical gaps, the disputed canon, and a life lived that 'gives the electrifying impression of being in contact with both myth and reality' (Vieth, *Attribution*, p. 203) that Vieth thought it never would. Nevertheless, Johnson's *A Very Profane Wit*, though peppered with 'begun possibly', 'one can only conjecture', and 'we can imagine Rochester feeling', and laced with speculations, gives us a wealth of information and insight into his upbringing. It is particularly good at reconstructing Rochester's domestic and Court life while providing the most complete account and understanding that we are likely to have of his formidable mother, the Dowager Countess of Rochester.[46] This study also has the advantage of standing on the shoulders of others who have done scholarly work on Rochester since Griffin's book of 1973.[47] The findings have been big, Love wryly noting in 2000, for example, that 'we are still getting used to the idea that Rochester may have been the author of the anti-Danby satire *An Allusion to Tacitus* ('The Freeborn English Generous and Wise')'.[48] As Christopher Tilmouth has noted: 'much of the Earl's biography remains a matter of informed speculation. Even so, research has unearthed details of Rochester's political life as an associate of the Country Party faction emergent in the 1670s Britain, a discovery that poses significant questions for the interpretation of his poetry'.[49] And small, Fisher providing us with this gem of an insight into a playful, good-humoured Rochester in nailing down that the anecdote about Rochester encountering Isaac Barrow, first mentioned by Pinto, is probably true:

> As a proof of [Barrow's] wit, we are told the following story: Meeting lord Rochester one day at court, his lordship, by way of banter, thus accosted him: 'Doctor, I am your's to my shoe tie.' Barrow, seeing his aim, returned his salute as obsequiously, with 'My lord, I am your's to the ground.' Rochester, improving his blow, quickly returned it, with, 'Doctor, I am your's to the centre;' which was as smartly followed by Barrow, with 'My lord, I am your's to the antipodes.' Upon which, Rochester, scorning to be foiled by a musty old piece of divinity as he used to call him, exclaimed, 'Doctor, I am your's to the lowest pit of hell.' On which Barrow, turning on his heel, answered, 'There, my lord, I leave you.'[50]

In method, this book takes its cue from Kenneth Burke who observes in *The Philosophy of Literary Form*: 'The main ideal of criticism ... is to use all that there is to use.'[51] I try do just that with the goal of restoring the private grammar to the poems by reading them as much as possible in the context of their making. This method of reading the works in their biographical context reveals that Rochester's work clusters about a central theme, the pursuit of pleasure. This phrase is shorthand for a complex process in which so many of Rochester's mid-seventeenth century contemporaries were engaged. No longer sure under the old dispensation of their duties – religious, political, familial, or artistic – they sought new grounds for their motivations. For Rochester and perhaps for a number of his libertine companions this pursuit of pleasure was motivated by a courtship of purity that in all probability grew out of a religious neurosis. I argue that Rochester's work everywhere reflects his Christian and

God-fearing upbringing and provides evidence of an excessive preoccupation with, and acceptance of, Christianity. As the various speakers, and the man himself, pursue pleasure by courting king, wives, mistresses, and the craft of writing, they also often in perverse, even criminal, ways court God.

Some may feel that finding a thematic order in the work of an insouciant though obviously talented rake poet simply reflects the logic of the method and nothing essential about the work itself. I hope such is not the case here. In scope, this book goes beyond that of past critical studies, none of which puts Rochester's plays, prologues, epilogues, and letters in relationship to his poetry. Until recently no reliable text of the notorious *Sodom* existed. We now know a good deal more about the various texts of *Sodom*, and if Rochester did have a hand in this wickedly hilarious farce – and I speculate that he did – we may have found an important clue to his development as a satirist. *Lucina's Rape*, often categorized as no more than that oddity, a Restoration adaptation, received some attention from Griffin and more recently insightful commentary from Love and Fisher. When seen in the context of Rochester's intellectual development, it becomes a most significant work: Rochester's final attempt to make neo-classical art and its humanistic vision a viable alternative to self-destructive ironies and the scepticism that fuelled them. Whether this study will also meet the criteria of simplicity and fruitfulness remains to be seen.

I certainly would not claim that Rochester's work has meaning only in its biographical context. Nor is there any claim that such an approach avoids critical relativism, though I think this problem looms greater in theoretical discussions than in practical criticism. Several critics could, and no doubt will, have the same historical information, and they will come to quite different conclusions while still being accurate, consistent, comprehensive in scope, elegantly simple, and abundantly fruitful. Choosing among these critical models will be a matter of values not of philosophically verifiable criteria, and these values will have evolved in large part through experience. The contemporary critic, that is, finally confronts the epistemological dilemma out of which the poems themselves arose and which often become their subject matter. In trying to understand this dilemma the contemporary critic, like Rochester, learns that induction has no philosophical solution and that the critical act, like other acts of knowing, begins in experience and is finally an act of faith. Seen within the biographical context, Rochester's poetic career began in earnest when he confronted this epistemological paradox in the flesh while on a ramble in St James's Park.

Notes

1. Rosalie L. Colie, *Paradoxia Epidemica: The Renaissance Tradition of Paradox* (Hamden, CT: Archon Books, 1976), p. 360. Hereafter cited in the text as Colie.
2. Clifford Geertz, *The Interpretation of Cultures* (New York: Basic Books, 1973), p. 20.
3. Citations to Rochester's poetry, unless otherwise noted, are from *The Works of John Wilmot Earl of Rochester*, ed. Harold Love (Oxford: Oxford University Press) and will be cited in the text by line number.
4. Dustin H. Griffin, *Satires Against Man: The Poems of Rochester* (Berkeley: University of California Press, 1973), p. 24. Hereafter cited in the text as Griffin.
5. Wallace Stevens, 'Large Red Man Reading', *The Collected Poems of Wallace Stevens* (New York: Alfred A. Knoff: 1967), line 6.
6. David Vieth, ed., *The Complete Poems of John Wilmot, Earl of Rochester* (New Haven, CT: Yale University Press, 1968), p. xxxiii. Hereafter cited in the text as Vieth, *Poems*.
7. George Etherege, *The Man of Mode, or Sir Fopling Flutter: a comedy* (London: Printed by J. Macock for Henry Herringman, 1676), II. ii., line 15.
8. David Vieth, *Attribution in Restoration Poetry: A Study of Rochester's 'Poems' of 1680* (Yale Studies in English 153. New Haven, CT: Yale University Press, 1963), pp. 103–36. Hereafter cited in the text as Vieth, *Attribution*.
9. Vivian de Sola Pinto, *Enthusiast in Wit* (Lincoln, NE: University of Nebraska Press, 1962), p. 148.
10. Wayne Booth, *The Rhetoric of Irony* (Chicago: University of Chicago Press, 1974), p. 44.
11. Love places *Timon* among Rochester's 'Disputed Works'. For more on the authorship of *Timon* see Chapter 4, note 3.
12. See John Harold Wilson, *The Court Wits of the Restoration* (Princeton, NJ: Princeton University Press, 1948), pp. 30 and 117. And Vieth: 'The true character of the "Heroical Epistle" as a satire on Mulgrave was first pointed out by Wilson, whose insight evidently came through a combination of scholarship with criticism, since he was also the first to discover the allusions at the end of the poem to Mulgrave's affair with Mall Kirke' (Vieth, *Attribution*, p. 108).
13. 'If a speaker betrays ignorance or foolishness that is "simply incredible", the odds are comparatively high that the author … knows what he is doing' (Wayne Booth, *Rhetoric of Irony* (Chicago: University of Chicago Press, 1974), p. 57).
14. Mulgrave, John Sheffield, Earl of, *The works of John Sheffield, earl of Mulgrave, marquis of Normandy, and duke of Buckingham* (London: Printed for J.B., 1729), 2, pp. 8 and 10.
15. As Samuel Johnson wryly puts it: 'He had a quarrel with the Earl of Rochester, which he has perhaps too ostentatiously related' (*The Lives of the Poets*, ed. John H. Middendorf (New Haven, CT: Yale University Press, 2010), 22, p. 689).
16. I am quoting from Princeton University Library, MS AM 14401 and have more to say about *Sodom* in Chapter 3.

17 Graham Greene thinks that though Rochester may have 'induced his wife to turn Catholic for political reasons ... Certainly he never himself showed any inclination towards Catholicism' (*Lord Rochester's Monkey: Being the Life of John Wilmot, Second Earl of Rochester* (New York: Viking Press, 1974), p. 170). James William Johnson, however, observes that 'Rochester's reason for urging his wife to become a Recusant remain unclear. The simplest explanation would be that he himself had converted earlier and wanted her to share that faith' (*A Profane Wit: The Life of John Wilmot Earl of Rochester* (Rochester, NY: University of Rochester Press, 2004) p. 94). Hereafter Johnson's biography will be cited in the text as Johnson.

18 George deF. Lord, ed., *Poems on Affairs of State Augustan Satirical Verse, 1660–1714*, 1 (New Haven, CT: Yale University Press, 1963), lines 38–43. The authorship of 'Advice to Apollo' is unknown. Lord, citing John Harold Wilson, thinks it 'was probably produced by Rochester and his fellow wits who assembled at Woodstock in mid-October 1677' (Lord, p. 392; Wilson, *The Court Wits*, p. 195). Vieth finds that in its 'attitudes' the poem 'suggest[s] an origin in Rochester's circle of Wits' (*Attribution*, p. 188).

19 In a stylistic study of selected works of Dryden and Mulgrave, John Burrows concludes: 'It has been possible to establish consistent and wide-ranging differences between Dryden and Mulgrave. Set in that light, neither version of *An Essay upon Satire* resembles Dryden's unassisted work. If it is a collaboration, it would seem that Mulgrave had by far the major hand' ('Mulgrave, Dryden, and *An Essay upon Satire*', *Script & Print*, Special Issue, 33 (1–4) (2009), p. 89).

20 John Sheffield, *An Essay Upon Poetry* (London: Printed for *Joseph. Hindmarsh*, 1682), p. 6.

21 Mulgrave, *The Works of John Sheffield*, 2, p. 161.

22 Vivian de Sola Pinto, *Restoration Carnival* (London: The Folio Society, 1954), p. 215.

23 John Dryden, *The Works of John Dryden* (Berkeley, CA: University of California Press, 1978), 21, pp. 221–23. Hereafter cited in the text as Dryden.

24 Jeremy Treglown, ed., *The Letters of John Wilmot Earl of Rochester* (Chicago, IL: University of Chicago Press, 1980), pp. 87–88. Hereafter cited in the text as Treglown.

25 As Paul Hammond first noted in 'Two Echoes of Rochester's *A Satire against Reason and Mankind* in Dryden', *N&Q*, 233 (1988), p. 171.

26 Kenneth Burke, *A Grammar of Motives* (Prentice-Hall, 1945; Berkeley, CA: University of California Press, 1974), p. 514.

27 See 'Lord Rochester and the Tradition of Cyrenaic Hedonism, 1670–1790', *Studies on Voltaire and the Eighteenth Century*, 153 (1976), pp. 158–59.

28 Dale Underwood, *Etherege and the Seventeenth-Century Comedy of Manners* (New Haven, CT: Yale University Press, 1957; rpt. Archon Books, 1969), pp. 16–17.

29 Irvin Ehrenpreis, *Literary Meaning and Augustan Values* (Charlottesville, VA: University of Virginia Press, 1974), pp. 57–58.

30 Lord, *POAS*, 1, p. 348.

31 David Farley-Hills, ed., *Rochester: The Critical Heritage* (New York: Barnes & Noble, 1972), p. 26.
32 David Farley-Hill, *Rochester's Poetry* (Totowa, NJ: Rowman & Littlefield, 1978), p. 127.
33 Keith Walker, ed., *The Complete Poems of John Wilmot Earl of Rochester* (Oxford: Basil Blackwell, 1984), p. 293. Hereafter cited in the text as Walker.
34 Frank H. Ellis, ed., *John Wilmot, Earl of Rochester: The Complete Works* (London: Penguin Books, 1994), p. 408.
35 Keith Walker and Nicholas Fisher, eds, *John Wilmot, Earl of Rochester: The Poems and Lucina's Rape* (Oxford: Wiley-Blackwell, 2010), p. 119. Hereafter cited in the text as Walker and Fisher.
36 David Brooks, ed., *Lyrics & Satires of John Wilmot Earl of Rochester* (Sydney, Australia: Hale & Iremonger, 1980), pp. 23 and 207 footnote 6.
37 D.K. Alsop, '"An Epistolary Essay from M.G. to O.B. upon their Mutual Poem" and the Problem of Persona in Rochester's Poetry', *Restoration Studies in English Literary Culture, 1660–1700,* 12, 2 (Fall 1988), pp. 61 and 67.
38 Marianne Thormählen, *Rochester: The Poems in Context* (Cambridge University Press, 1993), p. 338. Hereafter cited in the text as Thormählen.
39 Christopher Tilmouth, 'Rochester and the Play of Values', in *Lord Rochester in the Restoration World*, eds Matthew C. Augustine and Steven N. Zwicker (Cambridge University Press, 2015), p. 155.
40 Steven N. Zwicker, 'Lord Rochester: A Life in Gossip', in *Lord Rochester in the Restoration World*, eds Matthew C. Augustine and Steven N. Zwicker (Cambridge University Press, 2015), pp. 80–81, 83, and 79.
41 Paul Hammond, *The Making of Restoration Poetry* (Cambridge: D.S. Brewer, 2006), p. 191.
42 Paddy Lyons, ed., *Rochester: Complete Poems and Plays* (London: J.M. Dent, 1993). p. xv.
43 Love, p. xlii; Love is quoting from his article, 'Refining Rochester: Private Texts and Public Readers', *Harvard Library Bulletin*, 7 (1996) p. 48.
44 In arranging Rochester's poems 'into three categories' – those almost assuredly 'attributed to him', those 'which could well be by Rochester', and 'those poems that are only weakly attributed but cannot be shown *not* to be by Rochester' – Love writes: 'It must be remembered that the assignment of a poem to one of these categories is in each case the result of an act of judgement by the editor, and one that the reader, on an independent reconsideration of the evidence, may wish to dissent from' (Love, pp. xxviii–xxix).
45 David M. Vieth, *Rochester Studies, 1925–1982: An Annotated Bibliography* (New York: Garland Publishing, 1984), p. xvi.
46 While highly critical of Johnson's biography, Love points out: 'Among its errors and eccentricities the book has assembled much information not given in earlier biographies. Rochester's activity as a member of the House of Lords, the interminable squabbles within his extended family over property and marriages, and the content of his early education are all usefully explored … The year-by-year narration of events allows the different streams of Rochester's life – family,

amorous, political, literary and religious – to be brought together in a mutually illuminating way which becomes more effective as the story advances into the late 1670s with their richer haul of primary materials. The Popish Plot years and the events leading up to Rochester's death are presented as engrossingly as one would wish. Johnson's identification of Hamilton's mysterious Miss Hobart as Lady Dorothy Howard is persuasive, and he is able to draw on new evidence for identifying the same author's "Miss Sarah" with the actress Sarah Cooke' (Rev. of *A Profane Wit: The Life of John Wilmot, Earl of Rochester* by James William Johnson in *Seventeenth-Century News*, 63 (2005), pp. 137–41).

47 Most notably Treglown (*Letters*, 1980); Walker (*Poems*, 1984); Thormählen (*Poems in Context*, 1993); Ellis (*Complete Works*, 1994); Love (*Works*, 1999 and numerous, informative, insightful books and articles); Greer (*John Wilmot, Earl of Rochester*, 2000); Hammond (*Making of Restoration Poetry*, 2006); Nicholas Fisher (his many articles and his edition with Walker, *The Poems and Lucina's Rape*, 2010); and the essays collected in Treglown's *Spirit of Wit: Reconsiderations of Rochester* (1982), Nicholas Fisher's *That Second Bottle: Essays on John Wilmot, Earl of Rochester* (2000), and Matthew C. Augustine and Steven N. Zwicker's *Lord Rochester and the Restoration World* (2015).

48 Harold Love, 'Was Lucina Betrayed at Whitehall?' in *That Second Bottle: Essays on John Wilmot, Earl of Rochester*, ed. Nicholas Fisher (Manchester: Manchester University Press, 2000), p. 189.

49 Christopher Tilmouth, 'John Wilmot, Second Earl of Rochester', *Oxford Bibliographies* (www.oxfordbibliographies.com) (accessed 17 March 2023).

50 Nicholas Fisher, 'Isaac Barrow and the Earl of Rochester', *N&Q*, 65, issue 2, June 2018, p. 208.

51 *The Philosophy of Literary Form: Studies in Symbolic Action* (Louisiana State University Press, 1941; rpt. Berkeley, CA: University of California Press, 1973), p. 23.

2

'A *Ramble in St.* James's Park': The fall of the well-bred man

He was exactly well bred ... (Burnet)

... that my Lord's constant living at Court, and the Conversation of Persons of Quality, to which from his greenest Youth both his Birth and his Choice had accustom'd him, gave him some great Advantages above this so much and so justly applauded Author [Fletcher], I mean, a nicer knowledge both of Men and Manners, an Air of good Breeding, and a Gentleman like easiness in all he writ. (Robert Wolseley, Preface to *Valentinian*)

When Charles II returned in 1660, the then 13-year-old Earl of Rochester greeted his sovereign with a poem, which in part reads:

> And though my youth, not patient yet to bear
> The weight of Armes, denies me to appear
> In Steel before You, yet, Great Sir, approve
> My manly wishes, and more vigorous love ....
> ('To His Sacred Majesty', lines 11–14)

Though probably written with the help of his tutor, Robert Whitehall, these lines reflect the values of the young Rochester and the social class into which he had been born. Rochester was after all '*WILMOT*'s son', son of Baron Henry Wilmot of Adderbury. A chief adviser to both Charles I and II, the elder Wilmot was a royalist general who had proved himself time and again in battle. He fought beside the King at the Battle of Edgehill in October of 1642 and was wounded twice at the battle of Cropredy Bridge in June of 1644. He played a key role in Charles II's escape from the Battle of Worcester in 1651, was created Earl of Rochester on 13 December 1652, and until his death in 1657, served as spy, trusted messenger, and adviser to the Court-in-Exile. That the young John Wilmot may never have seen his father, I suspect, made the example of the father warrior all the more compelling to the son, who concluded his poem on Charles II's homecoming with these lines:

Figure 2.1 John Wilmot, 2nd Earl of Rochester after Sir Peter Lely. National Trust Images/National Portrait Gallery London.

> In whom a cold respect were treason to
> A Fathers ashes, greater than to you;
> Whose one ambition 'tis for to be known,
> By daring Loyalty Your *WILMOT*'s Son.[1]
> (lines 15–18)

The young Rochester sought to emulate his father, to bear arms in service of his king, to prove his daring loyalty. In a few short years after penning these lines, he would do all three.

Serving on board Sir Thomas Teddiman's flagship the *Revenge*, Rochester underwent a literal trial by fire as the English navy tried to capture the Dutch East India ships in Bergen harbour. He proved to be his father's son, writing to his mother after the battle of 2 August 1665, that

> wee now lie off a little still expecting a wind that wee may send in fireshipps to make an end of the rest, Mr Mountegue & Thom: Windhams brother were both killed with one shott just by mee, but God Almyghty was pleased to preserve mee from any kind of hurt, Madam I have bin tedious but begg your La^{sps} pardon who am
>
> Your most obedient son
Rochester (Treglown, pp. 48–49)

Burnet, commenting on this episode, wrote that 'It was as desperate an Attempt as ever was made: during the whole Action, the Earl of *Rochester* shewed as brave and as resolute a Courage as was possible: A Person of Honour told me he heard the Lord *Clifford*, who was in the same Ship, often magnifie his Courage at that time very highly' (Burnet, p. 50). A month later Rochester was in battle again, and the Earl of Sandwich, in command of this entire expedition, reported back to the King that Rochester was '"brave, industrious; and of parts fit to be very useful in your Majesty's service"' (quoted in Treglown, p. 16).

During the next summer's campaign, the young Earl was again to perform well, exposing himself to heavy enemy fire in service aboard Sir Edward Spragge's ship. As Burnet later redacted the episode:

> During the Action, Sir *Edward Spragge* not being satisfied with the behaviour of one of the Captains, could not easily find a person that would chearfully venture through so much danger to carry his Commands to that Captain. This Lord offered himself to the Service; and went in a little Boat, through all the shot, and delivered his Message, and returned back to Sir *Edward*: which was much commended by all that saw it. (Burnet, p. 50)

These displays of courage in battle, the calm reports back home, and the charmingly deferential tone taken toward his mother reveal that Rochester was living up to his breeding, gracefully performing the duties of peace and war. He told Burnet that 'He thought it necessary to begin his life with these Demonstrations of his Courage in an Element and way of fighting, which is acknowledged to be the greatest trial of clear and undaunted Valour' (Burnet, p. 50). No doubt Rochester 'thought' such undertakings necessary because he was fashioned according to his parents' carefully laid out educational plan. Being the man of war was but one, though one extremely important, part of this education, the goal of which was to train the young Lord Wilmot to serve his king and country. His mother, who like her husband had sacrificed a good deal for the royalist cause and remained tenaciously loyal to the Court, saw to it that Rochester had the opportunity to develop himself as a man of war, but also as 'the man of learning, the statesman, the polished cavalier, and the virtuoso', the 'Five overlapping cultural ideals', according to Lawrence Stone, of the seventeenth-century English aristocracy.[2]

Rochester's education followed the pattern typical of his class and 'was carried on in all things suitably to his Quality' (Burnet, p. 48). It began at home, his tutor at Adderbury House for seven years being the clergyman, Francis Giffard. There is no question, given his mother's reputation for piety and her choice of tutors, that the young Rochester was soundly and thoroughly instructed in the Christian religion. He told Burnet that during his various bouts of sickness, 'he complied with his Friends in suffering Divines to be sent for ... He had no great mind to it: and that it was but a piece of his breeding, to desire them to pray by him, in which he joyned little himself' (Burnet, p. 53). It is this childhood breeding in the Christian religion that would stay with Rochester all of his life, manifesting itself most clearly at times of crisis.

From instruction at home, the young Earl, probably beginning in 1656, was enrolled at Burford Grammar School. From there he proceeded on to university, matriculating at Wadham College, Oxford, at the age of twelve. Two years later on 9 September 1661, he received a courtesy MA degree, conferred on him by one of his mother's relatives, the Earl of Clarendon. The King, solicitous of Wilmot's son, then appointed a Scottish physician, Dr Andrew Balfour, to serve as his tutor on a Grand Tour that was to last for three years. As a result of this exemplary aristocratic education, Rochester mastered the arts of horsemanship, dancing, and fencing, accomplishments that the Earl of Clarendon thought '"accompany good breeding"'.[3] He also developed a deep love of music, became skilled in French and Latin, read widely, and dabbled in chemistry and medical lore. Dr Balfour, an accomplished man who could discourse in Latin and collected ancient coins, apparently had studied medicine at Paris, Montpellier, and Caen.

When Rochester was presented at Court on Christmas Day 1664 to be welcomed home by his King, he was indeed an accomplished young man, in looks, demeanour, and training, the ideal courtier. Gifted in conversation, fashionable in conduct, he also possessed the aristocratic quality of judging matters of taste with assurance. By 1666 Charles II was sufficiently pleased with his surrogate son, this product of a royalist household, of Oxford, the Grand Tour, and of war, to further his alliance with 'the great beauty and fortune of the North, [actually West]', Elizabeth Malet.[4] On 29 January 1667, the lady married the Earl, and it would be hard to imagine a couple who at that moment better exemplified the ideals of the seventeenth-century English aristocracy.

'A Ramble in St. *James's Park*' 53

I have spent time rehearsing in small Rochester's upbringing because it is here that we find the basic orientation of his life, that 'bundle of judgments as to how things were, how they are, and how they may be'.[5] Rochester's orientation, like so many artists and writers, was, pious, piety here being defined as a *'yearning to conform with the "sources of one's being"'*.[6] The source of Rochester's being lay in that early childhood training and subsequent education, in a conglomerate of values that included love and honour for parents, governors, and princes, a belief in their authority, an equally deep belief in the truth of the Christian religion, of the honour claimed and due the aristocracy, and of the graceful performance of all the duties of peace and war that makes such honour, rooted in social origin, also a matter of merit. Rochester's aristocratic upbringing provided him with a strong sense of how things ought to be, with a sense that 'the social order is not circumstantial and arbitrary, but corresponds to and expresses an analogous, intrinsic moral order'.[7] The emotional links – emotional because they were formed in childhood – with this aristocratic and heroic world are everywhere present in Rochester's work and life, even when, perhaps most of all when, he or his personae are violating them.

One measure of the strength of this piety can be seen in the values Rochester wished to pass on to his son, whom tellingly enough he and his wife had given the name of Charles (Henry Wilmot's father also bore the name Charles). On having provided, as his mother had for him, a tutor for his son, Rochester exhorts the young Lord Wilmot that

> you are now grown bigg enough to bee a man if you can bee wise enough; & the way to bee truly wise is to serve god, learne y^r booke & observe the instructions of y^r Parents first and next y^r Tutour, to whom I have intirely resign'd you for this seven yeare, and according as you imploy that time you are to bee happy or unhappy for ever. but I have soe good an opinion of you y^t I am glad to thinke you will never deceive mee, deare Child. Learne y^r Booke, & bee obedient, & you shall see what a father I will bee to you [;] you shall want noe pleasure while you are good, & that you may be soe are my constant Prayers. (Treglown, p. 143)

In the only other extant letter to his son, Rochester once again mingles mild criticism with stern but obviously affectionate advice:

> Charles I take itt very kindly that you write to mee (though seldome) & wish heartily you would behave y^r selfe soe as that I myght show how much I love you wth out being asham'd; Obedience to y^r grandmother & those who instruct you in good things, is the way to make you happy here & for-ever, avoyde Idleness, scorne Lying, & god will Bless you, for wch I pray. (Treglown, p. 229)

Serve God, be obedient to your parents, to grandmother, to your tutor, study, do not lie – these are the ways to wisdom, to being happy, to making sure you shall want no pleasure. In these instructions to his son, we hear the voice of Anne St John Wilmot as she spoke to her son twenty-nine years earlier, instilling the same fear: not to obey is to be unhappy – forever. Speaking of his tutor on the Grand Tour, Dr Balfour, Rochester told Burnet that 'he [Rochester] was obliged to Love and Honour this his Governor, to whom he thought he owed more than to all the World, next after his Parents, for his Fidelity and Care of him' (Burnet, p. 49).

Rochester was in the process of providing the same education for his son as had been provided for him. That education and particularly the goals toward which it aimed – the aristocratic life in service to the monarch – had already, however, been severely questioned by the time of Rochester's birth in 1647. By the 1670s, it was part of a world rapidly being lost. Lawrence Stone has examined the many causes – from the early Stuarts' inflation of honours, to Puritanism, to the changing economic and demographic factors – that led to the 'erosion of respect for kings, bishops, noblemen, landlords, and fathers of families' in England during the years 1558–1641 when 'rust was eating into the shackles of the Great Chain of Being'.[8] The civil wars served only to hasten what Michael McKeon has called 'The Destabilization of Social Categories'.[9] As Susan Staves puts it:

> The display and triumph of raw force against ancient right had an impact that could not be forgotten. The king had been judicially executed, the social order of bishops, lords, and even marriage suspended, and, contrary to the expectations of many, the heavens had not fallen ... The only truly successful way to escape disillusion during the civil wars was to get killed in them. With the exception of a few people who had spent eighteen years in jail, the survivors of 1660 were those who had compromised or at least given up active resistance to their enemies or those whose cause had been defeated. Of the surviving writers, many seem to have been left with a strong suspicion that there were no heroes, or at least that whatever heroes there might be were really only imperfect men. Yet there was naturally also considerable resistance to accepting such an idea.[10]

Rochester naturally belonged to the group that resisted the disappearance of the traditional order. During the Restoration, particularly during the 1660s and into the 1670s, the Court and the writers who served it tried to reinscribe the aristocratic culture on a world that was rapidly becoming pluralistic, their very attempts, conscious and often strained as in the rhymed heroic drama, being one measure of the feeling that things were not as they ought to be.[11] When Rochester arrived at Court in 1664, he was a courtier serving a disappearing ideal. Christopher Hill rightly observes: 'The aristocrats who regained their privileged position after 1660 had no significant role to play in the reconstructed social order. Flocking to the court, they ceased even to take the traditional part in local government; and at court their role was decorative rather than functional.'[12] The aristocrats who did flourish as the society moved from laissez-faire to the bureaucratic were, in Roy Porter's words, a new breed, 'careerist peers such as Clarendon and Danby, Sunderland and Oxford', self-made men who 'climbed the greasy pole'.[13]

Following his participation in the Second Dutch War in 1665 and 1666 and his marriage in 1667, signs that Rochester keenly sensed what it means to be under-employed, to have your training prepare you for a world that no longer exists, begin to crop up everywhere. An equally important source of these symptoms of disillusionment lay no doubt in the debased nature of the actual Court Rochester had gone to serve. On his return from battle in 1666, Charles II had made Rochester a Gentleman of the Bed Chamber, and shortly thereafter the young earl entered into a service of his king that would prove far more destructive than actual combat. Perhaps all piety is a preparation for disillusionment, but the corrupt, cynical court of Charles II, with its near daily assaults upon piety of any sort, hastened and intensified Rochester's.

Rochester's debauchery had begun at Oxford under the tutelage of his Silenus, Robert Whitehall. According to Burnet, 'the general joy which over-ran the whole Nation upon his Majesty's *Restauration* ... was not regulated with that Sobriety and Temperance ... [and] produced some of its ill effects upon him' (Burnet, p. 48). But as Burnet went on to point out, Rochester 'had so entirely laid down the Intemperance that was growing on him before his Travels, that at his Return he hated nothing more' (Burnet, p. 50). As a warrior and lover in pursuit of Mistress Malet, he apparently kept his drinking under control. Service at Court, however, quickly ate away at whatever resolves he had made. It was probably in 1667 that he fell in with the 'Ballers', being 'chosen Generall' (Treglown, p. 63) of a group that, among others, included Henry Killigrew, Richard Newport, Henry Harris, and Sir Charles Sedley. According to Pepys, they 'were ready to take hold of every woman that came by them', and their 'mad bawdy talk' made the diarist's 'heart ake' (Pepys, vol. 9, p. 218, 30 May 1668).[14] This probably began the period during which, as Rochester told Burnet, 'he was continually Drunk: not all the while under the visible effect of it, but his blood was so inflamed, that he was not in all that time cool enough to be perfectly Master of himself' (Burnet, pp. 50–51).

In the process of having his basic orientation challenged at every point, Rochester was indeed not his own master, alcoholism being but one symptom. Sexual promiscuity, increasing pugnacity, fear of death, constipation, and temporary blindness, like the alcoholism, though often having many and complex causes, usually share the common psychological trait of being symbolic challenges to and substitutions for authority. 'Particularly in eras of great uncertainty', Kenneth Burke writes, 'we might expect disease to appear significantly as an occupation – for though one be in doubt about all else, he finds an unquestioned authority in the reality of his own discomfitures.'[15]

Rochester's experiments with bisexuality and his adoption of female roles in his life and art also fit into this pattern of symptoms. Both modes of behaviour reveal a questioning of one's identity as well as an ambivalence towards, or rejection of, authority. As Kenneth Burke points out: 'The profoundest way of symbolizing a change in identity is in the symbolic change of sex.'[16] In an observation applicable to Rochester but also to a great many members of the Restoration Court, Burke writes: 'A compensatory increase in sensuality generally accompanies a loss of faith in the reasonableness of a society's purposes. People try to combat alienation by immediacy, such as the senses alone provide.'[17]

Perhaps the most significant result of Rochester's disillusionment was the birth of a satirist, a master scourge of the world as well as of the self, because by 1671 he had become deeply implicated in the very impiety that outraged him. His orientation called into doubt, Rochester was open to new ways of accounting for his own and the motivations of others, was searching for new duties, new authorities. As Burnet insightfully noted:

> These Exercises [i.e. odd Adventures and *Frollicks*, *Libels* and *Satyrs*] in the course of his life were not always equally pleasant to him; he had often sad Intervals and severe Reflections on them: and though then he had not these awakened in him by any deep Principle of Religion, yet the horror that Nature raised in him, especially in some Sicknesses, made him too easie to receive some ill Principles, which others endeavoured to possess him with; so that he was too soon brought to set himself too secure, and fortifie his Mind against that, by dispossessing it all he could of the belief or apprehensions of Religion. (Burnet, p. 51)

Severe reflections, the horror and apprehensions they evoked, led Rochester to attempt to dispossess himself of all that he could of his beliefs in religion, of his linkages to his pious upbringing, and to replace those beliefs with other (for Burnet 'ill') principles. It is this attempt to banish the past and to replace its claims of authority with new ones that Rochester's poetry, though in no systematic way, was shortly to record.

'*A Ramble in St. James's Park*' was the first poem to record this process in all its complexity. Vieth considers the poem to be 'apparently a crucial work biographically' (Vieth, *Poems*, p. xxxvii), and I would add, apparently a deeply personal one. Corinna, the 'name of Ovid's mistress in the *Amores*', will also appear, as Love notes, as 'the partner in "The Imperfect enjoyment" and the revengeful whore in' *Artemiza to Chloe* (lines 189–251). Love thinks there is a historical person behind these three Corinnas, writing: 'Taken together these three poems could be considered as describing three stages in a single life. Here a prostitute is clearly intended, perhaps Sue Willis who is attacked in "Against the harms our Ballox have." The poem is too early to refer to Rochester's liaison with Elizabeth Barry.' Moreover, 'The First' of the 'Three *Knights*', 'Near Kin to th' *Mother* of the *Maids*' (lines 43 and 46), 'seems to be', according to Love, 'the future author, Charles Blount'. The '*Grays Inn Wit*' may be 'the poet Alexander Radcliffe' or 'Aphra Behn's lover, John Hoyle' (Love, pp. 412 and 413).

While the poem, in all probability, provides these glimpses and more of the day-to-day life Rochester experienced, the relationship of the speaker of the poem to the historical Rochester remains a contested issue.[18] Griffin finds that the speaker 'in several ways resembles the historical Rochester' (Griffin, p. 25); Warren Chernaik thinks that in some respects 'his values seem identical with Rochester's own'.[19] Germaine Greer tantalizingly observes that 'Rochester's interrogation of his own sexuality reached its apogee in "A Ramble in St James's Park" which was circulating in manuscript by March 1673', but offers no evidence.[20] Even more tantalizing is Johnson's conjecture that the impetus for '*A Ramble*' may have been Rochester's encounter in 1671 with Elizabeth Foster, a minor actress then little known and now nearly unknowable.[21] The evidence, however, is tenuous.[22]

As with so much of Rochester's work, we would very much like to know more about the context of this brilliant, maddeningly elusive poem that will come to be seen, I believe, as a central work in the Rochester canon.[23] Part anti-feminist jeremiad, '*A Ramble*' also satirizes Restoration society and its king, lampoons particular people, and scathingly excoriates the self while attempting self-exculpation. Mingling libertine swagger with pathos and anger, brimming with hatred for others and for the self, the poem is, nevertheless, narrated with an engaging humour and wit that often belie its obscenity and are intended to belie its seriousness. More than any other Rochester poem, '*A Ramble*' is a true 'satura', a medley of poetic models and styles, of intellectual cross-currents and intentions.

What we do know is that the man who, probably early in 1673, sat down with quill and foolscap to exorcise and explain this seemingly real-life, ludicrous yet altogether painful affair was in a high state of turmoil, domestically, poetically, and intellectually.[24] Incurably syphilitic, he had recently suffered lameness, impotence, and blindness. He had begotten a congenitally ill son, and was, quite understandably, estranged for the moment from his wife. Poetically, he was betwixt and between, a talented but insouciant amateur with a few works of obvious promise but hardly the accomplished poet he was about to become. His metres still hobbled between the native

58 *Rochester and the pursuit of pleasure*

four beat line and the artful iambic couplets he would soon fashion. He had tossed off a few songs, written two pastorals, translated some Ovid and Lucretius and borrowed from Petronius. He was seeking models. Intellectually, Rochester was also at a crossroads. Suspended between Christian orthodoxy and his classical mentors, he was fleeing the former while looking to the latter to provide him the mirror in which he might find self-recognition.

'*A Ramble*' reveals Rochester to be the rake everyone recognizes but also the classicist few have appreciated.[25] He seems intuitively to have turned to the past in search of models to make intelligible his ongoing present experiences. Such is the case with this affair as he drew upon the rhetorical topos of the world turned upside down, and as few have registered the havoc caused by false love better than Catullus, Rochester looked to him. '*A Ramble*' is, among many other things, a paraphrase with considerable additions of *Carmina* XXXVII.[26]

> Salax taberna uosque contubernales,
> a pilleatis nona fratribus pila,
> solis putatis esse mentulas uobis,
> solis licere, quidquid est puellarum,
> confutuere et putare ceteros hircos?
> an, continenter quod sedetis insulsi
> centum an ducenti, non putatis ausurum
> me una ducentos irrumare sessores?
> atqui putate: namque totius uobis
> frontem tabernae sopionibus scribam.
> puella nam mei, quae meo sinu fugit,
> amata tantum quantum amabitur nulla,
> pro qua mihi sunt magna bella pugnata,
> consedit istic. hanc boni beatique
> omnes amatis, et quidem, quod inidgnum est,
> omnes pusilli et semitarii moechi;
> tu praeter omnes une de capillatis,
> cuniculosae Celtiberiae fili,
> Egnati, opaca quem bonum facit barba
> et dens Hibera defricatus urina.

This translation by Barriss Mills captures the spirit of the poem:

> Disreputable tavern, and you gang
> who hang out in it, behind
> the ninth pillar from the temple
> of Castor and Pollux – do you think
> you're the only fellows with the right
> to tumble all the pretty girls

> and the rest of us are nothing
> but goats? Just because you sit
> together there like dummies
> a hundred or two, don't think
> I can't tackle all two hundred
> at a sitting. Believe me
> I'll scribble your names and epithets
> all over the front of the place
> For my girl's run out on me –
> the one I loved more than anyone
> will ever be loved, and for whom
> I've fought great wars – and come
> to stay there. Now all you fine
> noble fellows make love to her
> and what's even more shameful, every
> small-time lecher from the back streets
> and alleyways. You above all
> long-haired Egnatius – spawn
> of a Spanish rabbit-warren
> whose only claim to distinction
> is a bushy beard and teeth
> scrubbed with Spanish urine.

Like Catullus's bemused spokesman, Rochester had recently been to war, two of them, and though this Corinna was probably not the woman he loved more than anyone, he seems to have been deeply involved with her. She had betrayed him with fellows hanging around 'the *Bear*', and Rochester was sitting down to scribble their names with appropriate epithets. If Rochester's poem gives the illusion of being a window upon the raw experience of a most spectacular life, it is in part because he chose as a model another poet whose work gives much the same impression.

Seeing the poem through the topos of topsy-turveydom helps us to put its grotesqueries into proper perspective. Like Catullus's Lesbia, Corinna has turned 'damn'd abandon'd *Jade*' (line 99), and consequently the poet's world has become chaotic. The hierarchy and fecundity of God's plenteous creation is now disordered, perverted, and nasty. Two passages in particular come into clearer focus: the description of the park (lines 9–32) and the mock love feast (lines 111–24). Though both descriptions have other functions in the poem, both, surrealistic and monstrous, worthy of a Breughel or a Leonard Baskin, mirror the torment of the poet's mind. Both owe much to the paradox tradition of listing impossibilities, paradoxes because though impossible they describe the world better than any so-called realistic and accurate picture would. No 'Antient *Pict*' has 'Frigg[ed] upon his *Mothers* [i.e. the earth's] Face' (lines 14 and 18) nor have 'Rowes of

Mandrakes ... Fuck'd the very Skies' (lines 19–20), yet the world that the poet now sees, wonder by clear knowledge having been destroyed, can, impossible as it seems, have been engendered in no other way. To the disillusioned poet, the monstrous is the normal, as it would be for us if we could, like him, just see. Similarly, the Lais-like activities of Corinna and the credulity of the narrator who can find pleasure and love in them are impossible truths. In Catullus and in the rhetorical figure of the world turned upside down, Rochester found the realism and surrealism that could accurately reflect the life he was experiencing.

As critics have noted, '*A Ramble*' parodies Waller's 'On St. James's Park, As Lately Improved By His Majesty' while harpooning the Cavalier love song convention of elevating one's mistress to divine status. Rochester finds his goddess all too earthly and earthy, and as Griffin observes: 'Rochester's anti-pastoral satire ... measures the distance between Waller's old ideal and present reality by parodying the panegyric, importing its own imagined details and replacing allusions to a golden age with its own mythology, a jumble of sexual lore' (pp. 28–29). This is astute, but there is more. For Waller, the park is a second 'paradise'. It is a god-like creation, and he implicitly compares 'the first Paradise', created by God, with the second, created by his divine representative, Charles II.[27] The park is heaven come to dwell on earth. For Rochester, the park has its genesis not in any action analogous to divine fiat, to spirit informing matter, but in 'Antient *Pict* ... Frigg[ing] upon his *Mothers* Face'. The divine genealogy traditional to the panegyric has been replaced by an earthly one, the genesis of the park not being the responsibility of God, but a result of the sexual drives of a flesh-addicted line of North Britons, that is, the Stuarts. English life now consists of the seamy physicality found in the park – St James's here metonymically representing all England – which Charles II and his family (St James the first Apostle to be martyred being reduced to the first Stuart king of England), and not God, have engendered. A better way of putting this might be to say that the opening thirty-two lines of the poem do not so much assign responsibility for the world as it is but mock the very idea of beginnings and of causality. To say such a world was created by God, that king and poet in park and poem imitate God's initial creative act, is ludicrous. The aesthetic of pagan realism reveals the world to be what it is, a Lucretian atomism in which events just happen, all things being predetermined. In such a world sexual drives rule the king, and the poet writes from a drunken stupor and is not so much a creator but at best, like Aretine, an imitator of the realistic scene before him.

In its very form then the poem juxtaposes two ways of reading the world. The one, represented by Waller, is Christian and idealistic; the other, represented by Catullus, is pagan and materialistic.[28] The former embodies the way Rochester and a vast majority of his countrymen were brought up to decipher this world, being taught that in scripture they would find the patterns that give order to their experience. The latter reflects a humanistic and secular version of the former, the interpretative models being taken not from the Bible but from the classics of ancient Greece and Rome. These two ways of reading the world exist side by side in 'A Ramble', the one being systematically mocked, the other severely tested. Libertine realism is aesthetically satisfying in that it reflects accurately the experience of the poet whereas the idealism of the panegyric falsifies it. At a crucial moment in the poem, however, that realism is found to be neither psychologically nor philosophically acceptable.

Just as the form embodies this tension between idealism and materialism, so does the speaker. He is an idealist manqué, simultaneously a materialistic critic and debunker of his own performance. If my experience is indicative, this performance both tricks and shocks us. That is, having read the poem many times, I became convinced that the speaker in his libertine bravado is rather naive. He is a dupe whose angle of vision is much less than mine, a character I felt comfortable criticizing. But then came the awareness that all his statements ought to be taken as ironic. It is as though a smiling face had been there all along, taking a certain sardonic satisfaction in my misreading, making me a participant in the poem when I thought I was merely a spectator. Nothing is perhaps more typical of the experience of reading Rochester's poetry than this rabbit-duck illusion of suddenly realizing that the narrator is both actor and spectator, that he or she is simultaneously functioning in two different capacities, one of which assumes the perspective that the audience believed to be exclusively theirs. Though expected, these realizations always surprise, which may be one measure of Rochester's artistry.

Such a narrative and rhetorical strategy is part and parcel of what the poem means and how that is expressed, a point examined later, but suffice it now to say that through three-quarters of the poem (lines 1–132), the poet has created an exaggerated version of himself as he was. As he recounts in past tense the actions of the knights and Corinna and goes on in present tense to sort out their significance, he uses different interpretative models – Christianity, hedonism, and a willed self-deception taken from Ovid. It is as though the disillusioned Rochester had used this affair to recapitulate his intellectual history, testing each of his stances against his newly discovered norm of satiric realism that reduces all that exists to body and all that occurs to motion. Each stance is found wanting, the satiric process of attributing human motives to physical drives finally destroying the very persona (literally masked actor) the poet had fabricated in order to distance himself from, and understand, what he had experienced and finally threatening to do the same to the poet himself. Unable to find evidence for the idealism he desires but equally unable to accept the implications of the materialism he has evoked, the poet explodes in a vicious tirade.

The two voices of the poem are there from the beginning, the idealist manqué telling us as the poem opens: 'Much Wine had past with grave discourse/ Of who Fucks who, and who does worse.' The juxtaposition of 'grave discourse' with what follows sums up in little the question the poem raises, teases, seeks to resolve, does and does not do so, and that is: what happens when our logical formulations of experience do not match sense experience itself? The writing of 'grave discourses' on 'who Fucks who' is pretty much, in Rochester's estimation, what court poets, whether in heroic play or panegyric, had been doing. Such fabrications are ludicrous if one compares artistic representation with reality, not unlike Peter Lely's painting of Barbara Villiers with one of Charles II's bastards in the pose of the Madonna and Christ child. There is little doubt that we are meant to laugh at the narrator juxtaposing high with low, the hudibrastic rhyme (discourse/worse) also serving to deflate the lofty. Moreover, 'grave discourse' turns out to be just what it is, a verbal mask for the physical, 'grave' being a pun (pit, trench) on female genitalia as well as a comment on what happens to those who 'promiscuously ... swive' (line 32), ending up as Rochester put it a short time later 'To gett supplies for Age and Graves' ('*Love to a Woman*', line 8). From the perspective of the materialistic wit that underlies and mocks the idealism in the poem, men really do end where they began, in the 'grave'.

The speaker, despite the sordid physicality of the world he experiences – something that is so obvious to him now and should have been then – persists in reading this world in an Augustinian way. That is, what 'does not literally pertain to virtuous behavior or to the truth of faith' he takes to be 'figurative'. But he is simultaneously mocking himself from the perspective of his new understanding which 'is subjected to the flesh in pursuit of the letter', and which takes 'figurative expressions as though they were literal' and understands them 'carnally'.[29] To the speaker the park is 'consecrate to *Prick* and *Cunt*' (line 10), its walks 'hallow'd' (line 33), his mistress heavenly and divine (lines 38–39). Clearly, his language is at odds with experience. The consecration has not endowed the earthly with the spiritual; what takes place in the park being neither sacred nor holy. The religious vocabulary masks the physical, 'hallow' also being an archaic term from venery (which itself combines an archaic reference to hunting with the pursuit of sexual satisfaction), meaning, fittingly enough, 'the parts of the hare given to hounds as a reward or encouragement after a successful hunt' (*OED*). It is just such venery that is going on in 'these hallow'd Walks' as 'humble *Currs* ... obsequiously do hunt/ The sav'ry scent of Salt-swolne

Cunt' (lines 84–86). The pun on 'consecrate' is a synecdoche for the materialistic reading of the world underlying the poem in which the spiritual is seen as being really material rather than the material being elevated, consecrated, to the divine.[30]

But it is just not Christian idealism that this materialistic debunking destroys. The satire, for example, that the speaker directs at the fops and Corinna seems clear enough, its norms straightforwardly libertine. All have perverted nature and nature's end, pleasure. The fops are mere mechanical men who, like 'The First', one of 'your *Whitehall Blades*', have converted 'Abortive imitation/ To Universal affectation' (lines 46 and 57–58) and who look, live, and love 'by Rote' (line 61). They are 'Asses' but no more natural for that because 'confounded *Asses*' (line 81), somehow impure and corrupt; and their speech, somewhere ''twixt Tune and *Nonsense*' (line 75), is known neither to nature nor to art. Similarly, Corinna has perverted nature, turned it topsy-turvy, or as the speaker puts it in his accurate but obscene image, 'at her *Mouth* her *Cunt* says yes' (lines 78). If she 'Had ... pickt out to rub her Arse on/ Some stiff-Prick'd *Clown*, or well hung *Parson*' (lines 91–92), it would have been, the speaker assures us, all right. According to him, 'Such nat'rall freedoms are but just/ There's something gen'rous in meer Lust' (lines 97–98).

The speaker's argument from nature, however, is not so straightforward as it appears. He is measuring the fops by one definition of nature, but his own actions by quite a different one. If he applied the same norm to himself as he applies to the fops, he too would be found wanting. The satirist is being satirized. The speaker in criticizing Corinna and the fops has assumed that one in tune with the senses, with nature, will make choices that lead to the pleasurable. Yet, if anything, Corinna and the fops have done just that, followed, with comical alacrity, their physical desires. In condemning them for being unnatural, however, the speaker does not have in mind 'sense' (line 88), meaning natural processes, the physical reality, but 'common Sence' (line 55), meaning man's second nature, that is, his social and cultural values. In order to distinguish himself from the fops, he wants to say that the pursuit of pleasure is 'just' in some cases, but not so in others. Yet I think we are meant to see that there is little separating the 'humble Currs' (line 84) from 'humble fond, believing me' (line 108), save a certain self-delusion that tries to see human motivation in terms of the 'ought' of an idealistic morality, albeit a libertine one, rather than the 'is' of physical drives. For the speaker the knights are pavlovians whose bell is 'The sav'ry scent of Salt-swolne *Cunt*' (line 86). Yet what the speaker calls his love for Corinna has its pavlovian ring to it as well. He pursues Corinna – not as he later tells us out of love – but because he is driven by drink to lechery.

Though he attempts to see his actions in terms of human choice, that is, he takes 'care to see/ Drunkenness reliev'd by *Lechery*' (lines 5–6), any choice he may have had in the matter seems doubtful. Drink leads to lechery, experience telling us that in such cases the time for ratiocination between stimulus and response becomes greatly diminished. The speaker, no less than Corinna, the fops, and the other inhabitants of the park, participates in the pursuit of physical desires that is the poem's assessment of human motivation, something the speaker does not want to acknowledge. He is 'fond', that is, foolish, and wants to believe in transcendent values, love, the good, and the bad, but his 'common Sence' is no less a mask for natural appetites than the affectations of the fops. The oxymoronic 'nat'rall freedoms' (line 97) is unwitting testimony to the speaker's delusion as is the incongruity of 'just/Lust' (lines 97–98), lexically a true rhyme, but experientially an impossibility.

The failure of the speaker to set up an ethical hedonism, one that would condemn the fops but which would sanction his relationship with Corinna, becomes increasingly evident as he turns to an assessment of his own motives.

> But why was I of all *Mankind*,
> To so severe a fate design'd?
> Ungrateful! why this Treachery
> To humble fond, believing me?
> Who gave you priviledge above,
> The nice allowances of Love?
>   (lines 105–10)

The speaker's self-deception is great here; shortly it will become heroic, if mockingly so. Though he believes his libertine code to be an accurate description of the way things are, it is no less idealistic than the courtly, heroic code whose vocabulary he continues unwittingly to use. That love is a matter of 'Fate', an overwhelming passion impossible to resist, is an idea worthy of that 'tearing *Blade*' (line 74), the court fop. The speaker, moreover, has not been singled out from 'all *Mankind*', Corinna having dispensed her favours impartially and in so doing proving herself most 'grateful'. The speaker continues to believe in a world organized purposively and having ethical standards by which one can judge the ungrateful and the treacherous. But he is 'fond' in his beliefs, because the world he has described is 'promiscuous', without order or purpose and lacks standards of selection. Its inhabitants regardless of the linguistic labels attached to them are going to do what their appetites drive them to do. For him to make 'nice', that is, fine, distinctions or 'allowances' (line 110) when Corinna has come 'spewing home/ Drencht with the Seed of half the *Town*' (lines 113–14) is preposterous.

The speaker goes on to compare his relationship with Corinna to a meal, revealing further his delusions as well as the nature of his predicament. The comparison brings to the fore again the poem's ongoing debate between biblical upbringing and pagan learning. To eat, to make a vast meal of the senses, is an attempt to say 'no' to God's original interdiction; it is to assert that the feast of the senses is prologue to and analogue of love. But this 'vast *Meal*' is of 'Nasty Slime' (line 118). Following nature, indulging the senses, leads not to the Epicurean life filled with delightful sensation but to utter depravity.

Even though love has become in Corinna's hands sordidly debased, the narrator describes it in the language of ideal courtly love: 'tender hours', '*Knight Errant Paramours*', 'Faithless Breast', 'security, and rest', and 'Soft kindness' (lines 127–31). One wonders after the previous description just how tender these hours could have been, and we are meant to wonder, wonder at the massive incongruity between language and experience, wonder at the mock-heroic attempt of the speaker to sustain his illusion that his ideal conception of the world derived from language matches experience. The narrator, a libertine Don Quixote, has been betrayed not just by Corinna but by language itself, and thus the poem's attack on the ideal language of Christianity and panegyric, of romantic and courtly love, the breaking down of that language to show its physical origins ('hallow'd') or juxtaposing it with undeniably earthy words ('*Grace Cup*' with '*Cunt*') to show that religion, indeed any form of idealism, begins in and is but compensation for physical appetite. The ensuing curse suggests, however, that this last resort, this Ovidian posture of a willed self-deception, does not work. Even the narrator, foolish as he has shown himself to be, cannot sustain his illusion. While 'Reason lay dissolv'd in Love' (line 132), he could, but through the process of the poem 'wonder by clear knowledge' has been destroyed. The curse marks a turning point in the poem but also the poem turning against itself, for it is not just the narrator who makes a discovery here. The poet who has been mocking him throughout does so as well.

For the narrator the dilemma and the motive for his vitriolic outburst arise from being caught between credulity and reason. Reason has destroyed credulity by showing Corinna and the world to be what she and it really are. But in destroying credulity, reason has provided no acceptable alternative. Reason reveals a world of the ancient atomist, a material world in which events just happen, man being the product of predetermined drives. Given such a world, man, as the narrator has shown, attempts to avoid that reality by thinking or pretending that there is more, specifically that love is more than a physical appetite. Man can either be a fool or a knave; no wonder the narrator discharges a volley of invective. And he is joined by his other half, the poet, who also discovers that, for all his self-awareness, he too has been a dupe.

As I suggested, reading 'A Ramble' is like looking at a double-entendre painting. From one perspective, we see the naive idealist, from another, the materialistic debunker who mocks him. This process of narration is at once psychological, rhetorical, and philosophical in its purpose. The poem is in part a savage self-indictment, an extreme act of self-exposure and self-punishment. I have been a dupe; my idealistic thoughts were foolish and empty. At the same time, this is self-punishment to deflect criticism, an attempt to judge before being judged, to usurp the role of any possible audience, to anticipate their criticism and render it harmless through self-ridicule and laughter.

Rochester in this poem is trying to look around his own corner, to be absolutely self-contained. He attempts to come back from wherever his audience is going, to reverse the role between actor and spectator, so that it is not the actor who is naive, lacking in knowledge and therefore vulnerable, but the audience. Rhetorically, he traps his audience, inviting them to read one way while they should be reading quite another as if to show that they too are determined. Such a rhetorical strategy – perhaps motivated by a desire to assuage guilt, to foreclose criticism, to have power over one's audience, or all three – also has a philosophical purpose. In many ways, the narrator admits, there is nothing separating him and his motives from Corinna and her appetite-driven suitors. On the other hand, he is aware in a way they are not, and though he may perforce participate in this physical world, he also has a perspective which transcends it. Yet this attempt to gain a perspective of perspectives and thus raise oneself above the deterministic laws governing others contains an awareness of its own inadequacy.

The speaker laughs at the fops, but is blind to his own pretentions. Just as he was deceived, there is no reason to suspect that his new-found awareness is not simply another form of self-deception. He has a perspective on the fops and now on himself, but we have a perspective on him that sees his awareness, manifested in the double perspective of the story he has told, as another attempt at compensation for his reduced circumstances. In turn, though we laugh at him, our own myopia may prevent us from seeing that we share the same predicament of being determined by our circumstances and not knowing it. Though the poet has constructed the poem so that we would come to this awareness and thus has a perspective on us, we can in turn say that he has done so for compensatory reasons, and so go back and forth in an infinite regress. The point is, if one can stabilize the irony momentarily, that any perspective is necessarily inadequate. Thus the curse has all the marks of an idealist realizing finally that he has been betrayed, doubly so, and of no longer being able to distance that betrayal through a cynical belittling of himself. With the beginning of the curse, narrator and poet have become one, both reduced, along with the audience, to a physical world which provides no solace and from which there is no escape.[31]

The curse may be the final ironic testimony to the inability of man to be other than what his appetites dictate, the speaker, persona and poet, being prey to his anger as he was to his drink and lust, a driven man. That is, the curse – the vein of satire running deep in Rochester – takes away perhaps the one comfort that materialistic philosophies afford: that because of the very nature of his make-up, man cannot fall below a certain level of sloth and error. The sheer malice of the closing curse suggests, on the contrary, that only in depravity can man triumph over the physical, making what is far worse than it would naturally be.

On the other hand, we could read the curse idealistically, taking the poem's final thirty-four lines as blasphemy, which they are, and interpreting blasphemy, following Kenneth Burke, as an

> expression of the religious inclination in an intelligence which cannot believe. Since it is impossible to praise the divinities with sincerity, there is nothing left but to insult them. Blasphemy is a serious experiment, a transgression by means of the sins of others. To blaspheme is to restore the lost gods by renouncing them; blasphemy is the struggle of an emotional nature, a protest against the intellect which tends to make it sterile of religious ecstasy.[32]

The lost gods or God are not restored at the end of the poem, but the attempt may be to test whether that God exists and whether he understands his own religion. For when the speaker boastfully declares, '*And may no* Woman *better thrive/ That dares prophane the* Cunt *I Swive*' (lines 165–66), he is blatantly mocking God while offering himself up for punishment and salvation. In his debased world, he has assumed the role of mock-Christ, his act of swiving being a blessing, making that '*Grace Cup*' holy, capable of being profaned. If God does exist, the speaker surely will be punished, but his violation will have, paradoxically, established the existence of the holy. Moreover, he will then be candidate for salvation, not a mock-Christ, but a true Christ-like figure who has become a scapegoat so that God might exercise his love in redeeming him and thus 'prove' his religion.

To make such an argument is to be trapped by the logic of the poem; it is to become a fool by trying to make the sordid realities of the poem other than what they are. If there is no comfort to be had in a materialistic reading of the poem, there is certainly none in an idealistic one, both subject as they are to corrosive ironies. The poet must rail on in a language – 'grace', 'heaven', 'Jesus' – that promises an ideal world he cannot experience in order to reveal a material world he cannot accept.[33]

In purpose, theme, tone, and form '*A Ramble*' is a rehearsal for the poetry Rochester will write in the seven years that remain to him.[34] As a satirist, he will lash out at the Restoration world about him but punish himself for being implicated in and representative of that world. His speakers will continue to pursue pleasure, pleasure for them being life's goal and Rochester's principal theme. 'Pleasure(s)' and its cognate 'please(s)' ('pleasant', 'pleased', and 'pleasing') occur sixty-three times in the poems Vieth assigns to Rochester. After 'love' (126) and 'Man/men' (88), this group of words ranks third in frequency of use. 'Wit' (52) and 'make' (52) are next, followed by 'own' (48) and then by the various forms of 'nature' (42).[35] Pleasure, synonymous with love, is to be obtained through wit whose proper use guides man to a harmonious relationship with nature. Pleasure will serve as the norm for libertine satire as in the 'Epilogue to *Circe*' (1677):

> Some few from Wit have this true Maxime got,
> *That 'tis still better to be pleas'd then not,*
> And therefore never their own Torment plot.
> While the Malitious Criticks still agree
> *To loath each Play they come and pay to see;*
> ...
> *Poets and Women have an Equal Right*
> *To hate the Dull, who Dead to all Delight*
> Feel pain alone, and have no Joy but spite.
> 'Twas Impotence did first this Vice begin,
> Fooles censure Wit, as Old men raile of Sin,
> *Who Envy Pleasure, which they cannot tast,*
> And good for nothing, wou'd be wise at last.
> (lines 1–5 and 10–16)

Matters aesthetic and sexual should yield pleasure, and those who apply rationalistic categories to either – nit-picking criticism to the one and religion to the other – are wrong. Far more often, however, pleasure will remain an unattainable goal, and the poems will explore the ambiguities and paradoxes of life led in its pursuit. As the various speakers come up against paradoxes that challenge their way of looking at the world and their audience's assumptions, or both, their tone will range from arch, distant laughter to buffoonery, bitter mockery to comic acceptance, rage to cool judgment. And Rochester, as here in '*A Ramble*', will be looking for the proper form in which to express himself. Burnet interestingly observed that 'Sometimes other men's thoughts mixed with his Composures, but that flowed rather from the Impressions they made on him when he read them, by which they came to return upon him as his own thoughts, than that he servilely copied from any' (Burnet, p. 49). Robert Parsons would corroborate this insight in his sermon on Rochester's death:

His natural talent was excellent, but he had hugely improved it by Learning and Industry, being throughly acquainted with all Classick Authors, both Greek and Latin; a thing very rare, if not peculiar to him amongst those of his quality. Which yet he used not, as other Poets have done, to translate or steal from them, but rather to better, and improve them by his own natural fancy.[36]

In search of an intelligible world, Rochester turned to, among others, Ovid, Horace, Catullus, Lucretius, Petronius, Fletcher, Boileau, and Waller. They became a part of him, part of the ongoing story he told himself in order to live. At the same time, the biblical narratives with which he grown up were never far out of mind, always ready to provide an ironic, parodic perspective on a libertine's experiment.

Rochester's libertine code could never adequately account for the world it evoked. Being anti-rationalistic, he believed only in the truth of the senses, but the senses provided no norm by which to live. Rochester could never derive a satisfactory 'ought' from the only world he acknowledged as 'is'. He was not ready until the very end to accept absence and negation as proofs for the existence of the ideal, to agree with Tertullian that the ideal *'certum est quia impossible'*. The concept of *via negativa*, however, informs his mature poetry throughout. It is a concept he began to consider in earnest only after he fell while on *'A Ramble in St. James's Park'*.

Notes

1 C.S.L. Davies writes that Rochester 'may have seen his father during Henry Wilmot's clandestine visit to England in 1655, but, if so, only very briefly' ('John Wilmot, Earl of Rochester: His Childhood and Experience at Oxford', *HLQ*, 81, 2 (2018), p. 175). In his hypothesis about Rochester 'living with a false self' Ken Robinson zeroes in on 'one particular aspect of his false self which is clear for all to see, and that is his living through an identification with his father. The degree of identification is very marked. It points to Rochester as it were acting out a script written and already acted by his father' ('John Wilmot, Earl of Rochester: An Author in Search of a Character', in *The Art of Literary Biography*, ed. John Batchelor (Oxford: Oxford University Press, 1995), pp. 107 and 108).
2 Lawrence Stone, *The Crisis of the Aristocracy* (abridged edition; Oxford: Oxford University Press, 1967), p. 313.
3 Stone, *Crisis of the Aristocracy*, p. 315.
4 Samuel Pepys, *The Diary of Samuel Pepys*, eds Robert Latham and William Matthews (Berkeley, CA: University of California Press, 1979), 6, p. 110, 28 May 1665. Pepys recorded the location of Elizabeth's family estates incorrectly.
5 Kenneth Burke, *Permanence and Change: An Anatomy of Purpose* (Indianapolis, IN: Bobbs-Merrill, 1975), p. 14. For this account of Rochester's upbringing and early years, I am drawing upon Johnson, pp. 6–102 and also C.S.L. Davies,

'John Wilmot, Earl of Rochester: His Childhood and Experience at Oxford', *HLQ*, 81, 2 (2018), pp. 171–89.
6   Burke, *Permanence and Change*, p. 69.
7   Michael McKeon, *The Origins of the English Novel, 1600–1740* (Baltimore, MD: Johns Hopkins University Press, 1987), p. 131.
8   Stone, *Crisis of the Aristocracy*, p. 21.
9   McKeon, *Origins of the English Novel*, p. 131.
10 Susan Staves, *Players' Scepters: Fictions of Authority in the Restoration* (Lincoln, NE: University of Nebraska Press, 1979), p. 40.
11 I am echoing what remains one of the best, short discussions of this process, that by J. Douglas Canfield, 'The Significance of the Restoration Rhymed Heroic Play', *Eigtheenth Century Studies*, 13 (Fall 1979), pp. 49–62.
12 Christopher Hill, *The Collected Essays of Christopher Hill* (Amherst, MA: University of Massachusetts Press, 1985), 1, p. 301.
13 Roy Porter, *English Society in the Eighteenth Century* (Harmondsworth: Penguin Books, 1982; rpt. 1983), p. 69.
14 See David Vieth, 'Sir Charles Sedley and the Ballers Oath', *The Scriblerian*, 12, 1 (1979), pp. 47–49.
15 Burke, *Permanence and Change*, p. 244.
16 Kenneth Burke, *Attitudes Toward History* (Editorial Publications, 1937; rpt. Berkeley, CA: University of California Press, 1984), p. 211.
17 Burke, *Attitudes*, pp. 217–18.
18 One example: Sarah Ellenzweig in a wonderfully insightful reading takes the poem to be 'a particularly illustrative example of the conflict between the historical Rochester's elevated status and decreased material power', the poem revealing 'Rochester's cavalier stance ... assert[ing] certain age-old privileges of the aristocracy at the same time as it registers the demise of those privileges'. On what she rightly calls 'the always contested question of the relationship between poet and speaker', she 'concurs with Dustin Griffin's assertion that "the libertine speakers of [Rochester's] poems are too much like the historical Rochester to be personae, and too self-consciously, too knowingly, scandalous to be, simply, the man himself"'. Griffin's, however, is a distinction that allows him and Ellenzweig to have it both ways, the speaker being Rochester and not Rochester. But it is the 'stance' of the man himself, the historical Rochester, that Ellenzweig seeks to, and does, illuminate ('Hitherto Propertied: Rochester's Aristocratic Alienation and the Paradox of Class Formation in Restoration England', *ELH*, 69, 3 (2002), pp. 705 and 722).
19 Warren Chernaik, *Sexual Freedom in Restoration Literature* (Cambridge University Press, 1995), p. 75.
20 Germaine Greer, *John Wilmot, Earl of Rochester* (Devon: Northcote House Publishers, 2000), p. 44. Hereafter cited as Greer in the text.
21 Treglown captures pretty much all that we know: 'Some time in 1671 he had to extricate himself from an affair with a "damsel of low degree" called Foster, a tart who figures briefly in one of his later satires, and who seems to have passed herself off as a courtier' (Treglown, p. 20).

22 Johnson conjectures that in the summer of 1671 Rochester 'discovered that his mistress, Foster, had been betraying him with other lovers and that she had passed on more deadly forms of the pox to him. Infuriated, he threw the false Corinna out, subjecting her to a "treatment" that included castigating her to his friends and then making her the subject of one of his most vituperative and scurrilous verses, "A Ramble in Saint James's Park"' (Johnson, pp. 133 and 149; see also 153). Frank Ellis, however, thinks, quoting Love, that 'There is no reason to identify the speaker with Rochester, who would be unlikely to prowl in St. James's Park "unaccompanied by ... a purse bearer, a page, and couple of footmen" (Love, 1972, 161)' (*Complete Works*, p. 330). Love finds Johnson's 'assertion ... that Foster was the Corinna of "A Ramble in St. James's Park" (late 1672?) ... pure fantasy' (Rev. of *A Profane Wit: The Life of John Wilmot, Earl of Rochester* by James William Johnson in *Seventeenth-Century News*, 63 (2005), p. 139).

23 Critical commentary on the poem has been lively and insightful. See Griffin, pp. 25–35; Reba Wilcoxon, 'The Rhetoric of Sex in Rochester's Burlesque', *PLL* 12 (1976), pp. 279–84; Thomas K. Pasch, 'Concentricity, Christian Myth, and the Self-Incriminating Narrator in Rochester's *A Ramble in St. James's Park*', *Essays in Literature* (Spring, 1979), pp. 21–28; rpt. in *John Wilmot, Earl of Rochester: Critical Essays*, ed. David M. Vieth (New York: Garland Publishing, 1988), pp. 149–61; Thormählen, pp. 95–103; and Johnson, pp. 149 and 152–55. All treat the poem in depth as does Sarah Ellenzweig in the article cited above. For piecemeal but often illuminating comments on the poem see Ronald Berman, 'Rochester and the Defeat of the Senses', *Kenyon Review* 26 (1964), pp. 362–63; Carole Fabricant, 'Rochester's World of Imperfect Enjoyment', *Journal of English and Germanic Philology*, 73 (1974), pp. 338–50; John E. Sitter, 'Rochester's Reader and the Problem of Satiric Audience', *PLL*, 12 (1976), pp. 291–92; and Chernaik, *Sexual Freedom*, pp. 74–78.

24 The date of '*A Ramble*' is unknown. It is mentioned 'in a letter of 20 March 1673 from Godfrey Thacker to Theophilus Hastings, 7th Earl of Huntingdon' (Love, p. 410). Vieth thinks it was 'apparently composed early in 1673' (*Attribution*, p. 294).

25 On Rochester's education in the classics, see Johnson, pp. 21–27. Johnson concludes 'the evidence for John Wilmot's ability as an enthusiastic classicist is convincing' (p. 23).

26 Johnson notes this parallel p. 152, the first to do so; the use I make of it is, of course, my own.

27 Edmund Waller, 'On St. James's Park, As Lately Improved By His Majesty', *The Poems of Edmund Waller*, ed. G. Thorn Drury (Scribner's, 1893; rpt. New York: Greenwood Press, 1968), lines 1 and 4.

28 'Several scholars', Marianne Thormählen writes, 'have noticed the frequent use of biblical and otherwise Christian expressions in *A Ramble in St. James's Park* and have drawn different conclusions from it. As was the case with "Absent from thee", the religious element operates on more than one level. There are the deliberately debased "consecrate", and "hallow'd" in lines about the Park

itself (lines 10 and 13); the similarly blasphemous lines on the ambitious crab-louse and on the inability of doctors, doormen of life and death, to believe in the Incarnation (lines 147–49); and the representation of Corinna's vagina as a once-sacred vessel that has been *"prophan[d]"* (line 166). There is also the suggestion of human and divine love coalescing in the lines that end in "And Reason lay dissolv'd in Love" (line 132)' ('Dissolver of reason: Rochester and the nature of love', in *That Second Bottle: Essays on John Wilmot, Earl of Rochester*, ed. Nicholas Fisher (Manchester: Manchester University Press, 2000), p. 31). In a suggestive and intricate reading of the poem, Thomas K. Pasch explores how 'Biblical allusions are used extensively in the poem: the elevation of St. James's Park to Edenesque proportions through words like "honor" (l. 9), "consecrate" (l. 10), "all-sin-sheltering grove" (l. 25), and "hallowed walks" (l. 33); the concept of *felix culpa* (lines 91–96); free will (lines 109–10); the Twenty-Third Psalm (lines 129–30); and the parable of passing a camel through the eye of the needle (lines 143–53). Also, the central section ends with a paradox like the paradox central to Christian belief – the fortunate fall' ('Concentricity, Christian Myth, and the Self-Incriminating Narrator in Rochester's *A Ramble in St. James's* Park', *Essays in Literature* (Spring, 1979), pp. 21–28); rpt. in *John Wilmot, Earl of Rochester: Critical Essays*, ed. David M. Vieth (New York: Garland Publishing, 1988, pp. 149–61). See p. 159, footnote 9). In his edition, Frank Ellis notes: 'Throughout "this unprintable poem" (Ronald Berman, *Kenyon Review* 26 (1964), p. 362) in Hudibrastic verse there is a surprising leitmotif of Christian imagery: "consecrate (l. 10) … hallowed (l. 33) … heaven (lines 38, 148) … fall (l. 90) … Jesus (l. 149)" and a remarkable concentric structure turning round an axis of "natural freedoms" (l. 97)' (*Complete Works*, p. 330).

29 Augustine, *On Christian Doctrine*, trans. D.W. Robertson (New York: The Liberal Arts Press, 1958), pp. 88 and 94.
30 As Carole Fabricant notes: 'Consistently the poems reflect a conversion of spiritual and philosophical phenomena into concrete objects or actions: a kind of counter "transubstantiation" which exposes the wine as nothing but water after all' ('Rochester's World of Imperfect Enjoyment', p. 338).
31 Presumably the speaker could find solace in simply realizing that his materialistic vision is but one of an infinite number, none of which, given his terms, can be proven to be 'right'. Moreover, though he can claim he is a materialist, he cannot prove materialism any more than he could prove that he is a solipsist. But the speaker, if not Rochester, is looking for a dogma, and the modernistic one of seeing various conflicting perspectives as constituting reality and therefore making the interpretative attitude itself into a dogma is no more an alternative here than are the comforts of subtle philosophical distinction.
32 Kenneth Burke, *Counter-Statement* (Berkeley, CA: University of California Press, 1968), p. 25. James G. Turner writes: 'I would not want to overstate the religious dimension in libertinism; certainly not every wild rake was a devout believer led astray by the profligacy of his age. But the religious analogy does provide a useful model for deciphering the mental processes of the libertine; it

may even throw light on the problems of definition and chronology that have divided scholars. Blasphemy, for example, evidently depends on a core of emotional belief glowing within a mantle of intellectual doubt; a secure and conventional believer has no need for blasphemy, and a true atheist has no reason for it ... The somewhat tamer rakes of Restoration England may be seen as blasphemers in two senses. Not only do they mock Scripture and the liturgy, and thus attest to the importance of the religion they pretend to despise, but they are also social blasphemers, rebelling against the rules of upper-class civility even though it is precisely those rules that give them the license to be uncivil' ('The Properties of Libertinism', in *'Tis Nature's Fault: Unauthorized Sexuality during the Enlightenment*, ed. Robert Parks Maccubbin (Cambridge University Press, 1987), pp. 80–81).

33 As Warren Chernaik insightfully notes: 'The situation is a classic double-bind: what the mind perceives as true, the heart feels as an aching void. 'I rise at eleven', 'A Ramble in St. James's Park', and *A Satyr against Mankind* in their different ways all assert a freedom that mocks and entraps in its denial of value 'beyond material sense' (*Satyr against Mankind*, 67). The delicate balance of belief and unbelief, the yearning for a transcendence for which the analytical intellect, trained in habits of skepticism, can find no rational grounds, marks Rochester as the child of his time' (*Sexual Freedom*, p. 81).

34 *'The Imperfect Enjoyment'*, one of Rochester's most admired poems, a favourite among undergraduates, can be seen in turn as a rehearsal for '*A Ramble*'. 'A Ramble' was written before 20 March 1673, *'The Imperfect Enjoyment'* probably just before then. It contains a parody of lines from Dryden's *Conquest of Granada*, first acted in December 1670 and published in 1672. The speaker pursues pleasure through the senses with his *Corinna*. When he is about to succeed, at least momentarily, he experiences, however, a premature ejaculation.

> But whilst her buisy hand would guide that part
> Which shou'd convey my soul up to her heart
> In liquid raptures I dissolve all o're,
> Melt into sperm and spend at every pore.
> (lines 13–16)

The poem, like '*A Ramble*' ends in an extended curse, a 26-line rant the object being not *Corinna*, but the disillusioned speaker's 'Dart of Love' (line 37), which 'Now languid lies in this unhappy hour/ Shrunk up and sappless like a wither'd flower' (lines 44–45). The tone of the curse is not savage as in '*A Ramble*' but comic, if grotesquely so, laced with what John H. O'Neill calls 'its hyperbolic brilliance' ('Rochester's "Imperfect Enjoyment": "The True Veine of Satyre" in Sexual Poetry', *Tennessee Studies in Literature* 25 (1980); rpt. in *John Wilmot, Earl of Rochester: Critical Essays*, ed. David M. Vieth (New York: Garland Publishing, 1988), p. 135). As Griffin points out, some of the lines 'in part recall the boastful confessional of "To the Postboy". There, the speaker has "swived more whores more ways than Sodom's walls e'er knew," has broken houses, libeled kings and fled like a coward when courage was needed' (Griffin, p. 98).

> This Dart of Love whose peircing point oft Try'de
> With Virgin blood Ten Thowsand Mayds have dy'de,
> Which Nature still Directed with such Art
> That it through every Cunt reach't every heart,
> Stiffly Resolv'd t'would Carelesly invade
> Woman, nor Man, nor ought its fury stayd –
> Where ere it pierc'd a Cunt it found or made –
> ...
> What Oyster, Cynder, Beggar, Common whore
> Did'st thou ere fayle in all thy life before?
> When Vice, Disease, and scandall lead the way
> With what officious hast doest thou obey!
> Like a rude Roareing Hector in the streets
> Who scuffles, Cuffs and Justles all he meets
> But if his *King* or Countrey claime his Ayde
> The Rakehell villain shrinks and hides his head,
> Even so thy brutall vallour is display'd,
> Breaks every stew, does each smale whore invade ....
> (lines 37–43 and 50–59)

I would add the echoes of the poem found in 'The Disabled Debauchee': 'I'll tell of Whores attack'd, their Lords at home/ Bauds Quarters beaten up, and fortress won' (lines 33–34). *Sodom*, in which Rochester may have had a hand and which was probably written in the early 1670s, contains a comic scene in which Fuckadilla in her eagerness brings Virtuoso to a premature ejaculation (Scene B6, Act 4th Sc: 5th, lines 43–63, p. 328).

Perhaps Rochester's most cited, most remembered lines about pleasure also occur in *The Imperfect Enjoyment*:

> ... Is there then no more?
> She cries; All this to Love, and Raptures due—
> Must we not pay a Debt to pleasure too?
> (lines 22–24)

Serving as the title of John Adlard's 1974 book, *John Wilmot Earl of Rochester: The Debt to Pleasure*, the lines also make an appearance in the Inspector Morse episode 'Last Bus to Woodstock':

Morse:	Lewis, if anyone offered you a free holiday in the sun, what would you do?
Lewis:	Take it.
Morse:	Sensible fellow. Let's get out of here. I hate the smell of hospitals. "All this to love and rapture's due. Must we not pay a debt to pleasure, too?"
Lewis:	What?
Morse:	Rochester, Lewis.
Lewis:	I think maybe it's time I bought you a drink.

35 I am relying, somewhat anachronistically, on John Frederick Moehlmann's *A Concordance To The Complete Poems of John Wilmot, Earl of Rochester* (Ann

Arbor, MI: University Microfilms International, 1977) for these numbers. A concordance to Love's edition has yet to appear.

36 Robert Parsons, 'A Sermon Preached At the Funeral of the Rt Honorable John Earl of Rochester, Who died at *Woodstock*-Park, July 26. 1680, and was buried at *Spilsbury* in *Oxford-shire*, Aug. 9' (Oxford: Printed at the Theater for *Richard Davis* and *Tho: Bowman*. 1680), p. 7. Hereafter cited in the text as Parsons.

3

Development of the satirist

> But my business here was to see the inside of the Stage and all the tiring roomes and Machines; and endeed it was a sight worthy of seeing. But to see their clothes and the various sorts, and what a mixture of things there was, here a wooden leg, there a ruff, here a hobby-horse, there a Crowne, would make a man split himself to see with laughing – and particularly Lacys wardrobe, and Shotrell's. But then again, to think how fine they show on the stage by candle-light, and how poor things they are to look now too near-hand, is not pleasant at all.
>
> Samuel Pepys, 19 March 1666

The events of 1671–72 mark a major turning point in the life of John Wilmot and therefore in the art that it so keenly and accurately reflects. Among the significant changes that occurred during this winter of his discontent is that Rochester began to write satire. He had written parodies, engaged in mockery and low-key raillery, and he had shown flashes of satiric wit in the 'Epigram on Louis XIV' and in his lampoon on Miss Price, but during and following the winter of 1671–72, Rochester wrote social satires, lampoons, and finally the great self-reflective, philosophical satires. '*A Ramble*' is one of the key works in Rochester's development as a satirist. My conjecture is that the other, similar to '*A Ramble*' in so many respects, is *Sodom*.

'Among the Rochester *dubia*', Harold Love rightly points out, 'the case of *The Farce of Sodom* is agreed to be crucial'.[1] The play rests among Rochester's *dubia* because there is no conclusive evidence that John Wilmot, 2nd Earl of Rochester, wrote *Sodom* or that he collaborated with others to do so. Early pioneers of Rochester studies – L.S.A.M. von Römer, Johannes Prinz, Sidney Lee, and Montague Summers – thought he did, Summers asserting: 'Although the authorship has been disputed, there is no doubt that Rochester actually penned the piece.' And he concluded: 'I fear that the entirely conscientious editor of Rochester's work … cannot but include *Sodom* in his text.'[2] Others were not so sure, John Hayward having his doubts, Graham Greene finding 'The ascription … very doubtful', and Vivian de Sola Pinto thinking it improbable.[3] The critical debate over the authorship of *Sodom*, lively and insightful, has continued to this very day, that history canvased in the Appendix.

Thanks to the efforts of many, we now know, however, a great deal more about *Sodom* than did those early pioneers, though the author or authors so far continue to elude us. And despite the doubts of many, *Sodom* continues to be associated with John Wilmot, 2nd Earl of Rochester. Love includes it in his 1999 edition, knitting together, to my mind in a not altogether easily understandable way, the two versions of the play found in the Princeton manuscript. His rationale for including *Sodom* is that 'Stylistic tests conducted by John Burrows show the word usage as falling within the established Rochesterian parameters.' Love concludes, therefore, that 'there is no stylistic case for *rejecting* Rochester as a possible author, unless it be the clumping ungraciousness of the songs' (Love, p. 498). He places *Sodom*, however, 'not in the section of "Poems probably by Rochester" nor that of "Disputed Works", but in the *Appendix Roffensis* of works which for one reason or another are *associated with* Rochester' (last italics are mine).[4] The rationale that Love and Robert D. Hume give for using 'Associated With' in their magisterial edition of the *Plays, Poems, And Miscellaneous Writings Associated With George Villiers Second Duke of Buckingham* (2007) illuminates why Love's placement of *Sodom* in his edition is exactly right:

> Some readers may be disconcerted by 'associated with' in the title of this edition. That phrase was arrived at only after considerable debate and soul-searching. We want to signal as precisely as possible the highly unusual authorial status of the contents. 'Plays, Poems, and Miscellaneous Writings' seemed unexceptionable, and 'George Villiers, Second Duke of Buckingham' would be hard to avoid without abandoning the enterprise entirely, but how should the two be yoked? To say 'by' or 'of' would imply a claim for sole authorship that we are very far from making. If we said 'attributed to' we would be directing attention to precisely the issue we cannot solve, and might seem to be presuming attribution of the unthinking kind we wish to put under question. If we were to say 'from the circle of' we would make the contents seem arbitrary – why not include anything we can find of Clifford's, or whatever we fancy of Butler or Cowley? We considered 'by and associated with', but this seems to imply that we can distinguish the two, which is not true. If some readers are puzzled or irked by *Plays, Poems, and Miscellaneous Writings associated with George Villiers, Second Duke of Buckingham* then perhaps our title has served its function. Far from wanting to feign certainty or to hide the problems, we would like to invite users to recognize that we are dealing here with a concept of authorship radically foreign to the assumptions most of us bring to literary texts.[5]

Nicolas Nace speculates that 'Harold Love bends to necessity, not conviction, in giving *Sodom* a home in his Oxford edition of Rochester.'[6]

The 'necessity' arises, however, because Rochester has been, is, and will be for the foreseeable future 'associated' with *Sodom* and for some good reasons.[7] For all of his 'argument-by-conjecture',[8] one conjecture Johnson makes in *A Profane Wit* stands out as being particularly powerful and worthy of exploration: 'Indeed, most of the Earl's poems written between 1671 and 1674 constitute a sort of gloss on *Sodom*, which is the missing link in Rochester's development as a major satirist' (Johnson, p. 149).

The date of the composition of *Sodom*, like so much about the play, is, as Love points out, uncertain.

> Charles's declaration and its undignified revocation on 8 March 1673 (echoed by Bolloxinian's in scene B7) were too long-lasting in their effects to provide more than a *terminus a quo*. A reference to 'A tale of *Sodom*' in l. 24 of the epilogue of Part 1 of Crowne's *The destruction of Jerusalem* (January 1677) is much too general to be accepted as a proven reference to our *Sodom*. If scene B7, l. 63 is indeed a quotation from Dryden and Lee's *Oedipus*, that portion of the skit cannot have been written before September 1678. (Love, p. 497)

Nace thinks composition of the play occurred later, arguing that 'we have cause to imagine the composition of the play at distinctly different times: an initial, possibly longer version *c.*1678 and a shorter version *c.*1684, the time at which interest was resurrected by the now lost printed edition known from manuscript transcriptions'. And he cites Love: 'Otway may have encountered Fishbourne during military service in Flanders before "The Poet's Complaint" was written in January 1680 and after September 1678, the date that Love, on the authority of an allusion in *Sodom* to Dryden and Lee's *Oedipus*, supposes the earliest date that the farce might have been written.'[9] But Love, as quoted here, wrote '*If* scene B7, l. 63 is indeed a quotation from Dryden and Lee's *Oedipus*, *that portion of the skit* cannot have been written before September 1678' (italics mine). Love is probably right that allusions to Charles's Declaration of Indulgence in March of 1672 and its revocation a year later would continue to reverberate five to eleven years later, but I doubt that other objects of satire, for example, the Secret Treaty of Dover (May 1670) would have. Moreover, as Richard Elias points out: 'Besides two versions of *Sodom* (the five-act version found in other manuscripts and a unique three-act version) and a long erotic prose dialogue, the Princeton MS. Contains mostly political satires and libertine poems, none of which can be dated after 1676.'[10]

In all probability *Sodom*, like '*A Ramble*', was begun between 1672 and early 1673. Frighteningly ill in the autumn of 1671, Rochester had retreated to Woodstock, beginning a pattern of behaviour he would follow intermittently throughout the 1670s of going 'into the Country, and be for some months wholly imployed in Study, or the Sallies of his Wit: which

Development of the satirist

he came to direct chiefly to *Satyre*' (Burnet, p. 54). The two works, in effect companion pieces, share numerous characteristics, not the least of which being the recipients of their satiric venom. '*A Ramble*' had, however obliquely, registered Rochester's disgust with his King; it had also been his first blast at Restoration society, the

> *Whores* of the *Bulk*, and the *Alcove*,
> Great *Ladies*, *Chamber-Maids*, and *Drudges*,
> The *Rag-picker*, and *Heiress* trudges:
> *Carr-men*, *Divines*, great *Lords*, and *Taylors*,
> *Prentices*, *Poets*, *Pimps* and *Gaolers*;
> *Foot-Men*, fine *Fops*, do here arrive ....
> (lines 26–31)

Sodom too focuses on the King, the great ladies, lords, and fops and with an even greater vehemence, a searing hatred perhaps unmatched in English literature.

The story line is simple enough. The king of Sodom, Bolloxinian, has decided for various reasons ranging from hygiene to aesthetics that his subjects should give up heterosexuality for homosexuality. Accordingly, he instructs his minions to 'proclaim that Buggery may be vsd/ O're all the land so C—t be not abus'd' ([Scene I], lines 69–70, p. 305).[11] This decision, though popular with the army, leads to the nation's destruction. Women resort to dildoes but also make use of horses and dogs; in the Court disease and corruption spread. Finally, fflux, 'Phisician in ordinary to his Majesty', instructs the King;

> To love & nature all their rights restore:
> ffuck women & lett Bugg'ry be no more.
> Itt does that Propogable end destroy
> Which nature gave wth pleasure t'enjoy.
> Please her, & sheel be kind: if yo^u displeas,
> Shee turnes into Corrupcon & disease.
> ([Scene B7] lines 43–48, p. 330)

Bolloxinian, however, remains adamant, and true to biblical prophecy, he and his kingdom come to a sulfurous end:

> Enter Fire & Brimstone. A Cloud of smoak arises.
>   The curtain falls.
>   Finis
>   ([Scene B7] lines 86–88, p. 332)

The play has significance and value in three directions: as social and political satire, as literary parody, and if Rochester did have a hand in writing of *Sodom*, as a reflection of his intellectual and poetic development.

Sodom, in both its versions, opens to a gallery of vicious lampoons. Elias was the first 'to show that it [*Sodom*] refers to some important political events and public figures of the 1670's'.[12] He was cautious, however, in identifying the characters with real-life counterparts, writing: 'except for Bolloxinion and Pockanello, whose habits and political assumptions resemble those of Charles and his brother, none of the characters can be certainly identified with anyone in real life. *Sodom* provides few hints.'[13] He also noted that there is no evidence that at the time anyone 'read *Sodom* as a "key" drama'. Elias is, however, fairly certain that

> the Restoration reader who saw Borastus identified in the *dramatis personae* as 'Catamite of Honour' (or 'Buggermaster-General' in other texts) would, I believe, instantly think of Buckingham. It is Borastus who is given Bolloxinion's declaration with orders to promulgate it; it is Buckingham who was chosen to guide Charles's Declaration through the Privy Council. Moreover, the prominence accorded Borastus in the farce – 'Catamite of Honour' – brings to mind satirical descriptions of Buckingham as a sodomite *and* prime minister ... The Duke's public ambitions and private vices were notorious enough to make this cartoon sketch recognizable.[14]

Johnson was less cautious in linking characters with real-life counterparts as was I, finding the play

> A vicious satire on Charles II's (Bolloxinian's) omnivorous and varied sexual appetite, on this barren Queen, Catherine of Braganza (Cuntagratia), on the fading rival for the king's bed, Lady Castlemain (Fuckadilla), on the new, scheming French whore, Louise de Kéroualle (Clitoris), and on the royal pimps and hanger-on in this depraved court (William Chiffinch is perhaps the Buggermaster General Borastus; Pine is Churchill, Tewley perhaps is Jermyn, and Mulgrave Pockanello).[15]

Love is unconvinced: 'Attempts so far made (including that of Elias) to identify the characters with historical individuals have all had an unconvincingly gratuitous quality. Cuntagratia, for instance, has nothing at all in common with Charles's real queen, the pious and reclusive Catherine of Braganza. And Bolloxinian does not even have a brother' (Love, p. 497). The truth probably lies somewhere in between. There is no question that Bolloxinian is Charles II, Tarsehole, Louis XIV, and that some conjectural identifications, as I hope to show, are more plausible than others. Elias and Love, however, are right that the play provides few hints, 'almost no particularity in the satire' (Love, p. 487) and for good reason. As Love, citing Rochester, points out in *English Clandestine Satire, 1660–1702* (2004):

> Sodomy, with both sexes, was ineradicably associated in the minds of Protestant Britons with the Roman Catholic clergy and with Catholicism generally. In the obscene play *Sodom*, Charles's Declaration of Indulgence

of 1672, which gave Catholics a measure of religious freedom, is parodied as a universal legitimization of buggery. Elsewhere, Rochester, in a morbid piece of self-mockery, announces that he has

... swiv'd more whores more ways then sodoms walls
E're knew or the Colledge of Romes Cardinalls.

And he goes on to argue:

> In such ways the sexual invective endemic to the lampoons often asks to be construed as political allegory. I believe this was sensed by at least some of the writers of these pieces and that in their narratives of scandal they were interrogating problems in the exercise of power that could not at that period be addressed in any more satisfactory or intelligent way.
> One consequence of this emblematic use of sexual insults is that accusations of sodomy, whether heterosexual or homosexual, made in lampoons cannot, when they belong to the language of political allegory, be taken as a guide to actual patterns of sexual behavior at the court or elsewhere.[16]

Paddy Lyons, moreover, makes the interesting case that the satire in *Sodom* is not directed at particular faults of particular people, Catherine of Braganza not being satirized for being a nymphomaniac, but for being barren, the satire directed at issues of succession. *Sodom*, he writes,

> does not seem concerned to condemn or to condone in themselves any of the wildly varied sexual practices it canvasses, but it does deploy speculation about non-procreative sexual engagements, and so raises the political issue of dynasty. Once the 'Divine Right' argument had been discounted, the remaining justification for monarchy as opposed to republicanism was that monarchy gives continuity to the State; the play, however, devises a situation whereby sodomy is the sole permitted sexual practice, and no offspring can be produced to give legitimate continuation to the dynastic line. (Young Prince Prickett is far from manifesting any statesman-like aspect.) The play can then be read as making imaginative use of the coterie surrounding the French *non*-king (Monsieur), with Rochester posing in terms of fiction the situation of his own English monarch, who also had no legitimate offspring to succeed him. This is to view the play as addressing in its own fashion an issue taken up later by, for instance, Dryden's *Absalom and Achitophel*.[17]

Lucina's Rape will satirize Chylax, Lycias, Balbus, Proculus, and Lycinius, some of the same raffish crew of courtiers found in *Sodom*, and Love thinks Rochester may well have intended to target their real-life counterparts.

> The play's constant suggestion of veiled satire on the English court is part of its alliance with the lampoon culture. Indeed, if we knew more about such characters as Mall Howard, Mary Knight, William Chiffinch, Bab May, and Catharine Crofts, the bawds and procuresses of the play might be found to have been aligned in revision with originals from Whitehall. The character of

Proculus, of whom Rochester wrote more new dialogue than in the other cases of this kind, reads as if a personal model existed. His scene with Aecius in 5.1 is a gem of satirical portraiture.[18]

Of one of those real-life counterparts, John Harold Wilson writes, 'Chiffinch, Page of the Backstairs, was also pander-in-chief to the King. According the gossipers, he smuggled the fair and frail ladies in through his own lodgings in Whitehall, adjacent to the King's apartments, and opening on the Privy Stairs.'[19] If we only knew more.

The particularly scabrous early version of *Sodom* focuses on the king and the chief rivals for his bed in the spring and summer of 1670. Clitoris (perhaps Louise de Keroualle who arrived with the French delegation to Dover in May of 1670) vies with Fuckadilla (perhaps Barbara Villiers, Lady Castlemaine, the established but fading object of Charles's attention), and Cuntagratia (perhaps Catherine of Braganza) to lure the king from the practice of Sodomy and make him her own. Trying to convince the king that Cuntagratia has been unfaithful, Clitoris explains:

> Then, s^r, you swore if Cuntagracia e're
> Proud shew'd to you & did to others steer,
> You would to me the happiness bestow
> If e're yor Pr— to female C—t did bow.
> ([Scene A3], lines 46–49, p. 311)

Charles's barren queen is portrayed as a raving nymphomaniac, 'Resolu'd to swiue with e'ry one she meets' ([Scene A3], line 17, p. 310). Fuckadilla is a worthy rival, and though Rochester poured many a harsh phrase on his monarch's head, it may be in *Sodom* that he reserved his most vicious swipe for the king to whom he pandered when he put the following words in his mouth:

> But Buggerantes knows my will alone:
> To humid C—ts I am a stranger growne.
> Arse of all kinds I follow by the scent –
> My prick allows no spous but fundament.
> ([Scene A3], lines 25–28, p. 310)

Others also receive generous doses of venom. It would seem that Rochester cast the vain, sycophantic Mulgrave as Pockanello, a poxed puppet, who snitches on his friends and who declares to the King: 'Its all I wish that Pock^{os} arse/ May still find fauo^r from yor Royall Tarse' ([Scene I], lines 57–58, p. 305). Here we probably have Rochester's assessment of the reasons for Mulgrave's rapid rise at Court. The wits had dubbed the ambitious Mulgrave 'King John'; the early version of *Sodom* ends with Pockanello's mock apotheosis as Sodom's new king. Other salacious caricatures include, I believe, the Duke of York as Buggeranthes, the thoroughly poxed leader of the army. Monmouth is perhaps cast as the moronic Prince Pricket, and in a role also not far removed from life, Borastus (William Chiffinch?) as Buggermaster General, makes sure that the seamy desires of his monarch are fulfilled. The 'plot' in Act I in which Pine is accused of having an affair with Fuckadilla, the King's mistress, apparently refers to the actual Court imbroglio that eventuated in the daughter born to the Duchess of Cleveland in July 1672. John Churchill (Pine?) was almost surely the father. Ironically and sordidly, Tewly, one of the informants against Pine, is probably Henry Jermyn, Master of the Horse to the Duke of York, whose own affair with Barbara Villiers had caused an uproar at Court in 1667. Rochester, various leaves aside, had been at Court since 1665 and knew by now that the more things change, the more they remain the same. *Sodom* registers an enormous disgust with the staple fare of intrigues and sexual shenanigans.

We do not know Rochester's precise political leanings in the early 1670s, but he seems to have been moving toward the newly emerging Country Party, headed in a desultory way by Rochester's companion, the Duke of Buckingham. As Elias has rightly argued, the political stance behind the play is roughly congruent with the Country Party's line.[20] The play equates buggery with Catholicism, an object of fear among many seventeenth-century Englishmen, a fear upon which those in opposition played. In *Sodom*, Bolloxinian instructs Borastus to

> sett the Nation free:
> Let Conscience haue itts force of liberty.
> I do proclaim that Buggery may be vsd
> O're all the land so C—t be not abus'd.
> Thats the Prouiso; this shall be yor trust.
>   ([Scene I] lines 67–71, p. 305)

These lines refer to Charles II's Declaration of Indulgence, 15 March 1672, Borastus explicitly answering the King: 'Streight this indulgence shalbe issued forth' ([Scene I], line 75, p. 305). Political liberty is satirically reduced to a question of sexual liberty. Heterosexuality comes to stand for Anglicanism and the Clarendon Code with its restrictions on dissenters and Catholics. Sodomy, on the other hand, stands for Catholicism and political tyranny. In exercising arbitrary power the King is subverting not supporting 'native' liberty ('native' rather than 'force of' being the reading of the British Library, Harleian MS 7312). The play depicts the Declaration of Indulgence as a Catholic plot, a sodomizing of the country, which will lead to destruction.

The Declaration of Indulgence also brought centre stage an issue much debated in the late 1660s and 1670s, the extent of the King's prerogative, not only his ability to protect his ministers and to grant pardons but to suspend the 'enforcement of statutes where the forfeiture or part of it was the King's', a right the Declaration directly tested.[21] The issue is given several pointed, if sordid, send-ups. The king, declaring his intention to bugger Tewly and then Pine, receives from the latter these obsequious remarks:

> Oh! s^r you hono^r vs too much.
> Itt was enough when me you did entrust
> As harbinger vnto yor sacred lust.
> But, as from heauen, yor will cann make vs blest
> Though we're vnworthy when we do our best,
> Nor yor affections dare we clayme as right.
> ([Scene I], lines 60–65, p. 305)

The Stuarts' beloved fiction of divine right receives a glancing blow here, but the real target is the King's power to protect his ministers ('affections' is 'Protecion' in P2). To Pine's fawning, the King replies: 'Those who my pleasure serue I must requite' ([Scene I], line 66, p. 305). In this assessment the Declaration of Indulgence was literally just that, the King defending his rights only when they pertained to his indulgence in carnal pleasures. The prerogative receives similar treatment when Pockanello informs the King of a plot against him. Pine has been swiving Fuckadilla. The king insouciantly replies: 'Alas Poore Pine I cannot blame ye deed/ When nature vrges by impulse of seed?' ([Scene I], lines 90–91, p. 306). Pockanello obtusely insists: 'It was a trespasse without leaue to swiue/ Vpon his Soueraignes Prerogatiue' ([Scene I], lines 93–94, p. 306).[22]

How much Rochester knew about the secret Treaty of Dover signed 22 May 1670 is unknown. He carried messages to Charles's sister, Mary, the Duchess of Orleans, on his travels to France in 1669, the year of the secret negotiations. When Mary and the French delegation arrived at Dover on 16 May 1670, John Wilmot was there. Whether his duties included political and social responsibilities, we do not know, but the events of Act IV of *Sodom* (Scene B5 in Love) seem to have the Treaty as target. In order to bring about a perfect union between the kings of England and France and thus to ensure the felicity of their peoples, the Treaty called for England to declare war upon the Dutch and for Charles 'being convinced of the truth of the Roman Catholic religion' to declare it with a view to bringing his country once again into the Catholic fold.[23] In Act IV Bolloxinian receives a messenger from Gomorrah (France) with greetings from his brother king, Tarsehole (Louis XIV). Tarsehole wishes the King 'peace & pastime in abundance' ([Scene B5], line 118, p. 326) and towards that end includes gifts of dildoes and 'forty striplings' ([Scene B5], line 101, p. 325).

Whether the gifts have as their referent the attractive group of ladies-in-waiting Louis XIV had sent with Mary as persuasion for Charles to sign the Treaty; the secret subsidies of money Louis had been providing; the 6,000 troops the French king promised Charles in order to carry out his plans to make England Catholic; or all of these, the grand affairs of state are shown to be the ignoble and sordidly motivated transactions they often are and in this case surely were.

The play attacks other political targets that we plausibly associate with Rochester. The Earl was no longer enamoured with war and warriors, as he perhaps had been in 1665–66. Charles again declared war against the Dutch on 17 March 1672. That Buggeranthes (probably the Duke of York) suffers from syphilitic scars is but one manifestation of Rochester's attitude toward the jingoist party headed by York and supported by Mulgrave (probably Pockanello). There is also satire directed against a standing army, an English taboo during the period but again one associated with the Country Party. When Bolloxinian asks whether the army is 'pleas^d with w^t I did proclame?' Buggeranthes tells him:

They Practice it in hono^r of yor name.
If lust p^{r}vaile they want no womans aid:
Each Buggers with Content his owne Com'rade.
 ([Scene B5], lines 49–52, p. 324)

So much for martial dignity and boastful masculinity. Whether the play actually has the historical CABAL in mind, it does refer to a 'iuncto' and criticizes politics conducted by informal cabinet councils.[24] Underlying the play throughout is the appeal to a natural constitution that guarantees native rights and that in turn is being threatened by absolutism in politics and religion, that is, by French and Catholic ways. The play as such takes its own modest place in yet another document protesting the Norman Yoke',[25] a protest that plausibly would have drawn Rochester's sympathies.

Like 'A Ramble' with its attack on panegyric, Sodom satirizes the people and politics of the Stuart Court and also the artistic mode that served to flatter that Court, the heroic drama. The play has numerous affinities with, and grew out of, much the same milieu as The Rehearsal (first acted 7 December 1671) of which it is an underground version. Throughout the later 1660s and into the 1670s the stage had proffered the court a steady fare of flattery. Dedications proclaimed denizens of the Court to be patterns of virtue, and the stage reflected back to them their idealized image with the assurance that such idealizations were reality itself. Court tastes ran to the platonic as it assumed pastoral and heroic forms; playwrights scurried to satisfy them. Dryden's Secret Love was a particular favourite with

Charles II, and Fletcher's *The Island Princess* as well as Shadwell's *The Royal Shepherdess* also found favour at Court where Arminda, Cleantha, and even Strephon became adopted names. The romantic, courtly, *precieuse* code of love embodied in such names is duly debunked in the polysyllabic but emphatically Anglo-Saxon names in *Sodom* as well as in the play's mock-pastoral songs. In one stage direction, for example, 'A youth sitting under a Palm tree, in a melancholly posture, sings.' His song begins, 'O Gentle Venus, ease a Tarse' and proceeds in similar fashion ([Scene B7] line 1, p. 329).

Rochester's animus seems to have been focused on the idealistic aesthetic of John Dryden and perhaps to a lesser extent on that of Elkanah Settle. Dryden had dedicated *Tryannick Love* (24 January 1669) to Monmouth whom, he claimed, 'Heaven has already taken care to form ... for an Heroe' (Dryden, vol. 10, p. 107). As the editors of the California Dryden point out: 'The dedication implies that Monmouth might see in the story of Porhyrius and Berenice a model for an epic on the House of Stuart with the Duke as its hero, and in the verse and the rendering of "history" the suggestion of a poem glorifying himself and his wife' (Dryden, vol. 10, p. 387). Dryden went on in the 'Preface' to argue that his play had a moral purpose, writing that

> *pleasure was not the only end of Poesie; and that even the instructions of Morality were not so wholly the business of a Poet, as that the Precepts and Examples of Piety were to be omitted ... Yet far be it from me, to compare the use of Dramatique Poesie with that of Divinity: I only maintain, against the Enemies of the Stage, that patterns of piety, decently represented, and equally removed from the extremes of Superstition and Prophaneness, may be of excellent use to second the Precepts of our Religion.* (Dryden, vol. 10, p. 109)

In the dedication to *The Conquest of Granada* (December 1670), the poet laureate continued on in the same idealistic vein. The object of his praise was the dedicatee, the Duke of York, to whom he explained that

> Heroique Poesie has always been sacred to Princes, and to Heroes ... 'Tis, indeed, but justice, that the most excellent and most profitable kind of writing, should be addressed by Poets to such persons whose Characters have, for the most part, been the guides and patterns for their imitation. And Poets, while they imitate, instruct.

In Charles and James, Dryden contended, 'are eminent the Characters which *Homer* has given us of Heroique vertue' (Dryden, vol. 11, pp. 3 and 6). Settle's dedication to *Cambyses King of Persia* (acted, 1670; published, 1671) to the Duke and Duchess of Monmouth begins: '*Since the great Characters, and Subjects of serious Plays, are representations of the past Glories of the World, the arrogance of an Epistle Dedicatory may pretend to some Justice, in offering Heroick Stories of past Ages to their Hands, who are the Ornaments of the present.*'[26]

Rochester, very much on the other side of this battle of the playwrights, found such claims nauseous, the assertion that these plays were mimetic and moral being to him absurd if not hypocritical. He knew all too well that the objects of such praise, far from being patterns of virtue, were examples of debauchery, vainglory, and stupidity. Therefore he may well have cast Charles as the ranting, sexually omnivorous Bolloxinian, the Duke of York as a poxed warrior, and Monmouth as a booby. Moreover, Rochester would not have been convinced by Dryden's claims for the moral efficacy of his plays. Morality was hardly being served by the double entendres coyly couched in the elevated diction and plaintive songs of heroic drama. In *The Rehearsal* Bayes chortles: 'I made 'em all talk baudy; ha, ha, ha: beastly, downright baudry upon the Stage.'[27] *Sodom* exposes the incongruity between reality and representation, between Dryden's moral claims and the actual effect of his plays, by taking Bayes's formula to exponential extremes and making the salacious emphatically explicit. In Dryden's aesthetic Rochester found neither clarity nor common sense, neither moderation nor sincerity, neo-classical qualities he was coming to embrace. What claimed to be mimetic and moral was not and to show just how bogus these claims were, Rochester, I am hypothesizing, substituted for what he took to be the artificial and idealistic the harsh and vulgar realisms found in *Sodom*.

As critics have noted, the opening two lines of *Sodom* parody *The Conquest of Granada*. 'Thus in the Zenith of my lust I reigne/ I eat to swiue & Swiue to eat againe' declares Bolloxinian in an obscenely realistic rendering of Boabdelin's 'Thus, in the triumphs of soft peace, I reigne/ And, from my walls, defy the powers of Spain.' Similarly, the song in 'O Gentle Venus, ease a Tarse' ([Scene B7], lines 1–9, p. 329) is a loose parody of the Zambra dance in *The Conquest of Granada*, making the covert prurience of that song explicit.[28] When Bolloxinian gives orders that Clitoris should be tortured (Scene A3, lines 55–60, p. 311), he sounds very much like the ranting Maximin in *Tyrannick Love* calling for St. Catherine to be put upon the rack. Both tyrants trespass the laws of heaven and earth; both expire unrepentant, uttering defiance. Maximin: 'And shoving back this Earth on which I sit/ I'le mount – and scatter all the Gods I hit.'[29] Bolloxinian's speech, similar in rhetoric, is racier in content: 'Ile Heaven invade & bugger all the Gods/ And drain the spring of their imortall Cods' ([Scene B7], lines 12–13, p. 329). Such ribald deflations, which occur throughout *Sodom* and which are perhaps its best accomplishment, jarringly reveal just how heroically mad the rant of the Maximins really is.

Other passages in *Sodom* echo heroic plays of the day, but for the most part its humour and effectiveness as parody arise not because it points to specific passages but because it manages to sound in general like heroic drama. That is precisely one of the points Rochester probably wished to make. Heroic plays, whether by Boyle, Settle, or Dryden, are all alike. All share similar rhetorical solemnities and declamations, all share the same plots and attendant imbroglios, the same characters and themes. *Sodom* catalogues these commonplaces of heroic drama, mocks and deflates them. Its plot concerns the destruction of an empire and the fall of a king complete with court intrigues that, in the early version, include a poisoning. The main plot sports a king, his cast-off queen, her rivals, and her lover, a warrior hero. In Prince Pricket and Princess Swiuia the play has a sub-plot of exemplary love. To be sure, the King's downfall is due not to any evil machinations on his part or on the part of others but rather to his pursuit of sodomean pleasures. The queen and her warrior hero debate at length and with requisite casuistry the merits of passionate love and exalted honour. But in this parody of the heroic lover and heroine the roles are reversed, the female being the pursuer, the content explicitly rather than covertly sexual, and the denouement decidedly deflationary. Buggeranthes can no longer satisfy the voracious appetite of the Queen; he must retire for rest.

> *Cunt*: You must oblige me in this very howre –
> 'Gainst all Denyalls you know C—t has power!
>
> *Bugg*: Yo^r favours, Madam, are so farre above
> The vtmost merrits of my Vassall love
> That, should I court my letchery to obey
> And in obedience swive my soul away,
> All my endeavours would att best become
> A poore Oblacon to yor Royall womb.
>
> *Cuntag*: Still from my love you modestly wth draw:
> You are not by my fauo^{r}s kept in aw.
> When freindship does approach, you seem to fly.
> Doe you soe do before an Enemy?
>
> *Bug*: No, by my head & by this honor^d scarre;
> But toyles of C—t are more than toiles of warre.
>
> *Cunt*: ffucking a toyle? o my Lord you much mistake:
> Of ease and pleasure itt does all partake –
> 'tis all that wee can deare or hapy call.
>
> But loue like warre must haue its intervall:
> Nature Renews ye strength by kind repose,
> Which an vntimely drudgery would lose.
>
> *Bug*: Madam, wth sighs Ile celebrate y^t howre
> That stole my love & robd me of my power.
>   ([Scene B4], lines 22–43, pp. 321–22)

This sounds remarkably like similar encounters between Mustapha and the Queen of Hungary, between Porhyrius and Berenice, or Almanzor and Almahide. The startling incongruity between the mock formality and the salacious content expose the coy sexuality often present in the elevated language of such heroic lovers, and the parody is funny, if coarsely so. Similarly, Pricket and Swiuia are intended as a mockery of such exemplary lovers as Ozmyn and Benazyda, particularly in the often highly contrived episodes that serve to frustrate their love. Thus the moronic prince must be instructed in the mechanics of sex, and his affair with Swiuia really is incestuous. The test traditional to such heroic affairs is reduced to a game between Cunticula and Swiuia as to which one can 'by the power of her p^{r}vaileing hand/ Make Codds shrink vp & Pintle stifly stand' ([Scene B3], lines 97–98, p. 320).

Cliché after heroic cliché come in for *Sodom's* obscene ridicule. In diction and desire, Cuntagratia resembles Settle's Roxolana and Dryden's Lyndaraxa, a type that finds its quintessential embodiment in Laula, the Empress of Morocco. According to the critics of the heroic play – and Rochester was certainly among them – such productions had as their only excuse for existence the presentation of lavish spectacle. As Bayes puts it: 'you must ever interlard your Plays with Songs, Ghosts, and Dances'.[30] The distraught Cuntagratia, in keeping with the formula, seeks comfort in a song.

> Cuntag: Sing, Fuckadilla, charme me with a touch;
> So itt not treat of Chastity too much.
>
> *Fucka*: Thats a strange word; but, if youl baudy haue,
> Madam, Iue Choice.
> ([Scene B2], lines 80–83, p. 316)

Indeed, she does. The play contains three other songs, all of the blue variety, has two dances, a ghost, spirits, and to make the spectacle complete, smoke, clouds, and fire. Even the stage directions, in their elaborate particularity, mock their counterparts.

> A faire Portico Ioyned to a pleasant Garden adornd with many statues of naked men & women in Various postures. In the midle of the Garden a naked woman rep^{r}senting a fountaine bending and Pissing Bolt vpwards. Soft musick is plaid to the purling water, after which is sung this song that follows by a smal voice in a mournfull key. ([Scene 2], p. 306)

In addition there is the obligatory report from the army; untypically, they are not mutinous but rather overjoyed with their King as they revel in the pleasures of sodomy. True to generic expectations, a heroine confronts the paradox of having to destroy what she loves. In her eagerness Fuckadilla brings Virtuoso to a premature ejaculation; she consoles herself by weeping.

The Restoration prologues and epilogues too come in for similar treatment, though what hand Rochester had, if any, in concocting those that accompany *Sodom* we do not know.[31] The intention of the prologue was to gain the attention of the audience just as the epilogue attempted to win a final round of applause. In trying to make such openings original and to make their endings appealing, playwrights resorted to scolding the audience, condemning the times, mocking or making special pleas for poets and their work. In addition, they might lampoon fops, discuss the state of wit, lay down critical dicta, all with the intention of putting their audience in a good mood. Increasingly, though, whatever the topic, the playwright resorted to what was sure to gain attention and win applause: sex. Consequently, the prologues and epilogues to *Sodom* are openly salacious, frank in their acknowledgment that the audience, to quote Aphra Behn who undoubtedly knew, would rather *'hear a smutty Jest/ Spoken by* Nokes *or* Angel, *than a Scene/ Of the admir'd and well penn'd* Cataline.'[32]

The author of the opening prologue complains not about the traditional harping critic or ungenerous audience, but about being unable to write because of his unruly member. He makes no pretence that art is morally uplifting or pleasurable in any of the ways dictated by Horace. It provides the pleasure the audience really wants:

> Here's that will fit your Fancy with delight,
> 'Twill tickle every vein, and please your sight,
> Nay make your Prick to have an appetite:
> ([*First*] *Prologue*, lines 37–39, p. 678)

He scolds the audience not for being dull, religious, or unduly critical but for masturbating and thus depriving the many available women of pleasure. The poet goes on to attack the teasingly coy relationship of actress to role and between actress and audience that Restoration prologues and epilogues often exploited. Actresses pandered to an audience who encouraged them to do just that. The relationship of actress to role was often as incongruous as that between the heroic characters they assumed and their living models. In their notes to the California Dryden the editors of *Tyrannick Love* are of the opinion that 'The audience must have experienced a kind of perverse pleasure in seeing the roles of women of exemplary virtue played by actresses who were anything but that in everyday life.' They go on to point out that 'Mrs. Hughes, who played Saint Catherine, was, in Pepy's words "a mighty pretty woman, and seems, but is not, modest." She became the mistress of Prince Rupert shortly after the initial run of *Tyrannick Love*. Rebecca Marshall, who played Berenice, was, in the words of Nell Gwyn, "a whore to three or four, though a Presbyter's praying daughter", and was simply notorious' (Dryden, vol. 10, pp. 382–83). Nell, herself a woman of some reputation, played Valeria. Openly soliciting the audience, Cuntagratia and Fuckadilla assume the facetiously impudent tone of the Gwyns and Knepps. Fuckadilla's epilogue begins with the spirited: 'Damye my lads, what never a word to say/ in praise or commendation of the Play?' ('The Epilogue. *Spoken by fuckadilla*', lines 1–2, p. 679).

The author or authors of these prologues and epilogues apparently had to admit that satire's exaggeration often paled before the outrageous practices of Restoration society. Thus the notorious epilogue to *Tyrannick Love* could not be topped, only imitated. Nelly enticingly sent her audience off with a *'farewel, Gentlemen, make hast to me/ I'm sure e're long to have your company'* (Dryden, vol. 10, lines 25–26). Cuntagratia does the same, instructing her audience: 'Baffle not nature with yor silly hands/ But come to us when ere yor pintle stands' (BL MS, lines 31–32; not quoted in *Love*). Having read *Sodom*, one can only agree with the assessment of the *First Prologue*: 'It is the most debauch'd heroick Peice/ That e're was wrote, what dare compare with this?' (lines 35–36, p. 678).

The second prologue does have affinities with Rochester's known work and may provide evidence that *Sodom*, as well as being a literary and political satire, is also a deeply personal work. Assuredly part of the play as originally conceived, these 29 lines read less like a prologue than like the initial sketch of the play that they probably are.[33] The opening lines announce *Sodom*'s story line:

> Almighty Cunts, whom Bolloxinian here
> Tyr'd with their tedious toyle does quite Casheire;
> From thence to Arse hee hath his Pricke conueyed
> And thinks itt Treason to behold a maid.
> ('Prologue To Sodom & Gomorah by Bolloxinian', lines 1–4, p. 302)

In lines following Bolloxinian gives reasons for the new dispensation; what he relates should sound familiar.

> The sensuall Creature [i.e. a maid] apted for delight
> Will spend in dreames & so debauch all night;
>
> Begins with little finger, thrusts that in
> And teaches by Degrees whole hand to sin;
> The trickling nature from each vaine does sucke
> And turnes all ouer Proselite to ffucke;
> But yet this Saint shall on examinacon
> Swear shees the onely maid within ye nation.
> Some Gawdy ffoppe stoopes to the Creatures Eyes,
> Yields to the Magick of her ropy thighes
> And att the Church begins his miseries.
> Att night Conueyed to a well ordered bed
> The already Cuckold getts a maydenhead

>   Which is a toy made by a stringent aid –
>   Cunt washt with Allom makes a whore a maid.
>   Wanting that art, shee clings her thighs so fast,
>   Haueing spent thrice shee letts him in at last.
>   Often she Claps the vnacquainted Chicke
>   And draws his Reignes thro' his snotty Pr—.
>   This is the Cheat, twas this made me retire
>   From humid C—t to humaine Arse all fire.
>   (lines 5–25, p. 302)

Like '*A Ramble*', *Sodom* has its genesis partly in and is a retelling of what apparently happened to Rochester in his affair with Corinna, an event crucial to Rochester's life and work, not so much for the person involved but for all that it symbolized. The story of the young man being duped by the wily women came to stand for the failure of youthful expectations, the debunking of hedonism. In one form or another he would continue to retell this story of betrayal in an attempt to find an explanation for it (the most polished version will be Corinna's told at the end of 'Artemiza to Chloe').

Whether this sketch preceded '*A Ramble*' or vice versa, we do not know. But it is here that Rochester seems to have first used the word 'cheat', and it is with the Corinna affair and the works generated by it that 'cheat' and its many synonyms become thematic in his poetry. Rochester's satires in the 1670s will dwell on the 'affected', 'contrived', 'devised', 'false', 'fond', 'feigned', 'vain', and the 'pretended'; will dwell on that which is outwardly 'kind' and 'charming' but which is not, on that which draws belief but does not merit it. This theme perhaps culminates in the definition of man in 'A Satyre against Reason and Mankind' as 'the reasoning Engine' (line 29), a contriver of his own undoing, one who by his very nature deceives himself and others. In the 1670s Rochester, like Aureng-Zebe, considered life and found it all a cheat. Behind *Sodom* is rage at the cheats and betrayals practised by the politicians, courtiers, poets, and actresses, but the rage is directed inwards as well, the work, like '*A Ramble*' being an exercise in self-loathing. As a Gentleman of the Bedchamber, poet, and patron of actresses, Rochester was implicated in all that the play satirizes. *Sodom* reeks of self-hatred and reveals in its various and mingled tones a tormented mind. It is on the one hand jocular and playful; Rochester obviously delighted in parodying heroic bombast, perhaps delighted in the bombast itself. On the other hand, the play exhibits a juvenile imagination that wants to scribble the scabrous, to show off, and to flout authority, and one senses that the jocular stance conceals genuine fear arising from a childish, nightmare vision of having been unspeakably bad and of meriting severe punishment. The hatred for self and other is registered in the play's often pathological obscenities and in its apocalyptic conclusion.

In *Sodom*, if I am right, Rochester continued to explore the implications of hedonism. The political stance of *Sodom* could be, without much distortion, reduced to a critique of the widely used phrase 'the King's pleasure'. 'Nelly ... says that the King first spoiled Mrs Weaver – which is very mean methinks in a prince, and I am sorry for it – and can hope for no good to the State from having a Prince so devoted to his pleasure', wrote Pepys on 11 January 1668 (Pepys, vol. 9, pp. 19–20). Whatever hope Rochester may have had was pretty much gone by the time he wrote *Sodom*, an unstinting diatribe on the pursuit of pleasure. Pleasure is the key word in the play, used twenty-one times in the P2 version. Bolloxinian's fall and his country's woes result from his pursuit of pleasure. As he announces in his opening speech: 'My laws shall Act more pleasures then Comand/ And with my Prick I'le gouerne all the land' ([Scene 1], lines 7–8, p. 303). The only excuse for the existence of the sycophants who surround him is to pander to his pleasures. As Borastus puts it: 'May yor most gracious Pr— & Cods be still/ As boundless in their pleasure as yor will' ([Scene 1], lines 15–16, p. 304). Cuntagratia's dissatisfaction arises because 'In all his pleasures I haue not a share' ([Scene 2], line 19, p. 307). In the early version Clitoris tells the queen that her consort in 'His boundless pleasures bugg^{rs} all he meets/ As Linkboys, fidlers, friggs in open streets' (First Continuation [Scene A2], lines 85–86, pp. 308–9). She advises the queen to follow his example: 'Like him run on with pleasure, build yor throne/ff—ke, frig, spend, royot & the worlds yor owne' (First Continuation [Scene A2], lines 89–90, p. 309). Cuntagratia follows this counsel as do the other characters. Pockanello's boast speaks for all: 'Wee the kind Dictates of our sense pursue/ Wee study pleasures still & find out new' ([Scene B5], lines 25–26, p. 323). This heroically mad pursuit of pleasure, sordid in itself, ends in catastrophe.[34]

The play, however, does not condemn pleasure per se; rather it attempts to work out, as did '*A Ramble*', a limited form of hedonism, and like that work, it fails to do so and is aware of its failure. Aptly enough, fflux, the physician, is the play's normative spokesman. His name, which means to purge, is of course comic; he is probably meant to be taken as a caricature of Sir Alexander Frazier, the King's physician, whom Rochester later ironically called 'the Learned Physician' ('[Impromtu on court personages]', line 3). But I do not think we are meant to take his message ironically; at this period in Rochester's career, say 1672–75, the physician figure is not yet a fraud. During this period Rochester was seriously reading medical lore, seeking cures for his numerous maladies; apparently, he believed cure to be a possibility. It was a bit later, 1676 or so, that Rochester would lump the physician with the politician in the class of cheats. The would-be physician who could not cure himself would play Alexander Bendo, the mountebank, mocking man's desire for health, for a harmonious relationship with nature, and the pathetic credulity springing from what he increasingly considered a desire impossible to satisfy.

In Act V fflux comes on to explain how under the new order the country is suffering, teetering on disaster. After graphically describing the nation's scrofulous condition, fflux urges Bolloxinian

> To love & nature all their rights restore:
> ffuck women & lett Bugg'ry be no more.
> Itt does that Propogable end destroy
> Which nature gave wth pleasure t'enjoy.
> Please her, & sheel be kind: if yo^u displeas,
> Shee turnes into Corrupcon & disease.
> ([Scene B7], lines 43–48, p. 330)

Again, fflux is not an unambiguous character; nevertheless, his position seems to be one that Rochester would genuinely have liked to embrace. It is yet another version of the libertine code: man in tune with nature will find pleasure. The play attempts, however crudely, to show just what following nature means. In sex, politics, and religion there is a natural order – heterosexuality and presumably the King-in-Parliament and Anglicanism – that man violates through sodomy, tyranny, and Catholicism. But following nature remains more an ideal than a reality. Man in his pursuit of pleasure ends in self-destruction, Genesis 19 offering a more accurate reflection of man's experience than the teaching of Epicurus. While there is no evidence for the pagan promise of a harmonious relationship with this world, there is every evidence of the Old Testament assurance that the wicked will end in fire and brimstone. Thus the play exhibits the desire for an ideal relationship between man and nature, but can provide no evidence for it save through its absence, that is, save through the negative. *Sodom* is yet another work reflecting the ongoing debate Rochester entertained between Christian and pagan interpretations of experience. It is yet another work reflecting the torment of a mind whose beliefs and experience are frighteningly incongruous.

If in writing *Sodom* Rochester did not succeed in solving the ethical dilemma which had become and would continue to be the central theme of his work, he did succeed in experimenting with a number of poetic techniques that would contribute to his maturity as a poet. Vieth accurately noted that 'During the early months of 1674, Rochester attained his full growth as a poet.' While pointing out that the reasons for the flowering of artistic gifts can never be fully known, Vieth went on to hypothesize that this 'sudden burgeoning' had much to do with Rochester's banishment from Court in 1673 for his lampoon on Charles II and with his increasing familiarity with Roman satire through Boileau and his growing interest in drama. Yet Vieth remained puzzled that 'before 1674, Rochester was seemingly unable to write fully successful satires in heroic couplets' (*Poems*, pp. xxxviii–xxxix). Seemingly, the ability to write the impressive heroic couplets to be found in *Timon* and 'Tunbridge Wells' simply materialized. Vieth could roughly approximate the time when such a development had to have taken place, but could find no evidence for the apprentice at work. If Rochester, however, really did write or contribute to the writing of *Sodom*, then we may have gone a long way toward clearing up the puzzle.

That is, I am suggesting that it was during an absence from Court that Rochester began to master his craft, and though the process continued during his banishment in 1673, it most likely began in the winter of 1671–72. It was this two-year period that most likely gave birth to *Sodom*. This playlet with its Hebrew fable, Juvenalian rancour, and intense involvement in the contemporary drama, would prove to be Rochester's testing ground for writing the iambic pentameter line. To be sure, *Sodom* contains some dreadful verse, but with its hudibrastic rhymes, comically stilted diction, and hobbled metres, it is safe to infer that, though much of it is bad, Rochester was learning while playing. If one blocks out for a moment the distracting content, one can see in *Sodom* Rochester's couplet art coming to maturity. Moreover, though characterization in *Sodom* is minimal, here too Rochester was learning to create the narrator-personae and the conversational style upon which his reputation would be based. He learned to create dramatic characters by in fact writing a play. Speaking in their own voices, these characters were to become the perfect vehicle for his later ironic vision. One can never be sure how far they are to be trusted, whether their words are self-condemnatory or not. We can see in the characterization of Mulgrave as Pockanello and later as Bajazet the genesis and fulfilment of just such a development. The crude caricature who is indeed but a puppet becomes the polished courtier libertine whose act is very difficult to distinguish from Mulgrave of the life. Rochester was learning, moreover, to take the stuff of life, filter it through established patterns of experience, and create universal situations and types. This neo-classical process is discernible not only in the development of Pockanello to Bajazet but in Rochester's use of the Sodom fable and in his characterization of Charles II as Bolloxinian, then as the 'merry monarch', and finally as the debauched, raving Valentinian, last Roman emperor of the family of Theodosius.

Sodom, begun in 1671–72, was revised on and off over the next three to four years. It and 'A *Ramble*' mark, or so I am contending, Rochester's debut as satirist, and both works adumbrate the direction his other satire will take. Satire of self and of other is in Rochester, as perhaps in all satirists, a simultaneous activity. In 'A *Ramble*' Rochester attacks Court society and its foppish hangers-on only to discover that *inter pares* he is *primus* and thus fit object for his own excoriations. *Sodom* is also, as we have seen, an exercise in self-scourging. But Rochester did write a group of poems whose emphasis is on the depravity of the social world and not, as in later satires, on the satirist and the indeterminable degree to which he is part and parcel of that depraved world. It is as though Rochester in his development as a satirist recapitulated the history of satire not as we have come to know it but as the seventeenth century ideally conceived of it. That is, he seems to have moved from the harshness and vituperation of Juvenal to the more polished and ironic satire of Horace. To be sure, both '*A Ramble*' and *Sodom* fascinatingly intermingle both, but the other satires are divided in their emphasis on one or the other. The more Horatian satires form the subject of the next chapter; here we pursue Rochester's ongoing development as a social critic rubbing down his society with salt.

For the most part the poems under consideration precede the great satires, and in their obviously experimental rhythms they should be considered, like *Sodom*, as apprentice work. Indeed, in subject matter and technique these poems are so close to *Sodom* that they could be considered a part of it, part of an ongoing satiric comment on the Court that began with *Sodom*. His 'Lampoone', 'Too longe the Wise Commons have been in debate', written some time in April 1671 or March 1673 is, for example, *Sodom* in miniature.[35] It too originated as a comment on the question of Charles's prerogative. Parliament would not grant the King the money he so badly needed to continue his Dutch war and to support his own extravagances at home unless he cancelled his Declaration of Indulgence. He did, Parliament went on to pass the Test Act, and the King received his money. Rochester, recovered somewhat from his frightening and serious illness of the year before, sat through this parliament, and the poem is his sardonic comment on it and the state of the Court at the time.

> Too longe the Wise Commons have been in debate
> About Money, and Conscience (those Trifles of State)
> Whilst dangerous Greyvances daily increase,
> And the Subject can't riott in Safety, and Peace;
> Unlesse (as agaynst Irish Cattle before)
> You now make an Act, to forbid Irish whore.
>
> (lines 1–6)

The 'Wise Commons' has been directing its attention to Money, and Conscience', but these are 'Trifles of State' because the real issues, the real 'dangerous Greyvances' are to be found elsewhere, (i.e., in the King's boudoir). If one is to understand the politics of the Stuart Court, Rochester suggests, one needs to look at who is controlling the King's mistresses. The joke on Irish cattle and Irish whore is on one basic level clear enough, but one needs to know that when the Commons passed the Bill prohibiting Irish cattle 'they insisted on the insertion of the word "nuisance" into the Bill ... for it was generally accepted that the king could not dispense with a law prohibiting a common nuisance'.[36] The real issue of prerogative, the real nuisance, rests with Charles and his whores, that is, with Charles and his uncontrollable appetites. The same point had been made more bluntly in *Sodom* when Pockanello announces that 'It was a trespasse without leaue to swiue/ Vpon his Soueraignes Prerogatiue' ([Scene 1], lines 93–94, p. 306). Under the gilding of institutional ceremony and of high-flown diction, lies the carnal reality of 'The Cootes (blacke, and white), Clenbrazell, and Fox/ Invade us with Impudence, beauty, and Pox' (lines 7–8). As in *Sodom*, the country has been 'invaded', though by Irish not French whores. The result, however, has been the same: individuals, yes, but the nation as a whole has become diseased. fflux had given a pathological description of the effects of buggery (i.e., of Catholicism and political tyranny): 'The Pr—s are eaten off, ye womens parts/ Are witherd more y^{en} their dispareing hearts' ([Scene B7], lines 24–25, p. 330). The invasion of Irish whores similarly carries

> ... a Fate, which noe man can oppose;
> The losse of his heart, and the fall of's his Nose.
> Should he dully resist, yet would each take upon her,
> To beseech him to doe it, and engage him in honour.
> (lines 9–12)

In the Stuart Court ideal terms have no meaning save in a carnal frame of reference, 'honour' being a jaded courtly lover's euphemism for a condom.

The last lines share the imagery, theme, and tone of *Sodom*. The question again raised is why sensual indulgence should lead to disease and not to happiness.

> O! Yee mercifull powers, who of Mortalls take Care,
> Make Women more modest, more sound, or lesse fayre.
> Is it just, that with death cruell Love should conspire,
> And our Tayles be burnt by our hearts taking fire?
> There's an end of Communion, if humble Beleavers
> Must bee damn'd in the Cup, like unworthy Receavers.
> (lines 13–18)

The first two lines would seem to be highly ironic. From available evidence, such 'mercifull powers' do not exist. Man is confined to this world that does not yield him the transcendence he seeks. His attempt to make a religion of the senses winds up grimly parodying what Christianity promises but for which it provides no evidence. Man drinks of the unspeakable earthly cup seeking communion and love as promised in the Eucharist but encounters the little death and inexorably the great death. Here as in *Sodom* man ends in fiery damnation.

The entire poem is enormously clever, and its childish rhythms coupled with the alternating lines of twelve and eleven syllables give it a playfulness, doggerel set down to pass away tedious parliamentary time. But hatred, conflicting desires and beliefs lie just under the surface. On the one hand is the very desire for sensual indulgence coupled with a desire to mock the Christianity which condemns it. On the other is the desire to believe in that Christianity, to participate in its promised transcendence, and to have the moral basis it proffers to be able to call down fire and brimstone upon the sordid reality which the poem evokes.[37] In short, the same conflicting emotions we found in *Sodom* are in evidence here.

Rochester's other social satires share equally close affinities with *Sodom*. The same raffish crew, minus the disguise of their stage names, is paraded forth in this doggerel song:

> Quoth the *Dutchess* of *Cleveland*, to Counsellor *Knight*,
> I'd fain have a *Prick*, knew I how to come by't;
> I desire you'le be secret, and give your advice,
> Though Cunt be not coy, Reputation is nice.
>
> To some *Cellar*, in *Sodom*, your *Grace* must retire,
> Where *Porters*, with Black Pots, sit round a *Coal-fire*;
> There open your *Case*, and Your *Grace* cannot fail,
> Of a douzen of *Pricks*, for a douzen of *Ale*.
>
> Is't so quoth the *Dutchess*? Ay by God, quoth the *Whore*.
> Then give me the *Key*, that unlocks the Back-dore;
> For I had rather be fuckt by *Porters*, and *Car-men*,
> Then thus be abus'd by *Churchill* and *German*.

Barbara Palmer, née Villiers, the Duchess of Cleveland, Rochester's cousin, and Charles's chief mistress in the 1660s, was, in Rochester's jaundiced view, simply being herself in *Sodom*. She would 'fain have a *Prick*, knew I how to come by 't', and the essence of her nymphomania character is reflected in Fuckadilla's rhetorical question: 'What woman cann a standing Pri— refuse?' ([Scene 2], line 26, p. 307). She seeks advice from Mary Knight, a singer and minor mistress of Charles, who makes an entrance in *Sodom* by way of a pun, Pockanello telling the King that 'Yo^r Grace att once has from the powers aboue/ A knightly wisdome, & a princely loue' ([Scene 1], lines 9–10, p. 303).[38] Both are past mistresses of the corrupt coterie politics of Charles's Court, aptly and succinctly captured in the metaphor of 'the *Key*, that unlocks the Back-dore'. As in *Sodom*, Churchill (Pine) and German, Henry Jermyn (Tewly), abuse the royal mistress. The *Sodom* in this poem refers to an area of London known for its brothels and disreputable inns. Rochester apparently had already made it a metaphor for the Court.

Rochester's attacks on women, often real-life figures, Juvenalian in its ferocity, made its first appearance in 'A Ramble'. In *Sodom* it became focused on the liberated ladies of the Court; from then on it became a staple of his social satires, one of the more rollicking being 'Signior Dildo'.[39] The poem attacks the same ladies and their insatiably priapic desires. 'That Pattern of Virtue, her Grace of *Cleaveland*' (Version B, line 37) makes an obligatory appearance as does Mary Knight along with a plague of countesses, maids of honour, and actresses turned mistresses. The plot, such as it is, reverses that of *Sodom*. The new Duchess of York, Mary of Modena, whose arrival in England in November of 1673 may have led Rochester to write the poem, declares '"to the Duke I will go/ I have no more need of Signior *Dildo*"' (Version B, lines 7–8). But she is an exception; the other ladies find Signior Dildo an admirably useful and dependable substitute. Males suffer accordingly.

> A Rabble of Pricks, who were welcome before,
> Now finding the Porter deny'd 'em the Door;
> Mischeviously waited his coming below,
> And Inhumanly fell upon Signior *Dildo*.
>
> Nigh wearied out, the poor Stranger did fly,
> And along the *Pall-Mall* they follow'd full Cry:
> The Women concern'd, from every Window,
> Cry'd, Oh, for Heav'ns Sake, save Signior *Dildo*!
>   (Version B, lines 81–88)

Signior Dildo gets away, escaping the fate of his cousins that the Ballers tried to import in 1670 and that customs officials confiscated and burned (Treglown, p. 63). Though the satire is equally pointed – the Duchess of Cleveland is said to have 'swallow'd more Pricks, then the Ocean has sand' (Version B, line 38) – the tone is lighter here than in *Sodom*. The intention, however, is much the same. Personal lampoon combines with political and religious satire. Though primarily a catalogue of bawdy caricatures, 'Signior Dildo' may also be Rochester's sardonic assessment of the Duke of York's second marriage. The Duke had precipitously, without the permission of his brother, married the Catholic Princess of Modena, an event that proved vastly unpopular. Rochester, by now in a typical carnal reduction, equates Mary's arrival with the importation of dildoes. In this mock panegyric, the use of dildoes, like buggery in *Sodom*, is a practice foreign and Catholic.

> Were this Seignior but known to the Citizen Fops,
> He'd keep their fine Wives from their Foremen of Shops;

> But the Rascalls deserve their Horns shou'd still grow,
> For burning the Pope, and his Nephew *Dildo*.
> (Version B, lines 61–64)

This is praise doubly damning. Using dildoes would certainly help keep women from intriguing with shopkeepers, but it is not likely to improve the relationships between fops and their fine wives. The native and natural relationship among the sexes, like man's relationship with God, is already quite corrupt, but Mary of Modena, like Louis XIV with his striplings and the pro-Irish forces with their whores, brings with her a practice which would lead to even greater corruption.

'In the Isle of Brittain', for which Rochester was banished from Court in early 1673, obviously belongs to the group of satires we have been examining. Rochester had said worse things about his king in *Sodom*, but the King had not seen them. If he had, the punishment would probably have been a good deal more severe. In various guises, Charles II plays a central role in Rochester's work. Though we know little about the relationship between the two men, it is clear that when Rochester came to Court on Christmas Day 1664 Charles assumed the role of the father Rochester had never known and desperately desired. In Charles, it is furthermore safe to speculate, Rochester sought the real-life version of the hero who is so much a part of his imagination. This hero was no doubt based on his father, the cavalier Henry Wilmot, horseman and soldier, and took on an idealistic stature precisely because of the absence of this father. The boy's imagination conjured up a powerful figure who would return to set things right, a figure who remained with him all his life. Behind the vituperative satires, behind all of the self-doubts, lies a longing for just such a man. Indeed, Rochester would finally cast himself in this role when he came to write *Valentinian*. The hatred he directed at Charles II over the years, usually deflected by wit or hidden altogether, is one measure of how far Charles failed to live up to the expectations of his surrogate son. When he presented the King with a copy of this satire instead of another the King had apparently asked for, he committed one of what would become a series of Oedipal blunders.

Bolloxinian and the Charles II of this satire are one and the same, mock heroes indulging in priapic politics. Bolloxinian declares that 'My Pintle onely shall my scepter bee' ([Scene 1], line 6, p. 303), and it is said of Charles that 'His Scepter and his Prick were of a length' (line 11). For both the lure of sexual pleasure is irresistible, Bolloxinian boasting that 'My laws shall Act more pleasures then Comand/ And with my Prick I'le gouerne all the land' ([Scene 1] lines 7–8, p. 303). Similarly, 'no Ambition mov'd' Charles 'to get Renowne ... Peace was his Aime, his gentleness was such/ And Love, he lov'd, For he lov'd Fucking much' (lines 5 and 8–9). Unlike Bolloxinian,

Development of the satirist

Charles is portrayed as being heterosexual. But his specific sexual predilections make little difference; governed by his penis he also jeopardizes himself and the well-being of his country: 'Thô Safety, Law, Religion, Life lay on't [his penis]/ 'Twou'd breake thrô all to make it's way to C—t' (lines 18–19). The threat, however, is apparently more hypothetical than real, for the King is in 'my declineing yeares' (line 24), royally impotent. Mistress Nelly must take great pains and employ 'Hands, Armes, Fingers, Mouth and Thighs/ To raise the Limb which shee each Night enjoyes' (lines 31–32). Here we find the same, by now familiar, supporting cast.

Rochester takes a swipe at Louis XIV, 'a French Foole still wandring up and downe/ Starving his People, hazarding his Crowne' (lines 6–7). The poem also lampoons Louise de Kéroualle, Duchess of Portsmouth. By October of 1671 the French whore the English called Madam Carwell (Clitoris) had won her battle with the Duchess of Cleveland (Fuckadilla) for the King's affections and had become the 'dearest of all Deares!' (line 23). The politics of the bedchamber continued to flourish. In tone, the poem again mingles humour and utter contempt. The portrait of Charles has a certain old Rowley flavour to it, an affection for the declining stallion king, but it ends in unmediated animosity: 'I hate all Monarchs and the Thrones that they sitt on/ From the Hector of France to th'Cully of great Brittaine' (lines 33–34). It is as though the poem began in playful lubricity, but in the process of composing Rochester came face to face with the reality of the King and the Court that he served and his salacious jocularity turned to venom.

Rochester took up once more the subjects and themes of *Sodom*. The occasion was a shift of mistresses remarkably similar to the one in 1670 that had served as the initial plot of *Sodom*. Late in 1675 or early 1676 Hortense Mancini replaced Louise de Kéroualle as the mistress *en titre*. In Rochester's estimation, though the faces had changed, nothing else had, and in the '*Dialogue L:R.*' which begins, 'When to the King I bid good Morrow', he gave yet another obscene portrait of his pleasure-driven king surrounded by nymphomaniacal mistresses vying for his favour. In the last stanza the 'People' speak:

Now Heav'ns preserve our *Faiths Defendor*,
From *Paris* Plotts, and Roman Cunt,
From *Mazarine*, that new Pretendor,
And from that Politic *Gramount*.
              (lines 13–16)

Here in capsule form we have the negative rationale of Rochester's social satires, all being protests against tyranny, Catholicism, French influence, and the politics of intriguing mistresses and debauched courtiers.

Rochester wrote a handful of other social satires – the 'Impromptu on Charles II' ('God bless our good and gracious King'), the 'Impromptu on court personages' ('Here's Lauderdale the pretty'), 'Upon Betty Frazer 1677' ('Her Father gave her Dildoes six'), '*On Mrs Willis*' ('Against the Charms our *Bollox* have'), and '*On Poet Ninny*' – that belong to the same group we have been examining.[40] Like them, each attacks a Court figure or one closely related to Court, infamously so in the case of Madam Willis.[41] All mingle lampoon with satire: satire in that there is little irony and the norms by which the characters are measured and found wanting are clear. The values are public, and where they are not clearly delineated, the depravity is so obvious that the reader is made to feel that there must be something better than this lecherous king and his scrofulous court. But each of these poems is animated by the spirit of lampoon. They are personal, scurrilous attacks that coarsely exaggerate. The subjects are rendered ridiculous, bestial, and impotent, the poet wanting to hurt, wound, or in the case of *Sodom*, to kill his victims if only vicariously through language. Rochester, being candid about his motives in writing satire, told Burnet that 'A man could not write with life, unless he were heated by Revenge; For to make a *Satyre* without Resentments, upon the cold Notions of *Phylosophy*, was as if a man would in cold blood, cut men's throats who had never offended him.' With tongue-in-cheek he added: 'the lies in these Libels came often in as Ornaments that could not be spared without spoiling the beauty of the *Poem*' (Burnet, p. 54). He too perhaps told lies, but unlike those of the sycophantic court panegyrists, they at least had an aesthetic justification!

Desire for revenge fuels all of Rochester's satire, but in these ephemeral exercises in raillery and vituperation he learned to write deft heroic couplets, to gain perspective on himself, and to create out of personal animus complex characters of universal appeal. It is to that accomplishment that we now turn.

Notes

1 Harold Love, 'But Did Rochester *Really* Write "Sodom"?' *PBSA* 87, 3 (September 1993), p. 320.
2 Montague Summers, *The Playhouse of Pepys* (London: Kegan Paul, 1935), pp. 296–97; see also L.S.A.M. von Römer, *Rochester's Sodom* (Paris: H. Welter, 1904); Prinz argues that 'A critical investigation into the play will confirm Rochester's authorship', and goes on to opine: 'However moral and perverted the sphere of its ideas may be, *Sodom* is, after all, a work of remarkable literary talent. It is so well written that it may be called a masterpiece of its kind. It seems therefore very unlikely that Fishbourne, a totally obscurely person from whose pen otherwise not a single line has come down to us should be guilty of

this brilliant literary misdeed' (*John Wilmot Earl of Rochester: His Life and Writings* (Leipzig: Mayer & Müller, 1927), pp. 174 and 176).

3   John Hayward, ed., *Collected Works of John Wilmot, Earl of Rochester* (London: Nonesuch Press, 1926), p. xvii; Graham Greene, *Lord Rochester's Monkey: Being the Life of John Wilmot, Second Earl of Rochester* (New York: Viking Press, 1974), p. 188; and *Poems By John Wilmot Earl of Rochester*, ed. Vivian de Sola Pinto (London: Routledge & Kegan Paul, 1953), p. xlvii.
4   Rev. of *A Profane Wit*, pp. 136–37.
5   George Villiers, *Plays, Poems, and Miscellaneous Writings associated with George Villiers, Second Duke of Buckingham*, eds Robert D. Hume and Harold Love (Oxford: Oxford University Press, 2007, 1), pp. x–xi.
6   Nicolas Nace, 'The Author of *Sodom* Among the Smithfield Muses', *The Review of English Studies*, New Series, 68, 284 (2016), p. 298, n. 8.
7   In 'Did Rochester *Really* Write "*Sodom*"?' Love, who does not believe Rochester had a hand in writing *Sodom*, rather startlingly writes that 'Very probably Rochester read *Sodom*', but unfortunately gives no reasons for this tantalizing opinion (p. 33).
8   Nace, 'Author of *Sodom*', p. 297, n. 3.
9   Nace, 'Author of Sodom', pp. 321 and 311.
10 Richard Elias, 'Political Satire in *Sodom*', *SEL*, 18 (Summer 1978), p. 427.
11 All citations to *Sodom*, unless otherwise noted, are to Love's edition with page numbers included for ease of reference.
12 Elias, 'Political Satire', p. 424.
13 Elias, 'Political Satire', p. 433.
14 Elias, 'Political Satire', pp. 433–34.
15 See Carver, 'The Texts and the Text of *Sodom*', *PBSA*, 73, 1 (1979), p. 21; and also Johnson, 'Did Rochester Write "*Sodom*"?', *PBSA*, 81, 2 (1987), pp. 135–36 and Johnson, pp. 166–67.
16 Harold Love, *English Clandestine Satire, 1660–1702* (Oxford: Oxford University Press, 2004), pp. 59–60.
17 Paddy Lyons, ed., *Rochester: Compete Poems and Plays* (London, J.M. Dent, 1993), p. xvi.
18 Harold Love, '"The Rapes of Lucina"' in *Print, Manuscript & Performance: the Changing Relations of Media in Early Modern England*, eds Arthur F. Marotti and Michael D. Bristol (Columbus, OH: Ohio State University Press, 2000), p. 211.
19 John Harold Wilson, *Rochester–Savile Letters* (Columbus, OH: Ohio State University Press, 1941), p. 110.
20 'The political hits in *Sodom*, therefore, merely follow the associative logic of the Country Party: misusing the prerogative would lead to popery and arbitrary government on the model of France' (Elias, 'Political Satire', p. 436).
21 Quoted in David Ogg, *England in the Reign of Charles II* (London: Oxford University Press, 1956; rpt. 1967), p. 355.
22 Paul Hammond notes: 'One could not extract a very sophisticated political message from this particular work [*Sodom*], but it is at least symptomatic

of a general concern in the 1670s that Charles' private sexual obsessions are becoming a form of tyranny over the body politic' ('The King's Two Bodies: Representations of Charles II', in *Culture, Politics, and Society in Britain, 1660–1800*, eds Jeremy Black and Jeremy Gregory (Manchester: Manchester University Press, 1991), p. 190). Rachel Weil observes: 'Narratives about the king's body, its powers and vulnerabilities, its healthy and unhealthy states and its relationship to the body politic, provided writers with a way of dramatizing their deepest political concerns' ('Sometimes a Scepter is Only a Scepter', in *The Invention of Pornography: Obscenity and the Origins of Modernity, 1500–1800*, ed. Lynn Hunt (New York: Zone Books, 1993), p. 142).

23 Quoted in Ogg, *England in the Reign of Charles II*, p. 345.
24 Lines 21–22 of the opening scene in the Princeton manuscripts read: 'My Pr— Borast thy Iudememtt and thy Care/Requires in a nice iuncto of affaire.' Love emends 'iuncto' with 'iuncture', the reading of D and V.
25 See Christopher Hill, 'The Norman Yoke', in *Puritanism and Revolution* (1958; rpt. London: Panther Books, 1969), pp. 58–125.
26 Elkanah Settle, *Cambyses King of Persia* (London: Printed for *William Cademan*, 1671), A2–A3.
27 George Villiers, 2nd Duke of Buckingham, *The Rehearsal* in *Plays, Poems, and Miscellaneous Writings associated with George Villiers, Second Duke of Buckingham*, eds Robert D. Hume and Harold Love (Oxford: Oxford University Press, 2007, 1, III. ii., p. 429).
28 Dryden, 11, II. i. Jeremy Treglown, 'Rochester and Davenant', *N&Q*, 221 (December 1976), p. 555, points out another of Rochester's parodies of *The Conquest of Granada*, Part I. III, i. lines 70–71, read: '*Abdelmelech*: ... Dislodge betimes before you are beset./ *Abdalia*: Her tears, her smiles, her every look's a Net' (*Works*, xi, 47). In *The Imperfect Enjoyment*, this becomes: 'A touch from any part of her had don't:/ Her hand, her foot, her very look's a Cunt' (lines 17–18).
29 Dryden, *Tyrannick Love*, 10, V. i., lines 633–34.
30 Buckingham, *The Rehearsal*, III. i., line 421.
31 Of the *First Prologue* to *Sodom*, Greer writes: 'Seventeenth-century prologues were seldom if ever written by the authors of the play-texts; admirers of Rochester need to be told up front that the likelihood that Rochester penned this one is virtually nil' (Rev. of *The Works of John Wilmot, Earl of Rochester*, ed. Harold Love (*London Review of Books*, 16 September 1999), p. 9).
32 *The Amorous Prince. Prologue*, *The Works of Aphra Behn*, ed. Montague Summers (New York: Benjamin Blom, 1915; reissued 1967), 4, lines 22–24, p. 121.
33 P1 and P2 probably lie closest to *Sodom* as originally conceived. P2 contains neither of the prologues; P1 does not have the first prologue but does contain the second.
34 Pepys provides a running commentary on Charles II's real-life pursuit of pleasure, the details of which Rochester exaggerates but often not by much, this from 15 May 1663: 'After dinner I went up to Sir Tho. Crew ... and there I sat

talking with him all the afternoon, from one discourse to another. The most was upon the unhappy posture of things at this time; that the King doth mind nothing but pleasures and hates the very sight or thoughts of business. That my Lady Castlemayne rules him; who he says hath all the tricks of Aretin that are to be practiced to give pleasure – in which his too able, hav[ing] a large —' (4, pp. 136–37). See also 17 February 1667; 26 April 1667; and 24 June 1667.

35 Love finds either date plausible (p. 366). In an email correspondence, 2 April 2020, Nicholas Fisher argues for the earlier date, writing: 'I spent a good part of yesterday trying to firm up an unshakeable case for the traditional, later date of composition for "To[o] longe the wise Commons" and have come to the conclusion that the 1671 date is the correct one. The point that bothered me was Love's pointing to 1671 as the date when Lady Clanbrassil was in London, and in trying to further read round the subject discovered a reference to Lady Alice Clanbrassil "thinking to trip up Nell Guin's heels" in 1671, Barbara Palmer having ceased in mid-1670 to be the favoured chief mistress, and from more or less then onwards, and throughout 1671, Nell Gwin taking over that role. It appears that courtiers had realised the power that Barbara Palmer had to reward those she favoured, and that the apolitical Nell wasn't going to help them line their pockets. So thought was being given to finding a pliable Protestant chief mistress who would help them to line their pockets, and at this point Lady Clanbrassil, sponsored by the Earl of Arran, hove into view and came to London in June 1671 with a view to detaching the King from Nell. And two of the women who accompanied her were daughters of the late Charles Coote, Earl of Mountrath, Dorothy (32 yrs – and perhaps grey-haired) and Jane (19 years) and Mistress Fox, probably a gentlewoman as yet unidentified. The plan was unsuccessful, but interestingly the Earl of Arlington later had considerable personal benefit when he facilitated the development of Louise de Kerouaille's relationship with the King (she supplanted Nell). So I am sure that 1671 was the date of the shenanigans Rochester describes, and the references to the Commons' debates about money and religion, and the rioting can as equally apply to the earlier year as 1673. The two books that fully support this earlier date are Jane Ohlmeyer, *Making Ireland English: the Irish Aristocracy in the Seventeenth Century* (Yale University Press, 2012) and Sonya Wynne 'The Mistresses of Charles II and Restoration Court Politics' in *The Stuart Courts*, ed. Eveline Cruickshanks (Stroud, 2000).'

36 Ogg, *England in the Reign of Charles II*, p. 354.

37 Nicholas Fisher shows how the poem's 'topical political context ... is enriched by reference to the Bible and *The Book of Common Prayer*, expressed with a mixture of wit, irony and satire' ('"Damn'd in the Cup": Faith, Poetry, and the Earl of Rochester', *English: Journal of English Association*, 62, issue 237 (2013), p. 170).

38 'Knightly' is a reading unique to BL; all other MSS have 'princely', as does Love's edition.

39 While Vieth thought Rochester the author, recent scholarship has called this into question, Love writing: 'The currently accepted attribution to Rochester, while

not intrinsically impossible, rests ... on rather thin evidence' ('A Restoration Lampoon in Transmission and Revision: Rochester's (?) "Signior Dildo"', *Studies in Bibliography*, 46 (1993), pp. 250–51). He includes it in 'Disputed Works' in his edition. Walker and Fisher include what Love identifies as the 'A text', 'O! all yee young Ladyes of merry England', along with Love's 'Additions to Seigneur Dildoe', but not Love's 'B-version text', 'You Ladies all of merry *England*', in '*Poems Less Securely Attributed to Rochester*'.

40 Love places the 'Impromptu on Charles II', the 'Impromptu on court personages', and 'Upon Betty Frazer 1677' in his *Appendix Roffensis*, 'comprising poems that are only weakly attributed but cannot be shown *not* to be by Rochester' (p. xxviii).

41 For a deft reading of *On Mrs Willis*, see Katherine Mannheimer, 'Poetic Style and the Mind-Body Problem: Sound and Sense, Flesh and Spirit in the Work of John Wilmot, Second Earl of Rochester', *ELH*, 83, 2 (2016), pp. 493–96.

4

'Cripples in their Art': The major satires

Through pac'd ill Actors, may perhaps be cur'd,
Half Players like half Wits, can't be endur'd.
Yet these are they, who durst expose the Age
Of the great *Wonder* of our English Stage.
Whom Nature seem'd to form for your delight,
And bid him speak, as she bid *Shakespeare* write.
Those Blades indeed are Cripples in their Art,
Mimmick his Foot, but not his speaking part.
　　('Epilogue to *Love in the dark*', lines 28–35)

Following the winter of 1671–72 and his extended convalescence at Enmore in 1672, Rochester entered his most productive period as a poet. In the winter of 1676 he would again fall dreadfully ill with an illness from which he never fully recovered and that marked his decline as a poet. In the intervening four years, however, Rochester was to write the six poems – *Timon*, 'Tunbridge Wells', "An Allusion to Horace', 'A Satyr against Reason and Mankind', 'A Letter from Artemiza in the Towne to Chloe in the Countrey', and *The Disabled Debauchee* – that would form the basis of his reputation as the Restoration's major-minor poet. These poems, different as they are in structure, personae, and tone, share three interrelated characteristics.

Like the apprentice work that served as their prologue, these poems too lash the fools populating Restoration London. In defending the writing of satire, Rochester told Burnet that 'there were some people that could not be kept in Order, or admonished but in this way' (Burnet, p. 54). Robert Wolseley, in his 'Preface' to *Valentinian*, made the strongest case for Rochester as satirist-hero:

> He had a Wit that was accompanied with an unaffected greatness of Mind, and a natural Love to Justice and Truth; a Wit that was in perpetual War with Knavery, and ever attacking those kind of Vices most, whose malignity was likely to be most diffusive, such as tended most immediately to the prejudice of publick Bodies, and were of a common Nusance to the happiness of humane kind. Never was his Pen drawn but on the side of good Sence, and usually

Figure 4.1 John Wilmot, 2nd Earl of Rochester by unknown artist. National Portrait Gallery London.

imploy'd, like Arms of the ancient Heroes, to stop the progress of arbitrary Oppression, and beat down the Bruitishness of headstrong Will .... (A5v)

Writing in 1685 and confronting a hostile audience, one that included first and foremost John Sheffield, Earl of Mulgrave, Wolseley overstates his case. Nevertheless, the voice informing these satires is very much that of the satirist as hero, taking on society's foibles. More difficult to determine is the basis for this hero's judgments. How is the social order defined? Who are the knaves? What are the common nuisances? We tend to assume that Rochester's poetry, like Pope's, 'stands guard over morals: the systematic value codes of civilized behavior'[1] and often that is the case. Rochester, does not, of course, have Pope's range; the characters are fewer, the moral discriminations less complex. Nevertheless, 'Half-Witt, and Huffe/ Kickum, and Ding-Boy', 'The would-be witt, whose business was to woo', and 'a fine Lady with her humble Knight', like Pitholeon, the Baron, and Flavia, are measured and found wanting by a code of values that Rochester and Pope shared. The basis of judgment in Rochester's satires, however, often comes not from what the larger community would value, but from an aristocratic-heroic code and set of social conventions. In Rochester's hands, moreover, taste, refinement, social position, bearing, and wit become the measure of mankind.

'The right veine'[2] of satire, however, runs deep in Rochester, and in each of these poems the normative values, whatever their source, are themselves at some point called into question. The satirist ridicules the fops only to realize that not much separates him or her from them. The satirist becomes the object of his own satire or that of his creator as both search for a way to ground their judgments, to find a perspective from which to make sense of the satiric scene they confront and contribute to. Rochester's stumbling block in each poem inevitably arises from his pursuit of pleasure, his attempt to establish an ethical hedonism based on nature. The same question he raised, teased, and could not solve in '*A Ramble*' he explores again and again in these poems.

Here too Rochester fails in uniting grace and nature, but as he does so, he attempts – the third characteristic of these poems – to substitute aesthetic judgments for ethical ones, to make that which is well-acted, well-made, or well-performed the norm by which to evaluate human beings. This attempt to make the aesthetic the ground for satiric judgments has not been much explored in Rochester's work. It was Rochester's attempt to answer the materialistic arguments he used to debunk the affectations of the fops and fools.

Timon[3]

The speaker of *Timon*, Vieth tells us, 'resembles Rochester in his character, activities, and social position' (*Poems*, p. 65). Indeed he does.[4] Timon is a poet who counts among his peers the likes of Sedley, Buckhurst, and Savile. He is thought – as many must have taken Rochester strolling up Portugal Row – to have just come from a bout of debauchery or gambling.

Moreover, what he has actually experienced – being accosted by a fool who attributes a recently circulated satire to him – seems to have happened to Rochester often enough for Burnet to find the episode typical:

> his Composures came to be easily known, for few had such a way of tempering these together as he had; so that, when any thing extraordinary that way came out, as a Child is fathered sometimes by its Resemblance, so it was laid at his Door as its Parent and Author. (Burnet, p. 51)

Identifying Timon with Rochester and being able to date the poem in the spring of 1674 enables us to place *Timon* more in the immediate context of its making and to have, therefore, a better understanding of some of the issues Rochester was attempting to address.

As the poem opens, Timon, bemused, confronts an interlocutor who, knowing either Rochester or the growing Rochester legend, assumes that the poet 'droop'st under a Nights Debauch' (line 2) or has lost to rogues at gambling. The interlocutor obviously thinks he understands Timon, and he is expecting to be entertained by the latest exploit. Timon knows this, and tries not to disappoint. Debauchery? Gambling? 'Neither, alas' (line 5); these might titillate *you*, but both are commonplace though devoutly to be wished compared to what I have just been through. Having built up his listener's expectations, Timon is off on a 171-line performance.

What has happened is that 'a dull Dineing Sott' (line 5) has accosted Timon, told him that 'With me some Witts, of thy Acquaintance Dine' (line 8), and pressed the poet to join them. Reluctantly, Timon consents, and enters his host's coach only to be greeted by a poem, 'Insipid as the Praise, of Pious Queenes/ Or Shadwells, unassisted former Scenes' (lines 15–16). The host greatly admires this 'Libell, of a Sheete or Two' (line 14) and attributes it to Timon. 'Choakt with his flatt'ry', Timon leaves 'him to his deare mistake' (lines 27–28).

'But this was not the worst' (line 33). The promised company of Sedley, Buckhurst, and Savile is nowhere to be found, and in their place are 'Half-Witt, and Huffe/Kickum, and Ding-Boy' (lines 35–36). Timon sees his 'Errour, but 'twas now too late' (line 41), and he enters into one of satire's traditional scenes, *le repas ridicule*: a foolish host, his superannuated wife, a group of hectors ('blustering, turbulent, pervicacious, noisy fellow[s]' (Johnson, *Dictionary*), uneatable food, cheap drink, and prating. As the wine flows, the action becomes increasingly chaotic, degenerates into a fight, and promises in the whirligig logic of satire to repeat itself. At the end, we find Timon fleeing 'with a Vow never more/ To drinke Beare-Glasse, and heare the Hectors roare' (lines 176–77).

In seeking to explain these events to his audience, Timon adopts, on one level, a strategy of comic acceptance. Though affected, deceiving, and self-deceived, the actions of this motley crew have resulted in no great harm. Timon, moreover, gives the sense that in pursuit of a good meal, we are all subject to similar foibles, even himself. In entertaining the host's invitation he has prostituted himself, acting 'as a Whore', who 'With Modesty, enslaves her Sparke the more/ The longer I deny'd, the more he prest' (lines 9–11). His complicity has been there from the beginning and continues throughout. He sees his 'Errour' (line 41) in coming, but makes no effort to retreat, and continues to hope that the dinner will 'make some amends' (line 69). The dinner over, however, he becomes part of the group: 'Left to our selves, of severall things wee prate' (line 111). The company is clearly vulgar, but Timon descends to their level.

In his comic acceptance of his predicament, Timon ingratiates himself with his audience in two ways: Yes, just as you expected, I have allowed my 'violent love of Pleasure' and 'disposition to extravagant Mirth' to lead me again and against my best judgment into one of my many 'odd Adventures and *Frollicks*' (Burnet, p. 51). He has not disappointed his audience; he has been Timon or Rochester. At the same time, there is also a bid for sympathy here. This *repas ridicule* marks yet one more of Rochester's failed eating scenes, eating being emblematic of a hoped-for communion, a pursuit of the natural appetites that leads to a state of well-being and grace. Timon has prostituted himself, willingly deceived himself, been a vulgarian among the vulgarians, but in his wrong-headed pursuit of pleasure he had hopes of a dinner with fine conversation, of a real communion.

While seeking acceptance and understanding from his audience, Timon also wants to assure them, however, that he has not lost his capacity for judgment. He is still Timon, still Rochester, the elegant arbiter of social distinctions. To assure his audience of his superiority, he appeals to what seemingly are his own and their shared prejudices concerning the older generation, social position, and taste, particularly literary taste, the central theme of the poem. Timon, for all of his foibles, has it; the host, hostess, and hectors do not. They affect it; he has the real thing.[5]

The host and company are ridiculed in part because they date from the previous generation and come from the country. With elegant French cooking, 'Kickshaws, Cellery, and Champoone/ Ragous, and Fricasses' (lines 73–74), they have nothing to do. They dine on beef, 'Hard as the Arse of Mosely' (line 77), carrots the length of dildoes.

> Pigg, Goose, and Capon, follow'd in the Reare,
> With all that Countrey Bumpkins, call good Cheere,
> Serv'd up with Sawces, all of Eighty, Eight,
> When our tough youth Wrestled, and threw the Weight.
>   (lines 83–86)

But their chief fault is that they compound their affectations with hypocrisy. The host, a colonel during the civil wars, claims to have lost an estate 'For the Kings service' and 'He talkt much of a Plott, and Money lent/ In Cromwells tyme' (lines 98 and 100–101). He did lose the estate, Timon tells us, but it was to 'Whoreing and drinking' (line 99), and in his hints about having aided the Royalist cause during the Interregnum, he is clearly attempting to deceive himself, others, or both. Rochester, whose family had estates sequestered and whose father did plot for his King during Cromwell's time, must have had a particularly jaundiced view of these all too common retellings of the past. The host's would-be military exploits are of a piece with the drum beating about 1588, the tough youth of those times, and with the jingoism, posturing, and pugnacity of Half-Witt, Huffe, Kickum, and Ding-Boy. All are mock heroic and deserve ridicule.

While Timon does not spare his host or the guests, he does seem to have some sympathy for the hostess. She has her own version of the Cavalier past, a past of high-minded, elegant love as captured in the poetry of Lucius Cary and Sir John Suckling. A proto-Mrs Loveit, her constant talk of love masks a consuming carnality, and because 'Age, Beautyes incureable Disease/ Had left her more desire, than Pow'r to please' (lines 49–50), she is ridiculous enough. But her affectations and appetites seem rather innocent in the mist of the vulgarity of Huffe, who asked 'if Loves flame he never felt?/ He answered bluntly – Doe you thinke I'm Gelt?' (lines 61–62) and those of her husband:

> Falkland, she prais'd, and Sucklings easy Pen,
> And seem'd to taste their former Parts agen.
> Mine Host, drinkes to the best in Christendome,
> And decently my Lady quits the Roome.
> (lines 107–110)

If the lady does have a real understanding of Falkland and Suckling, and it would seem that she might, it would set her off from her husband and guests and may account for Timon's sympathy. For the group's lack of literary taste is the chief target of his scorn.

Disclaiming authorship of the libel foisted upon him, Timon tells his host:

> I vow'd, I was noe more a Witt than he,
> Unpractic'd, and unblest in Poetry:
> A Song to Phillis, I perhaps might make,
> But never Rhym'd but for my Pintles sake;
> I envy'd noe Mans Fortune, nor his Fame,
> Nor ever thought of a Revenge soe tame.
> (lines 19–24)

The host is simply incapable of understanding the scorn being directed at him, the scorn of someone of Timon's social class who is also a real poet: the professed humility that draws upon religious vocabulary, 'vow'd' and 'unblest' to make seem all the more humble what is in fact a witty boast and put down; the insouciant claim never to write but for one's 'Pintles sake' (something the enthusiastic host might well believe of a wit); being of a social position that precludes envy of this man's fortune or that man's fame; the seemingly off handed, but sharp judgment concerning revenge that at once reveals the true source of such poetry and provides a warning that the host has indeed made a 'deare mistake' (line 28). The host is a 'Sott' (lines 5 and 44), a 'dull, ignorant, stupid fellow' and 'A wretch stupified by drinking', Samuel Johnson's first and second definitions capturing his progress through the poem.

After dinner, the conversation turns to stage, and some of the early titles attributed to *Timon* provide us with an insight into Rochester's intentions here. One reads: '"Timon, a Satyr, In Imitation of Monsieur Boleau, upon several Passages in some new Plays then Acted upon the Stage"'; and another, '"The Rehearsal. A Satire"' (Vieth, *Attribution*, p. 453). Rochester was writing a 'rehearsal' in small, with the host and company serving as Bayes and Timon playing the role of Smith and Jones, the target being the heroic drama.

> Half-Witt, cryes up my Lord of Orrery;
> Ah how well Mustapha, and Zanger dye!
> His Sense soe little forc'd, that by one Line,
> You may the other easily Divine:
>
> 'And which is worse, if any worse can be,
> He never said one word of it to me.'
> There's fine Poetry! you'd sweare 'twere Prose,
> Soe little on the Sense, the Rhymes impose.
>   (lines 113–20)

Huffe, Kickum, and the host go on to cite and praise passages from Settle's *The Empress of Morocco*, Crowne's *The History of Charles the Eighth of France*, and Dryden's *Indian Emperor*. Timon shows the limitation of these enthusiastic judgments, briefly, but deftly pointing out Orrery's bad versification and insipid rhymes, Settle's bombast and fustian, and the strained metaphors of Crowne and Dryden. The company is either inattentive or Timon actually does not want them to hear his criticisms. Either way, Timon has constructed two audiences – those who know, those who do not. Those who do include his interlocutors, Sedley, Buckhurst, Savile, and others in the know among the Court. When Ding-Boy deviates into praise and a just, witty criticism of Etherege, Timon has nothing to say.

While it might appear strange to take a part (lines 113–50) of what seems to be a casually organized poem of 177 lines on disparate topics and make it stand for the whole, the question of literary judgment, in truth, underlies the entire poem and gives it a thematic coherence. *Timon* in effect turns the world into theatre and then uses aesthetic criteria to judge it. It is not just that the host is a bad judge of poetry; he is a poor performer, Timon judging him this way: 'Of a well meaning Foole, I'm most afraid/ Who sillily repeates, what was well said' (lines 31–32). The hostess, Timon goes on to tell us, 'Preserv'd the Affectation of her Prime' (line 54). As for Half-Witt, Huffe, Kickum, and Ding-Boy, they are not human beings so much as mechanical characters out of farce. The dinner itself, as we have seen, is poor performance, and the company winds up discussing matters of state, a potential military clash between the imperial forces and the French, because little separates that supposedly weighty affair and the heroics played upon the stage. Both are bad theatre, as farcical in their way as the foolish contretemps that closes the poem.

Meanwhile, the polished performance by which to judge the failures of the others has been delivered by Timon himself. He has told a good story, setting it up well by whetting our curiosity and by maintaining our interest throughout: 'a dull Dineing Sott/ Seiz'd me i' th' Mall'; 'But this was not the worst'; 'In comes my Lady strait'; 'And now the Wine began to work' and so on. For those really in the know, moreover, there is the satisfaction of having a poem by Boileau wittily adapted to the present concerns of their group. *Timon* is a central document in the battle of the playwrights and poets going on in the 1670s. It takes its cue from *The Rehearsal*, has obvious affinities with 'A Session of the Poets' ('Since the sons of the Muses grow num'rous and loud'), the 'Advice to Apollo' ('I've heard the Muses were still soft and kind'), both of which Rochester may have had a hand in writing, and looks forward to 'An Allusion to Horace'. On the one side stood the wits, Rochester, Buckingham, Sackville, Sedley *et al.* with their preference for comedy; on the other Orrery, the Howards, Settle, Crowne, and Dryden, champions of heroic drama. Rochester was attracted to these literary encounters in part because he felt on firm ground in judging them. Theatrical criticism comes to serve social and moral purposes.

'Tunbridge Wells'

'Tunbridge Wells'[6] and *Timon*, both written in the summer of 1674, share obvious similarities; Vieth rightly calls them 'pendant pieces' (*Poems*, p. xxxvii).[7] The speakers in both are libertines, closely resembling their creator. The settings are traditional to satire, in one *le repas ridicule*, in the other a tour through a gathering that represents society as a whole. In structure both have a unity that belies the seemingly episodic organization adopted to reflect the chaotic world of satire.[8] And finally, both share similar satiric norms. Timon, however, escapes the world of the fools, and his tone is comic. The speaker in 'Tunbridge Wells' cannot, and his tone is sharply satiric, his 'spleen' and 'malice' (line 26) directed at the motley crew he encounters but also at himself.

The speaker in 'Tunbridge Wells', though he does not have an interlocutor, is, like Timon, in the process of giving a dramatic account of one of his libertine escapades. Presumably because of his rakish ways, he needs 'To undertake the dose, it was prescrib'd' (line 7), and in search of health, he has risen 'Att five this Morn' (line 1) to take the waters. Instead of the hoped-for cure, he finds a scene that 'made me purge and spew' (line 10): a foppish knight descending from his 'Coach, and Six' (line 11) with a retinue 'all of the selfe same Stuffe' (line 25). Things get no better as he encounters in 'th' lower walk' (line 37) the 'Master of Ceremonies', 'As great a fop, though of another kind' (lines 49 and 41), and they continue to decline as the speaker moves along the walks and meets 'A Tribe of Curatts, Preists, Canonicall Elves' (line 53); 'a fulsome Irish Crew/ Of Silly Macks' (lines 83–84); 'Mother, and daughter, Mistress, and the Maid' (line 90); the 'Gallant' and 'young damsell' (line 98); 'two wifes with girl Just fitt for man' (line 127); and finally the mohawk-like 'Cadetts' (line 165). The speaker has sampled, with the exception of the 'Macks' who would appear to be out of place, the social hierarchy in descending order and found it greatly wanting. At the end, he passes this judgment on it and himself:

> Bless me thought I what thing is man that thus
> In all his shapes he is ridiculous:
> Our selves with noise of reason wee do please
> In vaine; Humanity's our worst disease.
> Thrice happy beasts are, who because they be
> Of reason void, are so of Foppery.
> Faith I was so asham'd that with remorse
> I us'd the insolence to mount my horse
> For he doing only things fitt for his nature
> Did seem to me, by much, the wiser Creature.
> (lines 178–87)

The speaker anticipates Rochester's more general indictment of reason and mankind, and in mounting his horse in insolence ('Pride exerted in contemptuous and overbearing treatment of others' Johnson, *Dictionary*), looks forward to Gulliver's misanthropy.

Fuelling the speaker's contempt for the thing called man is 'Foppery' – in Samuel Johnson's definition mankind's capacity for 'folly', 'Affectation of show or importance; showy folly', and 'Foolery; vain or idle practice; idle affectation'. Listening to the 'noise of reason', men and women get caught up in affectation and self-deception and, unlike the horse, do not do 'only things fitt for his nature'. The knight, who looks 'wise, as Calfe' (line 13), 'dares to Censure, as if he had witt' (line 16). The sententious 'Master of Ceremonies', 'grave as Owle' and wise as a 'woodcock' (lines 49 and 44), 'speakes all proverbs, Sentences, and Adage/ Can with as much solemnity buy eggs/ As a Caball can talk of theire Entreagues' (lines 46–48). The 'Tribe of Curatts, Preists, Canonicall Elves' (line 53) want 'learning, honesty, and brain' (line 60), yet 'call themselves Embassadors of heaven' (line 62).

> But should an Indian King whose small Command
> Seldome Extends beyond tenn miles of Land
> Send forth such wretched fools in an Embassage,
> Hee'd find but small effects of such a Message.
> (lines 64–67)

The 'Macks' are 'Silly' and 'beneath scorn' (lines 83 and 86). The 'Gallant' is a 'would-be witt' who having exhausted his store in one shopworn metaphor is not sure 'what next to say' (lines 100 and 115), and the 'young damsell' reacts 'With mouth screw'd up, conceited winking eyes/ And breasts thrust forward' (lines 98 and 110–11). The 'two wifes', with refined talk about the generative powers of the water, are, 'ten to one' in search of 'Cuffe, and Kick/ With brawny back, and leggs, and Potent Prick' (lines 127, 149, and 155–56). And the 'Cadetts' 'presume to swell/ This goes for Captain; that for Collonell' (lines 165 and 172–73).

Judged by this norm of affectation and self-deception, the speaker, however, finds himself to be as guilty as those he judges, which may in part account for his irascibility. He has gone to Tunbridge Wells knowing that it is 'The Rendevous of fooles, Buffoons, and Praters/ Cuckolds, whores, Citizens, their wives and daughters' (lines 4–5). He has sought out a cure, moreover, that he knows smacks of charlatanism, the restorative powers having little to do with the waters and everything to do with the sexual encounters going on among the 'herd' (lines 93). His self-deception is perhaps all the worse because it is willed and also because, as with Timon and so many of Rochester's speakers, it has its source in an idealism that has been destroyed. The speaker should know better, but he has gone to the waters, gone to nature for a cure that is not to be found.

In a similar way the speaker wants to believe that there is a natural order to society, but what he finds instead is 'a true Medley' (lines 93), 'A mixture; a miscellany; a mingled mass. It is commonly used with some degree of contempt' (Johnson, *Dictionary*).

> Here Lords, Knights, Squires, ladyes, and Countesses,
> Chandlers, mum-bacon women, semptressess
> Were mixt together, nor did they agree
> More in their humours, then their Quality.
>
> (lines 94–97)

The nature the speaker pursues is an ideal, the product of his own self-deception. Real nature is this place, is these people, this 'herd', who are simply being what nature has made them. 'Nature Contriv'd the fool should be a Knight' (line 18). With him and 'His train' (line 24), 'Nature has done the buisness of Lampoon/ And in their lookes theire Characters has shown' (lines 27–28). As for 'Pert Bays', nothing can make his 'nature or his manners good' (lines 69 and 79), and 'Nature has plac'd' the 'Silly Macks' 'beneath scorn' (lines 86 and 83). The foppery, the 'white wash and paint', the 'wigg, and Pantaloon displaid' (lines 89 and 91), turn out to be man's nature, his very humanity being his 'worst disease' (line 181). If man could just be like a horse and do things only fit for his nature, then he would find happiness, or so the speaker would like to believe. But, alas, man does follow nature and the results are far from happy. The generous Epicurean nature of his desires clashes sharply with the Hobbesian nature of his experience.

The speaker is aware of the dilemma. Ashamed, feeling remorse, he with insolence mounts his horse. It is insolent to do so given that the horse is the wiser animal. But little separates him here from his description of

> ... the beargarden Ape on his Steed mounted,
> No longer is a Jackanaps accounted,
> But is by vertue of his Trumpery then
> Call'd by the name of the young Gentleman.
>
> (lines 174–77)

The satire is directed at the 'Cadetts', animals, no better than apes, who through posturing hope to be seen as gentlemen. But given what the speaker knows about mankind, being an ape may be the wiser thing, and the juxtaposition of the ape on a horse with the speaker going off on his seems to be his ironic affirmation that it is. One thinks of the opening seven lines of 'A Satyre against Reason and Mankind' but also of the portrait of Rochester crowning a monkey with the bays.

The speaker's self-awareness may be his one consolation in this condemnation of mankind. At least he knows that his very humanity is a disease, but no one else in the poem does. The audience, moreover, is swept up in this condemnation as well and may not think awareness of the dilemma much of a consolation. The speaker's relationship with that audience has been irascible throughout. In this speaker we have the Rochester who could, in Gramont's words, pass for 'the most dangerous enemy in the universe'.⁹ There is, of course, the pleasure of being in the company of such a misanthrope as he wittily slices up various fools, but the pleasure is both heightened and made uneasy by the danger that the knife will be turned on you. For Rochester's more immediate audience there were, I think, other consolations, other pleasures.

First, the poem is quite personal, a work that one would give to immediate acquaintances. Pert Bays is Samuel Parker, Archdeacon of Canterbury, and the attack on the 'Master of Ceremonies' would seem to be aimed at Sir Francis Dorrell. While the other targets seem to be examples of a class, the bawling fop of a knight who opens the poem appears to be someone the Rochester crowd would recognize. The satire is specific and personal, attacking the knight's body, demeanour, and mind. Such identifications would appeal to those in the know, would make them feel on the side of the speaker.

So too would the speaker's use of theatrical allusions and techniques. The Knight is a 'meer Sir Nicholas Cully/ A Bawling Fopp, a naturall Nokes' (lines 14–15), a fool out of a comedy by Etherege. The 'Master of Ceremonies', a Buckeram Puppitt' (lines 49 and 43), comes from a Punch and Judy show. 'Pert Bays' suggests that Parker is the bold and garrulous director of all this Rabble' (lines 69 and 68), not unlike his counterpart in *The Rehearsal*. The comparison of the 'Tribe of Curatts' (line 53) to ambassadorial representatives of an Indian king evokes Dryden's heroic dramas with the suggestion that this tribe too is just so much theatrical bombast. The 'Mother, and daughter, Mistress, and the Maid/ And squire with wigg, and Pantaloon displaid' are more entertaining that anything that can be found in 'conventicle, play, or faire' (lines 90–92). The 'Gallant' and 'young damsell' (line 98) as well as the 'two wifes with girl Just fitt for man' (line 127) are, with their colloquial dialogue and miniature plots, cast as dramatic scenes and could be sketches, like Rochester's lines on Mr Daynty, for Restoration comedy.¹⁰ 'Cuffe, and Kick (line 155), characters in Shadwell's comedy *Epsom-Wells*, have walked right out of that comedy. As for the 'Cadetts', they are a Bear Garden spectacle (line 165). No doubt these references, this use of dramatic techniques, would have appealed to Rochester's coterie audience. They too were interested in and intimately knowledgeable about what was going on in Restoration theatre.

In drawing upon the drama, Rochester was doing at least two things: shaping a knowing, sympathetic audience by appealing to its interests but also, in drawing upon the theatre to make social and moral judgments, he was providing for both himself and that audience a shared satiric norm. Judged by the norm of nature, we are all, humanity being a disease, participants in a parade of fools. But these people – the stupid aristocrats, the foreigners, the clergy, the parvenus – are worse. They are the stuff of foolish heroic drama, of comedy and farce, and therefore just targets for malice and spleen.

'An Allusion to Horace 10 Sat: 1st Book. Nempe incomposito dixi etc.'

The aesthetic norms implicit in *Timon* and 'Tunbridge Wells' become explicit in 'An Allusion', the poem, written in the winter of 1675–76,[11] being, as several of its early titles tell us, 'A Satyr against the present poetts ...' and 'Rotchestrs censures of the poets' (Vieth, *Attribution*, pp. 386–87). The speaker, Rochester in the guise of the Restoration Horace, judiciously weighs the merits of his age's Lucilius and the ever-present Tegellius-like scribblers.[12] Rochester does not discuss his craft in his extant letters; nor does he do so anywhere else. It is in 'An Allusion' that we come as close as we ever will to Rochester's views on writing and on his audience. They are not, of course, spelled out as completely as we would like. What we have, however, supports the view of an aristocratic poet, who approves of the well-fashioned, who writes for a coterie audience that shares the prejudices and values of his class, and who feels masterful in judging poetry and drama.

Rochester's Lucilius is John Dryden, like his namesake, a good, but careless poet who writes hastily and in great quantities. We will go more fully into the nature of and reasons for this attack and also into the reasons for Rochester's choice of Horace's satire 1.10 in Chapter 5. Suffice it to say here that while Rochester arraigns Dryden on social and moral grounds, he for the most part ridicules him and his fellow poets and playwrights for bad writing.

The poem opens with a delightfully, if maliciously, cheerful indictment of Dryden and his patron, Rochester's inveterate enemy, John Sheffield, Earl of Mulgrave:

> Well Sir 'tis granted, I said Dryden's Rhymes
> Were stollen, unequal, nay dull many times.
> What foolish Patron is there found of his
> So blindly partial to deny me this?
> (lines 1–4)

Adopting the superior, but fair, tone that Horace employs, he goes on to aver:

> But that his Plays embroyder'd up and down
> With witt and learning justly pleasd the Town,
> In the same Paper I as freely own.
> (lines 5–7)

We do not know what, if anything, is behind the charge of 'stollen', which does not appear in the Latin original. In being dull, Dryden, however, is not alone. Crowne too produces 'tedious Scenes' (line 11), but at least both Dryden and Crowne occasionally 'divert the Rabble and the Court' (line 17), something that neither 'Blundering Settle' or 'puzzling Otway' can accomplish (lines 18–19).

The speaker then offers advice on writing well. It is questionable, given who these poets are, that they will be able to take advantage of such advice. The speaker nevertheless makes the gesture that at once establishes his good faith and shows how bad they really are:

> But within due proportions circumscribe
> What e're you write, that with a flowing Tyde
> The style may rise, yet in it's rise forbear
> With useless words to oppress the wearied Ear;
> Here be your Language lofty, there more light,
> Your Rhetorique with your Poetry unite.
> For Ellegance sake sometimes allay the force
> Of Epithets, 'twill soften the Discourse.
> A jest in scorn points out and hitts the thing
> More home than the morosest Satyrs sting.
> 					(lines 20–29)

The opening provides a perfect example of contempt disguised with disarming humour, and this passage, like the poem as a whole, embodies its own urbane advice, illustrating, without explicitly arguing for, the speaker's superiority. He belongs to the company of 'Shakespear and Johnson', and the 'refin'd Etheridge' (lines 30 and 32); Dryden, Crowne, and Settle are, on the other hand, to be grouped with the likes of Thomas Flatman, 'that slow Drudge' (line 34), and Nathaniel Lee, 'the hot-braind fustian foole' (line 39).

Next follows a catalogue of those who in this age have written well in particular kinds of poetry. Though but two 'have toucht upon true Comedy', 'hasty Shadwell and slow Wicherly' (lines 42–43), Waller 'In Panegyricks does excell Mankind' (line 56). 'For pointed Satyrs', Buckhurst is 'The best good Man, with the worst-natur'd Muse' (lines 59–60), and Sedley takes the palm 'For songs and verses mannerly Obscene' (line 61). Dryden himself has tried Sedley's 'nice way of Witt' (line 71), 'But when he would be sharp he still was blunt' (line 73). The speaker goes on to lash Dryden for his arrogance in finding faults in others that are abundantly present in his own work and in mistaking 'Five hundred Verses every morning writt' (line 93) for wit.

> Such scribbling Authors have been seen before:
> Mustapha, The English Princess, fourty more

> Were things perhaps compos'd in half an hour.
> To write what may securely stand the Test
> Of being well read over thrice at least,
> Compare each Phrase, Examine every Line,
> Weigh every word, and every thought refine.
>
> (lines 95–101)

Through advice and example, the speaker has advanced the requisites for good writing – appropriate subject matter and diction, smoothness and ease, brevity, pointedness, and humour. He has sought to convince his audience, not only through his own urbane tone, but also through his discriminating and fair judgments. Though Dryden has many faults, he is not without his virtues. Shadwell, on the other hand, is 'hasty' (line 43), and though his work shows 'great Mastery', it is done 'with little Care' (line 47). Wycherley is slow, but 'He frequently excells, and at the least/ Makes fewer faults than any of the best' (lines 52–53). The speaker ends with advice concerning the relationship of the poet to his audience, 'Scorn all applause the Vile Rout can bestow/ And be content to pleas those few who know' (lines 102–3), and holds up himself and his own audience as exemplary:

> Should I be troubled when the purblind Knight
> Who squints more in his Judgment than his sight
> Picks silly faults, and Censures what I write?
> Or when the poor led Poets of the Town
> For Scrapps and Coach-room crye my Verses down?
> I loathe the Rabble, 'tis enough for me
> If Sydley, Shadwell, Shepheard, Wicherley,
> Godolphin, Butler, Buckhurst, Buckinghame
> And some few more, whome I omitt to name
> Approve my sence, I count their Censure Fame.
>
> (lines 115–24)

The assured tone of 'An Allusion' arises in large part because Rochester thought, with obvious justification, that he understood his subject well.[13] In the winter of 1675–76, the probable date of the poem, Rochester was reaching the peak of his involvement in and influence upon the Restoration theatre. Four playwrights had dedicated plays to him; three more would do so shortly. He had written a prologue to Settle's *The Empress of Morocco*, had just finished an epilogue to Francis Fane's *Love in the Dark*, was in the process of coaching Elizabeth Barry for the stage, and was in all probability beginning his adaptation of Fletcher's *Valentinian*. Patron, poet, and playwright, Rochester was also himself becoming a subject for the stage. As Anne Righter has observed, 'the drama of the Restoration is filled with Rochester-figures, with (more or less garbled) memories of his conversation, refractions of his wit, attempts to mirror his style'.[14] In matters of poetry and theatre, Rochester knew his subject well. That his penetrating, aphoristic judgments of his contemporaries have held up over time testifies that his confidence was not misplaced. When dealing with Shadwell, we still have to come to terms with his being 'hasty', of showing 'Great proofs of force of Nature, none of Art' (line 45). And so too with Lee's 'fustian', the 'puzzling' nature of Otway's appeal, Crowne's tediousness, Settle's blundering. We must keep in mind, moreover, that the Dryden Rochester attacks had not yet written 'Mac Flecknoe', 'Absalom and Achitophel', or *Don Sebastian* and was not known as the author of the *Fables* or the translator of *The Aeneid*. Rochester displays a keen understanding of his fellow poets here, and he knows it, something that Tom Lockwood captures ever so well in his commentary on the poem's opening lines:

> The patrician hauteur of the poem's opening concessively grants the easy confidence of its ambiguously direct insult: was it that the speaker 'many times' said that 'Dryden's Rhymes/ Were stollen, unequal', or that he once said that they were, in general, 'stollen, unequal', and, in detail, many times 'dull'? That confidence in aesthetic judgement and poetic craft is of a piece with the speaker's social confidence later in the poem, where an ease in writing 'songs and verses mannerly Obscene' (line 61) is held up as an emblem of sexual and civil confidence among, and with, men and women.[15]

Rochester's assured tone is also related to his audience. He is writing for an audience he knows and trusts, one that shares his interests in and evaluations of the current literary scene. In the war of the theatres going on in the mid-1670s, Dryden, Mulgrave, Crowne, Lee, and Otway were generally connected with the King's players and favoured heroic drama, pastorals, masques, musicals, and non-satirical drama. Rochester and his 'few who know' were identified primarily with the Duke's players and championed classical subjects, high tragedy, the comedy of manners, and satire.

Though Shadwell and Butler are commoners, the others named by Rochester share his aristocratic background, and the poem's confident tone is securely grounded in class distinctions concerning style, wit, taste, judgment, learning, even physical demeanour. A sense of style, of the well-formed were part of an aristocrat's breeding. While Rochester's letters do not comment on poetry, they do reveal his sensitivity to matters of style. He thanks Savile for 'a fine letter from Mr. Savile which never wants wit and good nature' (Treglown, p. 166); another letter to Savile opens with a complaint that 'The lousiness of affairs in this place is such (forgive the unmannerly phrase! Expressions must descend to the nature of the things expressed) 'tis not fit to entertain a private gentleman, much less one a public character, with the retail of them' (Treglown, p. 232); he jokes with Savile that 'Mr. Shepherd is a man of a fluent style and coherent thought, if, as I suspect, he writ your postscript' (Treglown, p. 109); and in commenting upon 'the libel you speak of upon that most unwitty generation the present poets', Rochester tells Savile, 'I rejoice in it with all my heart and shall take it for a favour if you will send me a copy. He cannot want wit utterly that has a spleen to those rogues, though never so dully expressed. And now dear Mr Savile, forgive me if I do not wind up myself with an handsome period' (Treglown, p. 167). Rochester and his audience have style; the commoners, that 'unwitty generation of the present poets' – Dryden, Crowne, Settle, Otway, Flatman, and Lee – do not. These poets seek to please the 'Rabble', 'clapping fools', the 'vast Crowd', the 'Vile Rout', Fopps', and 'Ladyes'. Rochester writes 'to pleas those few who know' (line 103). When Dryden does try to imitate his betters in wittily obscene verse, he is only coarse. Dryden, the parvenu, is arrogant and proud in his criticism, finding fault with Shakespeare and Jonson, Beaumont and Fletcher. In criticizing even the likes of Dryden, Rochester is fair and gracious:

> But to be just, 'twill to his prais be found
> His Excellencys more than faults abound;
> Nor dare I from his sacred Temples tear
> That Lawrell which he best deservs to wear.
> (lines 77–80)

Dryden wears his learning heavily, using Horace to write a carping essay. Rochester has brought Horace's urbane, insightful criticism to life in a witty, humorous poem. From the perspective of Rochester and his audience, the scrambling to please the many, the writing of large quantities of bad verse, and the arrogance can be understood, if not forgiven, because Dryden and his fellow scribblers are among 'the poor led Poets of the Town' writing 'For Scrapps and Coach-room' (lines 118–19). The epithet, 'Poet Squobb' (line 76), captures in small Rochester's aristocratic judgment of Dryden, Johnson in the *Dictionary* defining squab as an adjective, 'Unfeathered; newly hatched', and 'Fat; thick and stout; awkwardly bulky;' as a noun, 'A kind of sofa or couch; a stuffed cushion;' and as an adverb, 'With a heavy sudden fall; plump and flat'. 'Poet Squobb' sums up, in Rochester's eyes, Dryden's social position, physical appearance, and poetry.

Rochester's aristocratic stance allows him to have it both ways, to be fair, or seemingly so, to Dryden and his fellow poets, while holding him and them in lofty contempt. It is also the source of the many arch judgments and ironies in the poem. Dryden possesses 'witt and learning' that 'justly pleasd the Town' (line 6). With what we have learned about the town, we are not likely to think much of the laureate's wit or learning. The justice seems to be that a foolish poet has found his fit audience, though many. Similarly, the speaker would not tear the bays from Dryden's 'sacred Temples' (line 79). Poet Squobb with sacred temples? Again, given the audience, given the poet, perhaps Dryden does 'best' deserve to wear 'That Lawrell' (line 80). The perspective here is olympian. It is not enough that Dryden and Crowne have a 'false sence' that

> Hitts the false Judgment of an Audience
> Of clapping fools, assembling a vast Crowd
> Till the throng'd Playhous crack with the dull load.
> Thô even that Talent merits in some sort,
> That can divert the Rabble and the Court.
> (lines 12–17)

The speaker has all society in purview, from rabble to court, would treat Lee as a schoolboy, points out the irony of Waller using his talent 'to prais great Conquerors or to flatter Kings' (line 58), and makes in-jokes about verses that warm the Queen' (line 63).

At the beginning of 'Book Two' of *De Rerum Naturae*, Lucretius wrote:

> But nothing is sweeter than to occupy the high and quiet places fortified by the teachings of the wise, from which you can look down upon other men and watch them as they wander to and fro, seeking in their wanderings a way of life, rivaling each other in genius, contending in rank, and struggling day and night with unceasing effort to rise to the greatest wealth and to become powerful in the state.[16]

This is a view of the follies of man that Rochester can occasionally sustain in his letters. In a letter to Savile, for example, written not long after he completed 'An Allusion', Rochester mentions both Mulgrave and Dryden.

> For my own part, I am not at all stung with my Lord M—'s mean ambition ... They who would be great in our little government seem as ridiculous to me as schoolboys who with much endeavour and some danger climb a crab-tree, venturing their necks for fruit which solid pigs would disdain if they were not starving ... You write me word that I'm out of favour with a certain poet whom I have ever admired for the disproportion of him and his attributes. He is a rarity which I cannot but be fond of, as one would be of a hog that could fiddle, or a singing owl. (Treglown, pp. 119–20)

This letter ends with a reference to the Duchess of Portsmouth with whom Rochester had been seriously quarreling: 'I am sorry for the declining D—ss and would have you generous to her at this time, for that is true pride and I delight in it' (Treglown, p. 120). The hauteur is breathtaking.

It is this tone of judging from the heights of Olympus that critics have in mind when they argue that 'An Allusion to Horace' is 'one of the few poems in which Rochester faces the world with assurance' (Griffin, p. 257). 'An Allusion', or so the argument runs, focuses on matters of poetry and the drama, areas where Rochester felt confident in his judgments. It raises no troubling questions concerning the nature of man, no spectres of 'the horror that Nature raised in him', no 'apprehensions of Religion' (Burnet, p. 51), no questions that would cause the speaker to doubt his judgment. But the line between aesthetic and ethical judgments is difficult to draw, and as we saw in *Timon* and 'Tunbridge Wells', the former moves in the direction of replacing the latter. Even in 'An Allusion' where judgment of poetry is the central concern, ethical considerations hover about. Dryden is not a very good poet, an overachiever at best, but he is also a stupid if not really a bad man. In those poems where the speakers are implicated in the wandering, seeking, rivalling, contending, and struggling of life, where ethical judgments are central, the aesthetic norm is never missing. But it manifests itself in two different ways in Rochester's poetry, and it is important to distinguish between them.

In the one the aesthetic is equated with the natural. The '*Whitehall Blade*' in '*A Ramble in St. James's Park*'

> Converts Abortive imitation,
> To Universal affectation;
> So he not only eats, and talks,
> But feels, and smells, sits down and walks;
> Nay looks, and lives, and loves by Rote,
> In an old tawdrey *Birth-Day-Coat*.
> (lines 57–62)

He is unnatural, an abortion, an imitation rather than the real thing. So too those actors at the Duke's Theatre satirized in the 'Epilogue to *Love in the dark*'. The speaker tells us that though

> Through pac'd ill Actors, may perhaps be cur'd,
> Half players like half Wits, can't be endur'd.
> Yet these are they, who durst expose the Age
> Of the great *Wonder* of our English Stage.
> Whom Nature seem'd to form for your delight,
> And bid him speak, as she bid *Shakespeare* write.
> These Blades indeed are Cripples in their Art,
> Mimmick his Foot, but not his speaking part.
> (lines 28–34)

There is a natural order that, if thoroughly trained in his art, man should be able to follow. But these blades are 'Cripples' in that art. Rochester held up two of his enemies to just such a standard and found them wanting. Sir Carr Scroope has 'grown up the most ungracefull wight' ('*On The Suppos'd*

Author of A late Poem in Defence of SATYR', line 13), 'The just Reverse of Nokes', the accomplished comic actor (*'On Poet Ninny'*, line 14). Mulgrave is a '*Punchinello*' who

> set's up for a Spark.
> With equal self-conceit too, he bears arms,
> But with that vile successe his part perform's,
> That he burlesque's his trade, and what is best
> In others, turn's like *Harlequin* to jest.
> ('*My Lord* All-Pride', lines 18–22)

This is the same charge, as in Chapter 1, that Rochester levels at Mulgrave in 'A very heroical epistle' and 'An Epistolary Essay': he is a bad actor.

In this form the aesthetic becomes a way of reuniting man with nature through grace, though the case for this happening is usually made in the negative. Those actors at the Duke's House have

> False accent and neglectful Actions too
> They have both so nigh good, yet neither true,
> That both together, like an Ape's mock face,
> By near resembling Man, do Man disgrace.
> ('Epilogue to *Love in the dark*', lines 24–27)

Implicit here is a standard of men, not aping, not being crippled, but truly acting their parts and doing so with grace.

In those poems where nature as a satiric norm is called into doubt, the aesthetic remains normative but in complex, often paradoxical ways, as we shall see as we move to examine two of Rochester's most accomplished poems and one of his most clever. Crimes, faults, and foibles are paraded with the intention of shifting the focus from them to the performance of them.

'A Satyre against Reason and Mankind'

We do not know much about the circumstances surrounding the writing of 'A Satyre'. The first ascription of the poem to Rochester occurs in a letter dated 23 March 1675/76 from John Verney to John Wilmot's godfather, Sir Ralph Verney: 'I have a sheet or two of Verses (s^d to be Rochesters) of Faith & Reason, much after ye sense of his Satyr ag^t man, If you have not seen them I'le next weeke send you a coppy' (Vieth, *Attribution*, p. 374).

The letter assumes that Sir Ralph is already familiar with the 'Satyr ag^t man', and he probably was because the manuscript was in circulation by the summer of 1675, Shadwell using phrases from it in the opening scene of *The Libertine*, which made its debut in June of that year.[17] Quickly and widely disseminated, it became, then as now, Rochester's best-known poem, and at the time seemingly one of his most notorious. Alexander Radcliffe, writing in 1682, would recall 'that which made 'em curse and ban/ Was for his Satyr against Man' (Vieth, *Attribution*, p. 374). One can well imagine why this poem would have raised the ire of a general audience. A witty, paradoxical, arch attack on man in general, his pride in his reason and humanity, the 'Satyre' makes its appeal to the libertines by ridiculing the clergy, by asserting the role of the senses as providing the only accurate view of reality, and by drawing upon Hobbes for an anatomy of human motivation. But the poem should have caused as well some uneasiness among the Rochester crowd. The hedonistic, libertine spokesman is himself the object of satire, the poem being Rochester's fullest exploration and criticism of efforts to find in nature the basis of an ethical hedonism.[18]

In the famous opening lines, the speaker declares:

Were I (who to my cost already am
One of those strange prodigious Creatures Man)
A spirit free to choose for my own share,
What case of flesh and blood I pleas'd to wear;
I'de be a Dog, a Monky, or a Bear.
Or any thing but that vain Animal
Who is so proud of being Rational.
(lines 1–7)

He would make such a dramatic choice because man, rather than paying attention to his senses and following nature, as do the beasts, 'contrive[s]' a sixth sense, reason, 'And before certain Instinct will preferre/ Reason, which fifty times for one does erre' (lines 10–11). 'Contrive' (line 8) is the key word here: '1. To invent, devise, excogitate with ingenuity and cleverness ... b. *esp*. used of the planning or plotting of evil devices, treason, treachery, murder, etc. 3. To devise, invent, design' (*OED*). The word, as verb and noun ('contrivance') is used fifteen times in the poems Vieth attributes to Rochester, and with one exception, has bad connotations. It belongs to a family of words – 'affected' (6 times), 'fancy' (11), 'fantastic' (4), 'cheat (6), 'trick (5), and 'charms' (17) – Rochester uses to indict man as either a fool or dupe, for being by his own devising or that of others caught up in the false, the artificial, or learned, metaphysical speculations. Instead of following the 'Light of Nature, sense' (line 13) – nature here being the order, disposition, or essence of all entities composing the physical universe but also the normal instincts or affections – man misguidedly follows his own contrivances, 'Mountains of whimseys heapt in his own brain' (line 17). Man uses his reason not to gain an accurate assessment of the world, as he should; rather he turns that faculty into 'an Ignis fatuus of the Mind' (line 12), which in turns leads into the artificial, the affected, the speculative and away from what should really concern him.

As the entire poem shows, Rochester had been reading, perhaps talking with, Hobbes. In discussing 'the use of Metaphors, tropes and other Rhetoricall figures, instead of proper words', Hobbes writes:

> To conclude, The light of humane minds is Perspicuous Words, but by exact definitions first snuffed, and purged from ambiguity; *Reason* is the *place*; Encrease of *Science*, the *way*; and the Benefit of man-kind, the *end*. And on the contrary, Metaphors, and senslesse and ambiguous words, are like *ignes fatui*; and reasoning upon them, is wandering amongst innumerable absurdities; and their end, contention, sedition, or contempt.[19]

The parallel is not exact. Rochester uses reason to mean both the process of reasoning and the results of that process, the *ignes fatui*, the whimseys. But for Hobbes, as for the speaker, the misuse of reason that occurs through 'metaphors, and senseless and ambiguous words' has a similar result, a 'wandering amongst innumerable absurdities' that ends in 'contempt'. The speaker's

> misguided follower climbs with pain
> Mountains of whimseys heapt in his own brain;
> Stumbling from thought to thought, falls headlong down
> Into doubts boundless Sea, where like to drown,
> Books bear him up a while, and make him try
> To swim with bladders of Philosophy:
> In hopes still to o'retake th' escaping Light,
> The Vapour dances in his dazled sight,
> Till spent, it leaves him to Eternal night.
> Then old Age and Experience hand in hand,
> Lead him to Death, and make him understand,
> After a search so painfull and so long
> That all his life he has been in the wrong.
> Hudled in dirt the reasoning Engine lies,
> Who was so proud, so witty and so wise.
>
> (lines 16–30)

Having lost, or deliberately forfeited, his right relationship with nature, the speaker's 'misguided follower', mankind in general, goes from error to error, looks to philosophy to correct his way, only to end in 'Eternal night', totally in the wrong.

Man's predicament, the speaker argues, is rooted in his pride, in his attempts to exceed the limits of his own nature.

> Pride drew him in (as Cheats their Bubbles catch)
> And made him venture to be made a Wretch.

> His Wisedome did his Happiness destroy,
> Ayming to know that World he should enjoy;
> And Witt was his vain frivolous pretence,
> Of pleasing others at his own expence:
> For Witts are treated just like common Whores,
> First they're enjoy'd and then kickt out of doors.
> The Pleasure past, a threatning doubt remains,
> That frights th' enjoyer with succeeding pains.
>   (lines 31–40)

Man seeks to know the world and please others in a way that destroys the very pleasure he pursues and would otherwise enjoy. The speaker is not raising the paradox of credulity versus reason that appears in 'Artemiza to Chloe' and to which Swift would later give a lasting formulation, but rather pointing out that man forgoes pleasure in order to please others and in turn feed his own pretentions. Man, that is, perversely follows his misguided reason in large part because it makes him feel important, a point the speaker makes following the *adversarius*'s interruption:

> This supernatural Gift, that makes a mite
> Think hee's the Image of the Infinite;
> Comparing his short life, voyd of all rest,
> To the Eternall, and the ever blest.
> This busy puzzling stirrer up of doubt,
> That frames deep Mysteries, then finds them out;
> Filling with frantick crowds of thinking Fools
> Those Reverend Bedlams, Colledges and Schools;
> Born on whose wings each heavy Sott can pierce
> The limits of the boundless Universe.
> So charming Ointments make an old Witch fly,
> And bear a crippled carcass through the sky.
>   (lines 76–87)

Like the philosopher Diogenes, man often forgoes pleasure and unnecessarily complicates his life because has nothing to do. But he also seeks the charms of 'Non-sense and Impossibilities' (line 89) in order to feel exalted and profound. He seeks them, too, because they give him power. In summing up his indictment, the speaker rails:

> All this with Indignation have I hurl'd
> At the pretending part of the proud World,
> Who swoln with selfish Vanity, devise
> False Freedomes, Holy Cheats and formal Lyes,
> Over their fellow Slaves to tyrannize.
>   (lines 174–78)

If man were to follow not reason but 'right reason', the speaker claims, such would not be the case:

> That Reason which distinguishes by Sense,
> And gives us Rules of Good and Ill from thence:
> That bounds Desires with a reforming Will,
> To keep them more in vigour, not to kill.
> (lines 99–103)

If man were to do so, he would like the beasts, become wise:

> Those Creatures are the wisest who attain
> By surest means, the ends at which they aime:
> If therefore *Jowler* finds and kills his Hares,
> Better than *Meeres* supplies Committee chaires;
> Though one's a Statesman, th' other but a Hound,
> *Jowler* in Justice would be wiser found.
> (lines 117–22)

The passage recalls the monkey portrait and the ending of 'Tunbridge Wells'. Compared to what is being written today, compared to man's affectations, the monkey and the horse are to be preferred. Compared to a bureaucrat, who would not find Jowler the wiser beast!

The central 'Paradox to them' (line 221) upon which the poem is built begins to emerge, however, as the speaker moves from his vision of man harmoniously united with nature through 'right reason' to the reality of actual human nature. When man really does follow his nature, he finds not the Edenic world of pleasure, of eating whenever he wants, of appetite and will united, but rather a Hobbesian world of man, driven by fear, pitted in perpetual war against his fellow man. As Vieth noted, 'A Satyre' 'splits into two nearly equal halves whose content cannot be reconciled logically'. This split arises, Vieth acutely observed, because

> the libertine section presents an *attainable* positive standard, whereas the standard in the Hobbesian section is *unattainable*. Animal imagery helps convey this contradiction. In the libertine section, 'a dog, a monkey, or a bear' (line 5) or 'Jowler' (lines 119–22) represents a norm of pleasure which true wisdom makes theoretically accessible to man. In the Hobbesian section, however, man, victimized by his depraved nature, cannot rise to the moral level of animals.[20]

The split arises, that is, from the two senses of nature that Rochester explores and that we have been tracing throughout his work. In the first half of 'A Satyre' (lines 1–122) nature, represented by the animals, is the senses; theoretically – and I would stress the theoretically – man can live in tune with this nature and find pleasure. The second section (lines 123–221) treats man in society and interprets nature as a cultural norm that he fails to live up to because he is unnatural, that is, not refined, orderly, and well-bred. To live naturally in the second part, man must not follow instinct, nature as defined in part one, but subordinate his instinct to discipline for the social good, which he is unable to do because he is driven by those very natural appetites.

In having presented this bitter paradox to mankind – that he can conceive of an ideal but not attain it – the speaker, however, would seem to be hoisted by his own satiric petard. His criticism has been that man prefers 'Mountains of whimseys', 'Non-sense and Impossibilities', to the reality of following 'certain Instinct' to 'that World he should enjoy'. Man does so because he has nothing to do, or worse, as a pretentious being, he seeks power over others. Yet the 'right reason', 'nature', and the ethical system the speaker attempts to draw from them turn out themselves to be whimsical.

Our first clue that the speaker is being oddly fanciful occurs in the very opening: 'Were I ... A spirit free to choose.' But he is not free to choose; he is already a 'prodigious' creature, prodigious here meaning 'unnatural', 'monstrous', but also ironically, 'marvelous'. The speaker would have that which is unnatural become natural; he would be a spirit, which hardly accords with his own materialistic view of reality. The main point here is the issue of choice. The speaker attributes free choice to man: 'will preferre' (line 10) and 'Ayming to know' (line 34). He would rather be a Dog, a Monky, or a Bear' (line 5) because, like Jowler, 'Those Creatures are the wisest who attain/ By surest means, the ends at which they aime' (lines 117–18). To aim assumes purposiveness and choice, and the speaker argues that one in tune with the senses will be guided so that his will can make good choices, choices that lead to the pleasurable:

> I own right reason, which I would obey;
> That Reason which distinguishes by Sense,
> And gives us Rules of Good and Ill from thence:
> That bounds Desires with a reforming Will,
> To keep them more in vigour, not to kill.
> Your Reason hinders, mine helps to enjoy,
> Renewing appetites yours would destroy.
> My Reason is my friend, Yours is a cheat,
> Hunger calls out, my Reason bids me eat;
> Perversly yours your appetites does mock,
> They ask for food, that answers what's a clock.
>   (lines 99–109)

This example, along with those comparing man to animals, suggests instinct, not choice. Man with right reason receives the stimulus to eat and he responds, eating being like the prelapsarian sex depicted in *The Fall*. From the standpoint of any kind of meaningful ethical choice, however, the man who asks the time appears to have the best of it. He controls his response to the stimulus. He has a choice. The speaker's illogical logic goes something like this: if man were free, he would choose; not being free, he nevertheless has the choice of being something that he cannot be, and if he could be that, it would not give him the freedom of choice that he supposedly had.

Other examples of the speaker's tortuous, fanciful logic abound. He would have man act in accord with nature, but when man does act according to his nature, the results are much worst than bestial. The speaker declares that 'Thoughts are given for Actions government/ Where Action ceases, Thought's impertinent' (lines 94–95). Yet there is no way that one could act on his thoughts concerning 'Reason righted' (line 112); man simply cannot become a beast, except, ironically, in a way that contradicts what the speaker says. The speaker, who advocates living in the world of the five senses, the world as is, discourses nevertheless in the conditional. The poem begins with 'Were I ... a spirit free to choose (lines 1 and 3), but he is not. And the poem's closing section begins with 'But if' (line 179), the speaker hypothesizing about a just statesman and faithful churchman who do not exist save in the conditional.

The conditional nature of the speaker's position, its contradictions, are meant to undermine his position, to show ironically enough that little separates him from the *adversarius*. The speaker has presented an ideal, a norm by which to measure man that is no more real than the *adversarius*'s conception of man, the one being simply a secularized version of the other. The *adversarius* evokes 'Blest glorious Man! to whom alone kind Heaven/ An Everlasting Soul has freely given' (lines 60–61). The *adversarius* would dignify man by attributing to him a reason that raises 'his Nature above Beast' (line 65). The speaker would dignify man by holding out the exercise of right reason that would raise him to the level of the beast. But when confronted with man's actual nature, both are chimerical. The *adversarius* draws upon 'Mysterious Truths, which no man can conceive' (line 219) and the speaker on 'Books' and 'bladders of Philosophy' (lines 20–21) that dazzle but leave man in the dark. The speaker, no less than the *adversarius*, would seem to be a member of 'the pretending part of the proud World' (line 175) against which he rails. He is a satirist satirized, the hedonist, libertine view of man he espouses, like the Christian, humanist view of the *adversarius*, consisting of 'False Freedomes', if not of 'Holy Cheats and formal Lyes' (line 177). The churchman and the satirist, 'blown up with vain Prelatick pride' (line 193) and guilty of the very sins they would deride, seek to tyrannize over their fellow man, the one through false piety and the other through ridicule and laughter.

The speaker of 'A Satyre' partakes of a certain poignant futility often found in Rochester's poetry. He, like the speaker of 'A Ramble' and of 'Tunbridge Wells', like Timon and Artemiza, conceives of ideals and of positive modes of behaviour that the awful shape of circumstances never allows him to realize. In each case it is difficult to determine how aware the speakers are, whether each is not in fact a target and in turn victim of the satire. Rochester's speakers are constantly trying to look around the corner, to make awareness a shield against the corrosive powers of the satiric attack they themselves have launched. For the speaker of 'A Satyre', there seems to be no such shield. Moreover, in advancing the ideal of right reason, he exemplifies ironically the very fault he finds in mankind, his belligerent attack against man being as dogmatic and as little founded in empirical truth as that of the *adversarius*'s praise of reason and mankind. His position is speculative, a product of that sixth sense, that intellectual pride, he has ridiculed.

The various paradoxes and contradictions in the poem provide evidence that the speaker is being undermined by his creator, but they also suggest that the creator himself had not thought through the implications of the libertine credo that what is true in discourse is not true in experience. Common sense may be used to call into question Christian faith and philosophical rationalism, but in turn the generous world of Epicurean nature is unknowable to the sceptic. What Rochester was doing was standing against – against needless, metaphysical speculation, against human rapaciousness, against the hypocrisy of traditional morality. That his criticisms are not rationally coherent would suggest that he was using whatever he could find to be against. Such is often the nature of satire. We do not ask of the satirist a coherent philosophical position. And often the confusions involved in his attack fuel further disgust with the human condition because they themselves reveal the limited nature of man's ability to solve his problems and the infinite nature of his desire to do so. In this awareness 'A Satyre' edges toward tragedy. The poem is unleavened by comic self-awareness or the exhibitionistic displays of aristocratic obscenity. The witty archness with which the poem begins gives way to the pleadings of the honest man, who if he is a libertine differs little from his traditional moralist counterpart. The poem expresses a longing for what the senses cannot provide and for which neither traditional Christian, humanistic, nor libertine thought can give consolation.

'A Letter from Artemiza in the Towne to Chloe in the Countrey'

The date and circumstances surrounding Rochester's writing of 'Artemiza to Chloe' remain uncertain.[21] Vieth finds that it and 'A Satyre against

Reason and Mankind' may have been composed about the same time, 'probably between the middle of 1674 and the end of 1675' (Vieth, *Attribution*, p. 293). Paul Hammond, while acknowledging that 'The chronology of Rochester's poems is not easy to establish', thinks the poem was probably written 'Between November 1673 and February 1675'.[22] Nicholas Fisher, having discovered a new manuscript of the poem, argues, however, 'that an earlier date of composition for *Artemiza to Chlöe* is entirely plausible', perhaps before 7 May 1669.[23] While there is no evidence to show that 'Artemiza to Chloe' was written after 'A Satyre' – and some powerful evidence to suggest it was not – thematically 'Artemiza to Chloe' seems to take up where 'A Satyre' leaves off, the poem being an exploration of a world of individuals craving love but united only by 'the deceptions of an idealistic rhetoric'.[24]

The opening thirty-one lines, playful, vivacious, and clever, capture the spirit of two young women caught up in a correspondence about intimate subjects, the most important being that of love. Artemiza, charmingly voluble, is writing to her friend in the country, Chloe, who has 'commande[d]' (line 1) that Artemiza write in verse. Write in verse! Do you really understand what that means? 'Shortly you'l bid mee ride astride, and fight' (line 2). In comparing the writing of poetry to riding like a man and going into battle, Artemiza is providing herself with a witty opening to her letter, having fun with her own name (Artemis and Diana), and making a facetious comment on what is and is not appropriate for women to do in her society. She is also addressing, in a serious way, one of the poem's central concerns: the nature of poetry in a fallen world. Her opening couplet suggests that being a poet, like being a warrior, is a heroic activity. Though it seems preposterous, women have a better chance of succeeding at the latter than the former, the pursuit of the bays being genuinely dangerous. Even among men of wit,

> How many bold Advent'rers for the Bayes,
> (Proudly designing large returnes of Prayse)
> Who durst that stormy pathlesse World explore,
> Were soone dash't backe, and wreck't on the dull Shore,
> Broke of that Little Stocke, they had before?
>   (lines 7–11)

The writing of poetry is a like an epic voyage, a perilous journey into the unknown. Few succeed, and 'How would a Womans tott'ring Barke be tost/ Where stoutest Ships (the Men of Witt) are lost?' (lines 12–13).

Artemiza's view of poetry is heroic, but also as will shortly become clear, idealistic. She conceives of it, as did her culture, as an activity capable of rendering a 'pure expression of the eternally human', particularly of love and valor.[25] But Artemiza is also well aware of the actual rhetorical setting for poetry in her world, and in that world

> Poetry's a snare:
> Bedlam has many Mansions: have a Care.
> Your Muse diverts you, makes the Reader sad;
> You fancy, you'r inspir'd, he thinkes you mad.
> Consider too, 'twill be discreetly done,
> To make your Selfe the Fiddle of the Towne,
> To fynd th'ill-humour'd pleasure att their need,
> Curst, if you fayle, and scorn'd, though you succeede.
> (lines 16–23)

The poet who is truly inspired will be taken as mad. The only way to succeed in such a world is not to tell people the truth, which would make them sad, but to become a 'Fiddle', in Vieth's gloss a 'mirth-maker' or 'jester', that is, to become performer, an entertainer.[26] Even if one does succeed in pandering to the taste of the town, she will be the object of scorn. Given the actual state of poetry, 'Whore is scarce a more reproachfull name/ Then Poetesse:' (lines 26–27). Being a poet is 'As Men, that marry, or as Maydes, that woe/ Because 'tis the worst thinge, that they can doe' (lines 28–29). The poet, like men and women pursuing love, begins with an ideal and inevitably winds up with the sordidly real. Artemiza knows this; nevertheless, she readily plunges into poetry. Calling herself 'an Arrant Woman' (line 24), that is a woman who is 'bad in a high degree' (Johnson, *Dictionary*), she is 'Pleas'd with the Contradiction, and the Sin' and stands 'on Thornes, till I begin' (lines 30–31). She is pleased because in her youthful exuberance she believes she can succeed in being a true poet where others have failed. She calls herself arrant (errant) and sinful in part to forestall criticism. She knows what she is doing is wrong, goes against, contradicts what she knows to be true. And she wants her audience to know that she knows. Whether she succeeds in keeping the ideal of poetry alive in a fallen world, is simply naive, or worse, is being a 'knave of the first rate' are questions that critics continue to debate and ones the poem was written to evoke. For if one of the poem's major themes concerns the role of the poet, the other, inextricably bound up with the first, is how to judge the performance of another.

This latter theme is embodied in the poem's very structure. Artemiza's narrative, charmingly entertaining, finally has only itself as referent. It contains much – her self-contradictions for example – that makes us question what she is doing, the charm itself being itself troublesome. Her inclusion of the fine lady's narration increases doubts about how to take Artemiza, both by what she has chosen to include and by her reaction to it. Furthermore, the fine lady's indirect narrative of Corinna's fate and that of the young master qualify our judgment of her as well as that of Artemiza and raise questions about Corinna, the young master, and the mysterious man of wit. The poem takes its structure from the drama, the play within the play, and gives rise to all the ambiguities that form induces.

Artemiza begins her dangerous voyage into poetry heroically, with the subject of love, but she does so in an unexpected way. To write of love in 'this lewd Towne' (line 33), she laments, is to do little more than to recount 'What change has happen'd of Intrigues, and whether/ The Old ones last, and who, and who's togeather' (line 34–35). Artemiza's is a delicate version of what the speaker in '*A Ramble*' describes as 'who Fucks who, and who does worse' (line 2). This debauched love Artemiza 'would faine forgett' (line 37). She would prefer to write of true love:

> *Love*, the most gen'rous Passion of the mynde,
> The softest refuge Innocence can fynde,
> The safe directour of unguided youth,
> Fraught with kind wishes, and secur'd by Trueth,
> That Cordiall dropp Heav'n in our Cup has throwne,
> To make the nauseous draught of Life goe downe,
> On which one onely blessing God might rayse
> In lands of Atheists Subsidyes of Prayse
> (For none did e're soe dull, and stupid prove,
> But felt a God, and blest his pow'r in *Love*).
>   (lines 40–49)

This ideal love, however, has become a 'lost thing' (line 38), an 'Arrant Trade' (line 51), cheats using its rhetoric to cash in.

What vexes Artemiza is that this trade is 'cheifely carry'd on by our owne Sexe' (line 55). In the pursuit of liberty – they 'hate restraint, though but from Infamy' (line 58) – women have become 'deafe to Natures rule, or *Loves* advice' and 'Forsake the Pleasure, to pursue the Vice' (lines 60–61). Like the speaker in 'A Satyre', Artemiza satirizes her fellow women for not following nature and the pleasure it proffers. Enamored of their own wit, they have turned love into a mechanical operation: 'To an exact perfection they have wrought/ The Action *Love*, the Passion is forgott' (lines 62–63). They too have become affected, making their choices not on the basis of morality or taste but on the public voice, on what is fashionable. They have become women of mode, deciding on whimsy, the form itself being all.

The nature that Artemiza holds out as norm here, however, is not the libertine one of freedom and pleasure. It is rather nature as a product of culture and intensive training that has been internalized and therefore taken to be natural. Women are by nature born into a monarchy, but in pursuit of liberty they turn 'Gipsyes' (line 57). They perversely forgo the pleasure afforded by restraint and hierarchy. Similarly, they have within them, by nature, the rules, advice, and taste to determine what is good or bad. But they have so perverted nature 'that with their Eares they see' (line 72). As an example of such perversion, Artemiza tells of her encounter with the fine lady. The fine lady is a performer; even

> As the Coach stop't, wee heard her Voyce more loud,
> Then a great belly'd Womans in a Crowd,
> Telling the Knight, that her affayres require,
> Hee for some houres obsequiously retire.
> (lines 78–81)

Artemiza's initial, naive reaction was that the fine lady 'was asham'd, to have [her husband] seene' (line 82). But as she later learns, the fine lady performs to manipulate and control. Such performances have led her to London

> her humble Knight,
> Who had prevayl'd on her, through her owne skill,
> At his request, though much against his will,
> (lines 74–76)

At least with her husband, her act is skilful enough. Her bellowing at the coach, her dramatic dismissal of her 'necessary thing' is a bid to show others that she is in control:

> Dispatch, sayes shee, that bus'nesse you pretend,
> Your beastly Visitt to your drunken freind;
> A Bottle ever makes you looke soe fine!
> Mee-thinkes I long, to smell you stinke of Wine.
> Your Countrey-drinking-breath's enough, to kill –
> Sowre Ale corrected with a Lemmon Pill.
> Prithy farewell – Wee'le meete againe anon;
> The necessary thing bows, and is gone.
> (lines 85–92)

She is a woman of 'fifty Antick postures' (line 94), a clown, a merry-andrew, capable of ludicrous or extravagant acts and gestures. Some of these at least she has adapted from the stage itself, Vieth pointing out how 'her character resembles that of Melantha in Dryden's comedy *Marriage À-la-Mode*' (*Poems*, p. 106). Declaring that she is 'Rude, and untaught, like any Indian Queene' (line 99), she compares herself to another of Dryden's dramatic characters. But far from being rude or untaught, she has thoroughly internalized the 'publicke Voyce', become a woman of 'Fashions' and 'Formes' (lines 66 and 68).

Her breathless, animated account of why women, even women of wit, should in matters of love prefer fools to men of wit is in large part a self-justification for her theatrical performance. As she explains, men of wit

> With searching Wisedome fatall to their ease
> They still fynde out, why, what may, should not please;
> Nay take themselves for injur'd, when Wee dare,
> Make 'em think better of Us, then Wee are:
> And if Wee hide Our frailtyes from their sights,
> Call Us deceitefull Gilts, and Hypocrites.
> They little guesse, who att Our Arts are greiv'd,
> The perfect Joy of being well deceaved.
> Inquisitive, as jealous Cuckolds, grow,
> Rather, then not bee knowing, they will know,
> What being knowne creates their certaine woe.
> Women should these of all Mankind avoyd;
> For Wonder by cleare knowledge is destroy'd.
> Woman, who is an Arrant Bird of night,
> Bold in the Duske, before a Fooles dull sight,
> Should flye, when Reason brings the glaring light.
>   (lines 108–23)

The fine lady gives a libertine critique of man's 'searching Wisedome', 'cleare knowledge', and the 'glaring light' of 'Reason'. These are 'contrivances' by which man forgoes 'what may ... please' (line 109). But the fine lady is a libertine without faith in a nature that yields pleasure if properly pursued. For by nature, woman is 'an Arrant Bird of night' (line 121). Given that fact, the only satisfactory relationship between women and men is one of deception.

The fine lady is also, as Artemiza tells us, learned, one 'who had turn'd o're/ As many Bookes, as Men, lov'd much, reade more/ Had a discerning Witt' (lines 162–64). As we might suspect of a wit, her mind runs to paradox. In support of her paradox that women of wit should prefer fools to men of wit, she offers yet another one: that to know joy in this life is to be well deceived. Men of wit who are undeceived, who know, create 'their certaine woe' (line 118). But what about women of wit of which the fine lady is one? She does not say just yet; she simply asserts that 'the Kinde easy Foole apt, to admire/ Himselfe', 'These are true Womens Men' (lines 124–25 and 135).

The implication seems to be, however, that being a woman of wit, though preferable, is not an altogether admirable state. As soon as the fine lady finishes her speech, she races to embrace 'Her much esteem'd deare Freind the Monkey ti'de' (line 138) and evokes yet another paradox. Given the deceptive relationship between men and women and the kind of men women can attract and keep, it would be better, so the fine lady's actions suggest, to have a relationship with a beast.

> Kisse mee, thou curious Miniature of Man;
> How odde thou art? How pritty? How Japan?
> Oh I could live, and dye with thee – then on
> For halfe an houre in Complement shee runne.
> (lines 143–46)

Artemiza takes 'this tyme, to thinke, what Nature meant/ When this mixt thinge into the World shee sent' (lines 147–48). By 'Nature' here Artemiza means the forces and processes of the physical world, not the hierarchical nature of human culture. By this definition, 'Nature's as lame, in making a true Fopp/ As a Philosopher' (lines 154–55). Paradoxically, the fine lady has turned herself into a brute, into an 'Asse' (line 151) by perverting human nature. According to Artemiza,

> the very topp,
> And Dignity of Folly wee attaine
> By studious Search, and labour of the Braine,
> By observation, Councell, and deepe thought:
> God never made a Coxecombe worth a groate.
> Wee owe that name to Industry, and Arts:
> An Eminent Foole must bee a Foole of Parts;
> And such a One was shee, who had turnd o're
> As many Bookes, as Men, lov'd much, reade more,
> Had a discerning Witt, to her was knowne
> Ev'ry Ones fault, and meritt, but her owne.
> All the good qualityes, that ever blest
> A Woman, soe distinguisht from the rest,
> Except discretion onely; she possest.
> (lines 155–68)

The fine lady's faults, Artemiza suggests, are all the worse for not being natural, but rather for being the result of human corruption, of 'choyce, not want of Witt' (line 151). Here is a highly cultivated, well-educated lady who should be a rational creature in a harmonious relationship with the world, but she is not. She is 'impertinent' (line 149) and lacks 'discretion' (line 168). To our ears, these judgments may not seem all that severe. But Artemiza appears to be working out of a highly cultivated, aristocratic sense of values where to lack prudence, circumspection, and control is to lack moral values as well. By Artemiza's standards, the fine lady's performance, up until now, has been a highly flawed one.

The fine lady senses that Artemiza is being critical of her, and responds:

> You smile, to see mee, whom the World perchance
> Mistakes, to have some Witt, soe far advance

> The Interest of Fooles, that I approve
> Their Meritt more, then Mens of Witt, in Love.
> (lines 171–74)

To support her contention the fine lady cites the case of Corinna who, when she first came on the scene, was anything but 'That wretched thinge' (line 189) she has become.

> Gay were the houres, and wing'd with Joy they flew,
> When first the Towne her early Beautyes knew,
> Courted, admir'd, and lov'd, with Presents fedd,
> Youth in her lookes, and pleasure in her bed,
> (lines 193–96)

Corinna's life was an Epicurean idyll, until she had the misfortune to

> doate upon a Man of Witt,
> Who found, 't was dull, to love above a day,
> Made his ill-natur'd Jest, and went his way.
> Now scorn'd by all, forsaken, and opprest,
> Shee's a Memento Mori to the rest.
> Diseas'd, decay'd, to take up halfe a Crowne,
> Must morgage her long Scarfe, and Mantua Gowne.
> (lines 198–204)

Corinna's fall results from her having been 'Couzen'd att first by Love' (line 191). Corinna believed in the ideal of love. The man of wit used the rhetoric of love simply to get what he wanted. Corinna has been left disillusioned and undone, the victim of a confidence game. But if she has not found real love, she has learned her lesson. She goes on to make her 'living then/ By turning the too-deare-bought trick on Men' (lines 191–92). That is, she has learned to use an idealistic rhetoric to take advantage of others.

As fortune would have it, she has recently encountered an excellent candidate upon whom to practise her artifice, a young master, who 'From Pedagogue, and Mother just sett free' (line 211) has come to town.

> This o'regrowne Schooleboy lost-Corinna wins,
> And att first dash, to make an Asse, begins:
> Pretends, to like a Man, who has not knowne
> The Vanityes, nor Vices of the Towne,
> Fresh in his youth, and faithfull in his Love,
> Eager of Joyes, which he does seldome prove,
> Healthfull, and strong, he does noe paynes endure,
> But what the Fayre One, he adores, can cure.
> Gratefull for favours does the Sexe esteeme,
> And Libells none, for being kind to him.
> (lines 226–35)

Corinna, now a product of the city, is probably older than her would-be victim. She flatters him for being from the country and young, two areas where he would have his greatest insecurities. She also entices him and tests him in a way that flatters him as a man of integrity. He is, she says, no doubt eager for joys a country cousin wife seldom offers; healthful and strong, he knows no pain, but one, and that can be cured by an adoring fair woman. Being grateful and having esteem for women, he is one who can enjoy such pleasures without having to tell the world about them. While holding out the promise of sexual pleasure, she at the same time wants to assure him that she is no common woman of the town and therefore

> ... of the Lewdnesse of the tymes complaines,
> Rayles att the Witts, and Atheists, and mainteynes,
> 'tis better, then good Sense, then pow'r, or Wealth,
> To have alone untainted youth, and health.
> (lines 236–39)

Corinna's artful speech has its desired end:

> The unbred puppy, who had never seene
> A Creature looke soe gay, or talke soe fine,
> Beleaves, then falls in Love, and then in Debt
> (lines 240–42)

The young master, like Corinna herself, becomes the victim of an idealistic rhetoric.

> And when to the height of fondnesse he is growne,
> 'Tis tyme, to poyson him, and all's her owne.
> Thus meeting in her Common Armes his Fate,
> Hee leaves her Bastard Heyre to his Estate;
> And as the Race of such an Owle deserves,
> His owne dull lawfull Progeny he starves.
> (lines 246–51)

Concerning this sordid tale of squalor, deception, and criminality, the fine lady chillingly concludes:

> Nature, who never made a thinge in vayne,
> But does each Insect to some ende ordeyne,
> Wisely provides kind-keeping Fooles, noe doubt,
> To patch up Vices, Men of Witt weare out.
> (lines 252–55)

Having told her tale of Corinna, the fine lady appears to us in a far different light. In the performance of a rattle, we see a woman with a steely assessment of reality. Her account of Corinna is, as they say, a worse case scenario.

Corinna is a whore; but in hearing her story, we extend sympathy to her, even in her criminality. The fine lady, though the wife of a knight, distinguished, and well-educated, has seen 'too many proofes ... / Of such, whom Witts undoe' (lines 175–76) to think that what has happened to Corinna is confined to the class of whores. Corinna's fall and that of the young master have an impressive inevitability about them as though this were the way of the world. And so it seems to be. There are the fools, the fops, the dupes. They trust, believe, fall in love, and then into debt. Paradoxically, being deceived, they know the only joy apparently available to mankind. In this schema of things, the 'necessary thing' as well as the young master are the joyful ones. Clearly, theirs is a joy unavailable and unacceptable to men and women of wit who, if the fine lady is typical, have no positive course to follow. The fine lady embraces the monkey, but his instinctual life and the pleasure it presumably brings cannot be hers. Men do turn themselves into animals, asses and puppies; into birds, rooks, arrant birds of night, and owls; and even into insects but without finding the instinctual pleasure these lesser, paradoxically yet theoretically higher, forms of life enjoy. Because life does go on, because men and women do seek to satisfy their appetites, the only alternative left to those of wit seems to be that of becoming, as the speaker of 'A Satyre' puts it, 'a Knave of the first rate' (line 173).

To be honest, to play fair, is to be undone. The only satisfaction the witty have is to control others before they control them. Life becomes a series of confidence games, one trying to undo others before they undo you, and even at its best, it is always an uneasy affair, as the nervous volubility of the fine lady indicates. Though the mysterious man of wit escapes in this poem, no one it seems is ever totally immune to mankind's disease of being taken in, of being deceived. Given this view of life, Corinna, though not honest or exemplary in any traditional sense, takes on a certain admirable authenticity as does the fine lady. They are survivors in a tough world, or so the fine lady would have us believe. But she does not have the last word. That belongs to Artemiza.

Artemiza had given an explicit and lengthy condemnation of the fine lady following her first speech. After the second, Artemiza says little, observing simply that there were 'some graynes of Sense/ Still mixt with Volleys of Impertinence' (lines 256–57). Then in a brief seven lines, she closes, decorously observing the proprieties of the *ars dicendi*. She will write again soon, but does not wish at present to further try the patience of her reader. Artemiza's cryptic remarks and abrupt closing provide us with few clues about her final judgment of the fine lady, fewer still about how she wants her audience to judge her.

The 'graynes of Sense' would seem to imply that Artemiza has some understanding of why the fine lady and Corinna have adopted their affectations. Nevertheless, she merely reiterates her criticism that the fine lady is impertinent, a woman who says a great many things that she should not. Even if we take Artemiza to be the refined young woman whom I have posited and that her social criticism of the fine lady also carries a moral censure, this reaction seems inadequate to what she and we have just heard. Despite the evidence before her, she clings to a view of love and of values that has no place in the world of real men and women. She is, in the fine lady's division of mankind, one of the deceived and her future is ominous.

But Artemiza has shown herself, particularly in the opening thirty-one lines, to be remarkably self-aware. It seems plausible, therefore, that her abrupt ending reveals that she has understood the fine lady all too well. Having listened to the fine lady's narrative, she has been led to sympathize, perhaps even to justify, the fine lady's treatment of her necessary thing or Corinna's appalling acts. What we have is the education of Artemiza who, having understood the plight of women in a world without essential values, promises to write Chloe 'By the next Post such storyes … / As joyn'd with these shall to a Volume swell/ As true, as Heaven, more infamous, then Hell' (lines 261–63). From Artemiza's own traditional values, she would be seen as becoming corrupt and spreading the corruption to Chloe in the country; from the view of the values of the real world as revealed in Corinna's story, she would be seen as becoming a pragmatic feminist.

Though this is a plausible reading, a third interpretation, which emerges if we focus on the relationship between Artemiza and the fine lady, may move us closer to what is actually going on. Artemiza is a bright young woman, a fledgling poet much troubled about the nature of love. 'The other night' she met a most unusual woman who had a great deal to say about it. Artemiza cannot wait to get home and write to her friend in the country. She wants her friend to admire her for writing in verse but also to be forgiving if she does not do it all that well. At the same time, she wants to assure her friend that what she is going to describe about love is not what she thinks love is or should be. She knows better, but then her friend has not been to the city, has not met this particular fine lady. As she writes the poem, however, exuberance gives ways to indignation, and finally to weariness, 'But you are tyr'd, and soe am I' (line 264). The content and implications of her story have come to overwhelm the framework she has provided for it. She has discovered too much; sympathy has come to undermine judgment.

From the beginning, Artemiza has attempted to interpret her experience through the framework of Christianity. In jesting that 'Bedlam has many Mansions: have a Care' (line 17), she is alluding to John 14:1–2: 'Let not your heart be troubled: ye believe in God, believe also in me. In my Father's house are many mansions: if it were not so, I would have told you. I go to prepare a place for you.' This along with her gleeful admission to committing a sin by writing in verse seems to be a playful way of bidding for sympathy for her venture while asserting its ultimate significance. In the process of writing her poem, however, she really has discovered a world which from a Christian perspective – God (lines 46, 150, and 159), 'Heav'n' (line 44), and 'blest' (line 166) – has been turned upside down and is indeed full of sin. Her criticism that the women have become so affected that 'with their Eares they see' may allude to Matthew 13:15: 'For this people's heart is waxed gross, and their ears are dull of hearing, and their eyes they have closed; lest at any time they should see with their eyes, and hear with their ears, and should understand with their heart, and should be converted, and I should heal them.' Her judgment at the end that 'Readers must reape the dullnesse, writers sow' (line 260) evokes Galatians 6:7: 'Be not deceived; God is not mocked: for whatsoever a man soweth, that shall he also reap.' Artemiza, well aware of what she has witnessed, has attempted, however obliquely, to judge it. Like Conrad's Kurtz, she has confronted the heart of darkness, and at least has spoken.

She also seems to be aware that her efforts to write heroic poetry are doomed. The values underlying such a poetry – love and honour – like Christianity itself seem to belong to a world passing away. She apparently came up from the Country; Chloe lives there. But that bastion of values has already been invaded by the fine lady, and the example of the young master would suggest that traditional country values have been in decay for some time. The poet in this fallen world will write stories 'more infamous, then Hell' (line 263). The would-be heroic poet in such a world must perforce become a satirist.

Artemiza's position, even and perhaps most of all, as a satirist may, however, be more tenuous than she knows. In having evoked the fine lady and her story so powerfully, she has allowed her reader to sympathize with both and in turn to render her own judgment as questionable. Perhaps, given this world, it is better to be a fine lady, to be a Corinna. That is, the fine lady's libertine relativism where all values are readily manipulated by the winds of rhetoric has a corrosive effect on Artemiza's own values, or at least our assessment of those values. Though ostensibly opposites, the one a romantic, the other a realist, Artemiza and the fine lady become increasingly identified one with the other as the poem unfolds and they come finally to share similar dilemmas. Artemiza describes herself as an 'Arrant Woman' (line 24); the fine lady characterizes all women as 'Arrant Bird[s] of night' (line 121); both are impertinent, confront similar dilemmas, and are involved in elaborate attempts at self-justification. Both, being 'arrant', err or fail. If the fine lady represents the cynical end of libertinism in its attempts to provide a satisfactory account of the way of the world, Artemiza's weak response to the fine lady's second narrative and her final weariness represent the failure of traditional social and moral values in such a world and of a poetry that would represent that world. Both are rationalist, whose rational schemas are shown in the light of experience to be inadequate. Given our experience of that world, there is no reason to trust either one. The fine lady is involved in the 'Arrant Trade' of using love to dupe others. Artemiza is, however wittingly or unwittingly, involved in a similar trade, passing along her tales of Hell under the guise of heroic and Christian values.

As we sift through the possible implications of Artemiza's abrupt ending, we come to the realization that we really cannot know whether to champion Artemiza, the fine lady, or to call both into question because 'Artemiza to Chloe', like 'A Satyre', is deeply and deliberately paradoxical. 'One element common to all ... kinds of paradox', Rosalie Colie has written, 'is their exploitation of the fact of relative, or competing, value systems'. She goes on to observe that 'The paradox is always somehow involved in dialectic: challenging some orthodoxy, the paradox is an oblique criticism of absolute judgment or absolute convention' (Colie, p. 10). The very occasion of 'Artemiza to Chloe' has a paradoxical air: a woman writing a poem. It is a thing that will not be done well, or such is the expectation. Yet in pursuing the paradox, one learns perhaps more truth than one wants to. This woman, seemingly trapped in romantic conventions, provides a most accurate and compelling description of the way things are. The poem challenges our assumptions about women and not just in the figure of Artemiza.

The poem is also riddled with numerous other paradoxes that inevitably arise where what is true in the realm of discourse is not true in the realm of experience. For Artemiza, the writing of poetry is a 'Contradiction' and a 'Sin', yet she is pleased to plunge into verse. Are we to judge her by what she says, or by her actions and the poem she has written? By the love she professes, or the one she so graphically encounters? For the fine lady, 'perfect Joy' comes from being 'well deceaved'. Are we to judge her by what she says or by the experience we have of Corinna and of the young master who have been so deceived? The poem exploits most fully the gap on the one hand between Artemiza's Christian, heroic tradition and experience and, on the other, the gap between the fine lady's libertinism and that same stubborn experience. As is the nature of paradoxes, they tend to proliferate when pressed. For example, the fine lady, a moral relativist, is very much interested in 'patch[ing] up Vices' (line 255) in having things righted. Artemiza, the Christian moralist, is engaged in spreading subversive tales of moral relativism, the very work of Hell.

Paradoxes are designed to call into question the ways we know. In 'Artemiza to Chloe', as in 'A Satyre', it would seem that Rochester was calling into question the powers of both Christianity as well as libertinism to provide a satisfying understanding of the world. Finally, of course, we simply cannot know to what degree to trust our judgments of either poem because both play upon logical paradox of self-reference. While it is true, as Clifford Gertz has reminded us, that all Cretans are not liars, in both poems the internal evidence is ambiguous and no outside evidence is available to cast light upon it. Chloe, so far as we know, never wrote back.

Rochester, like Artemiza and the fine lady, seems himself to have delighted in entertaining these paradoxes. He would go on to write 'A very heroical epistle' (1675) and 'An Epistolary Essay' (probably as late as 1679, but perhaps as early as 1676), both poems, as we saw in Chapter 1, exploiting the paradox of self-reference. 'Upon Nothinge' would soon follow, and it is probably during this period, 1675–78, that Rochester would write a number of poems, *The Fall*, 'Absent from thee I languish still', and '*Love* and *Life*' among others, that exploit Christian paradoxes, a subject I take up in the last chapter. We might speculate that his fascination with paradox arose from at least four motives. Paradox allowed the sceptic, the materialist, and nominalist to call into question all sorts of rationalisms, beliefs, and expectations, including those, paradoxically enough, of scepticism, materialism, and nominalism. At the same time, it allowed him to explore the various objects of his ridicule, in a paradoxical way to negate while expressing a yearning for them, to have by not having. In the very being against, I detect in 'Artemiza to Chloe' as in 'A Satyre' a longing for the positive, be it Christian or libertine. As Dale Underwood astutely noted in his indispensable study:

> We shall find increasing evidence that what the libertine, particularly in the Restoration, selected from these [classical] sources was determined chiefly by the extent to which the ideas negated conventional thought and values. The irrational element in such a controlling impulse toward negation suggests not merely a disenchantment with but a psychological and spiritual privation of what it seeks to destroy.[27]

Paradox also provided a perfect stage upon which the witty Rochester could perform. Around both poems hovers a tone of showing off, of being too clever by half. Granted, Artemiza is weary by the end of her performance but not too weary to flourish a triplet that imitates the very action of her poem. She promises letters that will 'to a Volume swell' that will be more 'infamous, then Hell', and so 'Farewell'. The speaker of 'A Satyre' is at the end more than a little bemused, yet he piques his audience by still taking an assured pride in his 'Paradox', offering to 'Recant' only in the face of evidence impossible to attain, and with a nod to Montaigne deftly restating in a couplet his theriophilic paradox. 'When the rhetorical paradox moved out of the classical languages into the vernacular literatures', Colie writes, 'it remained a sophisticated form, written for a learned and experienced coterie, an audience of men and women in the know, who could be expected to understand the paradoxists' learned wit and to admire the rhetorical skills demonstrated in the paradoxes themselves' (Colie, p. 33). The fine lady has put on just such a performance for Artemiza as has Artemiza for Chloe, and the speaker of 'A Satyre' for the 'proud World'.

Behind all three can be glimpsed Rochester himself in performance, cleverly contradicting, often outraging, his audience's expectations, his ultimate motive being a desire for acceptance, for affirmation, if through nothing else, than through the performance. The greater the outrage, the more daring the paradox, the greater the potential for testing the truths and conventions under scrutiny, and the greater the occasion for gaining applause and acceptance. A woman poet, I am on thorns until I begin, 'pleas'd with the Contradiction, and the Sin'. Had I a choice, 'I'de be a Dog, a Monky, or a Bear/ Or any thing but that vain Animal.' Such a rhetorical strategy informs nearly all of Rochester's poems and in its virtuosity was designed to elicit something like the response of Mrs Loveit to Dorimant in George Etherege's *The Man of Mode*: 'I know he is a Devil, but he has something of the Angel yet undefac'd in him, which makes him so charming and agreeable that I must love him, he be never so wicked' (Act II, scene ii., lines 15–16). Perhaps nowhere did Rochester employ such a strategy more skilfully and with more winning results than in '*The Disabled Debauchee*, a parading of aristocratic vice and crime that seeks acceptance and transcendence of both.

The Disabled Debauchee

The speaker of *The Disabled Debauchee* is the voice of aristocratic vice, crime that has the appeal of style, or as he puts it, of 'handsome Ills, by my contrivance, done' (line 36). As he compares his rakish accomplishments with those of 'some brave Admiral' (line 1), it becomes impossible to separate the 'pleasing Billows of Debauch' (line 15) from the waves of sea battle; bold, explosive naval engagements from 'Fleets of Glasses Sail[ing] about the Board/ From whose broad sides Volleys of Wit shall Rain' (lines 19–20); the scars of war from those of syphilis, 'honorable Scars/ Which my too forward valor did procure' (lines 21–22). The heroic is reduced, shown to be but an outlet for sexual energies, its violence and quest for glory no different in kind from that of the rake with his 'Whores attack'd, their Lords at home/ Bauds Quarters beaten up, and Fortress won' (lines 33–34). At the same time, the debauchee's 'bold Night-Alarms' (line 30), when he 'was strong, and able to bear Arms' (line 32), take on the character of being truly heroic, exercises of a 'too forward valor' (line 22). The speaker's sexual and bibulous bouts are splendidly wicked, and all the more so because so candidly and wittily related. They have the added appeal of a manly, paternal air as the older man passes on his wisdom to his protégé, a warrior to a would-be warrior.

> With Tales like these, I will such thoughts inspire
> As to important mischief shall incline;
> I'll make him long some Ancient Church to fire,
> And fear no lewdness he's call'd to by Wine.
> (lines 41–44)

The very profane – firing an ancient church – takes on the character of the truly sacred, mischief so important that it becomes inspiring. So too lewdness, transformed by the spirit of wine, becomes inspirational. 'S'il importe d'être sublime en quelque genre', says Diderot's Lui, 'c'est surtout en mal'.[28]

That is, of course, the whole point, the poem being an exercise in the art of the rhetorical paradox, a praise of 'mal'. In keeping with the nature of paradox, the speaker seeks to dazzle his audience with his cleverness: the brave admiral, 'Depriv'd of force', 'Crawls' (lines 2 and 4) as though suffering from the syphilitic ills the speaker proleptically sees for himself; the admiral takes on the countenance of an angry Zeus, with 'his fierce eyes flashes of Rage he throws/ As from black Clouds when Lightning breaks away' (lines 9–10) and like the god of those old stories he is ineffectual; naval battles are juxtaposed to the skirmishes on top a tavern table; honourable scars are 'procure[d]' (line 22); and sordid sexual escapades become heroic, even divinely inspired.

In keeping with the nature of paradox, the speaker's witty conceit advances an implicit argument that is not without its telling points. Compared to the conformity and hypocrisy of him who 'prove[s] nice' and 'meanly shrink[s]' (lines 25–26), of the 'cold complexion'd Sot ... With his Dull Morals' (lines 29–30), there is something generous and admirable about the open pursuit of wine, women, and boys. It may be, moreover, that little really does separate war conducted on the waves from the sexual wars within doors; on both battle grounds, ills are made handsome through contrivance. While wisdom grows out of experience, it has little power to affect that experience, whether it be war or whoring. It comes too late and is in some sense the offspring of impotence. As another ironist, La Rochefoucauld, put it, 'Les vieillard aiment à donner de bons préceptes pour se consoler de n'être plus en état de donner de mauvais exemples.'[29]

The speaker challenges, outrageously, the accepted wisdom concerning the warrior, the rake, and wisdom itself. He is also in his audacious parading of his own mortifications seeking to transcend them. If the audience is not convinced by his clever relativizing of heroic values, they will at least be charmed by his stylish performance. He may be a knave, but he is a knave of the first rate. There is another curious dimension in this process of bearing witness to one's crimes, of addressing an audience so that these crimes might be seen as an act of martyrdom, done in a heroic cause and in the pursuit of wisdom. The speaker in advancing such a case is being utterly facetious, yet wholly serious. The actions of the poem, however, have not taken place. The poem is proleptic: 'So, when my days of Impotence approach' (line 13). The speaker is anticipating and answering a charge before his audience has a chance to do so. In William Empson's words, this is 'pseudo-parody to disarm criticism'.[30] It is truly a performance, and as such less threatening; its case, therefore, is all the more likely to be entertained and accepted by the audience.

One of the manuscripts of *The Disabled Debauchee* bears the title 'The Lord Rochester upoon himselfe' (Walker, p. 203). The poem, like 'To the Post Boy' which it resembles in so many ways, would seem to be one of Rochester's attempts to answer his critics. Burnet tells us 'he would often break forth into such hard Expressions concerning himself, as would be indecent for another to repeat' (Burnet, p. 54). Knowing with La Rochefoucauld that 'Les véritable mortifications sont celles qui ne sont point connues; la vanité rend les autres faciles',[31] he would parade his faults, seek an audience, seek its judgment but ameliorate that judgment through the exercise of his wit. A letter he wrote to Savile, certainly one of the funniest and perhaps most revealing of the extant letters, sheds light on this process of performing one's trespasses in seeking to transcend them. It opens:

> Were I as idle as ever, which I should not fail of being if health permitted, I would write a small romance, and make the sun with his dishevelled rays gild the tops of the palaces in Leather Lane. Then should those vile enchanters Barten and Ginman lead forth their illustrious captives in chains of quicksilver, and confining 'em by charms to the loathsome banks of a dead lake of diet-drink, you, as my friend, should break the horrid silence and speak the most passionate fine things that ever heroic lover uttered, which, being softly and sweetly replied to by Mrs. Roberts, should rudely be interrupted by the envious F—. Thus would I lead the mournful tale along, till the gentle reader bathed with the tribute of his eyes the names of such unfortunate lovers – and this, I take it, would be a most excellent way of celebrating the memories of my most pocky friends, companions and mistresses.

Having received a letter from Savile relating his trials and tribulations while undergoing yet another cure for the pox in a sweatshop in Leather Lane, Rochester replies, turning that luridly real world of seamy sexuality, ghastly infection, and mercury poisoning into a playlet, a heroic romance. 'But it is a miraculous thing', Rochester goes on to write, '(as the wise have it) when a man half in the grave cannot leave off playing the fool and the buffoon' (Treglown, pp. 201–2). There is something indeed miraculous about his 'small romance', being as it is at once unflinchingly accurate in its assessment, yet comic, and quite touching, a transformation of a sordid reality into a celebration of friendship. By playing the fool and buffoon, though in a most witty and wise way, one overcomes the 'grave', or that is at least the hope. Though it irritated him, Sir Carr Scroope showed that he understood ever so well Rochester's aristocratic rhetorical strategy of dramatizing crime as style. In his 'In defence of Satyr' Scroope scathingly depicted Rochester as a man

> Who for the sake of some ill natur'd Jeast,
> Tells what he shou'd conceal, Invents the rest;
> To fatal *Mid-night* quarrels, can betray,
> His brave *Companion*, and then run away;
> Leaving him to be murder'd in the *Street*,
> Then put it off, with some *Buffoone* Conceit;
> (lines 50–55, Love, p. 104)

Scroope probably has 'To the Post Boy' in mind, but *The Disabled Debauchee* is another such '*Buffoone* Conceit', a self-accusation that accepts the judgments made against one while trying to transcend them. Rochester's performances, often the target of satire, would also become part of the standard fare of the Restoration stage. In yet another attempt to bear witness to his life and yet transcend it, he would in turn imitate the playwrights by casting himself in *Lucina's Rape Or The Tragedy of Vallentinian* as the wicked, appetite driven Emperor but also as the virtuous, though tragic, Petronius Maximus.

Notes

1 Maynard Mack, *Collected in Himself: Essays Critical, Biographical, and Bibliographical on Pope and Some of His Contemporaries* (Newark, NJ: University of Delaware Press, 1982), 1, p. 70.
2 The quotation is from John Aubrey's brief life of Rochester: 'Mr Andrew Marvell (who was a good Judge of Witt) was wont to say that he [Rochester] was the best English Satyrist: and had the right veine' (*Brief Lives* (London: Penguin Books, 2000), p. 345).
3 In trying to determine 'the authorship of 'Timon', one encounters, as Vieth points out, 'difficulties'. After examining the case for the poem being by Buckingham or Sedley, Vieth, while not 'pretend[ing] to identify the author of "Timon" with full certainty', concluded that Rochester was probably the

author and 'that "Timon" should be retained in the Rochester canon until new evidence either confirms or disproves his authorship' (Vieth, *Attribution*, pp. 281–95). Citing Vieth, both Lyons (*Complete Poems*, pp. 281–82) and Ellis (*Complete Works*, p. 349) attribute the poem to Rochester. Love places *Timon* among the 'Disputed Works', though as he points out 'Stylistic tests conducted by John Burrows suggest that Rochester is more likely to be the author than Sedley but do not locate it conclusively within the Rochesterian parameters' (Love, p. 482). Burrows himself is 'of the opinion that 'Timon' is primarily Rochester's but that Sedley played a secondary part in its composition' (Love, p. 686). Walker and Fisher place *Timon* in '*Poems Less Securely Attributed to Rochester*', citing Burrows but also Paul Hammond's opinion that Rochester's authorship 'is probable, but not beyond question' (Fisher and Walker, *Poems*, p. 157 and Hammond, ed. *John Wilmot, Earl of Rochester: Selected Poems* (The School of English, University of Leeds, 1982), p. 91). Paul Davis includes *Timon* in his Oxford World's Classics selection, noting that 'in three manuscripts the poem is attributed to R.'s friend and fellow wit Sir Charles Sedley, but it is not within Sedley's ken, as the stylometric analyses of John Burrows confirm. The two copyists who assigned it to R. were almost certainly better informed, but an element of collaboration is possible' (*Rochester: Selected Poems* (Oxford: Oxford University Press, 2013), p. 110).

4 How far to identify, if at all, Timon with Rochester is a vexed issue in Rochester criticism. John Harold Wilson took Timon to be Rochester, writing '"Timon, a Satyr" (*ca.* 1673) is a narrative piece which is almost jovial in tone. Timon (Rochester, of course) is tricked into dining with a bore on the promise of Sedley, Savile and Buckhurst as his companions' (Wilson, *The Court Wits*, p. 130). Pinto, though not explicitly, identifies the one with the other: 'This description ["He takes me to his *Coach*, and as we go"] is certainly a transcript of Rochester's own dearly bought experience' (Pinto, *Enthusiast*, p. 128). Vieth finds 'The identification of Timon with Rochester … at least plausible. Timon's personality resembles Rochester's, and his name as well as his attitudes suggest the misanthropy which was associated with the Earl' (*Attribution*, p. 286). Griffin agreed. While troubled that 'none of these critics has faced the problems raised by the poet's unpleasant characterization of the speaker', Griffin writes that 'Doubtless, as Wilson, Thorpe, and Vieth agree, Timon represents Rochester, or at least embodies "the norm of values by which judgment is passed upon other characters in the poem"' (Griffin, pp. 42–43, quoting Vieth, *Attribution*, p. 286). So, too, David Farley-Hills. 'In *Timon* he is closest to his satiric mouthpiece. Timon, for instance, shares his creator's fondness for debauchery … and the attitudes expressed are seemingly shared by poet and persona' (*The Benevolence in Laughter: Comic Poetry of the Commonwealth and Restoration* (London and Totowa, NJ: Macmillan and Rowan & Littlefield, 1974), p. 161; see also his *Rochester's Poetry* (Totowa, NJ: Rowan & Littlefield, 1978), p. 188). Johnson finds 'The "I" narrative voice and tone of "Timon" are similar to the "I" libertine-rake in "A Ramble", to which in some ways "Timon" appears to be an extension'. He also yokes Timon with Rochester:

'He [the "dull dining *Sot*"] shows Timon a "Libel", wanting to know whether they [*sic*] are his. Timon replies that he might make a "Song to Phillis" (as Rochester had) "for my *Pintle's* sake" ... Timon calls the libel insipid as the praise of virtuous Queens (a hit at Dryden's tributes to Queen Catherine) or Shadwell's lines before Sedley helped him with *Epson Wells*. These details and his libertine sentiments equate the Timon-persona with Rochester' (Johnson, p. 189).

Other critics have found the identification of Timon with Rochester problematic, if not wrong. Thormählen thinks Vieth's 'identification of Timon with Rochester' not all that plausible. For her Timon is a stock figure, one possessing little 'personality;' he resembles 'All his six fellow-diners (including the lady)' in being 'something of a bore himself' (Thormählen, pp. 278 and 283). For Ellis the identification is not even plausible, asserting 'Nor is the speaker Rochester.' He cites Love's argument that '"Rochester, as a peer, would hardly have been seized in the street, addressed in the familiar form of the second person, and dragged off to dinner by a down-at-heel ex-colonel whom he has never met before" (Love, 1972, 161)' (*Complete Works*, p. 349). Paul Hammond captures with great insight the problems one faces in equating Timon with Rochester. Having quoted lines 13–30 of the poem, Hammond writes: 'In this passage Rochester recounts the experience of being accosted by an admirer who has come across an anonymous satire and recognized it as his by its style. Though Rochester denies authorship, the admirer refuses to believe him, and circulates the poem through the town with this erroneous attribution. It is a vivid example of the way poetry circulated in the period, and of the hazards of attribution, especially when a major name like Rochester's is speculatively attached to all manner of verse. Except that this is not Rochester speaking: it is the persona of Timon in a satire modelled on Boileau's adaptation of Horace, and so the voice is both a fictional Restoration voice and one which echoes the complaints of French and Roman poets. All too often editors and critics have assimilated the voice in Rochester's poems to that of the historical John Wilmot, regardless of the games which are played with voice and role right across his oeuvre. Moreover, this poem, though it appears in every twentieth-century edition of his work, may not even have been written by Rochester' (*The Making of Restoration Poetry* (Cambridge: D.S. Brewer, 2006), pp. 190–91).

But in one of the best, recent commentaries on *Timon* Steven Zwicker makes the case that Timon may be Rochester: 'Think of Rochester's *Satyr*. [*Timon*] with its imitations of Boileau and Regnier, its echoes of Horace and Lucian, its allusions to Falkland and Suckling and to Rochester's own intimates – Sedley, Buckhurst, and Savile – and its quotations and misquotations of Restoration theatre – Settle, Orrery, Dryden, and Crowne. The character "Timon" may not be Lord Rochester, but how beguiling to think of Rochester imagining himself trapped by the noisy and vulgar host or squirming with discomfort under the pathetic assault of the host's aging wife, a woman with "more desire, than Pow'r to please"(line 50).' Zwicker goes on to note: 'Rochester is hardly alone in this multivocality, but there is a quickness to this verse that seems Rochester's own,

'Cripples in their Art' 153

even as we remember that Rochester is adapting and imitating other's voices and stories' ('Lord Rochester: A Life in Gossip', pp. 84 and 85).

5 Cf. Treglown. Quoting lines 13–22 and 25–30, he notes: 'It's an effective way in to the story, establishing as it does a reason for what we will find is a special interest of Timon's: good judgment, whether in literature, food and drink, conversation or manners generally. This is the subject of the poem' (p. 77). Treglown goes on to observe, acutely to my mind: 'These are moments – there are scores of them in the poems – when Rochester depends on the reader to recognize a literary reference in order to catch his tone, to feel the full weight of his otherwise unobtrusive irony. This is an elusive kind of art, and to be alert to what he is doing, it is helpful to know his views on tone. For a writer so resistant to theory and so unsystematic in his thinking he is remarkably clear on the subject. There is, as has often been pointed out, his Augustan support of reason and common sense. But this takes a particular form in his scorn for the effortful' ('"He knew my style, he swore"', in *Spirit of Wit: Reconsiderations of Rochester*, ed. Jeremy Treglown (Hamden, CT: Archon Books, 1982), pp. 77 and 79).

6 The authorship of 'Tunbridge Wells', like that of *Timon,* is disputed. Vieth found 'the case for Rochester's authorship of "Tunbridge Wells" ... weaker than is traditionally assumed' (*Attribution*, p. 279). After reviewing the then available evidence, he concluded, however, that 'in the absence of further arguments to the contrary, the six independent ascriptions in early texts – five manuscripts and *Poems on Affairs of State* – support the conclusion that Rochester probably composed "Tunbridge Wells"' (*Attribution*, p. 281). Lyons, Ellis, Love, and Davis include the poem in the canon. Love notes, however, that though 'Solidly attributed to Rochester in the manuscript sources ... yet stylistic tests by John Burrows find it uncharacteristic of Rochester. If another author, or a co-author, were to be sought, it might well be Henry Savile ... ' (Love, p. 373). Davis writes that the poem's '"casual accretive structure" (quoting Walker) led to considerable textual confusion among the surviving manuscript copies, and whilst collaborative authorship is again likely (as with "Of Marriage" and "Timon"), this is a uniquely puzzling case ... ' (*Selected Poems*, p. 119). Walker, too, attributes the poem to Rochester, but notes that 'The poem is texturally very confusing. Its casual accretive structure makes possible, and seems to have led to, several additions by Rochester and others' (Walker, p. 266). In their 'revised and updated version' of the *Poems* Walker and Fisher, however, have moved 'Tunbridge Wells' to the category of 'Poems Less Securely Attributed to Rochester', arguing that 'What weakens this otherwise firm attribution ... is the fact that "computational analyses do not favour Rochester's authorship" (John Burrows and Harold Love, "Attribution Tests and the Editing of Seventeenth-Century Poetry", *The Yearbook of English Studies*, 29 (1999), pp. 151–76 and 161)' (Walker and Fisher, p. 144).

7 For an informed, fine-grained account of the historical context, date, and objects of satire in 'Tunbridge Wells' see Thormählen, pp. 241–65. Her 'study of the historical context of *Tunbridge Wells*' does indeed 'help[] a present-day

reader develop a greater awareness of the ironical dimensions that Rochester's contemporaries recognized and enjoyed' (pp. 264–65).

8 As David Farley-Hills points out, 'It is a commonplace of the criticism of the poem that it suffers from what Ellis calls "a ramshackle structure" ... ' (Farley-Hills, 'Rochester and the theatre in the satires', in *That Second Bottle: Essays on John Wilmot, Earl of Rochester,* ed. Nicholas Fisher (Manchester: Manchester University Press, 2000), p. 161, quoting Ellis, *Complete Works*, p. 341). But as Harold Love observed, 'In "Tunbridge Wells" Rochester is not yet concerned to transcend list structure, but he is using it like a virtuoso. The skill with which narrative and descriptive style are varied from portrait to portrait and the vivid realization of speaker and scene reveal an artist completely in command of the possibilities, albeit restricted, of his elected mode' ('Rochester and the Traditions of Satire', in *Restoration Literature: Critical Approaches* (London: Methuen, 1972), p. 150). Love goes on to write: 'Driven by an almost Gulliverian repugnance from the purge-swilling yahoos of Tunbridge, the claret-drinker flies from the pump to the lower walk, from the lower walk to the upper end, and from the upper end to the heart of the crowd, at each turn encountering a new squadron of fools. Everywhere there is a sense of movement, mirrored and reinforced by the splendidly flexible verse' (pp. 155–56). Thormählen picks up on this insight into the unity of the poem, noting 'the verbs of movement which describe the speaker's involuntary encounters with pretentious fools and hypocrites ... "trotted", "turns his head", "silently slinks", "runs", "evade", "conveys himself", "runs away", and "gets a nearer view".' She also observes that 'The beginning and the ending are not without a certain symmetry. The third line of *Tunbridge Wells*, as well as the third line from the end, refers to the speaker mounting his horse' (Thormählen, p. 241).

9 Anthony Hamilton, *Memoirs of the Count De Gramont* (London: Vizetelly & Co., 1889) 2, p. 39.

10 See '*Scaene 1st. Mr. Daynty's chamber—Enter Daynty in his Night gown singing—*' (Love, pp. 123–24).

11 See John Harold Wilson, 'Rochester, Dryden, and the Rose-Street Affair', *Review of English Studies*, 15 (1939), pp. 294–301, and Vieth, *Attributions*, pp. 156–59.

12 The relationship of the poem to its Horatian model has been illuminatingly explored by Howard D. Weinbrot, 'The "Allusion to Horace": Rochester's Imitative Mode', *Studies in Philology,* 69.3, pp. 348–68; Jos. A. Johnson, Jr., '"An Allusion to Horace": The Poetics of John Wilmot, Earl of Rochester', *The Durham University Journal,* 66, 1 (n.s. 35.1; December 1973), pp. 52–59); Griffin, pp. 246–57; Farley-Hills, *Rochester's Poetry*, pp. 197–204; Pat Rogers, '"An Allusion to Horace"', in *Spirit of Wit*, ed. Jeremy Treglown, pp. 166–76; and Thormählen, pp. 311–19.

13 In a recent, hugely insightful article, Matthew C. Augustine provides a revisionist account of a view long held by literary historians of the relationship of Rochester and Dryden, 'the bourgeois professional versus the gentleman amateur, crowd-pleasing rhymester versus disinterested satirist, Tory flunky versus opposition

maverick' (p. 73). In doing so he calls into question the poem's 'air of assurance and authority' (p. 65). Following Love who 'identified the *Allusion* "as an attempt on behalf of the leading court patrons ... to reassert their waning authority over matters of literary judgment and the making and breaking of reputations"', Augustine finds that the poem 'far from revealing a Rochester who "looks out on a rabble of hacks and critics, confident of his own powers, surrounded by a few like-minded friends, protected by lofty contempt", the *Allusion* is more suggestively read as a brilliant simulacrum of devotion to a rapidly dissipating ideal' (p. 65, quoting Love, 'Shadwell, Rochester and the Crisis of Amateurism', p. 122 and Griffin, p. 257). Augustine is surely right that the relationship between the two poets is much more nuanced than it has been taken to be, one of 'dialogue and mutual adjustment rather than one of opposition and distinction' (p. 60). I will be exploring that relationship in the following chapter. Augustine's reading that Dryden's praise of Rochester has ironic undertones, that the speaker in '*An Allusion*' may be aware that he shares faults of writers he criticizes, notably that his 'literary identity too was conditioned by dependency' (p. 74), and that the speaker here, as so often in Rochester's poetry, is a satirist satirized, are powerfully suggestive. My point about the 'assured' tone of 'An Allusion' – and the tone is assured – is that it is Rochester's quest, one of many, qualified or not, to find a satiric norm. See Matthew C. Augustine, 'Trading Places: Lord Rochester, the Laureate and the Making of Literary Reputation', in *Lord Rochester in the Restoration World*, eds Matthew C. Augustine and Steven N. Zwicker (Cambridge University Press, 2015), pp. 58–78.

14 'John Wilmot, Earl of Rochester', *Proceedings of the British Academy*, 13 (1967), p. 51.
15 Tom Lockwood, 'Rochester and Rhyme', in *Lord Rochester in the Restoration World*, eds Matthew C. Augustine and Steven N. Zwicker (Cambridge University Press, 2015), p. 274. Lockwood's entire discussion of rhyme in 'An Allusion' is excellent and relevant to understanding Rochester's tone (pp. 274–76).
16 Lucretius, *On Nature*, trans. by Russel M. Geer (New York: Bobbs-Merrill, 1965), p. 40.
17 For the uses that dramatists of the 1670s – notably John Crowne in *Calisto*, Thomas Shadwell in *The Libertine* and *Timon*, and Rochester himself in *Valentinian* – made of the 'Satyre's' libertine arguments, see Brean Hammond and Paulinea Kewes, '*A Satyre against Reason and Mankind* from page to stage', in *That Second Bottle: Essays on John Wilmot, Earl of Rochester*, ed. Nicholas Fisher (Manchester: Manchester University Press, 2000), pp. 133–52.
18 For an understanding of the social, political, religious, and philosophical contexts of 'A Satyre', the works of Griffin (pp. 156–241), Thormählen (pp. 162–239), and more recently of Christopher Tilmouth (*Passion's Triumph*, pp. 345–60) are essential reading.
19 Thomas Hobbes, *Leviathan* (London: Andrew Crooke, 1651), Part I, pp. 21–22.
20 David Veith, 'Toward an Anti-Aristotelian Poetic: Rochester's *Satyr Against Mankind* and *Artemisia to Chloe*, with Notes on Swift's *Tale of a Tub* and *Gulliver's Travels*', *Language and Style*, 5 (1972), p. 127.

21 Bror Danielson and David M. Vieth, eds, *The Gyldenstolpe Manuscript Miscellany of Poems by John Wilmot, Earl of Rochester, and Other Restoration Authors,* Stockholm Studies in English 17 (Stockholm: Almqvist & Wiksell, 1967), p. 321.
22 Hammond, *Selected Poems,* p. xi. See also Paul Hammond, 'The dating of three poems by Rochester from the evidence of Bodleian MS. Don. B. 8', *Bodleian Library Record,* 11 (1982), pp. 58–59.
23 Nicholas Fisher, 'A New Dating of Rochester's *Artemiza to Chlöe*', *English Manuscript Studies 1100–1700,* 8 (2000), p. 304.
24 Kenneth Burke, *Grammar of Motives,* p. 251. Thormählen usefully canvases the scholarship on the poem, quarrelling with much of it (pp. 104–18), before going on to explore 'Wit, Folly And Sexual Politics In *Artemiza to Chloe*' (pp. 118–29), 'Woman Scholar And Woman Poet' (pp. 129–35), and '*Artemiza To Chloe* As A Reflection Of Its Time' (pp. 135–40).
25 Erich Auerbach, *Mimesis: The Representation of Reality in Western Literature,* trans. Willard Trask (New York: Doubleday Anchor Books, 1957), p. 343. The entire passage is relevant: 'It seemed the highest mission of the art of literature to render a pure expression of the eternally human. And it was thought that the eternally human appeared clearer and less contaminated on isolated heights of life than in the base and confused turmoil of history. But this at the same time implied a restriction within the concept of the eternally human: only the "great" passions remained as possible subjects, and love too could be represented only in those forms which were in keeping with the contemporary concepts of the highest seemliness.'
26 As Love points out, 'Fiddlers were the human juke-boxes of the time, called into homes and taverns to provide entertainment but often the victims of drunken violence' (Love, p. 397). See also Ashley Chantlet, 'The Meaning of "Scotch Fiddle" in Rochester's "Tunbridge Wells"', *Restoration,* 26 (2) (2002), pp. 81–84.
27 Dale Underwood, *Etherege and the Seventeenth-Century Comedy of Manners* (New Haven, CT: Yale University Press, 1957; rpt. Archon Books, 1969), p. 24.
28 Denis Diderot, *Le Neveu De Rameau,* in *Diderot Oeuvres* (Paris, Éditions Gallimard: 1951), p. 446. The entire passage is relevant: 'On crache sur un petit filou, mais on ne peut refuser une sorte de consideration à un grand criminel. Son courage vous étonne; son atrocité vous fait frémir. On prise en tout l'unité de caractère.'
29 Francois, Duc de La Rochefoucauld, *Oeuvres complètes* (Paris: Éditions Gallimard, 1964), p. 415.
30 William Empson, *Some Versions of Pastoral* (New York: New Directions, 1968), p. 57.
31 La Rochefoucauld, *Oeuvres,* p. 62.

5

'Wise about my owne follyes': *Lucina's Rape Or The Tragedy of Vallentinian*

'Tis not an easy thing to bee intirely happy, But to bee kind is very easy and that is the greatest measure of happiness; I say nott this to putt you in mind of being kind to mee, you have practis'd that soe long that I have a joyfull confidence you will never forgett itt, but to show that I myself have a sence of what the methods of my Life seeme soe utterly to contradict, I must not be too wise about my owne follyes, or els this Letter had bin a booke dedicated to you & publish'd to the world ....

Rochester to his wife

... if there bee a reall good upon Earth 'tis in the Name of freind, without wch all others are meerly fantasticall, how few of us are fitt stuff to make that thing, wee have dayly the melancholy experience ....

Rochester to Savile

A true friend and a tender faithfull Wife,
The two blest miracles of humane Life.

Maximus in *Lucina's Rape*

In his Preface to the 1685 quarto Robert Wolseley tells us that '*my late Lord Rochester intended to have alter'd and corrected this Play much more than it is, before it had come abroad*' (A2r). Though left unfinished, this adaptation in the judgment of Vivian de Sola Pinto 'is certainly one of' Rochester's 'most interesting and revealing works' (Pinto, *Enthusiast*, p. 159). The play would hold great interest if only for the fact that it adds some 1,300 lines to the Rochester canon. But there is more. Dramatically, it helps to shed light on the workings of the Mulgrave and Rochester factions in the mid-1670s and is in itself a contribution to the 'political tragedies' of the late 1670s and early 1680s. Historically, it rehearses the political stance of the emerging Country Party, and biographically, the play corroborates and adds to the evidence we have concerning what Vieth has called that 'subtle yet definite change in the direction' of Rochester's life that occurred during the spring of 1676 (Vieth, *Attribution*, p. 177).[1]

The impetus for Rochester's undertaking *Lucina's Rape* seems to have been his rivalry with Dryden, a rivalry that probably dates from Dryden's essay 'A Defence of an Essay of Dramatique Poesie', published in the second edition of *The Indian Emperour* in 1668.² Dryden was defending 'Of Dramatique Poesie' from an attack made on it by Sir Robert Howard, his brother-in-law, in the Preface to *The Great Favourite, or the Duke of Lerma* published in the summer of 1668. Howard criticized, among other things, Dryden's use of rhyme and his penchant for trying to find rules for writing. The gentleman relied on an argument from 'taste'. The middle-class professional defended himself more than ably with an argument based on rules and reason. Dryden's skilful use of evidence, his deferential tone barely masking laughter, and his telling criticism of Howard's ignorance of classical languages must have stung.³ Howard, increasingly involved in affairs of state, never replied, at least not in public. But some three years later, following Dryden's triumph with *The Conquest of Granada* late in 1671 and early in 1672, Howard apparently began a collaboration with Rochester (they may have brought in Settle sometime later) to write a heroic play based on the recently published *History of China* (1671) by Father Palafox. Evidently the gentlemen set out to show the middle-class upstart how it was to be done. Rochester completed 'A Scaen of Sir Robert Hoard's Play' and that is as far as the project went until it was turned over completely to Settle who in 1675 came out with *The Conquest of China* (28 May 1675).⁴

Whether the 'Defence of the Epilogue. Or, An Essay on the Dramatic Poetry of the last Age', which Dryden appended to *The Conquest of Granada* in 1672, further fuelled Howard's interest in putting his brother-in-law in his place, we do not know. This essay did repeat, even less deferentially, some of the arguments Dryden had made earlier in 'A Defence of an Essay of Dramatique Poesie'. We do know, however, that it caught Rochester's attention. In *Timon* (1674) he mocked (lines 147–50) the opening lines of *The Indian Emperour*, whose publication had been Dryden's vehicle for his first attack on Howard.

'Defence of the Epilogue' may also have contributed to Rochester's decision to work on a play by Fletcher. In his essay Dryden had done two things potentially irritating to Rochester.⁵ He took Fletcher to task for the 'redundancy of his matter', 'the incorrectness of his language' (Dryden, vol. 11, p. 217), his lack of characterization, and his faulty use of syntax – all errors Rochester saw in Dryden's own work and would later catalogue in 'An Allusion to Horace'. Then Dryden added another sin to what Rochester and others saw as hypocrisy by citing Buckingham's adaptation of Fletcher's *The Chances* as an example in which Fletcher had been greatly improved, something Dryden says 'I may affirm, without suspition of flattery'. '*Don John*', he goes on to observe, now 'speaks better and that his Character is maintain'd with much more vigour in the fourth and fifth Acts than it was by Fletcher in the three former' (Dryden, vol. 11, p. 215). Rochester probably had no objection to the content of this; the unctuous tone, however, was a different matter.

Dryden had been trying to enter into the court circle since 1666 and the essay *Of Dramatic Poesie*, attempting as Rochester later put it, 'to be a tearing Blade' ('An Allusion to Horace', line 72). By 1668 he had made some progress; he had become poet laureate and was soon to dedicate plays to the dukes of York and Monmouth. By 1673 he was in a position to banter with the most glittering of the court set, dedicating *Marriage à la Mode* to Rochester, writing to the Earl with patronizing in-jokes about Buckingham (see Treglown, p. 88), and dedicating *The Assignation* to Sedley (1672).[6] To be sure, Dryden knew he did not belong to this set, and his rhetoric is dutifully deferent. Once Rochester and Dryden had fallen out, however, the Earl likely overlooked any attempts at ingratiation or, worse, saw them as sycophantic. In the spring of 1676 Rochester observed, with aristocratic hauteur, that he was fond of Dryden 'whom I have ever admired for the disproportion of him and his attributes. He is a rarity which I cannot but be fond of, as one would be of a hog that could fiddle, or a singing owl' (Treglown, pp. 119–20). The growing animosity between the two, Dryden's criticism of Fletcher, and the precedent set by Buckingham's *The Chances* made it all the more likely that Rochester would choose a work by Fletcher for adaptation.

The choice also reflected Rochester's involvement in the battle of the theatres going on in the mid-1670s, a battle inextricably bound up with his quarrel with Dryden. As Vieth has pointed out, 'literary London' was divided 'during the mid 1670s into two broad factions, one led by Rochester and the other by Dryden' (Vieth, *Attribution*, p. 138). In part theirs was a battle of the books. 'When *Shakespeare, Jonson, Fletcher*, rul'd the Stage', begins Sir Carr Scroope in his 'In defence of Satyr' (Love, p. 102). Each of these father figures had his faithful sons, Shadwell being loyal to Jonson, Buckingham and Rochester siding with Fletcher, and Dryden, when not pointing out the virtues and faults of all three, standing up for Shakespeare. Between 1674 and 1679 Dryden adapted *Antony and Cleopatra* and *Troilus*. His version of *The Tempest*, originally done with Davenant, had a revival in 1674, this time with Shadwell's collaboration. The year 1677 saw Shadwell's *Timon* (dedicated to Buckingham and containing a glancing blow at Dryden). Early in 1677, Sedley came out with his version of *Antony and Cleopatra* (12 February 1677), a play designed to compete with Dryden's, which did not see the stage until 12 December of that year. Clearly there was some competition going on to bring out adaptations of

Shakespeare. There may also have been competition between Rochester and Dryden over bringing out an adaptation of Shakespeare versus one of Fletcher.

The Preface to *All for Love* published in 1678 has rightly been seen in the context of Dryden's response to 'An Allusion to Horace' and possibly to 'A Session of the Poets' ('Since the sons of the Muses grow num'rous and loud') and 'Advice to Apollo' ('I've heard the Muses were still soft and kind').[7] It also shows, I believe, Dryden's awareness that Rochester had been working on *Lucina's Rape*. Dryden had from time to time seen Rochester's work; he refers to Rochester's translation of Lucretius in the letter of 1673. In the 'Preface' he tags Rochester as 'this Legitimate Son of *Sternhold*' (Dryden, vol. 13, p. 17). Thomas Sternhold had become proverbial for bad poetry, but it is possible that Dryden had also heard or read Rochester's distich, 'Sternhold and Hopkins had such qualms/ When they translated Davids Psalms.'[8] Furthermore, this sentence from the Preface, 'there are many witty men, but few Poets; neither have all Poets a taste of Tragedy' (p. 14), would seem to refer directly to Rochester and *Lucina's Rape*.

Dryden, working with the King's men, would probably have known of Rochester's project (Fletcher's play had been assigned to this company in 1669). At the end of the Preface, moreover, Dryden, in defending Shakespeare, states that 'The occasion is fair, and the subject would be pleasant to handle the difference of Stiles betwixt him [Shakespeare] and *Fletcher*, and wherein, and how far they are both to be imitated' (p. 18). The sentence is rather gratuitous; Dryden had been discussing his style in imitating Shakespeare and Shakespeare's native genius. The comparison to Fletcher may have come to mind because the words he applies to Shakespeare had been conventionally applied to Fletcher. But the sentence has quite a different meaning if taken to be one last fillip to Rochester in a preface designed to denigrate the Earl. Rightly, Dryden sensed his own superiority: if one were to compare his work with Rochester's, one could discern easily enough who had the better product. Dryden, however, knew not to press his advantage, or at least he knew how to make it look as though he were pulling his punches while knocking his opponent flat. He follows, therefore, with this sentence: 'But since I must not be over-confident of my own performance after him, it will be prudence in me to be silent' (p. 18). 'Him' is first of all Shakespeare, but the 'him' is probably Rochester as well. In a preface which had classified Rochester among the 'flatterers after the third Bottle' and the 'little *Zanies*' (pp. 14 and 16), Dryden was hardly being prudent or silent, and his self-effacing rhetoric says as much while proclaiming the opposite. Rochester, who knew that 'A jest in scorn points out and hitts the thing/ More home than the morosest Satyrs sting' ('An Allusion to Horace', lines 28–29), would not have missed the hit.

The evidence for a rivalry going on between Rochester and Dryden, one that led in part to Rochester writing *Lucina's Rape*, though admittedly circumstantial, becomes, when put into context, rather telling. Rochester probably began work on *Lucina's Rape* early in 1675. The cast given in the manuscripts suggests that it was intended for the 1675–76, possibly the 1676–77, season. It apparently did not play then, and Rochester may have continued to work on it until late in 1677. This period marked Rochester's triumph in the world of the theatre. He served as patron, arbiter of taste, and finally as the subject of the plays themselves. Lee dedicated *Nero* and Fane *Love in the Dark* to Rochester in 1675; Otway followed with the dedication to *Titus and Berenice* in 1677. Rochester recommended Otway's *Don Carlos* to the King in 1676 and in his 'Epilogue' to *Love in the Dark* ridiculed the dramatic extravaganzas put on by the Duke's House and those attending them. Wycherley's Horner (January 1675), Shadwell's Don John (June 1675), and Otway's Alcibiades (September 1675) all imitate characteristics of Rochester. In March 1676, as Vieth has felicitously put it, came 'Rochester's apotheosis as the half-angelic, half-diabolical Dorimant' (Vieth, *Attribution*, p. 177).

During this period, Rochester also had Dryden on his mind. He tarred him in 'An Allusion to Horace', and it is in this poem that Rochester refers to Dryden's criticism of Fletcher in the 'Defence of the Epilogue' ('But does not Dryden finde even Johnson dull/ Fletcher and Beaumont uncorrect, and full/ Of Lewd lines (as he calls 'em)', lines 81–84). He based the poem, moreover, on Horace's Satire l. 10, ironically reversing the use that Dryden had made of Horace in his essay. Rochester may also have been instrumental in having Crowne, instead of the poet laureate, commissioned to write a masque for the Court, *Calisto* being first given 15 February 1674/75.[9] Other events exacerbated the relationship between the two. Dryden dedicated *Aureng-Zebe* (pub. February 1675–76) to Rochester's inveterate enemy, Sheffield, Earl of Mulgrave. This dedication obliquely, but bitterly criticized Rochester; Rochester, in turn, jestingly referred to it in 'An Allusion to Horace' ('What foolish Patron is there found of his/ So blindly partial to deny me this?', lines 3–4) and made it the subject of his 'An Epistolary Essay, from M.G. to O.B. upon their mutuall Poems'. Given Rochester's engagement with the stage and his quarrel with Dryden, it seems probable that he would have undertaken a play and would have done so with Dryden in mind.[10] If I am right, 'An Allusion to Horace' was Rochester's manifesto on heroic drama, *Lucina's Rape* was intended to be the exemplary play itself, and the audience for both was in part 'Poet Squobb' ('An Allusion to Horace', line 76).[11]

Rochester's revisions – Sprague called them 'sweeping changes' and Love writes of them as 'radical' – suggest such was the case.[12] The Earl turned playwright eliminated Act V of the original; cut three scenes, III. ii. and iii. and IV. ii.; added two of his own, V. i. and v.; added 245 lines to I. i., 75 lines to II. i., 77 lines to III. ii., and 219 lines to III. iii.; and substantially rewrote IV. i. and ii. and V. ii. He sought to unify the plot further by cutting the role of Eudoxia, the Emperor's wife, the parts of Afranius, Paulus, and Licippus and the tangentially related machinations of these three. With an eye to satire, Rochester enhanced the part of the eunuch, Lycias, and emphasized the seamy side of court intrigue. In addition, he gave Vallentinian and Maximus considerable psychological depth. Maximus is no longer the flat Machiavellian villain, but a patriot tormented by conflicting loyalties and metaphysical questions. Evidently meant to be a satirical portrait of Charles II, Vallentinian becomes a complex study of duty at war with lust.

Others have made the point that Rochester moved Fletcher's Jacobean mélange of rant, poisonings, and rape in the direction of neo-classical unity.[13] Let me add that in the 'Defence of the Epilogue' Dryden draws upon exactly these principles of neo-classical decorum to criticize Fletcher. 'Let us imitate', Dryden wrote,

> the quickness and easiness of *Fletcher*, without proposing him as a pattern to us, either in the redundancy of his matter, or the incorrectness of his language. Let us admire his wit and sharpness of conceit; but, let us at the same time acknowledge that it was seldome so fix'd, and made proper to his characters, as that the same things might not be spoken by any person in the Play.

Dryden also taxed Fletcher with not understanding 'correct Plotting'. Fletcher, that is, possessed wit, but lacked '*the Decorum of the Stage*' in language (Dryden cited his 'Luxuriance'), character, and plot (Dryden, vol. 11, pp. 217 and 206).

In 'An Allusion to Horace' Rochester repeated this criticism, only he applied it to Dryden without crediting the Poet Laureate for wit or ease. The first is 'embroyder'd' (line 5), that is, ornamental, artificial, the second suitable only as the subject of scatological joking. Dryden's 'masse' 'stuffs up his loose Volumns' and 'must not pass' (lines 8–9). Such 'masse' is owing to his 'loose slattern Muse' who inspires him to 'Five hundred Verses every morning writt' which 'Proves you no more a Poet than a Witt' (lines 92–94). Another rhyme comes to mind and was meant to; Dryden produces both in the morning and they resemble one another. Clearly Dryden's work lacks decorum. But perhaps the more damning criticism Rochester makes of Dryden (and of several others) is the failure to unite 'Your Rhetorique with your Poetry' (line 25). Dryden's plays, that is, lack the art and elegance that would allow them to communicate effectively. Empty in content, they are also inept in presentation. In adapting *The Tragedie of Valentinian* Rochester focused on precisely the faults Dryden had cited in Fletcher with the aim of exposing Dryden's hypocrisy and of providing him with an example of the way a heroic play should be written, ironically employing Fletcher to do so.[14]

Rochester perhaps succeeded all too well in making his play an effective piece of rhetoric. Although we do not know why *Lucina's Rape* never played during the seasons for which it seems to have been intended, we can imagine that Rochester himself, already in trouble with the Court, would not have wanted this thinly disguised satire on the boards.[15] John Harold Wilson has glossed much of the play's satire, making the convincing case that the Emperor is intended to be a satire on Charles II by showing that Rochester in Act I changed Fletcher's harsh, militant tyrant to reflect the more lenient, easy-going character of Charles II. But the play's satire on the King and his politics has dimensions that Wilson did not explore.

The play attacks, as Wilson points out, the King's physical pleasures, but it also reserves abundant salt for his political 'pleasures', that is, the King's prerogative, a widely debated topic throughout the 1670s. When the Emperor tells Lucina that her 'husbands right' to her belongs to him 'Who justly may recall my owne at pleasure' (I. i., lines 218 and 220), he is using 'pleasure' to assert a political right. 'Impunity is the highest Tyranny' (I. i., line 104) is Maximus's mocking summation of the royalist claim that the King is above the law. The Emperor has also violated his divinely given charge. Throughout the play, the exemplary characters – Maximus, Pontius, Aecius, and Lucina – evoke the past, the time of heroic fathers, to condemn the present. Maximus asks:

> And to what End are wee the sonnes of Fathers
> Famous and fast to Rome? why are their vertues
> Stampt in the dangers of a thousand Battails
> For goodness sake, their honours time out daring
> (I thinke for our Example)
> (I. i. 80–84, Fletcher's lines)

Pontius echoes these sentiments, complaining that Rome has forgotten 'with what Winde their feathers sayl'd/ And under whose protection their soft Pleasures/ Grow full and numberless' (V. iv., lines 203–5, Fletcher's lines). Lucina chastises the court ladies for having forgotten the nobility of their 'Fathers', 'Mothers', and 'Ancesters' (II. i., lines 49–50 and 52). The charge against the Emperor and his court is impiety, the Emperor having become a bad father. Divine right, whose spokesman in the play is Aecius, was a sensitive issue in the 1670s, perhaps more so than in 1614, and patriarchalism with its evocation of the *pater patria* and its derivation of legitimate political power from that granted to Adam by God and passed down through inheritance was one of the principal arguments used by royalists to support the King's authority.[16] Here an argument traditionally made to support the King is simply turned against him.

The play advances, in no systematic way, other 'Country Party' criticisms of Charles II. At one point, Maximus compares the Emperor unfavourably to 'our severer, warlike Emperours' (I. i., line 96), perhaps a reference to Cromwell.[17] In III. i., lines 32–41, Rochester introduced a rebellion of the army; the Emperor's solution is to buy off soldiers. The issue of the standing army and of Danby's briberies may be the targets here. In V. v., lines 82–87 the Emperor in an act of self-castigation laments over the dead Aecius:

> Ah what a Lamentable Wretch is hee
> Who urg'd by feare or sloth yields up his pow'r
> To hope protection from his favourite,
> Wallowing in Ease, and Vice, feels noe contempt
> But weares the empty name of Prince with scorne
> And lives a poore Led Pageant to his Slave?

As Love writes:

> It would have been impossible in the mid-1670s not to recognize these lines as a critique of Charles's dependence on his then chief minister, Thomas Osborne, Earl of Danby. This had led the king to support a policy, in which he did not himself believe, of enforced conformity to the Church of England. Rochester writes as a supporter of Buckingham's campaign to secure greater accommodation within the Church for Dissenters, a price that Charles had earlier been prepared to pay in order to advance his own project of removing penal sanctions against Catholics. (Love, pp. 471–72)

Rochester had begun to take a genuine interest in Parliament in 1676–77.[18] His friend Buckingham had already gone over to the opposition. Evidence from the play and from the life suggests a Rochester leaning toward the 'Country Party'. The evidence does not indicate that he embraced 'classical republicanism', but the play's political satire evokes some of the common arguments of the republican opposition, arguments that have their culmination in the story Rochester chose to adapt.[19]

Between 1675 and 1677 Rochester had begun to read Livy, writing to Savile that 'Livy and sickness has a little inclined me to policy' (Treglown, p. 117). Livy attributes the end of monarchical government and the rise of the republic to the corruption of tyrannical kings, a corruption culminating in the rape of Lucrece by Sextus Tarquinius. The reign of kings, always a foreign growth to the classical republicans, ends with this rape and the expulsion of Tarquinius Superbus. Balbus, Lycinus, and Lucina herself point to the parallels – Tarquin and the Emperor, Lucrece and Lucina – in their equation uniting the office of the father and the crime of the son

(II. ii., lines 87–93; IV. ii., lines 195–96; and IV. iv., line 60). In his final confrontation with the Emperor, Maximus too makes the comparison, asking: 'Why was the Lustfull Tarquin with his house/ Expell'd; but for the Rape of Bleeding Lucrece?' (V. v., lines 159–60).[20] He goes on to declare that his motives for revenge are greater than Brutus's, for Lucina was his wife.

These parallels suggest that the death of Tarquin/Vallentinian will lead to a new political order. Valentinian was the last Roman emperor of the family of Theodosius, and c.1677 there was every possibility that Charles II would be the last king of the house of Stuart. Rochester never fully explores these political implications.[21] The play does end with the death of Tarquin/Emperor, with Maximus being cast as a new Brutus, but it does not conclude triumphantly as the political theme indicates it might. It ends sadly, not on a public but a private note. It does so because the play, while being political satire, is also a dialogue that Rochester was having with himself about himself.

Biographical criticism, always a precarious enterprise, is never more so than when it addresses the drama. Wellek and Warren have made the point succinctly: 'One cannot, from fictional statements, especially those made in plays, draw any valid inference as to the biography of a writer.' Harriet Hawkins, moreover, has repeatedly admonished critics of seventeenth-century drama and poetry for taking the conventional and making it mean whatever they want it to mean.[22] Wellek and Warren, having pointed out the pitfalls of using biography to illuminate literature and vice versa, conclude, however, that

> Still, there are connecting links, parallelisms, oblique resemblances, topsy-turvy mirrors. The poet's work may be a mask, a dramatized conventionalization, but it is frequently a conventionalization of his own experiences, his own life. If used with a sense of these distinctions, there is use in biographical study. First, no doubt, it has exegetical value: it may explain a great many allusions or even words in an author's work. The biographical framework will also help us in studying the most obvious of all strictly developmental problems in the history of literature – the growth, maturing, and possible decline of an author's art.[23]

Lucina's Rape does indeed contain 'connecting links, parallelisms, oblique resemblances, topsy-turvy mirrors' of Rochester's life. These connections do not make *Lucina's Rape* a better work – more unified, more moving, or whatever – but they do allow us to account for changes Rochester made in the play which would remain inexplicable if we were to rely only on arguments from formalistic standards such as the generic demands of the heroic drama or of satire. These parallels between life and work also shed light on Rochester's 'growth, maturing, and ... decline' as a poet.[24]

To begin with there is the remarkable fact that Lucina is, as Germaine Greer points out, 'lured to a court that Rochester has transformed with a few deft touches into Whitehall' (Greer, p. 59), a transformation that Love has cleverly laid out and explored in 'Was Lucina betrayed at Whitehall?' As Love explains, the play tells us about

> the Emperor's 'closet' (II. ii. 176), 'the garden gate' (II. ii. 173), the 'Councell dore' (III. iii. 127); 'the old hall' (IV. ii. 190), the 'great Chamber' (IV. ii. 4), the 'Lobby' (IV. ii. 18) and a staircase leading to the royal apartments (IV. ii. 78). There are galleries, both public and private, and an 'Appartment ... that lies upon the Garden' (III. ii. 523) that is so close to the public gallery that a crime committed in it might be overheard there. All of these locations had counterparts at Whitehall.

When the Emperor orders Proculus to 'see the Appartment made very fine/ That lies upon the Garden' (III. ii., lines 52–53), 'we are being told not about an imaginary palace in fifth-century Rome but about a very specific palace in England. The rape of Lucina is to take place in Rochester's own bedroom.'[25] That Elizabeth Barry played Lucina in the 1684 United Company's production may have given those in the know a certain frisson. Love notes that 'Barry, who created the part for the United Company, may well have been in Rochester's mind at the time of writing, since she was, or shortly became his mistress, and in December 1677 gave birth to a daughter by him. He had personally trained her for her career after her initial failure' (Love, p. 451). It gives a twenty-first-century critic shivers to speculate with Love that Rochester may have worked on the play in that very apartment.

Maximus, moreover, speaks for Rochester through most of the play, perhaps nowhere more so than in his final speech when he affirms that 'A true friend and a tender faithfull Wife' are 'The two blest miracles of humane Life' (V. v., lines 259–60). Expressions of love for his wife and of the value of friendship can be found throughout his letters, but by 1675–77, the probable time of his working on *Lucina's Rape*, he needed to affirm these values all the more. He had just emerged from perhaps the most productive and triumphant period of his life. The years 1674–76 witnessed the writing of his finest work, 'A Satyre against Reason and Mankind', 'An Allusion to Horace', and probably *The Disabled Debauchee* and 'A Letter from Artemiza in the Towne to Chloe in the Countrey'. He was also enjoying, as we have seen, his power and notoriety in the world of the theatre.

This period, however, culminated in three sobering disasters. On 25 June 1675, he and a group of fellow rakes destroyed the King's Sun Dial in the Privy Garden at Whitehall, a particularly symbolic action given that the 'Sun Dial featured glass portraits of King Charles, Queen

Catherine, the Duke of York, the Queen Mother, and Prince Rupert. In smashing the images of the Stuarts physically, Rochester was translating into action on one occasion the iconoclasm he had verbally expressed on others' (Johnson, p. 220). Later that summer, he offended the Duchess of Portsmouth and was banished from Court, one result of this contretemps being the instigation of an action, probably by the King himself, which led to Rochester's loss of the 'reversion' of Woodstock Park. Then in June 1676 he participated in the ruckus that led to the death of Mr Downs at Epsom. Throughout this period, moreover, Rochester experienced periodic bouts of prolonged illness. As early as 1673, the youthful Earl's earlier decisions to sacrifice principle, health, friendship, love – indeed everything but money – for Charles Stuart's 'pleasures' already had begun to show their tragic consequences. By the winter of 1676 Rochester fully understood these consequences, and like Maximus, could cry out:

> Tis then a certaine truth that I am wrong'd,
> Wrong'd in that Barberous manner as I imagin'd:
> Alas I was in hopes I had been mad –
> And that these horrours which invade my heart
> Were but distracted, Melancholly Whimseys
> But they are reall truths (it seems) and I
> The last of men, and vilest of all beings!
> ...
> Wrong'd by my Lawfull Prince, rob'd of my Love,
> Branded with everlasting infamy:
>   (IV. iv., lines 289–95 and 298–99)[26]

During this season of tribulations, Rochester was feeling more than ever wronged by his prince. He wrote to Savile, for example, concerning the loss of the 'reversion' that 'The King, who knows me to be a very ill-natured man, will not think it an easy matter for me to die now I live chiefly out of spite' (Treglown, p. 114). Although Charles certainly did not in any sense rob Rochester of his love, Rochester's service to King and Court had been a constant source of irritation between the Earl and his wife, and by 1676 the syphilitic consequences of that service had been communicated to Elizabeth and to their son. Rochester was, in more ways than one, feeling the heat of his infamous acts.

Religion provided neither Maximus nor Rochester much comfort, Maximus's conclusions on this subject resembling closely what Rochester was to tell Burnet. In IV. iv. Maximus *'falls to the ground'* and cries out:

> Supreme first causes! You whence althings flow,
> Whose Infiniteness must each title fill,
> You who decree each seeming chance below

(Soe great in power) were you soe good in will
How cou'd you ever have produce'd such ill?

Had your eternall mindes been bent to good,
Cou'd humane happiness have prov'd so Lame?
Rapine, Revenge, Injustice, thirst of Bloud
Griefe, Anguish, Horrour, want, despair, nor shame
Had never found a being nor a name.

'Tis therefore less Impiety to say,
Evill with you has Coeternity!
Than Blindly taking it the tother way,
That Mercyfull, and of Election free,
You did Create these Mischiefes you decree.
(lines 306–20)

A few years later, Burnet was to tell us that when Rochester 'explained his Notion of this Being [God], it amounted to no more than a vast power, that had none of the Attributes of Goodness or Justice we ascribe to the Deity' (Burnet, p. 53).[27] Rochester's works of the previous two years afforded little solace either. They had questioned the possibility of man being anything more than a Hobbesian compound of self-interest and fear. *Lucina's Rape* reflects his attempt to move beyond the attitudes taken in these satires. In it he cast himself in a role he would have liked to have played, meditated on and finally condemned his life of the past ten years, and affirmed the three values central to his life: married love, friendship, and, in the crafting of the play, art itself.

The Restoration Petronius took the historical Petronius Maximus, stripped away his ambition and seamy machinations, and moulded him into a model husband, citizen, and warrior. At the same time as he presented an idealized conception of himself, Rochester gave a realistic assessment of his predicament. Rochester, like Maximus, was a servant at Court. There he made his living, and he could not leave it any more than could Maximus, though both longed to do so and though both paid a high price for remaining.

If for Rochester/Maximus the Court is 'Hell', the home of 'the Devill' who 'entred into him, and never left him till he came to Alderbury or Woodstock again',[28] so the country house of Lucina represents that feminine, pastoral ideal Rochester dreamed of and occasionally realized with his wife and family at Adderbury. Lucina is an idealized portrait of Elizabeth. She withstands the temptations of the flesh and of worldly gain; she provides evidence that virtues are not masks for the appetites. Lucina, moreover, resides in the country, a setting of 'Deare sollitary Groves where Peace does dwell/ Sweet Harbours of pure Love and Innocence' (III. i., lines 1–2). A master of the mock-pastoral, Rochester nevertheless longed for the tranquility the country afforded him and the values it represented. He writes to Savile:

> Deare Harry let us not give out nor despaire of bringing that [friendship] about wch as it is the most difficult & rare accident of life, is allsoe the Best, nay perhaps the only good one; this thought has soe intirely possest mee since I came into the Country (where only one can think, for you att Court thinke not att all or att least as if you were shutt up in a Drumme, you can thinke of nothing but the noise is made about you). (Treglown, p. 93)

Act III. i. written entirely by Rochester, evokes the pastoral with no ironic qualifications.[29] It is in this scene, moreover, that Lucina says she will 'fondly' chide Maximus,

> make his heart confesse
> How far my busy idleness excels
> The idle business Hee pursues all day
> At the contentious Court or clamorous Camp ...
>   (III. i., lines 14–17)

Elizabeth chided Rochester, often not so fondly, for his prolonged stays at Court and at Woodstock.

Vallentinian is the snake in this garden, the play being an enactment of the Oedipal drama Rochester found himself caught up in with Charles II. The Emperor is for Maximus, as Charles was for Rochester, a 'mangled Figure of a Ruin'd Greatness!' (V. v., line 113). The play heaps opprobrium upon the hated father, finally kills him off, though Rochester carefully does not place responsibility for the Emperor's death on the surrogate son. That the Oedipal wish to kill the father was much on Rochester's mind is evidenced by a speech he gives to Vallentinian, who, after killing Aecius, grieves 'for Aecius, yes, I mourn him Gods/ As if I'd met my Father in the dark/ And striving for the way had murder'd him' (V. v., lines 217–19). The speech is not inappropriate. Aecius, the old, faithful warrior, represents the world of the fathers, a world of promises kept, of faith maintained. Rochester gives him this speech at the beginning of Act V:

> As well might I kill my offended Friend
> As thinke to punish my offending Prince.
> The Laws of Frindship we our selves create
> And tis but Simple Villany to break 'em;
> But faith to Princes broke is Sacriledge,
>   (V. i., lines 4–8)

The Emperor, a Hobbesian man, has destroyed this world of trust; he has 'murdered' the father. But it is as though a speech expressing the wishes of Maximus to murder the father/Emperor had been given to the Emperor himself.

In Fletcher, Aretus, a brave, loyal soldier much concerned by the corruption he sees about him, poisons Valentinian. In Rochester, no one character bears responsibility for the Emperor's death. Aretus has a diminished role, and Rochester's stage direction reads: '*Enter Aretus and Souldiers. They kill the Emperour*' (V. v., line 252). On the level of the play's political commentary, to have the Emperor die at the hands of a group allows the audience to infer that the act represents the will of the people in general, not simply the revenge of one person. Rhetorically, Rochester would not have wanted any one character to bear this responsibility in a work that surely would be taken as a *drame à clé*. Rochester had yet other reasons for the deflection. The logical candidate to kill the Emperor is Maximus, that is, Rochester. It is one thing, however, to wish the father dead, quite another to see yourself as being instrumental in that wish.

While Wilson is right that the Emperor represents aspects of Charles II, Sprague's comment that the character of the Emperor 'suggests not infrequently Rochester's own' contains its own truth, the two views in the logic of satire being complementary not contradictory.[30] As Kenneth Burke reminds us, 'the satirist attacks *in others* the weaknesses and temptations that are really *within himself*'.[31] Rochester's excoriations of self were notorious. Burnet observes that 'he would often break forth into such hard Expressions concerning himself, as would be indecent for another to repeat' (Burnet, p. 54).[32] I do not think we can account for the viciousness of the attack upon Vallentinian and the courtiers who surround him unless we see that in them Rochester is lashing what he himself had practised, the play being, perhaps above all else, a condemnation of life he had led in the pursuit of pleasure.[33]

The Emperor is a militant hedonist.[34] 'Pleasures Slave' (I. i., line 27), he goes where 'appetite directs' (IV. ii., line 197), proclaiming that 'Noe glories vaine which do's from pleasure spring' (I. i., line 338). Maximus sardonically comments that 'the whole World dissolv'd into a Peace/ Owes its security to this mans pleasures' (I. i., lines 99–100) and that he is ready to serve 'when the Emperour pleases to afford/ Time from his pleasures' (I. i., lines 146–47). The Emperor, like the younger Rochester, conceives of pleasure as physical, though he, again like Rochester, is troubled that his pleasures may be sinful. 'Is it', he asks at the end of Act I, 'a Sin to Love this Lovely Woman?' (I. i., line 479). He knows that the world censures him 'extreamly for my pleasures' (I. i., line 342), but he seeks approval on a higher level, the moral codes of men being merely conventional and originating in self-interest. He wants, that is, to say 'Noe' to this question of pleasure being a sin, because 'she is such a pleasure being good/ That though I were a God shee'd fire my Blood' (I. i., lines 481–82, Fletcher's lines). The Emperor seeks to unite the pleasurable and the good. If the gods, like the society he inhabits, try to prevent him, he will

> ... scorne those Gods who seek to cross my wishes
> And will in spite of them be happy ...
> I'le plunge into a Sea of my desires
> And quench my Fever though I drowne my Fame
> And tear up pleasure by the roots ....
> (IV. ii., lines 201–2 and 206–8)

In the Emperor's pursuit of pleasure Rochester exaggerates for the purposes of satire the moral position by which he had directed his own life. As he later told Burnet:

> the two *Maxims* of his *Morality* then were, that he should do nothing to the hurt of any other, or that might prejudice his own health: And he thought that all pleasure, when it did not interfere with these, was to be indulged as the gratification of our natural Appetites. It seemed unreasonable to imagine these were put into a man only to be restrained, or curbed to such a narrowness: This he applied to the free use of Wine and Women. (Burnet, p. 57)

But he often violated his own, moderate Epicurean principles, and consequently, as Wolseley acknowledged in the Preface to *Valentinian*, '*he hurt himself by a wrong pursuit of Pleasure*' (A3r).

Equally reflective of Rochester's life is the trade of those who serve the Emperor's pleasures. Chylax, Lycias, Balbus, Proculus, and Lycinius resemble their Court counterparts – Will Chiffinch, Bab Wallis, Robert Montagu, and Rochester himself, each being 'the humble slave of Caesars will/ By my ambition bound to his commands/ As by my Duty' (III. ii., lines 63–65).[35] Each plays the courtier's game, the object being 'to destroy thy enemyes, delude thy friends, enrich thy self, enslave the World, raise thy kindred, humble thy Master and Governe him' (III. i., lines 61–63). The way to this goal is to pander to the Emperor's pleasures. Satire on, and disgust with, courtiers pervades the play. Chylax and his cohorts have a scene devoted to them and their plans to corrupt Lucina and figure prominently in three others. The schemes of the ambitious Lycias fuel the plot of much of the play; he serves as messenger between Lucina and Vallentinian, betrays the former, and dies while serving the latter's homosexual desires. His role marks one of the major changes Rochester made in Fletcher's play.

Rochester knew his subject matter well, for he was attacking what he himself had practised. Appointed Gentleman of the Bedchamber in 1667, he still served in that capacity, among his duties being to minister to the King's pleasures. He writes, for example, to Savile concerning the impending visit of the Prince of Orange and wishes 'myself in town to serve him in some refined pleasures which I fear you are too much a Dutchman to think of'. He goes on to write that

> The best present I can make at this time is the bearer [James Paisible, fashionable French musician and bisexual], whom I beg you to take care of that the King may hear his tunes when he is easy and private, because I am sure they will divert him extremely. And may he ever have harmony in his mind, as this fellow will pour it into his ears. May he dream pleasantly, wake joyfully, love safely and tenderly, live long and happily, ever prays, dear Savile, un bougre lasse qui era toute sa fouture reste de vie votre fidèle ami et très humble serviteur. (Treglown, p. 160)

In another letter Rochester recommends that Savile make the acquaintance of 'this pretty fool the bearer' of the letter, Jean Baptiste de Belle-Fasse, Rochester's valet, for 'the happy consequence would be singing ... The greatest and gravest of this Court of both sexes have tasted his beauties' (Treglown, p. 230). It would be more than we know to say that Rochester had Paisible or Baptiste de Belle-Fasse in mind when fashioning Lycias, 'That sweet fac'd Eunuch that sung/ In Maximus'es grove the other day' whom the Emperor orders to his 'closet' (II. ii., lines 174–76). But the exchange between the Emperor and Chylax in II. ii., lines 113–25 and of the Emperor and Lycias at the end of III. ii., lines 61–65 as well as the plans for the rape itself echo the seamier side of Court life captured in Rochester's letters. Compare Lucina's plight with this description in a letter from Rochester to Savile:

> I doubt shee [identity unknown] is a great object of charity, I am sure shee had had mine if shee had sent for it for I allwayes thaught her one of the most unfortunate and most meritorious of all the numerous traine of clean and unclean that gone into Will. Chiffinch his Arke or my Ld Manchester's chamber. (Treglown, p. 222)

In both play and life courtiers seek to gratify the Emperor's/ King's pleasures. Rochester's letter to Savile with advice to Nell Gwyn on how to get along with the King describes the courtier's art satirized in *Lucina's Rape*: 'my advice to the lady you wot of has ever been this ... with hand, body, head, heart and all the faculties you have, contribute to his pleasure all you can and comply with his desires throughout'. He goes on to add that 'Besides this, you may judge whether I was a good pimp or no. But some thought otherwise and so, truly, I have renounced business; let abler men try it. More a great deal I would say, but upon this subject and for this time I beg this may suffice' (Treglown, p. 189). By June 1678, the probable date of this letter, Rochester had already said a great deal on the subject of the King's pleasures and those who served them in his adaptation of Fletcher's play.

Other characters repeat and explore further this theme of pleasure. Rochester inserted into Act III. iii., for example, a long dialogue in which Marcellina and Claudia rehearse an argument central to *Lucina's Rape* and to Rochester's work as a whole (lines 1–75). Up to the writing of *Lucina's Rape*, it had received its fullest expression in 'A Satyre Against Reason and Mankind'. To follow 'nature', so the argument runs, is to know 'pleasure' and be 'happy'. To do otherwise is to live a slave to arbitrary and artificial conventions and to fear the very things a person should enjoy. Marcellina is one 'That Honour nere thought fitt to chuse mee out/ His Champion against Pleasure' (III. iii., lines 28–29). For her

> ... what Nature prompts us to
> And Reason seconds why should wee avoyd?
> This Honour is the veriest Mountebanke –
> It fills our fancies with affected Tricks
> And makes us freakish, what a cheate must that bee
> Which robbs our lives of all their softer howres.
> (III. iii., lines 54–59)

The key Rochesterian vocabulary is all here: 'Nature', 'Reason', 'Honour', 'fancies', 'affected', 'Tricks', 'cheate', and even 'Mountebanke' itself. The argument as presented in the play, however, does not, as in 'A Satyre', end by mocking those 'sway'd by Rules not naturall but affected' (III. iii., line 50) while paradoxically defending and pulling the rug out from under those who follow nature. It unequivocally condemns the latter; the Emperor, his infernal crew, and Marcellina all end in corruption and death. That is, experientially such a pursuit is shown to be wrong; but the play condemns it on moral and intellectual grounds as well. The Court is, in Lucina's words, a paradise to those 'Who know no Paradice but guilty pleasure', 'guilty' being Rochester's addition (IV. ii., line 116). The virtuous Claudia, moreover, has the last word in her debate with Marcellina, in a striking passage warning:

> Yet glory not too much in cheating witt,
> 'Tis but false wisdome, and its property,
> Has ever been to take the part of Vice,
> Which though the fancy with vaine shews it pleases
> Yet wants a pow'r to justifie the mind –
> (III. iii., lines 71–75)

This was written by an older, wiser Rochester and corroborates Pinto's insight that

> Rochester's mind was not an ordinary one. It had in it what ... must be fed with living experience, by significant emotion. He had found that emotion

once in love-making and the aesthetic satisfactions of the life of pleasure. But those satisfactions could no longer content his restless and aspiring spirit. Already, we have seen in his satires, he had come to see through the world of pleasure and to recognize and despise the ugliness and folly that lay behind it. (*Enthusiast*, p. 150)

At the end of the play when the Emperor confesses to, among other things, the vanity of the 'worlds contrivance/ Where Solid paines succeed our sensless joyes/ And short liv'd pleasures fleet like passing dreames', Maximus, who has been catechizing him, says 'Why this is right my Lord' (V. v., lines 199–201 and 207). In this concluding dialogue it is as though the 'good' Rochester were arraigning the 'bad'. And it is Maximus who in the play's closing speech declares that:

Bring power and pleasure on the wings of Fame
And heap this treasure upon Maximus,
You'l make a great man not a happy one:
(V. v., lines 263–65)

The play not only condemns the pursuit of pleasure; it offers an alternative, though a tragically limited one. The exemplary characters suffer, but as the play moves beyond what seems to have been its original purpose, satire, to genuine tragedy, they triumph in their loss. Lucina dies, but she, if only one 'mongst millions of thy sex' has been and has remained 'Unfeinedly virtuous' (IV. iii., lines 151–52). Aecius will not compromise his values for worldly gain, nor will Pontius. In the end Maximus prefers death to the gaining of an empire. The values of these exemplary characters appear to be genuine, not affected. That is, the characters have shown the capacity to remain loyal to these values despite the assaults of the passions and the reality of death; despite the tragic realization that these values are subject to time and perhaps to evil forces beyond human control.

'It is surprising, perhaps', writes Dustin Griffin, that Rochester was 'attracted as a dramatist more to heroic drama than to comedy'. Griffin goes on to solve part of what seems puzzling by suggesting that Rochester 'Perhaps ... wanted to show he was capable of matching Dryden on his own terms', a suggestion I have expanded upon here (Griffin, p. 288). The other part of the puzzle lies in understanding *Lucina's Rape* in its biographical context. Up to his undertaking *Lucina's Rape*, Rochester had in both life and work violated cultural and religious standards in a quest to find, in Claudia's phrase, that which would 'justifie the mind' (III. iii., line 75). His scepticism and impiety, in my reading at least, always disguised a desire for authority. His search, however, had gone unfulfilled; there remained, as he poignantly wrote to his wife, 'soe greate a disproportion t'wixt our desires & what is ordained to content them' (Treglown, pp. 241–42).

Lucina's Rape represents an attempt to mitigate that disproportion, 'poetic forms' in Kenneth Burke's terms being 'symbolic structures designed to equip us for confronting given historical or personal situations'.[36] *Lucina's Rape* represents Rochester's experiment with humanism, his attempt to look for patterns of value in the past, not to explode them as he had in his satires, but to affirm them.

For all their differences Rochester and Dryden were in 1676–77 engaged, ironically enough, in much the same endeavour and for much the same reasons, though going about it in opposite ways. Both were suffering from heroic memories and desires at war with satirical propensities and scepticism.[37] In *All for Love* Dryden abandoned his attempt to provide patterns of the heroic for his society and entered into the period when he would write his greatest satires, breaking down old beliefs in search of new. Rochester had just emerged from a satirical period and was seeking something to affirm. In *Lucina's Rape* he evoked that heroic world where promises are kept, where friendship and love can thrive, but he also said farewell to it. At the end of *Lucina's Rape*, Aecius, representative of the heroic, is dead; his successor, Maximus, has no place to go. Rochester wrote little after *Lucina's Rape*, and two years later he was talking to Gilbert Burnet and exchanging letters with Charles Blount, seeking not the limited truths of humanism but the eternal ones of religion.

Notes

1 *Lucina's Rape* exists in three manuscript versions, British Library, Add. MS 28692; Folger Shakespeare Library, MS V b 233; and a more recent discovery, Yale University Beinecke Library, MS Osborn b334 ('Hartwell' MS). None is in Rochester's hand, all three having been done by professional scribes. The play was also published in a quarto bearing the date 1685; the quarto introduces numerous changes not found in the manuscripts. As Love notes, 'each of the four surviving sources is terminal, which is to say that it contains unique variants which are not shared with any other source. The important feature for our purpose is that the sources also tend strongly to agree in pairs, *BLa92* with *Fv33* and Yo34 with 85va' (Love, p. 626). For a detailed, fascinating account of the manuscripts and the relationship of the sources, see Love, pp. 623–29. All citations are to Love's edition. Unless otherwise noted, the lines cited are Rochester's.

Both Love's edition and that of Walker and Fisher use the British Library manuscript with its two corrections by Rochester's mother as their source text, and Fisher and Walker present the text 'in a format that for the first time makes Rochester's alterations to John Fletcher's *The Tragedie of Valentinian* (1613 or 1614) immediately recognizable to the reader' (Walker and Fisher, p. xxiv).

The publication of these two editions has renewed critical interest in the *Lucina's Rape*. See Germaine Greer, *John Wilmot, Earl of Rochester* (Devon: Northcote House Publishers, 2000), pp. 22 and 58–63; Jeremy W. Webster, *Performing Libertinism in Charles II's Court: Politics, Drama, and Sexuality* (New York: Palgrave Macmillian, 2005), chapters 5–7; Sandra Clark, 'Sex and Tyranny Revisited: Waller's "The Maid's Tragedy" and Rochester's "Valentinian"', in *Theatre and Culture in Early Modern England, 1650–1737: From Leviathan to Licensing Act*, ed. Catie Gill (Farnham: Ashgate, 2010), pp. 75–86; Warren Chernaik, 'Sex, Tyranny, and the Problem of Allegiance: Political Drama During the Restoration', in *Theatre and Culture in Early Modern England, 1650–1737: From Leviathan to Licensing Act*, ed. Catie Gill (Farnham: Ashgate, 2010), pp. 87–105; and particularly Harold Love, 'Was Lucina betrayed at Whitehall?', in *That Second Bottle: Essays on John Wilmot, Earl of Rochester*, ed. Nicholas Fisher (Manchester: Manchester University Press, 2000), pp. 179–90; Harold Love, 'The Rapes of Lucina', in *Print, Manuscript, & Performance: The Changing Relations of the Media in Early Modern England*, eds Arthur F. Marotti and Michael D. Bristol (Columbus, OH: Ohio State University Press, 2000), pp. 200–14; Nicholas Fisher, 'Mending What Fletcher Wrote: Rochester's Reworking of Fletcher's *Valentinian*', *Script & Print*, Special Issue, 33 (1–4) (2009), pp. 61–75; and Melissa E. Sanchez, 'Sex and sovereignty in Rochester's writing', in *Lord Rochester in the Restoration World*, eds Matthew C. Augustine and Steven N. Zwicker (Cambridge University Press, 2015), pp. 184–206. For earlier commentary see Arthur Colby Sprague, *Beaumont and Fletcher on the Restoration Stage* (New York: 1926; rpt. New York: B. Blom, 1965), pp. 71–74 and 165–78; Montague Summers, *The Playhouse of Pepys* (London: Kegan Paul, 1935), pp. 290–92; J. Harold Wilson, 'Satiric Elements in Rochester's *Valentinian*', *PQ*, 16 (1937), pp. 41–48; and J. Harold Wilson, 'Rochester's *Valentinian* and Heroic Sentiment', *ELH*, 4 (1937), pp. 265–73. In addition see Lucyle Hook, 'The Publication Date of Rochester's *Valentinian*', *HLQ*, 19 (1956), pp. 401–7; Allardyce Nicoll, 'Dryden, Howard, and Rochester', *London Times Literary Supplement*, 13 January 1921, p. 27; Summers responding to Nicoll, *London Times Literary Supplement*, 27 January 1921, p. 60; and Richard Braverman, *Politics and Counterplots: Sexual Politics and the Body Politic in English Literature, 1660–1730* (Cambridge University Press, 1993), pp. 158–60. I discuss the relationship of *BLA92* and *Fv33*, then the only known manuscripts, to the 1685 quarto in 'Rochester's *Valentinian*', *Restoration and 18th Century Theatre Research,* 2nd series 4, 1 (1989), pp. 25–38.

2 James Winn in his elegant biography, *John Dryden and His World* (New Haven, CT: Yale University Press, 1987), provides to my mind the best, most comprehensive, and nuanced account of the relationship between Rochester and Dryden, noting for example, that 'Rochester's later attempt to denigrate Dryden for obscenity is more likely to be a complex example of class prejudice his friend Buckingham held for both Arlington and Dryden' (p. 226); and that 'Dryden's own constancy to James, which would cost him dearly in the turmoil of the 1680s, owed something to the distaste he developed for the mercurial Rochester.

Yet Dryden managed to learn literary lessons even from Rochester; it is surely no accident that his first couplet satire, *MacFlecknoe*, probably written late in 1676, follows the path marked out by Rochester's "Allusion to Horace", which was circulating earlier in the same year' (p. 255). See particularly pp. 225–328.

3 For an invaluable discussion of the relationship between Dryden and Howard, see George McFadden, *Dryden The Public Writer* (Princeton, NJ: Princeton University Press, 1978), particularly pp. 59–87. McFadden describes the 'Defence of an Essay of Dramatic Poesie' as a 'deadly, contemptuous attack on Howard's literacy, intelligence, and reliability' (p. 65).

4 I am following Pinto's dating of the 'Scaen' (*Enthusiast*, pp. 108–9). For the controversy surrounding the dating of this work, see J. Harold Wilson, 'The Dating of Rochester's "Scaen"', *RES*, 13 (1937), pp. 455–58; Jeremy Treglown, 'The Date of Rochester's "Scaen"', *RES*, N.S. 30 (1979), pp. 434–36; Howard's letter to Rochester dated by month and day but not by year, contains all the evidence we have concerning this collaboration (Treglown, p. 115). Good arguments have been made for 1672 and 1676. I would just add that it seems improbable that Rochester and Howard would have collaborated on such a work in 1676 given that Settle's version had just played.

5 Dryden clearly intended Rochester to be among the audience for this essay, giving credit to the refinement of language to 'the Court' and 'particularly to the King' and couching his praise in similar terms he would use in his dedication of *Marriage à la Mode* to Rochester.

6 This dedication perhaps provides the best evidence of Dryden's desire to be counted among the Wits. At one point, he writes: 'Certainly the Poets [Ovid, Horace et al.] of that Age enjoy'd much happiness in the Conversation and Friendship of one another. They imitated the best way of Living, which was to pursue an innocent and inoffensive Pleasure; that which one of the Ancients called *Eruditam voluptatem*. We have, like them, our Genial Nights; where our discourse is neither too serious, nor too light; but alwayes pleasant, and for the most part instructive: the raillery neither too sharp upon the present, nor too censorious on the absent; and the Cups onely such as will raise the Conversation of the Night, without disturbing the business of the Morrow ... I have often Laugh'd at the ignorant and ridiculous Descriptions which some Pedants have given of the Wits ... which are a Generation of Men as unknown to them, as the People of *Tartary* or the *terra Australis* are to us' (Dryden, 5, pp. 320–21).

7 McFadden also sees the Preface as referring to *Valentinian*, but he thinks Dryden's chief concern was the collaboration of Rochester and Howard on *The Conquest of China* (pp. 173–76). For my reservations about this latter point, see note 4.

8 Love thinks it unlikely that Rochester wrote this impromptu, placing *Lord Rochester upon hearing the singing in a Country Church* in the Appendix Roffensis.

9 McFadden raises the interesting possibility that Rochester may have assisted 'in the extensive additions to *The Rehearsal* that appear in the 1675 edition' (p. 213). Robert D. Hume and Harold Love in their edition of the *Plays, Poems,*

And Miscellaneous Writings Associated with George Villiers Second Duke of Buckingham, however, do not include Rochester among those who may have had a hand in *The Rehearsal*.

10 Matthew C. Augustine also makes the case that *Lucina's Rape* may well have arisen out of the competition between Rochester and the Poet Laureate, writing: 'What I would urge is that we view Rochester's adaptation of Fletcher too as significantly inflected by the larger literary dialogue carried on between the two poets over the span of half a decade, from c.1673–9. This conversation, if we may call it that, is fueled by competitiveness and overlain with instinctive dislike or distrust, but the lessons given and the lessons learned are nonetheless mutual, hardly a matter of Dryden merely taking his medicine from Rochester in the *Allusion to Horace*. Rochester's choice to refurbish a blank verse tragedy unmistakably reproves the fashion for rhymed heroic entertainments with which Dryden was inextricably associated. But there is in Rochester's dramaturgy much that harmonizes superbly with the positions staked out by Dryden in the *Essay of Dramatick Poesie* and elsewhere' (Augustine, 'Trading Places', pp. 70–71). Augustine goes on to observe: 'Rochester was not often given to sustained literary endeavour ... and the fact that he put as much of himself into *Lucina's Rape* as he did suggests something of the seriousness with which Rochester mounted this challenge to the laureate within the fraught sphere of dramatic poesy, a field in which both men had reputations at stake. That Dryden – into whose hands, we can be sure, *Lucina's Rape* made its way – was spurred on by Rochester's effort seems obvious, the result of course being *All for Love*, which sees Dryden adapting, almost tit for tat, a Jacobean blank verse tragedy, infamously irregular in the original, celebratedly unified in the alteration, with another dissipated and all too Carolean Roman at its centre' (pp. 72–73).

11 As Love points out, 'Such revisions were a good way of learning how to write an original play: that may well have been Rochester's long-term ambition' ('Was Lucina betrayed at Whitehall?', p. 187).

12 Sprague, *Beaumont and Fletcher*, p. 167. Love, 'The Rapes of Lucina', p. 200.

13 Wolseley was the first in *The Preface*; see also Summers, *The Playhouse of Pepys*, pp. 291–92; Sprague, *Beaumont and Fletcher*, p. 167; and Wilson, 'Rochester's *Valentinian* and Heroic Sentiment', pp. 265–67 and 273. There is some evidence that Rochester thought of writing *Lucina's Rape* in heroic couplets. The earlier 'Scaen' is in couplets, and Rochester breaks into couplets from time to time in *Lucina's Rape* (see III. iii., lines 78–115). Maximus's speech in IV. iii. lines 296–330 is in stanzas rhyming ababb.

14 In *Performing Libertinism in Charles II's Court: Politics, Drama, and Sexuality* (New York: Palgrave Macmillian, 2005), Jeremy W. Webster, drawing upon the work of Laura Brown, argues that *Lucina's Rape* 'is not a heroic drama' but an 'affective tragedy' (p. 161). 'According to Brown, "Restoration affective tragedy substitutes the unfortunate and undeserved situation of its central character for the aristocratic status of the heroic protagonists." As a result of this substitution, "The characters and episodes of affective tragedy are comprehensible not in terms of an internal standard of judgment that directs our assessments and

expectations, but rather in terms of the expressed pathos of the situation"' (p. 144 and quoting Brown, *English Dramatic Form*, pp. 69 and 70). This leads Webster to conclude: 'It is, thus, Valentinian's fate to love Lucina rather than pursue traditional heroism, and like the protagonist of affective tragedy, he is meant to be pitied rather than scorned by the audience' (p. 159). This is not my experience of reading the play. I agree with Love: 'Onto Fletcher's not fully successful blend of a Roman play of the kind pioneered by Shakespeare and Jonson with a full-blooded Jacobean revenge tragedy, Rochester imposed the mode of the Restoration heroic play of Dryden and Lee, in which characters cease to be multifaceted and are reconstituted as quasi-allegorical embodiments of a particular vice, virtue, or "passion"' ('The Rapes of Lucina', pp. 208–9).

15 Fisher makes a good case that a performance of *Lucina's Rape* may have taken place during Rochester's lifetime: 'a date late in 1676 for the first performance or intended performance of Rochester's play cannot be discounted, and it is worth stressing that with records existing for between just 7% and 13% of all theatrical performances during the later seventeenth century, the lack of documentary evidence (as is the case with the public performances of *Lucina's Rape* in late 1683 or early 1684) does not fatally undermine the thesis' (Fisher, 'Mending What Fletcher Wrote: Rochester's Reworking of Fletcher's *Valentinian*', p. 64). Love, however, thinks such a performance improbable, 'The most likely reason for the play's failure to reach the stage in the late 1670s [being] political. There can be little doubt that Rochester intended a covert attack on his royal master, Charles II, and that his motive for this was one of sympathy with his close friend, Buckingham, who had been dismissed from most of his offices at the beginning of 1674 and was thereafter in open opposition to the anti-tolerationist policies of the new chief minister, the Earl of Danby. (Buckingham had himself had an adaptation of Fletcher's *The chances* performed by the King's Company in 1667.) The reflections on Charles are qualified by Rochester's awareness that the king was himself an unwilling captive of Danby's programme; but a play about a lust-besotted autocrat had implications that could not be disguised, and at I. i. 97–100 and V. v. 89–90 ... to look no further, there are passages that a contemporary could hardly not have accepted as directed at Charles. Rochester also removes the scenes in which regicide is punished, leaving Maximus a successful usurper' (Love, pp. 449–50). Love goes on to note: 'But it would have been difficult for a theatre dependent on the king to accept the play at a time of sharply intensifying oppositional activity fueled by the passions that were to erupt in the Popish Plot panic' (Love, p. 450).

16 As Rachel Weil points out: 'The cuckolding of male subjects is the quintessential tyrannical act, a deprivation of their property and manhood. (This is why, when Charles's ministers are attacked, it is often said that they are pimping for their own wives and daughters.) It was also an implicit parody of Robert Filmer's patriarchal justification of absolutism: the joke being that Charles was trying to become, literally, the father of his country' ('Sometimes a Scepter is Only a Scepter', in *The Invention of Pornography: Obscenity and the Origins of Modernity, 1500–1800*, ed. Lynn Hunt (New York: Zone Books, 1993), p. 142.

For more on patriarchalism at this time, see Larry Carver, 'The Restoration Poets and Their Father King', *HLQ*, 40 (1977), pp. 333–51. Melissa E. Sanchez explores the 'debate over the origin and limits of sovereignty' that are at the heart of *Lucina's Rape*, concluding that Rochester 'absorbed principles crucial to the discourses that would emerge in Whig political theory: sovereignty is a human rather than a divine creation; sovereignty exists for the good of the subjects and the state not that of the monarch; and the sovereign who endangers rather than protects his subjects loses his claim to their obedience' ('Sex and sovereignty', pp. 184 and 185).

17 This entire speech, I. i., lines 85–108, a clever mock-encomium on Charles II, is characteristic of the play's tone as a whole. Maximus begins in irony but cannot sustain it. Thus he breaks out with this: 'But Aecius be sincere, doe not defend/ Actions and principles your Soule abhors' (lines 101–2). The play reveals a great desire to be done with wit and casuistry, to be sincere.

18 Wolseley writes that *'a considerable time before his last Sickness, his Wit began to take a more serious Bent, and to frame and fashion it self to publick Business; he begun to inform himself of the Wisdom of our Laws and the excellent Constitution of the* English *Government, and to speak in the House of Peers with general approbation; he was inquisitive after all kind of Histories, that concern'd* England, *both ancient and modern, and set himself to read the Journals of Parliament Proceedings. In effect, he seem'd to study nothing more, than which way to make that great Understanding God had given him, most useful to his Countrey*' ('Preface', A4r).

19 In 1679 Rochester would write 'To The Reader', a 'short skit', that introduces 'a projected edition' of 'The Satyr', his intention being 'to rectify the errors of the 1679 folio'. In the skit, which Love accepts as 'a genuine late work by Rochester', the Earl casts himself as the vicar, 'Lovesey', who as Love points out 'is to be understood as a sympathizer with the Exclusionist cause who has come to feel disgust at the extreme measures being adopted by the Whig leadership' (Love, p. 380). 'An Allusion to Tacitus' may also shed light on Rochester's political stance late in his life and provide an insightful gloss on the politics of *Lucina's Rape*. Here the opening eighteen lines:

> The freeborn English Generous and wise
> Hate chains but do not government despise:
> Rights of the Crown, Tributes and taxes they,
> When lawfully exacted freely pay.
> Force they abhor, and wrongs they scorn to beare.
> More guided by their judgement than their fear,
> Justice with them is never held severe.
> Here pow'r by Tyranny was never got,
> Laws may perhaps enslave 'em, force cannot.
> Rash councells here have still the worst effect,
> The surest way to Reigne is to protect.
> Kings are least safe in their unbounded will
> Joyn'd with the wretched pow'r of doing ill.
> Forsaken most when they'r most absolute

> Laws guard the Man and only bind the Brute.
> To force that guard, with the worst foe to joyn
> Can never be a prudent Kings designe.
> What King wou'd change to be a Catiline ….

In a gloss on 'distinction', I. i., line 116 of *Lucina's Rape*, Love notes: 'The capacity to distinguish between severe but loyal criticism of the ruler and outright treason – a tightrope that Rochester must often have walked himself' (Love, p. 452).

Love includes the 'An Allusion to Tacitus', written 'possibly winter of 1678/9' (Walker and Fisher, p. 158), among Rochester's 'Disputed Works', but finds there to be 'a strong presumption of Rochester's authorship. It seems most likely that he wrote the shorter version first and then expanded it for scribal publication as a political separate. Only the fact that stylistic tests by John Burrows have found the poem uncharacteristic have prevented it from being claimed as a secure addition to the canon' (Love, p. 481). Nicholas Fisher, having examined evidence that has come to light since Love's edition – 'three further manuscript texts … and two early printings of the satire' – concludes that there is 'a compelling case for Rochester's authorship' ('Rochester's *An Allusion To Tacitus*', *N&Q*, (October 2010), pp. 503–6). Fisher provides a valuable version of the poem in which 'The lines that expanded Rochester's "short" version are underlined; the couplets enclosed in square brackets are lines omitted from *The Anti-Roman Pacquet* and are supplied from the "Harbin" MS; and the new conclusion is marked by bold type' (p. 505). In 'Recovering a Restoration Scribal Poet: The Life and Work of Robert Wolseley, with Notes on His Association with Rochester', Paul Davis makes the case, however, for Wolseley being the author 'in part or all of the "Allusion to Tacitus"' (*HLQ*, 79, 4 (2016), pp. 677–704).

20 Balbus's reference to Lucrece is Fletcher's; the other three allusions are Rochester's.
21 Gibbon, drawing upon Procopius, possibly one of Rochester's sources, writes that during the reign of Valentinian: 'A republican spirit was insensibly revived in the senate, as their authority, and even their supplies, became necessary for the support of his feeble government. The stately demeanour of an hereditary monarch offended their pride; and the pleasures of Valentinian were injurious to the peace and honour of noble families' (*The Decline and Fall of the Roman Empire* (London, 1909; rpt. New York: AMS Press, 1974), 3, pp. 504–5).
22 *Likeness of Truth in Elizabethan and Restoration Drama* (Oxford: Clarendon Press, 1972), particularly pp. 103–7.
23 René Welleck and Austin Warren, *Theory of Literature* (New York: Harcourt, Brace & World, 1942; rpt. 1956), pp. 76 and 79.
24 I am not the first to point out parallels between the play and Rochester's life. See Sprague, *Beaumont and Fletcher*, p. 168; Wilson, 'Satiric Elements', *passim*; and Pinto, *Enthusiast*, pp. 159–61. Quoting Vallentinian's speech V. ii., lines 140–44 ('What an affected Conscience doe I live with'), Matthew C. Augustine

writes: 'As Sprague, John Harold Wilson, and others have variously argued, touches such as this also produce a frisson of resemblance with John Wilmot's world – to Charles II, to Rochester himself, and to the "hot-house" atmosphere of the Stuart Court' (Augustine, 'Trading Places', p. 70).
25 Love, 'Was Lucina betrayed at Whitehall?', pp. 180–81 and 187.
26 Cf. 'The last of men, and vilest of Beings' to the opening two lines of the dramatic fragment, 'Sab: Lost': 'Shee yields, she yields, Pale Envy said Amen/ The first of woemen to the Last of men.' There may also be, as Paul Hammond pointed out to me, an echo of 'Whilst the misguided follower climbs with pain/ Mountains of whimseys heapt in his own brain' ('A Satyre', lines 16–17), though for Maximus the 'Melancholly Whimseys' turn out to be 'real truths (it seems)'.
27 Christopher Hill notes that 'Those who write about Rochester are apt to attribute his materialist ideas to Hobbes: his contemporaries saw their connection with the ideas of Ranters and "mechanic" (i.e. lower-class) sectaries as well.' He goes on to write: 'Rochester translated lines from Lucretius which suggested that the gods took no notice of human life on earth ... This was a doctrine elaborated by the Ranter Laurence Clarkson and taken over by the Muggletonian sect which he joined. Even in Burnet's account Rochester was not persuaded "that prayers were of much use", since God would not "be overcome with importunities ... He doubted much of rewards or punishments" – i.e. of the Christian doctrine of heaven and hell, another familiar Ranter heresy. In revising *Valentinian* Rochester added some lines asking how the gods could permit evil to exist. His answer there was Manichaean: evil was co-eternal with the gods. Rochester, again like the Ranters, could believe the Biblical stories of the Creation and the Fall only if they were parable' (*The Collected Essays of Christopher Hill, Writing and Revolution in 17th Century England* (Brighton: Harvester Press, 1985), 1, pp. 304–5).
28 John Aubrey, *Brief Lives*, (London: Penguin Books, 2000), p. 345.
29 Melissa E. Sanchez acutely observes: 'Rochester's poetry ultimately demonstrates the inadequacy of the romance of libertinism to compensate for human transience. As seemingly opposite modes of understanding the human predicament, romance and libertinism both strive to find a lasting joy, but both rely on ever-fleeting pleasure – whether the spiritual contemplation of love or the physical immersion of lust. Aspiration to the ideal world of pleasure and love posited by the pastoral conjunction of the two discourses is the last straw at which the poet can grasp, the compensation that allows the world, political or private to function. Yet "the perfect joy of being well deceaved" described in *Artemiza to Chloe* (115) exists only in the extremes of psychosis. Rochester's poetry insists that we can never be well deceived enough, that the joy provided by delusion, like all other human enjoyment, remains decidedly inadequate – even so, it is such coerced, compromised desire that sustains the order of personal and political life' ('Libertinism and Romance in Rochester's Poetry', *Eighteenth-Century Studies,* 38, 3 (Spring, 2005), p. 456).
30 Sprague, *Beaumont and Fletcher*, p. 168.
31 Burke, *Attitudes Toward History*, p. 49.

32 Burke writes of Wyndham Lewis: 'there are symptoms to indicate that his excoriations arise from a suppressed fear of death, or, in other words, from religiosity frustrated by disbelief, though it must be admitted that our reasons for such diagnosis are tenuous' (*Attitudes Toward History,* p. 50). With the same reservations, I think the observations true of Rochester as well.

33 In summing up his account of *Lucina's Rape,* Tilmouth writes: 'However, the intuition that behind the composition of this play sits a shared self, passion, and villainy, yoking together Emperor and servant; the intuition, too, that the vigour of the attack upon Vallentinian reflects a protégé's *Oedipal* turn against his monarch-father, and a turn against his own likeness, surely does point to Rochester's relationship with Charles' (*Passion's Triumph,* p. 367).

34 The words 'pleasure' and 'pleasures' appear 31 times in the play, 13 of the uses being Rochester's. For more on Rochester and pleasure, see James William Johnson, 'Lord Rochester and the tradition of Cyrenaic hedonism, 1670–1790', *Studies on Voltaire and the Eighteenth Century,* 153 (1976), pp. 151–67.

35 As Love notes: 'The play's constant suggestion of veiled satire on the English court is part of its alliance with the lampoon culture. Indeed, if we knew more about such characters as Mall Howard, Mary Knight, William Chiffinch, Bab May, and Catharine Crofts, the bawds and procuresses of the play might be found to have been aligned in revision with originals from Whitehall. The character of Proculus, of whom Rochester wrote more new dialogue than in the other cases of this kind, reads as if a personal model existed. His scene with Aecius in 5.1 is a gem of satirical portraiture' ('The Rapes of Lucina', p. 211).

36 Burke, *Attitudes Toward History,* p. 57.

37 Pinto juxtaposes Aureng-Zebe's speech, 'When I consider life, 'tis all a cheat' with lines 6–28 of 'The Satyre', observing: 'It is impossible to say whether Rochester's misanthropic outburst or Dryden's fine rhetorical piece of pessimism came first. They seem to represent a moment when the two most creative imaginations of the day were confronted with the terrible vision of emptiness, the "universe of death" that followed the collapse of the hopes of rebuilding a new Christian humanism after the Restoration' ('Rochester and Dryden', pp. 40–41).

6

'The principal Disputant against God and Piety'

One day at an Atheistical Meeting, at a person
of Qualitie's, I undertook to manage the Cause,
and was the principal Disputant against God
and Piety, and for my performances received
the applause of the whole company ....
Rochester to Robert Parsons

In a word, he was neither perswaded that there
was a special Providence about humane Affairs;
nor that Prayers were of much use, since that was
to look on God as a weak Being, that would be
overcome with Importunities.
Gilbert Burnet

Is that an Object fit for my desires
Which lies within the reach of your perswasions?
Vallentinian

In a sense he had never stopped seeking those eternal truths. This 'very prophane Wit'[1] was always just outside his Father's house, seeking entrance, albeit in his own complex way.

Information about the role Christianity played in Rochester's life and work comes from five sources: his childhood upbringing; the biblical and liturgical allusions found in his letters, poems, and plays; his conversations with Burnet; his correspondence with Blount; and the various testimonials concerning the Earl that can be gleaned from, among others, Rochester's mother, the antiquarian Thomas Hearne, Robert Parsons who preached the sermon at Rochester's funeral, his old friend Robert Wolseley, and one of his great admirers, Sir Francis Fane. In Chapter 2 we canvassed what is known and can safely be inferred concerning Rochester's upbringing. Both parents were extremely devout Protestants, and there is little doubt, given their choice of a clergyman tutor, Francis Giffard, that their son was soundly inculcated with the principles of the Christian religion.

'The principal Disputant against God and Piety' 185

Figure 6.1 John Wilmot, 2nd Earl of Rochester, artist unknown. Collection of the Earl Bathurst, Cirencester Park.

While there is widespread agreement that Rochester received a Christian upbringing, there is little agreement on how to interpret the other evidence. In correspondence and poetry, Rochester does echo the Bible and prayer book, does draw upon snatches of church services he heard in his youth at Ditchley, Adderbury, Banbury, and Oxford, but he does so in a seemingly desultory, often ironic fashion. He returned in a conscious, open way to a consideration of Christianity in the last years of his life, but with Burnet, he remained sceptical and with Blount he tried to disprove the immortality of the soul. As for those who testified to Rochester's beliefs, they usually did so after he was dead when there seemed to be a concerted effort on the part of the family and friends to salvage for memory what the life perhaps never supported. Taking this evidence into account, Dustin Griffin sketched a Rochester who is a sceptic, partaking fully in the libertine heterodoxy described by Bredvold and Underwood. Reba Wilcoxon painted a similar portrait of Rochester and concluded that though Rochester believed in a Supreme Being and in the immortality of the soul his work shows a 'rejection of Christian orthodoxy'.[2]

The arguments of Griffin and Wilcoxon are part of a lively debate that began the day Rochester died and has continued into modern criticism. Assessing Prinz's biography, Montague Summers wrote:

> for all his boundless and indeed exaggerated enthusiasm Herr Prinz has certainly not gone to the lengths of proclaiming that Rochester had a 'religious' mind, that he was a man who 'pondered long and deeply on the ultimate problems of philosophy and religion.' This absurdity was put forward in all apparent seriousness by a writer in an article 'Unpublished Poem Attributed to Rochester in *The Times Literary Supplement*, 22nd November, 1934'.[3]

The author of this 'absurdity' was Vivian de Sola Pinto. Undaunted by Summers's withering scorn, he went on to make his case in book-length form, one of the central arguments of *Rochester: Portrait of a Restoration Poet* (1935) being that Rochester's 'celebrated conversion to religion was no sudden *volte-face*; it was the culminating point of a dialectical process which had been going on in his mind for years'.[4]

A year before Pinto's study came out, Graham Greene was completing his biography of Rochester and coming to a similar conclusion that Rochester's 'spirit was always at war with the flesh; and his unbelief was quite as religious as the Dean of St Paul's faith'. Greene's biography, though drawing upon some poems we no longer attribute to Rochester, remains one of the most penetrating accounts of this complex man. It was Greene who first pointed out that Christianity dominated the life of this seemingly most impious of poets and that the 'language of the Bible, however satirically used, is part of Rochester's style'.[5] Since the mid-1930s a number of commentators have continued to sense that in Rochester's case at least, the libertine and Christian are inextricably bound together. In *The Sun at Noon: Three Biographical Sketches*, Kenneth B. Murdock portrays Rochester as a 'wit' who was 'consumed by longing for some sufficing faith', which he finds 'in the last troubled months of his life'.[6] Anne Righter detected in the last four years of his life 'an attraction towards a kind of mystical Christianity'.[7] George Williamson found that 'For all his agnostic wit, Rochester's best love poems are haunted by ideas of religion'.[8] Howard Weinbrot quoted this observation in his essay on '*Artemiza to Chloe*' and labelled it 'shrewd'.[9] In Raman Selden's judgment, 'Much of Rochester's finest poetry takes the form of inverted religion'.[10] Jeremy Treglown came to much the same conclusion concerning the place of religion in the letters: 'The hold particular ideas had on him usually seems related to how far they reversed the Christian notions which had dyed his mind' (Treglown, p. 14).

Though Treglown's fine ear and erudition enabled him to go further than anyone in showing how Rochester 'constantly draws on the Bible and the Anglican liturgy for phrases, using them as points of contrast, or as intensifying points of resemblance' (Treglown, p. 14), the place of Christianity in Rochester's life and work remains moot. As with so much else concerning Rochester, the hard evidence is fragmentary and often open to diverse, even contradictory, interpretations. Marianne Thormählen opined that 'Rochester the man may not have been an atheist', but found it 'difficult to see how *Upon Nothing* could be saved from the imputation of atheism' (Thormählen, p. 147). Revisiting the issue a few years later in 2000, Thormählen would argue that 'There is evidence that Rochester always had what might be called a religious temperament', concluding:

> There will be many readers who feel that that is where the 'real' Rochester is and that, in so far as his poems ever address true love, they do not have anything very interesting to say about it. Likewise, a case could be made out for the view that the Christian elements mentioned here are part and parcel of a project of merry blasphemy, as impish as it was impious. But as I have traced what seemed to me to be the impulses of emotion to their synapses, I have become more and more convinced of one thing: to Rochester, love, like religion, 'was either a mere Contrivance, or the most important thing that could be'.[11]

Meanwhile two editors of Rochester's work, Paddy Lyons (1993) and Frank Ellis (1994) were concluding that 'Rochester is a poet of unbelief' and that 'Rochester himself was not a closet Puritan, as some of his biographers have made out. He was an atheist.'[12] In his 1995 study, however, Warren Chernaik in commenting on lines 22–30 of the '*Satyr*', writes: 'These lines are self-evidently the work of a religious poet, who presents man's life, here and in other poems, as an endless yearning after a satisfaction he can never find.' He goes on to conclude: 'Rochester then was an unbeliever who desperately wanted to believe – if not in God, in something.'[13] For Germaine Greer writing five years a later, Rochester's 'faith was', however, 'as instinctive as his skepticism was rational'. And she goes on to write:

Anne Rochester had bred her son on the Protestant Bible; biblical ideas and tenets had formed the very fabric of his personality. His poems and letters are full of echoes of the biblical readings and prayers of his youth, often turned upside down or used ironically. Like the devil, Rochester could cite scripture to his purpose, and, like the devil, he was a believer. Rochester's belief was not of the complacent kind that sees its justification in everyday phenomena. All about him but above all at court he saw God being mocked, and by none more impudently than the clerics who accumulated wealth and power through the church of which the dissolute and faithless King was the head. In retreat from conventional hypocrisies Rochester found himself driven into a byroad of English thought, that finds more merit in faith because it is irrational. (Greer, p. 67)

More recently Sarah Ellenzweig and Nicholas Fisher have made invaluable contributions to understanding the role that religion plays in Rochester's life and work. 'Reading Rochester's distinctive aristocratic heterodoxy' and 'his freethinking in the context of English deism', Ellenzweig concludes:

Not only does it provide a more accurate account of the content of Rochester's ideas about religion; it also affords a more nuanced view of the heterodox aristocrat's always uneasy relationship to a radical tradition. To the extent that the critique of enthusiasm is fueled by class anxiety, it is no coincidence that deism began as a largely aristocratic, even politically conservative, movement. It is also little wonder that Hobbes's distinctive mixture of freethinking and authoritarian absolutism served as an appropriate inspiration. In its anti-enthusiasm, in its nostalgia for a pure religion untainted by the corruptions of interest and politics, deism was radically conservative, a fitting home for an alienated aristocrat like Rochester.[14]

While exploring 'the validity of Rochester's assertion that he was "no atheist" through an investigation of some representative poems and the principal instances which reveal the vocabulary and literature of the Christian faith acting as the foundation of Rochester's poetic imagination', Fisher finds 'not only a further than expected layer of complexity and meaning but also a surprising concern and respect for religion that he would only fully realize on his deathbed'.[15]

Needless to say, more information about Rochester's beliefs would be welcomed. As Christopher Tilmouth has rightly pointed out, 'whereas [Rochester's] misogyny and apparent atheism might once have been thought straightforward matters, analysis now suggests that the contorted structure of Rochester's thinking about gender and sexuality and the parallel intricacy of his relationship to Christianity demand subtler comment'.[16] If Christopher Hill's speculations that Rochester's interest in the reality of Heaven and Hell are linked to debates that 'raged in the sixteen-forties' among specific sects could, for example, be substantiated, we would obviously have gained an invaluable interpretive context.[17] But the evidence we do have can be made to yield more information than it has if we begin to take into account that Rochester's engagement with religion is less a matter of specific doctrine than a particular rhetorical stance. That is, rhetoric is part and parcel of Rochester's religious concerns, being in itself a sixth and heretofore unexamined source of information concerning the place of religion in Rochester's life and work.[18] If we first focus on the rhetoric of the letters, then examine the rhetorical stance of the songs and love poems, and finally focus on Rochester's rhetorical use of Christian language, metaphors, and paradoxes we will be able to see that Rochester's work everywhere reflects his Christian and God-fearing upbringing and provides evidence of an excessive preoccupation with, and acceptance of, Christianity that Rochester, for all his efforts, could never banish with arguments drawn from pagan writers.

Rochester's *Letters* have proved nearly as vexatious to commentators as his poetry and for many of the same reasons. There are so few of them; they are difficult, and in some cases, impossible to date, but most troublesome of all, the correspondence, to quote Christopher Hill, does not reveal 'a unified personality ... behind the turbulent rake and the agonized poet, behind the courtier and friend of Charles II who wrote savage republican verse'.[19] Robert D. Hume, in reviewing Treglown's edition, agrees. While we learn 'quite a lot about Court Wit mentality' and gossip, about Rochester's affection for Savile, his penchant for parody, his seemingly genuine passion for Elizabeth Barry, the many voices with which he writes to his wife, his cutting scorn, and 'fantastical sexual humor', Hume concludes that 'These scrappy and occasional letters give us little more than a few random pieces of a huge puzzle'.[20] With Hill and Hume, I too would like to know more, but would argue that if we focus on the voice, the rhetorical stance of the speaker, we will find in the letters a remarkable unity and purposiveness. That voice, that stance, is one of courtship, and while identifying and exploring it will not finally solve the puzzle or give us the key to what Rochester's 'mind was up to, how original it was and how consistent',[21] it will cast light on Rochester's motives in the letters and in his work as a whole.

From the earliest extant letter (to his mother), to the last one (to the Reverend Dr Thomas Pierce), Rochester can be seen exercising the chief art for which he had been bred, the art of appeal, the motive being to advance through pleasing and being accepted by others. In that first letter the young Earl shows off the values and arts his mother instilled in him, and that he now displays for her approval: duty to king, country, and parents, courage under fire, the ability to write in an understated, yet utterly charming, style. Like the brilliant rhetorician he is on his way to becoming, Rochester wants to assure his mother that, whatever doubts she might have, he is like her, one of her kind, even and perhaps most of all, sharing her keen instinct for worldly gain:

> there wee lay all night and by twelve a clock next day gott off and sailed to Bergen full of hopes and expectation, having allready shared amongst us the rich lading of the Eastindia merchants some for diamonds some for spices others for rich silkes & I for shirts and gould wch I had most neede of, but reckoning without our Hoast wee were faine to reckon twice. (Treglown, pp. 47–48)

Don't count your chickens until they are hatched. The point, and the humour, would not have been lost on his mother, who held together the Lee and Wilmot estates during the Interregnum, and continued until her death to be sharp with a shilling. Rochester, who never lost a certain childhood awe for his mother, courts in every way he knows how Anne Wilmot's approval. You have educated me well; we are two of a kind. I am doing my duty, and 'I know noe body hath more reason to express theire duty to you, than I have, & certainly I will never bee soe imprudent as to omitt the occasions of doing it' (Treglown, pp. 46–47). Similarly, in the letter to Dr Pierce, Rochester marshals his powers of appeal, seeking the approval of other authority figures, of Dr Pierce and, through him, of God, 'that Holy One I have so often offended' (Treglown, p. 246).[22] But that is getting ahead of our story.

The point is that whether writing to Elizabeth Barry, his wife, his son, Savile, Buckingham, Burnet, or Blount, Rochester's goal is the same: be of my persuasion. 'Would I could bring you to my opinion in this point' (Treglown, p. 123), he writes to Elizabeth Barry. In letters written to wife, mistress, and friends one would expect the rhetorical motive to be present. In these letters, however, it is heightened, often becoming the subject itself. Rochester goes to great lengths to assure those to whom he is writing of his sincerity and that they may and ought to believe him. To his wife he writes that 'it will content mee if you beleive mee & love mee' (Treglown, p. 50). He is 'much troubled that' she 'should beleive I have not writ to you all this while' (Treglown, pp. 53–54). He asks her to 'beleive of every thing that it is as you would have it' (Treglown, p. 55). To Elizabeth Barry, he writes, 'Believe all I say' and 'Believe me, dearest of all pleasures.' 'You will scarce believe me in this particular as you should do', he writes, 'but I will convince you of the truth when I wait on you' (Treglown, pp. 102–4). In yet another letter, he assures his mistress that 'I am perhaps very dull, but withal very sincere ... These inconveniences you must bear with from those that love you with greater regard to you than themselves. Such a one I pretend to be, and I hope if you do not yet believe it, you will in time find it' (Treglown, p. 132). He beseeches her 'to believe the last thing possible in the world is the least omission of either kindness or service to you' (Treglown, p. 139); closes one letter requesting 'that you believe and use me like the most faithful of all your servants, etc'. (Treglown, p. 133); and another with, 'pray believe me sincere when I assure you that you are very dear to me' (Treglown, p. 156). To Savile, he writes, 'I have better compliments for you, but that may not look so sincere as I would have you believe I am when I profess myself/ Your faithful, affectionate, humble servant/ Rochester' (Treglown, p. 114).

The self-conscious nature of the rhetorical appeal reflects Rochester's solicitude for those to whom he is very close but also his awareness of how fragile and open to question such appeals are. Among courtiers, sincerity and the grounds for belief, were not, as Rochester well knew, to be taken for granted. In a letter to Savile we find Rochester praising 'that second bottle' as

> the sincerest, wisest, & most impartiall downwright freind we have, tells us truth of our selves, & forces us to speake truths of others, banishes flattery from our tongues and distrust from our Hearts, setts us above the meane Pollicy of Court prudence, wch makes us lye to one another all day, for feare of being betray'd by each other att night. (Treglown, p. 67)

In another letter, he tells Savile: 'I ever thought you an extraordinary man and must now think you such a friend who, being a courtier as you are, can love a man whom it is the great mode to hate' (Treglown, p. 158). It is possible, even for a courtier, to maintain bonds of love and friendship against the world's getting and spending, but that courtier is Savile, an extraordinary man. In a letter to his wife, probably written in the last few months of his life, Rochester summed up his jaundiced view of the courtier's life:

> soe greate a disproportion t'wixt our desires & what it
> has ordained to content them; but you will say this is pride
> & madness, for theire are those soe intirely satisfyed
> wth theire shares in this world, that theire wishes nor
> theire thoughts have not a farther prospect of felicity
> & glory, I'le tell you were that mans soule plac't in a
> body fitt for it, hee were a dogg, that could count
> any thing a benifitt obtain'd wth flattery, feare, & service,
>
> > Is there a man yee gods whome I doe hate
> > Dependance & Attendance bee his fate
>
> Cow:
>
> > Lett him bee busy still & in a crowde
> > And very much a slave & very proude.
>
> (Treglown, pp. 241–42)

At the time of his death, Rochester was holding the offices of Gentleman of the Bedchamber, Gamekeeper for the county of Oxford, Deputy Lieutenant of Somersetshire, Ranger and Keeper of Woodstock Park, and Alderman of Taunton. He had married the 'fortune of the North', had allied himself with the great and the powerful, including those who watched over the King's treasury, Sir Robert Howard, Thomas Clifford, and the Earl of Danby. And though he had not received as much as he liked from his impecunious king, he had done well. Despite his success, he clearly loathed the courtier's life, of making one's way in the world 'wth flattery, feare, & service'.

He could not, however, quit that life, nor did a part of him really want to, his feelings about the Court, like his feelings toward so many things in his life, being deeply at cross purposes. Life at Whitehall often made him, as he told his wife, 'soe weary of, that I may be said rather to languish than live in it' (Treglown, p. 52). In another letter to her he confesses 'I am allready soe weary of this place That upon my word I could bee Content To pass my winter att Cannington' (Treglown, pp. 82–83), Cannington being one of Elizabeth's family estates. The Court, nevertheless, was where he made his living. 'Court affaires', he explains to a wife imploring him to return to Adderbury, 'are more hardly sollicited now then ever, and having follow'd them till I had spent all my owne money & y^{rs} too, I was forc't to stay somthing longer here till I had contriv'd a supply' (Treglown, p. 80). At Court he also enjoyed the companionship of the likes of Sackville, Buckingham, Savile, and Sedley, drank, fornicated, and intrigued. Courtship itself, moreover, had become central to the very make-up of his character.

We catch a glimpse of just how important soliciting good opinion to gain favour and reward were to Rochester from his falling out with the Duchess of Portsmouth in the autumn and winter of 1675–76. The cause of their quarrel is unknown, but the Duchess, then mistress *en titre*, was a powerful person, a quarrel with her being a cause for worry. In a letter to Savile concerning the 'surprising account of my lady Duchess's more than ordinary indignation against me' Rochester complains:

> What ill star reigns over me, that I'm still marked out for ingratitude, and only used barbarously by those I am obliged to? Had I been troublesome to her in pinning the dependence of my fortune upon her solicitations to the King, or her unmerited recommendations of me to some great man, it would not have moved my wonder much if she had sought any occasion to be rid of a useless trouble. But a creature who had already received of her all the obligations he ever could pretend to, except the continuance of her good opinion, for the which he resolved and did direct every step of his life in duty and service to her and all who were concerned in her; why should she take the advantage of a false, idle story to hate such a man, as if it were an inconveniency to her

to be harmless, or a pain to continue just? By that God that made me, I have no more offended her in thought, word or deed, no more imagined or uttered the least thought to her contempt or prejudice, than I have plotted treason, concealed arms, trained regiments for a rebellion. (Treglown, pp. 106–7)

In what seems to be a quick follow-up letter to Savile on this potentially dangerous quarrel, surprise and vexation have become genuine anxiety and self-doubt:

> If it were the sign of an honest man to be happy in his friends, sure I were marked out for the worst of men, since no-one e'er lost so many as I have done or knew how to make so few. The severity you say the D. of P— shows to me is a proof that 'tis not in my power to deserve well of anybody, since (I call truth to witness) I have never been guilty of an error that I know to her. And this may be a warning to you that remain in the mistake of being kind to me, never to expect a grateful return, since I am so utterly ignorant how to make it. To value you in my thoughts, to prefer you in my wishes, to serve you in my words, to observe, study and obey you in all my actions is too little, since I have performed all this to her without so much as an offensive accident, and yet she thinks it just to use me ill. (Treglown, pp. 108–9)

Taking into account Rochester's capacity for exaggeration, self-parody, and playfulness, we still have here a man who is dumbfounded and more than a little hurt. His best performance has been rebuffed, and he is shaken, his capacity to make friends, 'to deserve well of anybody', called into doubt.

He goes on to put a brave face on this failure, telling Savile: 'I can as well support the hatred of the whole world as anybody, not being generally fond of it. Those whom I have obliged may use me with ingratitude and not afflict me much.' Then he returns to what really bothers him: 'but to be injured by those who have obliged me, and to whose service I am ever bound, is such a curse as I can only wish on them who wrong me to the Duchess' (Treglown, p. 109). His courtship has failed, and with the failure have come doubts about himself, even about his most trusted friendship, that with Savile. Though he declares that he is not 'at all afraid she can hurt me with you', he goes on: 'I dare swear you don't think I have dealt so indiscreetly in my service to her as to doubt me in the friendship I profess to you' (Treglown, pp. 107–8). Thoroughly shaken, he wants further assurances from Savile that he will talk once more to the Duchess on his behalf, but also that 'If you visit my Lord Treasurer, name the calamity of this matter to him and tell me sincerely how he takes it. And if you hear the King mention me, do the office of a friend' (Treglown, p. 108).

In this episode we see, in part at least, how much Rochester's sense of himself and of his well-being depends on his powers of persuasion.

His failure with the Duchess has called into question his relationship with those upon whom his very identity depends, the King, the Lord Treasurer, Savile, and his other friends. As Rochester himself puts it in what seems to be a genuine bid for Savile's sympathy:

> I hope ... within some time you will come and fetch me to London. I shall scarce think of coming till you call me, as not having many prevalent motives to draw me to the Court, if it be so that my master has no need of my service, nor my friends of my company. (Treglown, p. 109)

Rochester had every right to doubt Portsmouth's 'generous resolution of not hurting me to the King' (Treglown, p. 107) and therefore to be fearful of truly injurious consequences of this quarrel. Courtship was the way he made his living. A courtier for whom his 'master has no need of my service' quickly loses his place in preferment's line. But the rhetoric suggests that there is something more at stake for Rochester in this episode than worldly gain. He could understand the Duchess's indignation were he dependent on her for his fortune; in such a case she might well want to be rid of him. But he is not. He has sought her good opinion freely, indeed directed 'his every step of his life in duty and service to her' without thought of reward. On one level, then, he is worried about what the Duchess might do and what consequences her actions might have on his material well-being. On another level, he is concerned about his own prowess, his powers and abilities of appeal. We can also discern here another motive at work, a desire to court for the sake of courting. In all human affairs, let alone those of seventeenth-century courtiers, persuasion is never without its ulterior motives. But Rochester's interests here, as they so often do, move in the direction of what Kenneth Burke has called 'pure persuasion'.[23]

This interest in pure courtship, in taking 'delight in the sheer *forms* of courtship for their own sakes',[24] can also be detected in his letters to his wife and Elizabeth Barry. He sought both of them for any number of reasons, physical desire to worldly gain. But clearly one of the charms that Rochester found most attractive in both Elizabeths is that they too were adept in the art of courtship. They did not make it easy for the Earl. With Elizabeth Malet, Rochester had begun by eschewing the appeal of the word. 'My Lord of Rochester would have forced her', joked the heiress (Pepys, 25 November 1666), and on the evening of 26 May 1665, Rochester with a group of his henchman had done just that, kidnapping the heiress at Charing Cross. The Lady Malet married the impetuous Earl two years later, his verbal appeals apparently having greatly improved. She was to remain a match for him, however, throughout their fourteen years together.

> The Difficultyes of pleasing y^r La^{sp} doe encrease soe fast upon mee, & are growne soe numerous that to a man less resolv'd than my self never to give itt

over, itt would appeare a madness ever to Attempt itt more, but through your
frailtys myne ought nott to multiply; you may therefore secure y^r self that it
will not bee easy for you to put mee of[f] of my constant resolutions to satisfy
you in all I can. (Treglown, p. 77)

The very 'Difficultyes of pleasing', though perhaps a form of madness,
become for the true courtier a test of resolution, a woman's 'frailtys', in
turn, being an opportunity for exercising one's powers.

These same paradoxes lace Rochester's courtship of Elizabeth Barry.
'You are stark mad', he writes to her, 'and therefore the fitter for me to love;
and that is the reason I think I can never leave to be/ Your humble servant'
(Treglown, p. 98). In turn for her 'to pick out the wildest and most fantastical odd man alive, and to place your kindness there, is an act so brave
and daring as will show the greatness of your spirit and distinguish you in
love, as you are in all things else, from womankind' (Treglown, p. 99). In
yet another bravura attempt at persuading his mistress, Rochester contends
that:

> Sure, to be half kind is as bad as to be half-witted;
> and madness, both in love and reason, bears a better
> character than a moderate state of either. Would I
> could bring you to my opinion in this point. I would
> then confidently pretend you had too just exceptions
> either against me or my passion, the flesh and the
> devil; I mean, all the fools of my own sex, and that
> fat with the other lean one of yours whose prudent
> advice is daily concerning you, how dangerous it is
> to be kind to the man upon earth who loves you best.
> (Treglown, pp. 123–24)

Were you as madly in love with me as you should be, I would admit that
the gossip concerning me and my trafficking with 'passion, the flesh and the
devil' is true. But in your madness you would see such passion as proof that
it is indeed I who love you best. Teasing the same paradox in a different
way, he asks his mistress: 'Were men without frailties, how would you bring
it about to make 'em love you so blindly as they do?' (Treglown, p. 150).

In keeping with this logic, to give further opportunities for displays
of persuasive appeal, to test further the worth and steadfastness of the
pursued, and perhaps above all to keep the courtship going, we find
Rochester taking advantage of his own frailties, even introducing additional
complications and interferences. He writes to his wife:

> Runn away like a rascall without taking leave, deare wife, it is an unpollish't
> way of proceeding wch a modest man ought to be asham'd of, I have left
> you a prey to your owne immaginations, amongst my Relations, the worst

of damnations; but there will come an hower of deliverance, till when, may
my mother bee mercifull unto you, soe I committ you to what shall ensue,
woman to woman, wife to mother, in hopes of a future appearance in glory.
(Treglown, p. 73)

Rochester has been a rascal, and he is asking forgiveness. His being a rascal, however, has provided the occasion for this witty apology in which, as Treglown points out, he parodies the funeral service. He has created his own interference, creating the need for the apology. To a lesser or greater degree, Rochester was often doing just this: causing a breach, then trying to heal it. Rochester, in a parody of 'learned' style, writes to his Countess that 'Persons in Absence aught to notifie Returns reciprocrally, affectionately reconsell'd with humble Redentigration' (Treglown, p. 51). He had evidently done something that required that he take on this humorous pose in a bid for reconciliation, 'reconsell'd' having as Treglown points out 'a strong religious association, particularly of purification after prophanation' (Treglown, p. 51). In another letter to his wife, he adopts a similarly humorous strategy:

The last letter I received from y^r honour, was somthing
scandalous, soe that I knew not well how to answer it,
'twas my designe to have writ to my Lady Anne willmot
to intercede for mee, but now wth joy I find my selfe
againe in y^r favour, it shall bee my endeavours to
continue soe. (Treglown, p. 142)

Rochester plays the role of wife, who has heard 'somthing scandalous', in order to reconcile himself with his wife who often was wounded by news of her husband's extravagances. In a letter to Elizabeth Barry, we find Rochester confessing:

Till I have mended my manners I am ashamed to look
you in the face, but seeing you is as necessary to my
life as breathing, so that I must see you or be yours no
more, for that's the image I have of dying. The sight of
you, then, being my life, I cannot but confess with an
humble and sincere repentance that I have hitherto
lived very ill. Receive my confession and let the
promise of my future zeal and devotion obtain my
pardon for last night's blasphemy against you, my
heaven. So shall I hope hereafter to be made partaker
of such joys in your arms as meeting tongues but
faintly can express. Amen. (Treglown, pp. 131–32)

The greater the breach, the greater rhetorical effort needed to overcome it, greater the trust that can be placed in the person who agrees to the reconciliation, and greater too the chance to continue the courtship. Without division, without breach, there is no courtship. Rochester made this point to Elizabeth Barry in the form of a paradox: 'You need but continue to make it fit for me not to love you and you can never want something to upbraid me with' (Treglown, p. 181).

To be sure Rochester's relationship with the Duchess of Portsmouth, his wife, Elizabeth Barry, and the numerous others who peopled his various and busy life (a seventeenth-century aristocrat was never much alone), concerned real day-to-day problems and emotions – sufficient coal for winter, a nagging mother-in-law, a chronically sick son, genuine affection, unfaithfulness, and the ever-present need for the 'money you shall have as soone as ever I come to you' (Treglown, p. 96). On Rochester's part there was also, however, an interest in courtship for courtship's sake, a courtship often carried on in a paradoxical, negative way. His wife recognized, at least in part, what her husband was about. In reaction to what would seem to be typical example of Rochester's method of proceeding, she writes:

> If I could haue bin troubled att any thing when I had the happyness of resceiuing a letter from you I should be soe because you did not name a time when I might hope to see you: the uncertainty of which very much aflicts me whether this ode kind of proceeding be to try my patience or obedyence I cannot guesse but I will neuer faile of e[i]ther when my duty to you requier them. (Treglown, pp. 128–29)

In a genuinely moving letter to his wife he acknowledged that:

> 'Tis not an easy thing to bee intirely happy, But to bee kind is very easy and that is the greatest measure of happiness; I say nott this to putt you in mind of being kind to mee, you have practis'd that soe long that I have a joyfull confidence you will never forgett itt, but to show that I myself have a sence of what the methods of my Life seeme soe utterly to contradict ....
> (Treglown, p. 228)

A letter to Elizabeth Barry captures this 'sense of what the methods of my Life seeme soe utterly to contradict', but in a harsher tone. 'I assure you', he writes, that 'I am not half so faulty as unfortunate in serving you. I will not tell you my endeavours nor excuse my breach of promise, but leave it to you to find the cause of my doing so ill to one I wish so well to' (Treglown, p. 129).

We are close here to what is in part the motivation behind Rochester's exhibitionism and the parading of aristocratic vices and crime. He is seeking, in a paradoxical way, a purer form of preferment. 'If you distrust me and all my professions upon the score of truth and honour', Rochester writes to Elizabeth Barry, 'at least let 'em have credit on another, upon which my greatest enemies will not deny it me, and that is its being notorious that I mind nothing but my own satisfaction' (Treglown, p. 103). His very reputation for selfishness becomes a proof of his capacity to give totally of himself in this love relationship! Concerning the Portsmouth affair, Rochester icily notes, 'After this she need not forbid me to come to her; I have little pride or pleasure in showing myself where I am accused of a meanness I were not capable of even for her service, which would prove a shrewder trial of my honesty than any ambition I ever had to make my court to' (Treglown, p. 107). A meanness committed in her service would have shown a greater devotion than any honest courtship he has or could have made.

I want to explore further Rochester's exhibitionism and criminality, but the important point here is that Rochester's courtship is one, and one very important, manifestation of a generalized yearning for the ideal – friendship, truth, love, and communion – that suffuses the letters. He writes to Savile that

> if there bee a reall good upon Earth 'tis in the
> Name of freind, without wch all others are meerly
> fantasticall, how few of us are fitt stuff to make
> that thing, wee have dayly the melancholy experience;
> However Deare Harry let us not give out nor despaire
> of bringing that about wch as it is the most difficult &
> rare accident of life, is allsoe the Best, nay perhaps the
> only good one. (Treglown, p. 93)

To Savile he also writes of his desire for the 'truth of our selves', the 'truths of others', with 'flattery from our tongues and distrust from our Hearts' banished (Treglown, p. 67). 'Remember the hour', he instructs Elizabeth Barry, 'of a strict account, when both hearts are to be open and we obliged to speak freely' (Treglown, p. 99). He pursues his mistress, because her 'favours are to me the greatest bliss this world, or womankind – which I think Heaven – can bestow, but the hopes of it' (Treglown, p. 118).

But the ideal is rarely realized, the view of mankind and his condition Rochester gives in the letters differing little from that found in the poetry. Here too 'most human affairs are carried on at the same nonsensical rate, which makes me (who am now grown superstitious) think it a fault to laugh at the monkey we have here when I compare his condition with mankind' (Treglown, pp. 193–94). In this world 'few of us are fitt stuff' to sort out 'reall good' from all that is 'meerly fantasticall' (Treglown, p. 93). We are creatures of desire, but in this world there is 'soe greate a disproportion t'wixt our desires & what it has ordained to content them' (Treglown, pp. 241–42). As a result, one continues to court.

The rhetorical stance of courtship allows Rochester, then, to keep the ideal alive in a fallen world. Undoubtedly, other, often deeply ambivalent, motives are at work here as well. By continuing the courtship, even if one has to create one's own difficulties, one can avoid commitment and responsibility. But it is also a way of assuaging the guilt that arises from such avoidance. One can serve the ideal, yet acknowledge that one is unworthy of that ideal. Thus Rochester, whenever he approaches the ideal, expresses a seemingly heartfelt point, inevitably turns witty and humorous. Yes, I said this; take it seriously, but don't take it seriously. It comes from me, and after all, you know me. This is a way of asserting one's great worth: nothing human will quite do – while simultaneously acknowledging that one is totally unworthy – please accept me despite all that I have done. Thus we find what apparently are Rochester's most heartfelt sentiments couched with wit and humour. Thus too Rochester's tone in the letters ranges from the submissive and pleading to the imperious, cold, and sometimes mean, when one will not play the courtship game with him as he envisions it.

After the Duchess of Portsmouth had been ousted and had fallen ill, Rochester writes to Savile: 'I am sorry for the declining D—ss and would have you generous to her at this time, for that is true pride and I delight in it' (Treglown, p. 120). Addressing his wife's complaints, he warns her that she will not always have these problems. He will die, and 'when [that] time comes you will grow wiser, though I feare nott much Happyer' (Treglown, p. 171). Having taken their daughter, Betty, away from Elizabeth Barry, he warns his mistress: 'you would do well to think of the advice I gave you, for how little show soever my prudence makes in my own affairs, in yours it will prove very successful if you please to follow it. And since discretion is the thing alone you are like to want, pray study to get it' (Treglown, p. 217). While not discounting any of these motives, I would stress that around the edges of Rochester's letters, even those and perhaps most of all those which are perverse and paradoxical, hovers a yearning for the ideal.

Though they make up one third of the canon – of the seventy-six poems in the Love edition, sixteen lyrics are simply headed 'Song' in the manuscripts and for a further ten, contemporary musical settings survive – Rochester's songs have not, until recently, received much attention. Twentieth-century critics have lumped Rochester's lyrics with those by his fellow court wits, admired the craft but found the entire lot, with one or two notable exceptions, to be little more than smooth and easy redactions of the commonplace. For F.R. Leavis even the 'best things of Etherege, Sedley, Rochester and the rest' represented the 'decay of the Caroline courtly tradition'.[25] The lyrics of Charles II's court, in John Harold Wilson's estimation, were 'written to amuse, with no thought of profundity or moral instruction', though he concluded that 'Dorset, Etherege, Sedley, and Rochester were true poets in whose hands the merely fashionable themes and forms were new molded into verses of enduring worth.'[26]

For Pinto 'the tradition of the courtly lyric that began with Wyatt was dying' by 1660;[27] the only alternative left to the wits was to try to perfect the form. In pursuit of that decadent ideal, they often succumbed to 'aridity and insipidity'.[28] Neither Wilson nor Pinto, however, were entirely comfortable in judging Rochester to be just another writer of 'Love Songs to Phyllis'. Wilson, for example, observed that 'Rochester, the strangest and wildest genius of the period, occasionally used the standard poetic devices of his age for the expression of true emotion.' And he went on to cite 'My dear Mistress has a heart' as being 'one of the best lyrics of the century, and partly because it is so unlike the typical Restoration song to Phyllis.'[29] Pinto thought that 'in their best poems the wits are saved ... by their realistic temper, their humour and their irony', his chief example being, of course, a poem by Rochester, 'While on those lovely looks I gaze'.[30] Whether in subverting a genre, exploding romance conventions with realism, or restating the commonplace in a particularly memorable fashion, both Wilson and Pinto intuited that Rochester was somehow different. Recent critics have expanded upon their insights. Reba Wilcoxon devoted a fine article to Rochester's burlesque of the pastoral tradition.[31] In an analysis of four lyrics, Vieth gave a deft account of what he calls 'The Perverse Artistry of Rochester's Lyrics'.[32] And Griffin in his Clark Lecture on Rochester's songs observed that 'Rochester turns such conventional appeals into occasions for doubt, anxiousness, or mockery or even contempt; his songs rarely pursue the sexual goal singlemindedly or imagine that the end will be easily attained. Sometimes they are vexed by doubts or cross-purposes.' He went on to conclude that 'the conventional nature of the Restoration love song is in Rochester's hands typically subverted by coolly elegant wit or by an invasion of doubts and fears'.[33]

More recently, Nicholas Fisher has provided abundant and welcome evidence that 'Rochester was particularly recognized during his lifetime (and after his death) as a writer of songs.' And drawing upon the work of Harold Love, Fisher goes on to give equally compelling evidence of 'The probability of Rochester's songs having been "written for sung performance".'[34] It may well be that during his lifetime Rochester was admired as much for his lyrical as for his satirical skill. 'As *Chloris* full of harmless thought', 'All my past Life is mine no more', and 'Absent from thee I languish still' achieved particular popularity in his lifetime, the exquisite 'My dear Mistris has a heart' becoming arguably the poem most widely associated with Rochester and the Restoration period.

Burlesque, irony, incomparable voice, artistry and perverse artistry, mockery, subversion, cross-purposes – critics have sensed something in Rochester's songs that goes beyond the commonplace smoothly stated, something that indeed gives the songs, pace Dr Johnson, particular character. And they are right, though here I want to press the point further and describe the motives behind the doubt and anxiety, the mockery and contempt, the twisted logic and humour, the genuine emotion and tenderness in a genre central to Rochester's work. I want to do so not by reading the songs singly but collectively as one work and by reading them not as representative of a particular genre but rather as stylized attempts to answer certain questions.

As we might expect of poems written in the Cavalier tradition, Rochester's songs and love poems come suffused with the rhetoric of courtship, though that rhetoric, like its counterpart in the letters, bears the distinctive Rochester trait of being conducted through the negative. This similarity can readily be illustrated by looking at the one poetical correspondence between Rochester and Elizabeth Malet that has survived. At one point, perhaps during courtship or early on in his marriage, Rochester wrote to his lady this *Song*:

> Give me leave to raile at you,
> I aske nothing but my due;
> To call you false, and then to say,
> You shall not keepe my Heart a Day.
> But (Alas!) against my will,
> I must be your Captive still.
> Ah! be kinder then, for I,
> Cannot change, and wou'd not dye.
>
> Kindnesse has resistlesse Charmes,
> All besides but weakly move;
> Fiercest Anger it disarmes,
> And Clips the Wings of flying Love.
> Beauty does the Heart invade,
> Kindnesse only can perswade;
> It guilds the Lovers servile Chaine
> And makes the Slave grow pleas'd and vaine.

Rochester wishes to rail at his lover, to call her false. To do so would show that he is not her slave. But alas, his will is not his own; he can do neither; and he turns a paradoxical wish into a polished compliment. His lady is too appealing, his love for her too powerful for him to be anything but a captive. He can ask only that she 'be kinder'.

The conflict between 'will' and the forces of nature, indicative of Rochester's own internal divisiveness, is a theme that runs throughout the songs and love poems, but the important point to note for now is the use of 'kinder' and 'Kindnesse'. The 'kind family' – the words appear 39 times in the poems Vieth assigns to Rochester – with its root meanings of 'natural', 'native', and 'innate'; with denotations of 'affection', 'graciousness', 'good will', and with connotations of 'lubricity' – is centrally important in Rochester's poetry. Rochester wants the lady to be 'kinder', more generous, warm, open-hearted, but also more 'a kin' to him, more of his persuasion. 'Kindnesse has resistlesse Charmes' and 'Kindnesse only can perswade' because it points to the natural order of things, to the way things should be, with the implication that should the lady give in to him that would be only natural. The lover's appeal then is at once tender and explicitly sexual, pious in wishing to conform with the way things should be and impious in wishing to do so in a most impudent way. Kindness promises to overcome the breach between these lovers, to restore the natural order by bringing them together, by making them kin, the last line being on one level a bawdy joke. If his Countess is kind, Rochester, rather than railing, will become happy and docile. But 'Kindnesse' also 'makes the Slave [penis] grow pleas'd [ejaculate] and vaine [empty or flaccid]'.

It is just such lyrics that Samuel Johnson declared to 'have no particular character: they tell, like other songs, in smooth easy language, of scorn and kindness, dismission and desertion, absence and inconstancy, with the common places of artificial courtship. They are commonly smooth and easy; but have little nature, and little sentiment.'[35] While Johnson was surely right to point out the commonplace themes of these songs, he was wrong in all other respects. In Rochester's hands the Restoration love lyric comes laced with irony, wit, humour, and paradox, but more than anything else it is the speakers seeking to get what they want roundabout and at a distance that gives these songs their distinctively Rochester character. While Rochester's verse here as elsewhere can be smooth and easy, it is often, in keeping with the extravagant wit, the twists and turns of his thought, deliberately abrupt and harsh. The songs and love poems, moreover, are concerned with little else but nature, though not in the sense that Johnson meant. These poems, that is, give us another version of Rochester's principal theme: the pursuit of pleasure through a harmonious relationship with nature. And finally, it is precisely in the artful courtship of pleasure that we can come upon the genuine sentiments that motivated these poems, their very artifice being the major clue as to what Rochester was about.

Though Johnson did not understand Rochester's lyrics, Elizabeth Malet certainly did as we see from her answer to her lover's appeal for kindness:

> Nothing adds to your fond fire,
> More than Scorne, and cold disdaine:
> I to cherish your desire,
> Kindnesse us'd, but 'twas in vaine.
> You insulted on your Slave,
> Humble Love you soone refus'd:
> Hope not then a Pow'r to have
> Which Ingloriously you us'd.
>
> Thinke not Thirsis I will e're,
> By my Love, my Empire loose.
> You grow Constant through despair,
> Love return'd, you wou'd abuse.
> Tho' you still possesse my heart,
> Scorne, and Rigour, I must feigne.
> Ah! forgive that only Art,
> Love, has left your Love to gaine.

Kindness has not worked. When the lady has become kind, Rochester has 'insulted', that is, 'exulted' over her and refused to be hers. It is 'Scorne, and cold disdaine' that keep the courtship alive; only 'through despair' can the lady keep her 'fond fugitive'. She must court him, that is, through the negative: 'Scorne and Rigour I must feign.'

In this exchange, as in the other songs and love poems, pleasure is life's goal. That pleasure is, in turn, to be sought in sensual gratification. Those who would not follow nature, not indulge the senses, come in for various forms of ridicule, just as Rochester chides Mistress Malet here. That is, these poems, like the major satires, are crafted out of materialistic and nominalistic assumptions. The libertine feast of the senses, however, rarely becomes a reality. In their pursuit of pleasure, a number of speakers, like Elizabeth Malet, encounter a paradox: they find themselves seeking what they would have through not having it. Inhabitants of a purely materialistic and nominalistic world, they find themselves engaged in courting their love through that which is demonstrably not physical, that is, through the negative.

In this exchange of poetic epistles we also hear the two major voices that inform the other songs and love poems. Though these voices take on a local habitation and place in each individual poem, the clear sound of both is always there. The one is laughing, mocking, ironic, sometimes tender, more often arch, occasionally cruel. The other is less sure, more plaintive, exploring, yearning. The one has as its goal to ridicule those who do not follow libertine norms; the other attempts to deal with the irony of being unable to live up to those norms even if one wanted to do so.

In at least three of the songs, Rochester celebrates what he takes to be the ideal relationship of human beings to their world, a relationship where

'Witt has to Pleasure been ever a friend' and 'Delight, is Loves end' (Song: 'To this Moment a Rebell, I throw down my Arms', lines 11–12); where 'restless Jealiousy' aside, 'witt has taught us how' to Raise pleasure to the Topp' ('*To A Lady, in A* Letter', lines 3 and 5–6); and where '*Cupid and Bacchus*' are 'saints' and 'Drink and Love still Reign' ('*Nestor*', lines 21–22). This ideal, in turn, becomes the norm for the jagged bolt of libertine satire that cuts across the songs. In a 'Womans Honour', 'Love bad' the speaker to 'hope' (line 1). The love he has obeyed is clearly physical love, but Phyllis continues still 'unkind' (line 2), that is, unnatural. She remains loyal to what the speaker sees as empty abstractions; ignoring the pleasure she should pursue, she instead 'Lives a Wretch for honours sake' (line 18). Similarly, the woman in 'TO *The Honorable****In the *Pall-mall*' refuses the speaker's witty offer to fling away her book, to live by the word become flesh, and to ascend to heaven through the body rather than by the word '*That we by* easie *steps may rise/ Through all the* Joys *on Earth, to those Above*' (lines 16–17).[36] Like Corinna, these women take cruel pains 'Against kinde Nature to maintaine/ Affected Rules of Honour' (lines 11–12). In the judgment of the libertine speakers, theirs, like hers, is a 'Silly Art' 'ill-designd' by 'Vertue' (lines 7–8) that

> Poor Feeble Tyrant who in Vaine
> Wou'd proudly take upon her
> Against kinde Nature to maintaine
> Affected Rules of Honour.
> ('*To Corinna*', lines 9–12)

These ladies are 'fond of baubles' and of their 'Guegaw reputation' and therefore become fit objects for the libertine's curse to 'Live upon Modesty and empty fame/ Foregoeing sence for a fantastick name' ('The advice' lines 41–44), the satire being at once social, scientific, and philosophical, the ladies being unkind, unnatural, and nonsensical.

In the songs and love poems as in the major satires, however, the libertine norm of men and women reaping pleasure by being at one with nature is more ideal than real. Rochester's libertine idyll of an Elizabeth Malet, who loves pleasure as much as her suitor does, takes place in the conditional: 'How perfect Cloris, and how free/ Would these enjoyments prouve' ('Song', lines 1–2). This teases the same paradox with which 'A Satyre' opens: 'Were I … A spirit free to choose ….' In neither case are the speakers free, their versions of libertine pleasure taking place under the sign not of the indicative but of the conditional, the hortatory, and the optative. 'May Drink and Love still Reign' is Rochester's Anacreontic wish. Even in 'To this Moment a Rebell, I throw down my Arms' the only lyric in which the speaker's desired consummation takes place, the pleasure comes in a perverse form. The poem opens with the mild irony of the male being the reluctant object of female pursuit. Unlike the typically honourable Phyllis or artful Corinna, he has decided to give in despite being the object of what he feels is a conspiracy to lead him into self-betrayal:

> When innocence, Beauty and witt do conspire
> To betray and ingage, and enflame my Desire,
> Why shou'd I decline, what I cannot avoyd,
> And let pleasing Hope, by base Fear be destroy'd?
> (lines 5–8)

Whether his 'base Fear' has arisen out of Hobbesian nature, sheer cowardice, social decorum, respect for the lady, or concern for hygiene, he has, under the persuasion of her wit, set it aside.

> Her innocence cannot contrive to undo me,
> Her Beauty's inclin'd, or why shou'd it pursue me?
> And Witt has to Pleasure been ever a Friend,
> Then what Room for dispair, since Delight, is Loves end?
>
> There can be no danger in sweetnesse and Youth,
> Where Love is secured by good nature and Truth.
> (lines 9–14)

But this young man's pleasure comes in an unexpected way, the poem ending in *ejaculatio precox*: 'Help Love! I dissolve in a rapture of Charms/ At the Thought of those Joys, I shou'd meet in her Arms' (lines 23–24).

In one way or another, all of Rochester's lyrics and love poems rework the theme of imperfect enjoyment. Given Rochester's often satirical intentions, this is perhaps not surprising. The dilemma of the satiric targets in these songs is to find themselves seeking to persuade the world to conform to their desires while that world, because it is material and governed solely by the laws of motion, is immune to persuasion. They pursue what turns out to be illusions; disabused by the knowing libertine, they are the butt of an aristocratic, Hobbesian laughter. Because of the deterministic nature of the world they inhabit, the tone of these songs is rarely comic. On the contrary, it often borders on the cruel, if not brutal, even those moments of tenderness never being far from a mocking laugh. The audience is not immune to this debunking process either. It too has its assumptions exposed as illusions. One thing, for example, that makes Rochester's mock pastorals work so well is the assumption on the reader's part about the innocence of the pastoral. We too believe or want to believe in a '*Chloris* full of harmless thought'. Her innocence is such that it could survive the courtship of 'Princes' and 'all their pompous Train' (lines 21–22). But what seems to be genuine virtue is simply a product of circumstances. Her virtue does not depend upon her choice. Given the proper surprise, the 'lucky minute' (line 23), what princes have tried will be accomplished by shepherds.

The '*Faire Cloris*' who inhabits 'a Pigsty' is no more innocent and no less subject to circumstances than her pastoral sister of the same name. Had the swain in this poem been real, Cloris would have been undone. Judging from her wish-fulfilment dream and her subsequent masturbation, she really desired just that. She is 'Innocent and pleas'd' (line 40) because in her enthusiastic fit she has managed to satisfy her desires without violating her principles. Yet the joke is on Cloris – and us. She owes her chastity not to principle but to mere circumstance in which what she took to be real was not. The preservation of her honour depends not a bit on her choice; her honour, unbeknown to her, is a product of the pigsty with the suggestion that the reader's is as well.

The libertine alone can use his clear-eyed view of how things work to his advantage, ridiculing others and indulging his own appetites. The speaker in '*Love* and *Life*' attempts to answer his lover's question as to why he cannot be faithful to her. Because she frames her question in terms of free will and responsibility and speaks of 'Inconstancy', of being false, and of breaking vows, he cannot really answer her. For he frames his reply in terms of circumstances. He reduces will to motion:

> All my past Life is mine no more,
>   The flyeing houres are gone
> Like Transitory dreams given o're
> Whose Images are kept in store
>   By memory alone.
>
> What ever is to come is not:
>   How can it then be mine?
> The present moment's all my Lott
> And that as fast as it is gott
>   *Phillis* is wholly thine.
>
> Then talk not of Inconstancy,
>   False hearts and broken vows:
> If I by miracle can be
> This livelong Minute true to Thee
>   Tis' all that Heaven allowes.

She assumes he has free will. He replies that he does not; he is controlled by circumstances. Her question translated into his frame of discourse makes literally no sense. If allowed to hear her answer, we would probably be privy to mutterings about an evasion of responsibility. But in the poem, the libertine speaker, so he contends, cannot help his inconstancy, and according to him, if the woman only knew, she could not help it either.

She is a dupe. Her attempt to impose human categories on a world in Heraclitian flux is foolish.

The corrosive logic of satire, however, runs its entire course in these poems, the libertine speaker in turn becoming a victim of his own satirical strategy. In 'A Dialogue between Strephon and Daphne', Strephon, also wanting to shed himself of an unwanted lover, makes the libertine argument that Daphne should 'Faith to pleasure sacrifice' (line 64). She should recognize that constancy, love, and faith are but empty names; change is 'Natures Law'; 'Constancy alone is strange' (lines 31–32). But Strephon finds that his libertine persuasion depends on the assumption that Daphne really has been faithful, an assumption exploded by her sassy revelation:

> Silly swaine I'le have you know
> T'was my practice Long agoe:
> Whilst you Vainely thought me true
> I was falce in scorn of you.
> (65–68)

Strephon discovers, apparently to his consternation, that women as well as men do follow nature. In terms of our argument, he discovers that libertine rhetoric, with its materialistic and nominalistic assumptions, depends, paradoxically enough, on the reality of that which it seeks to prove unreal. To adapt words Anne Righter used to describe Rochester himself, the targets of satire in these poems seek from 'sense experience things which are not only in excess of what it can give, but inappropriate to it'.[37] In doing so, they come in for ridicule, satire being a guide to the distances between desire and reality, an art to measure imperfection.

While it is not surprising that the songs and love poems make use of the imperfect for satirical purposes, it comes as very much a surprise to see so many of the speakers deliberately court imperfection. One of the keys to understanding this paradox is to be found in Rochester's ingenious, miniature version of *Paradise Lost*, *The Fall*. 'Man and Woman er'e they fell' (line 2) lived in a state where enjoyment and desire were one, where there was no distance between human desires and what had been 'ordained to content them' (Treglown, p. 241).

> Naked beneath coole shades they lay:
>   Enjoyment waited on desire.
> Each member did their wills obey
>   Nor could a wish sett pleasure higher.
> (lines 5–8)

Because of his fallen state, however, this lover must persuade his lady that his 'frayler part' does not indicate his real desire and feelings for her.

On the contrary, his very frailty makes it possible that his real motives can be revealed through higher feelings, the love of his heart.

> Then *Cloris* while I Duly pay
>   The nobler Tribute of a heart,
> Be not you soe severe to say
> You Love me for a frayler part.
>   (lines 13–16)

This is, of course, an elaborate sexual joke, but paradoxically and cleverly enough, a most potent one. Paradise has no need for rhetoric, but man's fallen state makes persuasion possible by introducing the necessary interference. Persuasion perforce is based on the negative, but paradoxically, that negative becomes the means for developing positive values – loyalty, heart, and love. The greater the negative, the greater the chance to display human ingenuity but also human values. The clever seducer, the clever persuader, thus seeks the most impotent of positions. There is a sense in which the lady here should indeed love her man for his frailty.

In the song 'A Young Lady to her Antient Lover', the young lady does just that, and the haunting lyric derives a good deal of its poignancy from the rhetorical situation it exploits. It may well be that her 'Brooding kisses' (line 9) will restore her lover to a 'Second spring' (lines 12) and that

> Thy nobler parts which but to name
> In owr Sex would be Counted shame,
> By ages frozen grasp possest
> From their Ice shall be releast
> And sooth'd by my reviveing hand
> In former warmth and Vigour stand.
>   (lines 15–20)

But that has not happened yet, and she has so much to overcome. Though she loves 'without art' (line 25), that is, without ulterior motive or design, her song displays the greatest of rhetorical skill. The difference in age between herself and her lover becomes a powerfully persuasive way to show her love. Hovering around the edges of this poem, too, is that ever-lurking Rochester dilemma of being a creature of desire in a material world that cannot satisfy desire. If love depends solely on the body, then the young lady is deluded indeed. But it may be that her love, seemingly based on nothing, on a nobler part that no longer has potency, is proof itself that love really does exist and does so precisely because it is based on nothing.

'An Age in her Embraces pas'd' also teases the paradox that not having is having, the speaker announcing as the poem opens that:

An Age in her Embraces pas'd
Wou'd seem a winters Day
Where life and light with envious haste
Are torn and snatch'd away.
                    (lines 1–4)

On one level, we have the traditional theme that moments of love pass all too quickly; even an age would seem but one day. But that day, the poet tells us, would be a winter's day. The shortness is in keeping with his theme of the transitory quality of love, but the winter seems incongruous. Yet as the rest of the poem points out, being with the lover would indeed be wintry; it would be death. Their love can only be sustained by absence. This absence, paradoxically enough, contributes to the speaker's death but also makes him live. His 'breast, by absence made' becomes 'The living Tombe of Love' (lines 11–12). The speaker is well aware that such oxymoronic sentiments may be marked down by 'wiser men (line 13) as the ravings of 'lovesick fancy' (line 14). And they would be right, though not for the reasons they suppose. The speaker, as he goes on to explain, must entertain these fancies in order to keep his love alive. It cannot exist in any other way. To explain this apparent contradiction he switches the topic from absence to the sighs, laments, complaints, and griefs that exist between himself and his beloved. Do not, he warns, take such evidence as the basis for disagreement between lovers. On the contrary:

Alas! 'tis sacred Jealousy,
Love rais'd to an extream,
The only proof twixt her and me
We love and doe not Dream.
                    (lines 25–28)

Jealousy, a state contrary to love, validates love just as absence does. There may be something mad about arriving at love through negation, but it would be foolishness, if not outright madness, to imagine that love can exist in any other way.

Fantastick fancys fondly move
And in fraile joys believe,
Taking false pleasure for true love,
But pain can ne're deceive.
                    (lines 29–32)

The body is real; it knows pleasure as well as pain. But pleasure is apt to deceive. Pain alone provides the litmus paper for distinguishing true pleasure from false. In seeking pleasure then, one would deliberately seek interference, deliberately seek 'Kind Jealous doubt, tormenting fear/ And Anxious cares' (lines 33–34), for they 'Prove our Hearts Treasure fixt and Dear/ And makes us blest at last' (lines 35–36).

The beautifully fashioned 'Absent from thee I languish still' gives an even more probing account of the same theme. Absent from his lover, the speaker is in pain. Perversely, he wants nevertheless to be away from her, his reason being

> That my fantastick mind may prove,
> The torments it deservs to try
> That Tears my fixt heart from my love.
> (lines 6–8)

In his logic, however, he is not being perverse at all. Once absent, his mind can imagine the 'love and peace and truth' (line 11) that resides with his lover. That is, he can test whether these qualities really exist only by entertaining them from their opposite state of absence and the pain it brings. Once he has confirmed his love through love's opposite, he may be able to return to 'Where love and peace and truth doe flow … contented there Expire' (lines 11–12). To expire is an odd choice of felicity. It suggests sexual fulfilment, though such a reading is not it keeping with the quality of love that the speaker has been describing. Expire meaning death may get us closer to one of the predicaments the speaker is exploring. Contentment with his lover would be death; the love would lack the tension that defines it. On the other hand, if he continues to wander away in an attempt to define love through negation, there is every possibility that he will become lost. As the speaker puts its:

> Least once more wandring from that heav'n
> I fall on some Base heart unbles'd,
> Faithless to thee, false, unforgiv'n
> And loose my everlasting rest.
> (lines 14–16)

Either way the lover is doomed. To gain his love would be to die, to expire. Not to gain his love is to risk being lost, unblessed forever. The poem, on one level, suggests that to know that love exists, and in turn to keep that love alive, he must forever court it through absence, through the negative.

On another level, the poem is both an admission of and a bid to transcend guilt. I have been absent, but that absence and the suffering it has entailed have led me to realize how valuable our love is. In the very entertaining of the base, the faithless, and false, which in truth has been a 'world of woe' (line 9), I have come to know the heaven that you are. My absence, and the fall from grace that it has involved, is therefore justified by my own suffering but also by the knowledge it has brought. The religious vocabulary here – heav'n', 'fall', 'unbles'd', 'Faithless', unforgiv'n', 'everlasting rest' – may only be part of the arsenal commanded by a libertine rhetorician, the lady being flattered and in turn more easily persuaded by its use. And the orthodox argument of the fortunate fall that underlies the poem may be being used to the same libertine purposes. But whether one focuses on the libertine or spiritual reading of the poem, the important point to note is the negative courtship going on, the coming at what one wants by a roundabout way.

'The Platonick Lady' too would have what is most natural but only through the most artful of ways. She 'hate[s] the thing is calld enjoyment' (line 7). 'It cutts of all thats Life and fier' (line 9); converts the bee and its sting into a mere drone (lines 11–12); and brings a halt to 'desire' (line 10).[38] She wants to overcome the limitations of the physical. Her witty redefinition of what it means to be platonic in a physical world would turn the physical into a rhetorical exercise. She would

> ... sigh and looke with Eyes that wish
> For what if I could once obtaine,
> I would neglect with flat disdaine.
> (lines 16–18)

That which she can obtain is not the fit object for her desire. She wants to keep desire alive by foreplay that would have no end.

> I'de give him Liberty to toye,
> And play with mee and Count it Joy.
> Our freedomes should be full compleat,
> And nothing wanting but the feat.
> Lett's practise then and we shall prove,
> These are the only sweets of Love.
> (lines 19–24)

Not having would be having. Through the negative, this Lady would overcome the limitations of the purely physical; she would be free and would become, paradoxically enough, really Platonic. She knows, as the concluding couplet of 'Leave this gawdy guilded Stage' puts it, that ''Twixt strifes of Love and war the difference Lies in this/ When neither overcomes Loves triumph greater is' (lines 9–10).

'The Platonick Lady' can be profitably read as one more adaptation of Petronius's 'Foeda est in coitu et brevis voluptas' just as Rochester's other songs against constancy can be used to illustrate a genre or, in their twisting and turning logic, can be made to fit a thesis about a Cavalier tradition in decay or one about the quirks of a particular sexual pathology. One moves closer to Rochester's motives, however, in seeing these songs and love poems as variants of pure persuasion, the various speakers, like the Rochester in the letters, attempting to court forever. To be sure, other motives, as we have seen, are also at work in these poems: here are strategies for overcoming the distance between man's desires and the materialism that cannot satisfy them; strategies for acknowledging and transcending guilt, for expressing tenderness while guarding against being taken in; and strategies for dealing with closure of any sort, particularly the ultimate closure of death. But none perhaps is more important than the ever-present strategy of bidding for preferment. By not giving in, I show that I am special, worthy of special treatment. By implication you become worthy too because you also have passed the test. But there is more: by keeping the courtship open there is an appeal for an ideal audience, someone who will truly understand you as you wish to be understood.

I have traced this pattern of negative courtship in the letters and love poems not to argue that it provides in itself evidence for Rochester's religious motivation, but rather to corroborate the argument that behind Rochester's seemingly desultory use of religious language, metaphor, and paradox lies a similar pattern and a similar desire for an ideal audience. That is, Rochester courted his God as he courted his wife, mistress, and king, through the negative and for many of the same reasons.[39]

Rochester's conversations with Gilbert Burnet provide a fascinating glimpse into this courtship at work. As the talks began, the two evidently agreed, in what seems a rather comically formal way, not to enter into a debate. As Burnet explained it: 'He would conceal none of his Principles from me, but lay his thoughts open without any Disguise; nor would he do it to maintain Debate, or shew his Wit' (Burnet, p. 55). Given these two aggressive men, the agreement quickly broke down, Burnet being eager to persuade his infamous charge to return to the fold and the Earl, though ill, not about to give up the use of wit or disguise. He played the reluctant, coy object of Burnet's persuasion while he himself courted a higher audience.

At issue were Rochester's principles concerning the restraint of pleasure, how far that was to go.

> Upon this he told me the two *Maxims* of his *Morality* then were, that he should do nothing to hurt any other, or that might prejudice his own health: And he thought that all pleasure, when it did not interfere with these, was to be indulged as the gratification of our natural Appetites. It seemed unreasonable to imagine these were put into a man only to be restrained, or curbed to such a narrowness: This he applied to the free use of Wine and Women. (Burnet, p. 57)

Burnet countered with an argument for 'a higher and more lasting pleasure' available through the 'exercise' of 'Reason in the Restraint and Government' of the appetites (Burnet, p. 57). A few might be capable of exercising such restraint by drawing upon the principles of philosophy, but for most men this could not be achieved 'either steddily, or with any satisfaction, unless the Mind does inwardly comply with, and delight in the Dictates of Virtue.

And that could not be effected, except a man's nature were internally regenerated, and changed by a higher Principle' (Burnet, p. 59). While agreeing that the well-being of society demanded some such restraints, Rochester dryly observed that Burnet's support of them 'sounded to him like *Enthusiasme*, or *Canting*: He had no notion of it, and so could not understand it: He comprehended the Dictates of *Reason* and *Philosophy*, in which as the Mind became much conversant, there would soon follow as he believed, a greater easiness in obeying its precepts' (Burnet, p. 59). Burnet replied bluntly that 'all his Speculations of *Philosophy* would not serve him in any stead, to the reforming of his Nature and Life, till he applied himself to God for inward assistances' (Burnet, p. 59).

Burnet had clearly done his homework, for he went on to argue that armed only with philosophy Rochester, as Ovid had put it, would always '"see what is better, and approve it; but follow what is worse"' (Burnet, p. 59). Burnet's clever use of the pagan version of St Paul's lament that 'the good that I would I do not: but the evil which I would not, that I do' (Romans, 7:19) must have quickened Rochester's interest. This admirer of Ovid had an ever growing 'sence', as he wrote to his wife probably at about this same time, 'of what the methods of my Life seeme soe utterly to contradict' (Treglown, p. 228). In Burnet he clearly had a worthy opponent. Though ill, he would have to summon up the wit for which he was famous and of which the Anglican Divine, clearly forewarned, was rightfully wary. At this point in Burnet's account, he begins to do just that, replying with amused detachment that, though prayer might serve to fix one's principles and therefore help to resist temptation, 'if one could turn to a *Problem* in *Euclid*, or to Write a Copy of Verses, it would have the same effect' (Burnet, p. 59).

The debate was joined. At issue was Rochester's version of an ethical hedonism, but also the role of God in human affairs, and 'the Notion of Religion in general' (Burnet, p. 60). On the first, though Rochester hardly needed to be persuaded, he continued to press Burnet on two specific points, about 'restraining a man from the use of Women, Except one in the way of Marriage' and about 'denying the remedy of Divorce' (Burnet, p. 72). Burnet reiterated his general case against the 'mischiefs of being given up to pleasure' and in a rough paraphrase of 'To the Post Boy', warned 'of running inordinately into [pleasure], of breaking the quiet of our own Family at home, and of others abroad: the ingaging into much Passion, the doing many false and impious things to compass what is desired, the Wast of men's Estates, time, and health' (Burnet, p. 75). He concluded that while restraint obviously involved man in many 'Inconveniences', 'pleasure stood in opposition to other Considerations of great Weight, and so the decision was easie' (Burnet, p. 76). Rochester, never ceasing to needle the Divine, quipped that 'We are sure the terms are difficult, but are not so sure of the Rewards' (Burnet, p. 76). The specific points about many women and divorce never got resolved, but Rochester, having explored and experienced the consequences of unbridled hedonism in ways not dreamed of in Burnet's imagination, had long been ready to concede the general point, and in his last sickness he confessed that 'all the Pleasures he had ever known in Sin, were not worth that torture he had felt in his Mind' (Burnet, p. 79).

On the subject of God, Rochester proved, however, reluctant and wily. From the beginning, he artfully pinned Burnet into a rhetorical corner from which the clergyman never escaped. Rochester admitted that 'He believed there was a Supream Being: He could not think the World was made by chance, and the regular Course of Nature seemed to demonstrate the Eternal Power of its Author. This, he said, he could never shake off' (Burnet, p. 60). The implication is that he had tried to shake off such a belief, and to do so, as the language suggests, with arguments from Lucretius. Instead, he settled for Lucretian sense of the deity, Burnet telling us:

> when he came to explain his Notion of the Deity, he said, he looked on it as a vast Power that wrought every thing by the necessity of its Nature: and thought that God had none of those Affections of Love or Hatred, which breed perturbation in us, and by consequence he could not see that there was to be either reward or punishment. He thought our Conceptions of God were so low, that we had better not think much of him: And to love God seemed to him a presumptuous thing, and the heat of fanciful men. Therefore he believed there should be no other Religious Worship, but a general Celebration of that Being, in some short Hymn: All the other parts of Worship he esteemed the Inventions of Priests, to make the world believe they had a Secret of Incensing and Appeasing God as they pleased. In a word, he was neither perswaded that there was a special Providence about humane Affairs; nor that Prayers were of much use, since that was to look on God as a weak Being, that would be overcome with Importunities. (Burnet, pp. 60–61)

Rochester's God is remote, a supreme power but one who works through the regular course of nature. Any human conception of this 'vast Power' is inadequate, the human and the divine being of incommensurate orders. Those who think they can sway God in any way, through love, worship, or prayers, are 'presumptuous' and 'fanciful'. Such importunities are the contrivance of 'Priests' who would convince the credulous they possess a 'Secret of Incensing and Appeasing God'. This is Rochester at his satirical best. That which is beyond the proof of the senses is fanciful – a product of heated imaginations. Those who would seek God's favour inevitably work from self-serving motives. Therefore, anything Burnet would advance from here on in would have to overcome Rochester's wickedly satirical charge of being priest-like and smelling of incense. Moreover, whatever appeals Burnet might make would be to a lesser God, Rochester's God being by definition beyond 'Importunities'. Burnet had reason to fear Rochester's wit; he would win the philosophical argument but never overcome the rhetorical force of Rochester's satirically reductive arguments.

Sick and feeling himself near death, Rochester wanted to be persuaded,

> often confess[ing], that whether the business of
> Religion was true or not, he thought those who had the
> perswasions of it, and lived so that they had quiet in
> their Consciences, and believed God governed the World,
> and acquiesced in his Providence, and had the hope of
> an endless blessedness in another State, the happiest men
> in the World: And said, He would give all that he was
> Master of, to be under those Perswasions, and to have the
> Supports and Joys that must needs flow from them. (Burnet, p. 64)

He went on to tell Burnet that 'he was sure *Religion* was either a mere Contrivance, or the most important thing that could be: So that if he once believed, he would set himself in great earnest to live suitably to it' (Burnet, p. 77). But he did not want to be a dupe. He had already fully explored the paradoxes of 'The perfect Joy of being well deceaved' ('Artemiza to Chloe', line 115). The 'aspirings that he had observed at Court, of some of the Clergy, with the servile ways they took to attain to Preferment, and the Animosities among those of several Parties, about trifles, made him often think they suspected the things were not true, which in their Sermons and Discourses they so earnestly recommended' (Burnet, p. 77). To Burnet's arguments Rochester threw up all the tests his wit and sceptical materialism could supply. The burden lay with the clergyman to prove that he was not one of the contrivers, his doctrine not a cheat.

Clearly piqued by Rochester's characterization of God and of man's relationship to Him, Burnet shot back that 'his Notion of God was so low, that the Supreme Being seemed to be nothing but Nature' (Burnet, p. 61). If God were all powerful, then He must surely have the freedom to enter into human affairs. Burnet went on to sketch a God who is 'Wise and Good' and very much interested in rewards for those who follow his ways and punishments for those who do not. As all powerful, it is foolish to think that He cannot govern that world He created, just 'as among men, those of weaker Capacities are wholly taken up with some one thing, whereas those of more enlarged powers can, without distraction, have many things within their care' (Burnet, p. 62). Prayer, far from being a servile plea for favour, serves to strengthen man's 'Apprehensions of God ... And the Returns of Prayer are not to be considered as Favours extorted by mere Importunity, but as Rewards conferred on men so well disposed, and prepared for them' (Burnet, p. 63). With a sly dig at Rochester himself, Burnet observed that 'If some Men, have at several times, found out Inventions to corrupt this, and cheat the World; it is nothing but what occurs in every sort of Employment, to which men betake themselves. *Mountebanks* Corrupt *Physick* (Burnet, p. 63). Alexander Bendo was being given a dose of his own elixir.

Burnet argued in an exemplary manner. Shrewdly assessing his audience, he couched his appeal in terms of Rochester's own experience, common sense, and probability. Good men do feel 'secret Joys' at the approach of death while 'ill men' experience 'Horrours' (Burnet, p. 64). Rochester suggested that such was the effect of education not religion. It is true that 'we cannot have suitable Notions of the Divine Essence'. But 'we have no just *Idea* of any Essence whatsoever: Since we commonly consider all things, either by their outward *Figure*, or by their Effects: and from thence make Inferences what their Nature must be' (Burnet, p. 63). All perception, Burnet rightly argued, depends on inferences, depends on belief in things beyond the circumstances we actually perceive before us. The basis of this belief in the things beyond derives from the testimony of others or through a concurrence of individual parts we have been able to verify. As though having just returned from a meeting of the Royal Society, Rochester countered that 'believing was at highest but a probable Opinion' (Burnet, p. 66). Equally adept in the ways of contemporary polemic, Burnet told him that

> if the Evidence be but probable, it is so: but if it be such that it cannot be questioned, it grows as certain as knowledge: For we are no less certain that there is a great Town called *Constantinople* ... than that there is another called *London*. We as little doubt that Queen *Elizabeth* once reigned, as that King *Charles* now Reigns in *England*. So that believing may be as certain, and as little subject to doubting as seeing or knowing. (Burnet, p. 67)

To Rochester's catch-all list of doubts about the 'Penmen of the Scriptures' being inspired by God; about 'a Lapse derived from *Adam*'; 'Miracles'; the 'Incoherences of Style in the Scriptures, the odd transitions, the seeming Contradictions, chiefly about the Order of time, the Cruelties enjoined the *Israelites* in destroying the *Canaanites*, Circumcision ... many other Rites of the Jewish Worship'; and the creation of the world as chronicled in the first three chapters of Genesis, Burnet replied:

> that believing a thing upon the testimony of another, in other matters where there was no reason to suspect the testimony, chiefly where it was confirmed by other Circumstances, was not only a reasonable thing, but it was the hinge on which all the Government and Justice in the World depended. (Burnet, pp. 65–66)

For the miracles of the New Testament, for the Crucifixion and Resurrection, 'the innocence and disinterestedness of the Witnesses, the number of them, and the publickest Confirmations that could possibly be given, do concur to perswade us' (Burnet, p. 66). As for the prophecies of the Old Testament, given the evidence, 'it is at least as reasonable to believe this as any thing else in the World' (Burnet, p. 67). Just because we do not have 'a perfect account' of the 'Fall of Man, and other things' does not mean that we should believe nothing, that we should 'take on us to reject an excellent Systeme of good and holy Rules, because we cannot satisfie our selves about some difficulties in them'. 'Common Experience' (Burnet, p. 68) suggests as much. To ignore the testimony in the Bible and the corroborative evidence found in '*Jewish* and *Roman* Writers that lived in that time' 'by saying it is possible this might be a Contrivance, and to give no presumption to make it so much as probable, that it was so, is in plain *English* to say, We are resolved let the Evidence be what it will, We will not believe it' (Burnet, p. 66).

Despite his skilful arguments, Burnet could not overcome Rochester's damning suggestion that all 'this might be a Contrivance', 'All this ... might be fancy' (Burnet, pp. 66 and 68). He could not overcome the force of Rochester's reductive caricatures of his positions, his satirical method of reducing the human into the natural, the spirit into questions of opinion, moral virtues into the functioning of the appetites. And Rochester's mode of argument made him mad.

> Upon this and some such Occasions, I told him, I saw the ill use he made of his Wit, by which he slurred the gravest things with a slight dash of his Fancy: and the pleasure he found in such wanton Expressions, as calling the doing of Miracles, *the shewing of a trick*, did really keep him from examining them, with that care which such things required. (Burnet, p. 69)

When he came to write up these conversations, Burnet assured his audience that he had 'not concealed the strongest things [Rochester] said to me ... and as far as I could recollect, have used his own words'. He emphasized, however, that he had 'not enlarged on all the Excursions of his Wit in setting them off' (Burnet, p. 78). He did not want 'Impious Men' to 'make an ill use of' such wit, but clearly he also had had quite enough of the satirist. At the end, he wanted his audience to know that though he had not moved Rochester to 'a full perswasion of *Christianity*', he had wrung from him a promise that

> he would never employ his Wit more to run it [Christianity] down, or to corrupt others. Of which I have since a farther assurance, from a Person of Quality, who conversed much with him, the last year of his life; to whom he would often say, That he was happy, if he did believe, and that he would never endeavour to draw him from it. (Burnet, p. 79)

In 'That he was happy, if he did believe', we may hear a Rochester who was being an ironist to the end. But Burnet, perhaps illustrating Rochester's point, took it as a victory.

Though irritated with Rochester's use of wit, Burnet was shrewd enough to understand, in part at least, what motivated it. It was not so much the 'assumptions' of the Christian religion or Burnet's method of argument that Rochester opposed. What had set him against Christianity had been his own experience with those who practised it, the credulity, corruption, and hypocrisy of believers being a leitmotif of their talks.

> For Prophecies and Miracles, the World had been always full of strange Stories; for the boldness and cunning of Contrivers meeting with the Simplicity and Credulity of the People, things were easily received; and, being once received, passed down without contradiction. (Burnet, p. 65)

> And the business of the Clergy, and their Maintenance, with the belief of some Authority and Power conveyed in their Orders, lookt, as he thought, like a piece of Contrivance: and why, said he, must a man tell me, I cannot be saved, unless I believe things against my Reason, and then that I must pay him for telling me of them? (Burnet, pp. 72–73)

As he told Burnet at the end: 'There was nothing that gave him, and many others, a more secret encouragement in their ill ways, than that those who pretended to believe, lived so that they could not be thought to be in earnest, when they said it' (Burnet, p. 77). Burnet summed up Rochester's opposition to Christianity this way:

> For I found he was so possessed with the general conceit that a mixture of Knaves and Fools had made all extraordinary things be easily believed, that it carried him away to determine the matter, without so much as looking on the Historical Evidence for the truth of *Christianity*, which he had not enquired into, but had bent all his Wit and Study to the support of the other side. (Burnet, p. 67)

In directing his 'Wit and Study' against the hypocrisy and credulity of practising Christians, Burnet detected, rightly enough, a Rochester seeking purity of motive. So Burnet, in summing up his arguments on '*Revealed Religion*', appealed to the Earl to 'lay all these things together, and see what he could except to them, to make him think this was a Contrivance. Interest appears in all Humane contrivances' (Burnet, pp. 67 and 71). The exception was 'Our Saviour' who 'plainly had none; He avoided Applause, withdrew Himself from the Offers of a Crown: He submitted to Poverty and Reproach, and much Contradiction in his Life, and to a most ignominious and painful Death' (Burnet, p. 71). Burnet went on to make the case that the Apostles too had been without contrivance.

This moment in their talks looks back to the end of 'A Satyre' and the speaker's quest for 'God-like men' (line 220) and forward to Rochester's conversion while reading the account of the suffering servant in Isaiah 53, Rochester in both places, as here, seeking purity of motive. What Burnet may not have understood was that Rochester's rhetorical stance in the talks, his assumption about both God and man – the one impossible to approach, the other absolutely unworthy of approaching – was suffused with this motive. It posited a purity, but one impossible to attain.

Behind this theological standoffishness lies a number of complicated motives, not least is Rochester's attempt to deal with the guilt for a life badly led. He had wanted to 'shake off' a 'Notion of the Deity' (Burnet, p. 60). Unable to do that, he wanted to believe in a God 'Far off remov'd from us, and our Affairs', one neither 'pleas'd by *Good* Deeds; nor provok'd by *Bad*', as he put it in his translation from *De Rerum Natura* (lines 3 and 6). Such a God would not punish him in this life or the afterlife. But in this conception of God, we can also detect a desire to test as well as to seek preferment. I am not a dupe; I am not easily taken in. If belief is warranted, I am surely one who is able to tell. At the same time, I have not been hypocritical. I may have committed wrongs, but have sought a God worthy of being God. Here the motives of the libertine blur with those of the *honnêt homme*. In employing his 'Wit and Study to support the other side' against Christianity, Rochester was courting a relationship with God that would transcend the credulity, corruption, and hypocrisy he saw about him, but one that would also ease his anxieties about God's judgment. Such a God will judge on worth, not on the vulgar desire to please. He will understand Rochester on his own terms not on those of convention and custom. 'He did not deny', Burnet writes, 'but that, after the doing of some things, he felt great and severe Challenges within himself; But he said, He felt not these after some others which I would perhaps call far greater Sins, than those that affected him more sensibly' (Burnet, p. 65). Such a God will distinguish between foibles and real trespasses such as no mere clergyman can. By the time he spoke with Burnet, Rochester had been courting this aristocratic God for at least the last ten years and doing so through the negative.

As the major motifs of the poetry – the theme of pleasure, the scepticism and materialism, the satiric techniques, even the language of 'heats', 'fancy', and 'contrivance' – are woven into these conversations with Burnet so too is the ever-present pattern of Christianity woven into the fabric of the poetry. The latter is easier to pick out in retrospect, after having read Burnet's account, but in truth it was there from the beginning, the mock laureate's work, like the laureate's, being 'All, all of a piece throughout'.

Contriving clergymen and their credulous flock had long been objects of Rochester's satire. '*A Ramble*' casts scorn on the 'well hung *Parson*' (line 92). In 'Tunbridge Wells' the speaker comes across 'A Tribe of Curatts, Preists, Canonicall Elves' who 'call themselves Embassadors of heaven' (lines 53 and 62). The waters of Tunbridge, however, can be of little value to 'Their want of learning, honesty, and brain/ The generall diseases of that Traine' (lines 60–61). They are in need of other waters. The speaker of 'A Satyre' has 'with Indignation' 'hurl'd' his invectives

> At the pretending part of the proud World,
> Who swoln with selfish Vanity, devise
> False Freedomes, Holy Cheats and formal Lyes,
> Over their fellow Slaves to tyrannize.
> (lines 174–77)

Toward the end of this satire he sketches a damning portrait of the clergy, of

> that Sensual Tribe, whose Talents ly
> In Avarice, Pride, Sloth and Gluttony,
> Who hunt good Livings, but abhor good Lives,
> Whose Lust exalted to that height arrives,
> They act Adultery with their own Wives;
> And ere a score of Yeares completed be,
> Can from the lofty Pulpit proudly see
> Halfe a large Parish their own Progeny.
> (lines 202–9)

The speaker of 'What vain unnecessary things are men' admonishes members of her sex that in 'Theaters' as in 'Temples' 'Love is worshipt and his precepts taught' but

> You must goe home and practice, for 'tis here
> Just as in other preaching places, where
> Greate Eloquence is show'n 'gainst sin, and Papists
> By men who Live Idolaters and Atheists.
> These two were dainty trades indeed could each
> Live up to halfe the miracles they teach ....
> (lines 49–54)

In 'Upon Nothinge' we are told of the

> Nothinge whoe dwel'st with fooles in grave disguise,
> For whome they Reverend shapes and formes devise,
> Lawne Sleeves and furrs and gownes, when they like thee looke wise ....
> (lines 43–45)

'*On* Rome's *Pardons*' lashes the practice of buying and selling pardons, Rochester mocking the Catholic [mis]understanding of the paradox of the fortunate fall, as well as of the Church's [mis]use of the Beatitudes:

> At this rate they are happy'st that have most;
> They'll purchase *Heav'n*, at their own proper cost,
> Alas! the Poor! all that are so are lost.[40]
>
> (lines 7–9)

In perhaps one of the last pieces of verse he wrote, Rochester mocked 'the ambitious Zealot' and 'slavish Souls', declaring to them, and perhaps most of all to himself, that

> ... Hell and the foul Fiend that rules
> God's everlasting fiery Jayls,
> (Devis'd by Rogues, dreaded by Fools)
> With his grim grisly Dog that keeps the Door,
> Are sensless Stories, idle Tales,
> Dreams, Whimsies, and no more.
> ('Senec. Troas. Act. 2. Chor.', lines 3 and 5, 13–18)

As with his satires on politics or the theatre, Rochester carefully calibrated the distance between profession and practice, and blasted away at the incongruities he found in Christianity.

He clearly found, much to Burnet's irritation, 'pleasure' in doing so. Like a young Swift or Kafka, he seemed also to take delight in the discovery that because the language for spiritual and human values derives from the social and natural order it is subject to parody, often of the obscene variety, the language being the same, or punningly similar, in the one sphere as in the other. Spirit itself expires, 'Such feares in Lovers Breasts high vallue claimes/ And such expiring martyrs feele in flames' ('Could I but make my wishes insolent', lines 21–22), and in a comparison that Rochester returned to a number of times, communion cup and cunt are never far apart. Artemiza defines '*Love*' as 'That Cordiall dropp Heav'n in our Cup has throwne/ To make the nauseous draught of Life goe downe' (lines 44–45). Her reference to cup, supported by context of the poem, suggests the female anatomy that leads us to this world rather than the cup of communion that allows participation in spiritual or holy love. Similarly, the only '*Grace Cup*' the speaker in '*A Ramble*' can know is a 'devouring *Cunt*' (lines 122 and 119), and the 'Lampoone' beginning, 'Too longe the Wise Commons have been in debate', concludes with this mock prayer:

> O! Yee mercifull powers, who of Mortalls take Care,
> Make Women more modest, more sound, or less fayre.
> Is it just, that with death cruell Love should conspire,
> And our Tayles be burnt by our hearts taking fire?

> There's an end of Communion, if humble Beleavers
> Must be damn'd in the Cup, like unworthy Receavers.
>
> (lines 13–18)

Here too the Eucharistic cup, a promise of spiritual communion, becomes a parodic cup of flesh.

As Rochester discovered, there was no religious doctrine that could not be parodied, no language of the spirit that he could not 'slur' 'with a slight dash of his fancy' (Burnet, p. 69), the incarnation and salvation through faith being among his targets in '[Verses put into a Lady's Prayer-book]/ TO *The Honourable**** In the *Pall-mall*'.[41]

> *Fling this* useless *Book away,*
> *And* presume *no more to Pray;*
> *Heav'n is* just, *and can bestow*
> *Mercy on* none *but those that Mercy show.*
> *With a* proud *Heart* maliciously *inclin'd*
> *Not to* encrease, *but to* subdue *Mankind.*
> *In vain you* vex *the Gods with your Petition;*
> *Without Repentance and sincere Contrition,*
> *You're in a* Reprobate *Condition.*
> Phillis, *to* calm *the angry Powers,*
> *And* save *my Soul as well as yours,*
> *Relieve poor Mortals from Despair,*
> *And* justifie *the Gods that made you fair,*
> *And in those* bright *and* charming *Eyes*
>   *Let Pity* first *appear, then Love;*
> *That we by* easie *steps may rise*
>   *Through all the* Joys *on Earth, to those Above.*

Phillis believes one thing, the male speaker quite another, and he attempts to convince her about his attitude toward something of great importance, her salvation. For both, the words '*Heav'n*' and '*Mercy*', '*Repentance*' and '*Contrition*' ostensibly have the same meaning. As the speaker's argument progresses, these religious words, however, change meaning. The Christian heaven evoked at the beginning becomes sexual intercourse at the end. The speaker's definition of '*Mercy*' is equally topsy-turvy. His argument is one of plenitude where multiplication of the things of God's world is good, and he has the rhetoric if not the content of virtue. According to him, Phillis has erred because her 'proud *Heart*' is 'maliciously *inclin'd/ Not to* encrease, *but to* subdue *Mankind*.' What in a Christian framework of values – exercising control and being chaste – would be good, the speaker makes blameworthy. Perhaps Phillis's pride does make her culpable, but given the choice of sexual indulgence or chastity, she should clearly choose the latter, though according to the speaker she would be wrong to do so. Should the lady prove merciful on his terms, he would no doubt find her a 'heavenly reward', but then mercy would have quite a different meaning.

The clever redefinition of what it means to be merciful sets other definitions askew. As the speaker would have it, the woman is 'Reprobate', morally unprincipled, if she does not agree with his proposition. To repent and to be sincerely contrite would be, of all things, to give in to him. In a casuistical way the speaker is right. By giving into him, Phillis will have something about which to be contrite. She will have something to repent. Her religious vocabulary will have meaning only when it has been violated, Rochester here again teasing the paradox of the fortunate fall. There is yet another way in which the speaker's argument is wittily plausible. We along with Phillis no doubt take 'contrite' in its figurative sense, but the speaker has a literal sense in mind: 'contrite' meaning the action of rubbing things together, or against each other, grinding, pounding, or bruising. The sexual connotations are clear.

Just as mercy moves in definition from heavenly to fleshly reward in one line, so the other religious words become translated into the physical. The poem is a blasphemous parody on the word become flesh, on the incarnation. Phillis should not use her book and she should not pray. These are spiritual ways to salvation, and this seduction poem also satirizes the doctrine of salvation by faith. As we learn, the speaker wants the two of them to ascend to heaven through the flesh, not the word. Good deeds, at least as the speaker defines them, not faith, lead to salvation. In the speaker's logic, words, book, and prayer have all lost their efficacy, and the traditional dialectic of Christian-Platonism embodied in the movement from body to soul, from the senses to reason to understanding, from woman to beauty to the idea of God, has been turned upside down.

The Fall and 'Absent from thee I languish still' are both, as we have seen, equally ingenious in their use of theological paradox to further libertine ends. Even the most wanton Chloris might find the libertine's witty apology for the failure of his 'frayler part' a touching, 'nobler Tribute' than any experience of a 'perfect' enjoyment might have provided. Similarly, it is 'straying', experiencing a world of woe', and 'wandering from that heav'n' that has enabled the speaker, and in turn his lover, to know 'Where love and peace and truth doe flow'. Both poems play with the theological paradox of the sinner and are at once orthodox yet perverse. To the question, 'Shall we continue in sin, that grace may abound?' both poems answer with St Paul, 'God forbid' (Romans 6:1–2), but also say, yes.

The Christian paradox of fate and free will and the related paradox of time and eternity inform '*Love* and *Life*', Rochester's incomparable rendering of the standard Cavalier *topos* that inconstancy is constancy.

Rochester seems to have had Hobbes in mind, not only the philosopher's definition of memory as decaying sense, but also his account of the present, past, and future:

> The *Present* only has a being in Nature; things *Past* have a being in the memory only, but things *to come* have no being at all; the *Future* being but a fiction of the mind, applying the sequels of actions Past, to the actions that are Present. (*Leviathan*, Part I, p. 10)

The last stanza suggests that Rochester also had in mind his favourite English poet, Cowley:

> Then talk not of Inconstancy,
>   False hearts, and broken vows:
> If I by miracle can be
> This livelong Minute true to Thee
>   'Tis all that Heaven allowes.
>   (lines 11–15)

In the *Davideis* Cowley describes time as perceived in heaven: 'Nothing is there To come, and nothing Past/ But an Eternal Now does always last.'[42] Rochester is rendering Hobbesian time, all that exists is now, to further his libertine, Lucretian argument that 'whatever happens, happens by chance, and no one is responsible for events predetermined by an unknown, undiscoverable mechanist fate, in which all human values are relative and readily reduced to random insignificance' (Colie, p. 297). In doing so, however, he provides a parody of Christian eternity where 'All things, including the historical events that men experience and identify in time, happen at once and continually in the mind of God' (Colie, p. 172). That is the miracle: though seemingly fixed in time, men are free to love, to be true, to experience the eternity that is God. This libertine is only doing what heaven allows and that truly is a miracle. How can the woman possibly complain! Perversity and orthodoxy become so wittily commingled here that it is almost impossible to separate them.

Drawing upon yet another Christian paradox, 'Upon Nothinge' parodies God's creation of the universe out of nothing, but in doing so discovers a 'Somethinge' by which to judge satirically the all too present nothings of the world 'From princes Coffers and from Statesmens Braynes' (line 41) to

> French truth, Duch Prowesse, Brittish pollicy,
> Hibernian Learninge, Scotch Civility,
> Spaniards dispach, Danes' witt ...
>
> The Greate mans Gratitude to his best friend,
> Kings promisses, whoores vowes ....
>   (lines 46–50)

Several things should be noted about Rochester's various satires on and parodies of Christianity. First is their abundance; they run throughout his work. Rochester simply could not leave Christianity alone. Second, these attacks and parodies are vivid and urgent in their ingenuity. In his funeral sermon Robert Parsons astutely noted that Rochester

> seem'd to affect something singular and paradoxical in his Impieties, as well as his Writings, above the reach and thought of other men; taking as much pains to draw others in, and to pervert the right ways of virtue, as the Apostles and Primitive Saints, *to save their own souls and them that heard them*. For this was the heightening and amazing circumstances of his sins, that he was so diligent and industrious to recommend and propagate them ... framing Arguments for Sin, making Proselytes to it, and writing Panegyricks upon Vice; singing Praises to the great enemy of God, and casting down Coronets and Crowns before his Throne. (Parsons, p. 9)

All that a saint might wish to affirm, Rochester attempts to negate and with saintly zeal. Parsons may have been carried away a bit, but we remember to what lengths Burnet went in getting Rochester to promise that 'he would never employ his Wit more to run [Christianity] down, or to corrupt others' (Burnet, p. 79). This second point is related and leads to the third: in these 'Impieties' there is more than a little showing off. As Rochester told Parsons: '*One day at an Atheistical Meeting, at a person of Qualitie's, I undertook to manage the Cause, and was the principal Disputant against God and Piety, and for my performances received the applause of the whole company*' (Parsons, p. 23).

His satires and parodies of Christianity are just such performances, rhetorical paradoxes designed 'to show off the skill of an orator and to arouse the admiration of an audience, both at the outlandishness of the subject and the technical brilliance of the rhetorician' (Colie, p. 3). Rochester is mocking his audience, mocking Christianity, while bidding for that audience's acceptance and understanding. Those who really understand Christianity will see in his own outrageous way, that the witty Peer has a point: the Fall has made a greater love possible. As Burnet noted: 'He loved to talk and write of Speculative Matters, and did it with so fine a thread, that even those who hated the Subjects that his Fancy ran upon, yet could not but be charmed with his way of treating them' (Burnet, p. 49). The unknowing among the audience may hate the subject, but the knowing, the speaker gambles, will understand that these impious praises of libertinage, impotence, absence, and nothing are really most pious.

Rochester's use of biblical and liturgical allusions in his letters works much the same way. To his wife, suffering from dreadful mother-in-law problems and the prospect of being left with the dowager lady, Rochester quotes, as Treglown points out, the funeral service: 'but there will come an hower of deliverance, till when, may my mother bee mercifull unto you, soe I committ you to what shall ensue, woman to woman, wife to mother, in hopes of a future appearance in glory' (Treglown, p. 73). 'Absent from thee I languish still' is a poetic version of the opening of one Rochester's parodic letters to his wife. In a passage I quoted earlier, Rochester, seeking forgiveness, writes: 'Persons in Absence aught to notifie Returns reciprocrally, affectionately reconsell'd with humble Redentigration.' Again, 'reconsell'd', Trelown tells us, 'has a strong religious association, particularly of purification after prophanation' (Treglown, p. 51). To Elizabeth Barry in anticipation of their next meeting, he writes, echoing the Collect in the Anglican Ante-Communion: 'Remember the hour of a strict account, when both hearts are to be open and we obliged to speak freely' (Treglown, p. 99). To a Savile pretending to be scandalized by reports of the 'hideous deportment which you have heard of concerning running naked', Rochester reminds his fat friend of some of his own escapades and, quoting from Luke 6:41, writes: '"Pluck therefore the beam out of thine own eye", etc.' (Treglown, p. 159). In these and the other instances, there is a comic incongruity between allusion and actual context. At the same time, the quotations show that Rochester understands that context on a higher plane, that the relationship between writer and audience is a special one. Through comic incongruity, often of a perverse kind, comes an understanding on a higher level and almost always a bid for self-exculpation. I am guilty, but as you can see, I know I am guilty, so please forgive. In the letters, Rochester's audience is wife, mistress, and friend, but in his comic, often perverse, use of religious language he always had a higher audience in mind. He was testing his family and friends, building up through irony more intimate, more trustworthy bonds; he was doing the same thing with his God, testing his religion, looking for special understanding and forgiveness.

Evidence for this point is, admittedly, hard to come by. In the very negative of satire we can, and rightfully in Rochester's case, read a desire for the positive. In the blasphemous we often discover the truly religious. But my point is that Rochester understood this process, and at least two poems provide some evidence that this was actually the case.

The first, 'Rochester extempore', is ostensibly doggerel:

And after singing psalme the twelfth
He layd his booke uppon the shelfe,
And lookd much simply like himselfe;
   With eyes turn'd up as white as ghost,
   He cryd ah lard, ah lard of Hosts!
   I am a rascall, that thou know'st.[43]

This is rather complex, though the rhetoric outshines the poetry. There are a number of observations in Psalm 12 applicable to a rascal such as Rochester. The Psalm tells of those that 'speak vanity every one with his neighbor: with flattering lips and with a double heart do they speak', a blow at the courtier and ironist. The promise is that 'The Lord shall cut off all flattering lips, and the tongue that speaketh proud things.' The poem would seem, if hardly an Ignatian meditation, at least a recognition and condemnation, the speaker seeing himself in the mirror of the biblical text all too clearly. Yet the childish rhythm suggests a playfulness out of keeping with serious self-judgment. In his impudence, the speaker has all the makings of a true rascal.

We could leave it at that; our awareness is greater than the speaker's and his own words judge him. Yet, the theatricality – looking simply, white as a ghost, the mocking, 'lard' – also suggests that the speaker is aware of what he is doing. The poem is reported, and the observer is to the persona as we are to him and as presumably his other audience, the Lord, is also. Yes, the speaker is saying, I am bad, but I know it, and because I do, I am not really that bad. Mine is play, an act; you – the audience being the Lord – 'know'st' what I am really. In one sense, I suppose I am a 'rascall', but my awareness should make you see that in this charge there is no 'serious implication of bad qualities' (*OED*, definition 3). It is the rhetorical stance of a naughty boy before a chastising father, joking and clowning being a form of covert communication between father and son that allows them at once to acknowledge the interference between them created by the son and yet to overcome it. Indeed, the clowning itself is part of the interference that makes communication necessary; the son hopes the wit makes it also intimate. To others it may appear that I am just a rascal, a member of 'the rabble of an army or of the populace; common soldiers or camp-followers, persons of the lowest class' (*OED*, definition 1). But you know, Father, that I am of that army over which you as 'Lord of Hosts' preside, 'Hosts' referring to the 'armies of Israel' and by analogy to 'angels that attend God' (*OED*, definition 3). Self-debasement becomes self-enhancement; the negative becomes a positive. Rochester is clowning before the Lord and apparently in the process making his debased circumstances worse but actually through his own negative interference showing why he should march in his Father's army. Joking, ostensibly a form of impiety, becomes religious. Religion, 'religare', seeks to bind back, to unite once again man and God and as Freud reminds us, jokes can be, and are in Rochester's hands, a means of re-establishing the original power of words. Rochester's poem aptly fits into the category of jokes described by Freud as '"ready repartees." For repartee consists in the defense going to meet the aggression, in "turning the tables on someone" or "paying someone back in his own coin" – that is, in establishing an unexpected unity between attack and counter-attack.'⁴⁴ Through his wit, Rochester makes a bid to acknowledge his guilt while seeking redemption. He is wittily separating himself from God – the very separation being proof of God's existence – and binding himself to Him.

The magnificently wicked speaker in 'To the Post Boy' adopts a similar rhetorical stance of courting through the negative. Here Rochester once more plays on the paradox of the sinner, that the logic of Christianity leads to the perfect crime being redeemed by the perfect act of love. In a virtuoso display of rhetoric, Rochester offers himself as the 'greatest of sinners' (Parson's phrase) – drunkard, liar, whoremonger, murderer, a man who has 'Blasphem'd my God and Libelld Kings' (line 14). The ploy is that God, as Charles II often did, will see the wit, will perceive that here in corruption is conscientiousness, and will forgive him who is in reality his perfect servant. This speaker, seemingly the very sign of Hell, is on the same road as the 'Post-boy', who as Bunyan tells us,

> in this haste an Emblem is
> Of those that are set out for lasting Bliss.
> Nor Posts that glide the road from day to day,
> Have so much business, nor concerns as they.
> Make clear the road then, Post-boy, sound thy horn
> Miscarry here, and better n'ere be born.⁴⁵

The paradox of the sinner is given a further turn in the poem's last lines. Rochester asks:

> The Readyest way to Hell? come quick, nere stirr!
> The Readyest Way, my Lord's by Rochester.

The Lord's way is also Rochester's way, the road to Hell also being, paradoxically, the way to Heaven.

It is nearly impossible to paraphrase the rhetorical tone here, the combination of Christian humility with aristocratic pride, the simultaneous invoking of criticism and the guilt it involves with an attempt through self-awareness to foreclose that criticism, the seeking of understanding and acceptance through self-parody and debasement. Rochester audaciously challenges his conventional audience of Christian believers, saying in effect that if your religion is true, this is what it requires of you: to become great sinners. What is paradox to this audience, Rochester hopes, will in time prove orthodox to his other audience, the Lord.

In both these poems Rochester is courting God through the negative. Both mock the God of Christianity but do so with an ingenious perversity that shows that the speakers understand God's way ever so well. If He does exist, He will see such perversity for what it is, a perfection of His order, and thus He will forgive. Prodigal son psychology was perhaps not to be so finely or outrageously on display again until the days of Kierkegaard. Just as the materialistic determinism and the filthy words which inform and identify Rochester's work are a perverse imitation of God's holy order, so too the rhetorical stance of these two poems is a travesty of Christianity that seeks to affirm its possibilities.

Rochester grew up in a Christian household, his mind saturated with the language, stories, and teachings of the Anglican Church. As a young man, he had tried to shake off his Christian upbringing, his reading in Hobbes, in various classical authors, particularly Lucretius, and perhaps in the works of some of the French libertines served as both an impetus and a means for doing so. The episode with William Windham seems also to have significantly fuelled his scepticism, Burnet observing that that 'Gentleman's never appearing was a great snare to him, during the rest of his life' (Burnet, p. 52). Perhaps more than anything else it was, however, his day-to-day experience with the cynicism of the Court and the clergy that served to undermine his faith and turn his 'Wit and Study' against Christianity.

As Rochester engaged in these 'Sallies of his Wit' (Burnet, p. 54), he discovered in Empson's words that 'Everything spiritual and valuable has a gross and revolting parody' even, and perhaps most of all, Christianity.[46] This discovery seems to have delighted Rochester and no doubt further fed his scepticism of Christianity and those who professed a faith in it. At some point, however, he found, much to his astonishment, that these parodies led him into paradoxes that provided ways of harmonizing the various contradictions – philosophical, moral, and psychological – that so troubled him: how something could arise from nothing; how spirit could relate to flesh; how crime could relate to redemption; how he could live a life that so contradicted his desire; how 'so good a Being as the Deity would make him miserable' (Burnet, p. 65). By fits and starts and certainly in no systematic way, he was discovering, as Rosalie Colie has put it, that 'Christian paradoxes, in an ultimate oxymoron, are always orthodox, not only in the propriety of their doctrine but also in the fact that they appear to describe accurately feelings deeply rooted in human nature' (Colie, p. 32). In attacking Christianity, he was skewering the hypocrites as well as showing off; this showing off was in turn a bid for preferment, at once a test of Christianity and a desire for a special relationship with God. But he also returned, explored, and returned again to these Christian paradoxes, particularly those dealing with the negative, because they helped to explain his own experience, to show that 'it is a miraculous thing (as the wise have it) when a man half in the grave cannot leave off playing the fool and the buffoon' (Treglown, p. 202).

The last story the Earl of Rochester told to himself to make sense of his life was a version of what for Christians is the paradox of paradoxes. He told Burnet that he became 'perswaded both of the truth of *Christianity*, and of the power of inward Grace' as Robert Parsons 'read to him the fifty-third *Chapter* of the Prophecie of *Isaiah* and compared *that* with the History of our Saviour's Passion' (Burnet, p. 82). Rochester identified himself with the sceptics, glossing Isaiah 53:1, 'Who hath believed our Report?' by saying: '*Here ... was foretold the Opposition the Gospel was to meet with from such Wretches as he was*' (Burnet, p. 82). As Parson read the phrases, 'He is despised and rejected of men; a man of sorrows, and acquainted with grief', 'stricken, smitten of God, and afflicted' (Isaiah, 53:3–4), Rochester identified himself as well with the Suffering Servant. He was entering the house of a father he had long sought and who would finally understand him, his afflictions at last having purpose and meaning. The sinner and the saint were one. To be sure, even on his deathbed the Earl made peace with his radical, oxymoronic Christianity on his own terms. He described his conversion in materialistic language, as the workings of an '*inward force upon him*' (Burnet, p. 82), and in the last letter he ever wrote, he pleaded with the clergyman Thomas Pierce: 'Take heaven by force, and let me enter with you as it were in disguise, for I dare not appear before the dread majesty of that Holy One I have so often offended' (Treglown, p. 246). Even in Heaven, he would court his father through play, through a form of pure persuasion, coming disguised to mitigate past faults, but also to make his courtship, his performance, all the more attractive to the most critical audience he could imagine.[47]

Notes

1 John Evelyn, *The Diary of John Evelyn*, ed. E.S. de Beer (London: Oxford University Press, 1959), p. 547.
2 Griffin, p. 16; Reba Wilcoxon, 'Rochester's Philosophical Premises: A Case for Consistency', *Eighteenth Century Studies*, 8 (Winter 1974–75), p. 200.
3 Montague Summers, *Playhouse of Pepys* (London: Kegan Paul, 1935), p. 302.
4 Vivian de Sola Pinto, *Rochester: Portrait of a Restoration Poet* (London: The Bodley Head, 1935); rpt. as *Enthusiast in Wit* (Lincoln, NE: University of Nebraska Press, 1962), p. 186.
5 Grahame Greene, *Lord Rochester's Monkey: Being the Life of John Wilmot, Second Earl of Rochester* (New York: Viking Press, 1974), pp. 10 and 113.
6 Kenneth B. Murdock, *The Sun at Noon: Three Biographical Sketches* (New York: Macmillan, 1939), p. 271.
7 Anne Righter, 'William Wycherley', in *Restoration Theatre*, eds John Russell Brown and Bernard Harris (London: Edward Arnold, 1965; paperback 1973), p. 86.

8 George Williamson, *The Proper Wit of Poetry* (Chicago: University of Chicago Press, 1961), p. 126.
9 Howard D. Weinbrot, 'The Swelling Volume: The Apocalyptic Satire of Rochester's *Letter from Artemisia in the Town to Chloe in the Country*', *Studies in the Literary Imagination*, 5 (October 1972), p. 23.
10 Raman Selden, *English Verse Satire 1590–1765* (London: George Allen & Unwin, 1978), p. 94.
11 Marianne Thormählen, 'Dissolver of Reason: Rochester and the Nature of Love', in *That Second Bottle Essays on John Wilmot, Earl of Rochester*, ed. Nicholas Fisher (Manchester: Manchester University Press, 2000), pp. 32 and 33.
12 Lyons, *Complete Poems*, p. xii; Ellis, *Complete Works*, p. 15. One of those who finds Rochester 'still a Puritan at heart' is Roy Porter. See 'Mixed Feelings: The Enlightenment and Sexuality in Eighteenth-century Britain', in *Sexuality in Eighteenth-century Britain,* ed. Paul-Gabriel Boucé (Manchester: Manchester University Press, 1982), p. 3.
13 Warren Chernaik, *Sexual Freedom in Restoration Literature* (Cambridge University Press, 1995), pp. 98 and 102.
14 Sarah Ellenzweig, *The Fringes of Belief: English Literature, Ancient Heresy, and the Politics of Freethinking, 1660–1760* (Stanford University Press, 2008), p. 51. See also Ellenzweig's earlier study, 'The Faith of Unbelief: Rochester's *Satrye*, Deism, and Religious Free Thinking in Seventeenth-century England', *Journal of British Studies*, 44 (2005), pp. 27–45, where she writes: 'Rochester may well have had more faith than we thought and still have been a freethinker in the period's sense of the term' (p. 29).
15 Nicholas Fisher, '"Damn'd in the Cup": Faith, Poetry, and the Earl of Rochester', *English: Journal of English Association*, 62, issue 237 (2013), pp. 171 and 166. This article while providing a wealth of information on the role of religion in Rochester's life and work contains astute readings of two of Rochester's poems, 'Too longe the Wise Commons have been in debate' and *The Fall* as well as a highly useful 'Appendix' that gives the title and line number of poems where Rochester draws upon 'Judaeo-Christian' and 'classical/pagan' vocabulary. See also Fisher's insightful '"I abhor what I Soe long lov'd": An Exploration of Rochester's "death bed repentance"', *The Seventeenth Century*, 25, 2 (2010), pp. 323–49.
16 'John Wilmot, Second Earl of Rochester.' 'Introduction', *Oxford Bibliographies: British and Irish Literature* (www.oxfordbibliographies.com).
17 Christopher Hill, *The Collected Essays of Christopher Hill* (Amherst, MA: University of Massachusetts Press, 1985), 1, p. 299.
18 This chapter expands my argument in 'Rascal Before the Lord: Rochester's Religious Rhetoric', *Essays in Literature*, 9, 2 (Fall 1992), pp. 155–69; reprinted in *John Wilmot, Earl of Rochester: Critical Essays*, ed. David M. Vieth (New York: Garland Publishing), pp. 89–112.
19 Hill, *Collected Essays*, 1, p. 298.
20 Robert D. Hume, rev. of *The Letters of John Wilmot earl of Rochester*, ed. Jeremy Treglown in *Eighteenth Century Studies* (Spring, 1983), pp. 353–56.

21 Hill, *Collected Essays*, 1, p. 299.
22 Nicholas Fisher thinks this letter to Thomas Pierce is 'almost certainly inauthentic', and in a footnote explains: 'given the evidence of Rochester's physical deterioration in the weakness of his signature to the letter to Dr Burnet on 25 June 1680, it is inconceivable that he could have written the fluent and witty letter to Dr Pierce so close to his death' ('The Perspective of Rochester's letters', in *Lord Rochester in the Restoration World*, eds Matthew C. Augustine and Steven N. Zwicker (Cambridge University Press, 2015), p. 251 and note 5, p. 266. But as Treglown points out, 'While this letter cannot be attributed to Rochester with absolute certainty, the plea "Take heaven by force, and let me enter with you as it were in disguise" seems too idiosyncratic to have been invented' (Treglown, p. 258). Fisher's article, an astute reading of the letters, gives a brief account of the publication history of the letters, 'tease[s] out the classical and vernacular background that underpins letter writing in the Restoration period' (p. 251), and explores, while comparing and contrasting, the letters to Savile, Elizabeth Barry, and to his wife as opening 'a fascinating window onto Rochester's life and personality' (p. 255). Fisher concludes: 'Here is the witty, loyal and trusting friend; the ardent and impatient lover; and perhaps surprisingly a husband capable of profound and secure affection. The mercurial shifts of mood, stance, tone and pose within these sequences (and often within a single letter) are characteristic, too, of some of Rochester's most affecting poems; in prose as in verse he combined an unusual sensitivity to nuance with energy, intensity and humour' (p. 265).
23 Kenneth Burke, *Rhetoric of Motives* (Englewood Cliffs, NJ: Prentice-Hall; rpt. Berkeley, CA: University of California Press, 1969), pp. 267–94.
24 Kenneth Burke, *Rhetoric of Religion* (Boston: Beacon Press, 1961; rpt. Berkeley, CA: University of California Press, 1970), p. 34.
25 F.R. Leavis, *Revaluation: Tradition & Development in English Poetry* (New York: George W. Stewart, 1947), p. 33.
26 John Harold Wilson, *The Court Wits of the Restoration* (Princeton, NJ: Princeton University Press, 1948), pp. 87 and 108.
27 Pinto, 'John Wilmot, Earl of Rochester, and the Right Veine of Satire', *Essays and Studies* (The English Association) new ser. 6 (1953), pp. 56–70; rpt. *Seventeenth-Century English Poetry: Modern Essays in Criticism*, ed. William R. Keast (New York: Oxford University Press, 1962), p. 477.
28 Vivian de Sola Pinto, *Restoration Carnival* (London: The Folio Society, 1954), p. 18.
29 Wilson, *The Court Wits*, p. 88.
30 Pinto, *Restoration Carnival*, p. 19.
31 Reba Wilcoxon, 'The Rhetoric of Sex in Rochester's Burlesque', *PLL*, 12 (Summer 1976), pp. 273–84.
32 David Vieth, '"Pleased with the Contradiction and the Sin": The Perverse Artistry of Rochester's Lyrics', *Tennessee Studies in Literature* 25 (1980), pp. 35–56.
33 David Veith and Dustin Griffin, *Rochester and Court Poetry* (Los Angeles: William Andrews Clark Memorial Library, 1988), pp. 54 and 55.

34 'Love in the Ayre: Rochester's Songs and their Music', in *That Second Bottle: Essays on John Wilmot, Earl of Rochester,* ed. Nicholas Fisher (Manchester: Manchester University Press, 2000), p. 70. See Harold Love, 'The Scribal Transmission of Rochester's Songs', *Bibliographical Society of Australia and New Zealand Bulletin,* 20 (1996), pp. 161–80 and also *Charming Strephon: A Celebration of the Life and Times of John Wilmot, 2nd Earl of Rochester,* The Consort of Musicke (Ah Groot-Ammers, The Netherlands: Etcetera Record Company, 1997), CD.

35 Samuel Johnson, *The Lives of the Poets,* ed. John H. Middendorf (New Haven, CT: Yale University Press, 2010), 21, p. 231. In making this judgment Johnson probably drew upon the songs of Rochester published in Jacob Tonson's editions of 1714 or 1732, which included: 'Love bid me hope and I obey'd'; 'The utmost Grace the Greeks could shew'; 'An Age in her Embraces past'; 'Absent from thee I languish still'; 'What Cruel pains Corinna takes'; 'Ancient Person, for whom I'; 'Phillis be gentler, I advise'; 'How blest was the Created State'; 'All my past Life is mine no more'; 'While on those lovely looks I gaze'; 'Love a Woman! you're an Ass'; 'To this Moment a Rebel, I throw down my Arms'; 'As Cloris full of harmless thoughts'; 'Give me leave to rail at you'; 'Fair Cloris in a Pig-Stye lay'; 'I Cannot change, as others do'; and 'My dear Mistress has a Heart.' See Nicholas Fisher, 'Jacob Tonson and the Earl of Rochester', *The Library,* 7th series, 6, 2 (2005), pp. 154 and 158–60.

36 Love places this poem among 'Disputed Works'; Walker and Fisher among 'Poems Less Securely Attributed to Rochester'.

37 Anne Righter, 'John Wilmot, Earl of Rochester', *Proceedings of the British Academy,* 13 (1967), p. 50.

38 Love includes the poem as being by Rochester as do Walker and Fisher. Love notes, however, that 'If genuinely by Rochester, this is likely to be an early work' (Love, p. 361). Paul Hammond finds 'The authorship ... problematic', noting that 'It survives only in two Bodleian MSS, only one of which attributes it to Rochester, and when I examined the MSS long ago I could see no reason to think the attribution came from a reliable source' (personal email).

39 As Greer astutely notes, 'In its sophistry, "Absent from thee" is a typical Cavalier love lyric, but the love that it juggles with is not for woman but for God' (Greer, p. 73).

40 Love includes this poem in 'Disputed Works'. Walker and Fisher do not include it.

41 Love places this poem among the disputed work; Walker and Fisher place it among the '*Poems Less Securely Attributed to Rochester*'.

42 Abraham Cowley, *Poems,* ed. A.R. Waller (Cambridge: Cambridge University Press, 1905), Book 1, lines 360–61.

43 Love includes this impromptu in his 'Appendix Roffensis'. Walker and Fisher attribute it to Rochester.

44 Sigmund Freud, *Jokes and Their Relationship to the Unconscious,* trans. James Strachey (New York: Norton, 1963), p. 68.

45 John Bunyan, *A Book For Boys and Girls: or, Country Rhimes For Children* (London: Elliot Stock, 1890), p. 35. R.E. Pritchard thinks that Rochester had Bunyan's poem in mind but also a poem probably by Buckingham, 'A Notion Take out of *Tullie's* dialogue, *De Senectute*', a satire on the Duke of Monmouth ('Rochester's "Postboy" and Buckingham', *N&Q*, 257 of the continuous series [New Series, 59], 2 (June 2012), pp. 185–86).

46 William Empson, *Some Versions of the Pastoral* (New York: New Directions, 1968), p. 60.

47 Frank Ellis also finds Rochester performing to the very end. In his vivid account of what Rochester must have 'suffered in the last nine weeks of his life', Ellis casts this time as Rochester's 'last act', one in which 'Rochester threw himself into his final role'. Ellis's interpretation of Rochester's last theatrics, however, differs from mine, Ellis finding Rochester in Fanshaw's words, '"certainly delirious"', and probably mad. 'It seems unlikely that his mother, his chaplain, and Gilbert Burnet, three intelligent people with vested interests in the matter, should later spend so much effort denying that Rochester was mad, unless he was' ('Wilmot, John, second earl of Rochester', *Oxford Dictionary of National Biography* (https://doiorg.ezproxy.lib.utexas.edu/10.1093/ref:odnb/29623, 3 January 2008), last accessed 17 March 2023.

Appendix: Authorship of *Sodom*

In an article published in 1946, Rodney M. Baine made the case that Charles Gildon had it right all along when in 1698 he wrote that the author of *Sodom* '"was, I'm very well assured, one Mr. *Fishbourn*, an Inns of Court Gentleman"'.[1] Though Baine was able to identify in all probability the Fishbourne in question as Christopher rather than John, he cited no evidence to support Gildon's attribution, nor did Gildon. Nevertheless, Fishbourne entered into the list of likely candidates for the authorship of *Sodom*, John Harold Wilson (1948) citing Baine, writing: 'Many reputable historians, on very slender evidence, credit [Rochester] with the authorship of *Sodom, or The Quintessence of Debauchery*, a vulgar and worthless piece of pornography which was certainly never acted upon the public stage. It is quite likely that this was only one of the many obscene writings which were attributed to Rochester for want of a better culprit.'[2] Pinto, also citing Baine, wrote in the introduction to his *Poems by John Wilmot Earl of Rochester* (1953): *Sodom* 'was commonly attributed to Rochester, but there are strong reasons for believing that he had nothing to do with it, and that it is the work of a certain Christopher Fishbourne' (Pinto, *Poems*, p. xlvii). Fishbourne remains to this day a likely candidate, and among some critics the leading candidate, to have written or participated in the writing of *Sodom*. Vieth was not one of them. In his 'Preface' to *The Complete Poems* (1968), Vieth simply writes: '*Sodom*, I assume, is spurious' (Vieth, *Poems*, p. vi). But in 1973 Griffin, while agreeing with Vieth that 'the obscene play, *Sodom*, which though long attributed to him, was very probably not written by Rochester', cites in support Baine's article (Griffin, p. 89, n. 18).

A year later, 1974, John Adlard cast doubt on Baine's argument. Citing Vieth's comment about *Sodom* being a 'spurious' work, Adlard writes: 'and most people make the same assumption. But that assumption seems to be based on an article by Rodney M. Baine published as long ago as 1946.'[3] Baine contends that 'Baine seems over-anxious that Rochester should be 'exculpated', should not be 'damned with *Sodom*', and his anxiety seems utterly out of place when we consider that other works confidently attributed to Rochester contain ideas and words quite as likely to be offensive'. He goes on to argue that 'some of Baine's ideas are plainly silly. He tells us that *Sodom* "contains a good deal of military characters and atmosphere", and that this makes one Fishbourne a more likely author, since he had been in the army, whereas Rochester had served his King only at sea.' Adlard concludes: 'It will probably never be known whether Rochester or Fishbourne or someone else wrote *Sodom*, but we may say at least there is no reason why Rochester should not have written it.'[4]

It was Adlard's discounting of Baine's arguments and raising, 'with some cogency, the possibility of Rochester's authorship' that spurred A.S.G. Edwards in 1977 to revisit the issue. Finding the evidence for '*any* Fishbourne' to have authored *Sodom* 'slighter than has hitherto been supposed' and finding 'The evidence in favor of Rochester' to be 'equally insubstantial', Edwards in a groundbreaking article 'approach[ed] the problem of authorship from a new angle – the evidence afforded by the actual manuscripts of *Sodom* itself'.[5] Edwards knew of 'seven manuscripts containing texts of *Sodom*', which he identified as:

D: Victoria and Albert Museum, MS. Dyce 43, pp. 132–62.
F: Bibliothèque Nationale MS. Anglais 101, ff. 1–18^v.
H: Hamburg Staats and Universität Bibliothek MS., pp. 4–29.
L: British Library MS. Harley 7312, pp. 119–45.
N: Nottingham University Library MS. Portland PwV 40, pp. 1–22.
P: Princeton University MS. AM 14401, pp. 1–36, 37–108.
V: Vienna Österreichische Nationalbibliothek MS. 14090, pp. 137–68.[6]

Recently Nicholas Nace discovered two other manuscripts of the play, one in the 'Lowestoft branch of the Suffolk Record Office' and another 'privately held manuscript of the play in a miscellany transcribed by the Scottish writer and antiquary Robert Mylne (1643?–1747)'.[7] Exciting as Nace's discoveries are in themselves, and promising as they do that we may yet find out more about *Sodom* and about Rochester, they do not put into question Edwards's conclusion that a study of the manuscripts 'does not enable me to ascribe *Sodom* to Rochester, Fishbourne, or anyone else'. His study did, however, lead Edwards to surmise that 'the textual evidence afforded by the manuscripts raises serious doubts as to the utility of searching for a single author for *Sodom*. Such evidence seems rather to suggest that there were at least two separate and perhaps wholly unrelated hands at work in the creation of the play.'[8] Edwards's conjecture has in all probability turned out to be true.

The Princeton manuscript contains two versions of the play. The first follows closely the second and all other manuscripts of the play through act II., line 44, and then gives in three rather than five acts a completely

Appendix: Authorship of Sodom 237

different version. Stylistic tests conducted by John Burrows for Love's 1999 edition suggest the two versions 'would appear ... to be the work of two different authors' (Love, pp. 674–75). Given the shorter Princeton version and the incomplete four-act version, ending with 'Finis' recorded in the Nottingham MS, Edwards's article also raises, as Love points out, 'the interesting possibility that *Sodom* was composed in a series of stages ... How many authors were involved in this is one of the many mysteries that await solution' (Love, p. 675). Edwards suggested 'that there were at least three such hands working independently of each other'.[9]

That Rochester wrote or had a hand in the writing of *Sodom* continued, however, to crop up. While Keith Walker did not include Rochester's dramatic works in his 1984 edition, he notes in the introduction: 'Rochester adapted and improved a play by Fletcher called *Valentinian*, contributed a scene to a play by Robert Howard, began a prose comedy, and perhaps, collaborated in an obscene farce *Sodom*.' To this Walker adds a wry footnote: 'To assert this twenty years ago would have damaged Rochester's reputation as much as to deny it today' (Walker, p. x). In 1987 James William Johnson made an extensive case for Rochester's authorship of *Sodom*, arguing:

> A re-examination of the four relevant bodies of evidence – the publication history of the play, the extant manuscripts, the testimony of Rochester's contemporaries, and internal evidence – demonstrate as fully as it is epistemologically possible that John Wilmot was the writer responsible for *Sodom* as it has come down to us. From his own day to ours, evidence has been clear that nobody else was as likely to have written *Sodom* as Rochester was.[10]

Johnson would go on to make much the same argument when he published his biography of Rochester in 2004.[11]

Paddy Lyons found Johnson's argument 'definitive' and in his 1993 edition included *The Farce of Sodom, or the Quintessence of Debauchery*. While giving no rationale, he based 'his text on a transcription from Vienna MS 14090, emended as noted where Hamburg MS Cod. 115 or BL MS Harl. 7312 offer preferable readings. The subtitle is from BL MS Hafl. 7312, where it precedes the ascription: "By the Earl of Rochester for the Royal Company of Whoremasters"'.[12] Marianne Thormählen in her 1993 study of Rochester's poetry in the context of 'Restoration events, developments and personalities in the fields of national and international politics, religion, philosophy and social life' finds the authorship of *Sodom* 'uncertain'. She leaves it out in her discussion of Rochester's 'Court satires and lampoons', citing Griffin's doubts about the authorship (Thormählen, pp. 2 and 285). Even Frank Ellis, an authority on Restoration poetry and one of the editors of the Yale edition of *Poems on Affairs of State*, who published *John Wilmot, Earl of Rochester: The Complete Works* a year after Lyons's edition, excludes *Sodom*, does not even mention the play. He simply notes: 'In my opinion all the works in this edition are Rochester's; but *dubia* have been excluded. But opinion is not evidence.'[13]

The strongest case against Rochester having written or having had a hand in the writing of *Sodom* came in Harold Love's response to Johnson's arguments in 'But Did Rochester *Really* Write *Sodom*?' Finding Johnson's case conjectural – and it is, often wildly so – his sources at times given inaccurately, and his evidence, often with great leaps, made to fit the assumption that Rochester wrote *Sodom* in the first place, Love goes on to point out that none of the early ascriptions of the play, coming as they do after the printed edition of *Sodom* in 1684, have authority. Moreover, none of Rochester enemies, as one would expect, make satiric use of his authorship, to my mind Love's strongest argument. Then too, 'The play does not contain the detailed, specific references to events and personalities that we would expect from satire written by a court insider for the entertainment of other insiders.' Love goes on to argue, 'The satire of the play is assertively anti-court.' Rochester, being dependent on the Court, would not have implicated himself, an argument I find to be Love's weakest. For Love, 'The case for Fishbourne's authorship is still a defensible one.'[14] A decade later in reviewing *A Profane Wit*, Love continued to find Johnson's argument for the authorship of *Sodom* wanting in evidence and in scholarly rigour, concluding, a bit over the top, that Johnson's 'documentary evidence for [Rochester's] authorship of *Sodom* is about as convincing as that for *Hamlet* having been written by Marlowe'.[15]

Throughout the 1990s, however, other critics, despite the lack of hard evidence, continued to be intrigued by the parallels between Rochester's known work and *Sodom*, parallels hinting that perhaps John Wilmot after all had a hand in writing the notorious farce. In 'John Wilmot, Earl of Rochester: An Author in Search of a Character' (1995) Ken Robinson, citing the recent editions by Walker and Lyons, acknowledges 'The problems facing those who have worked on the Rochester canon ... Famous for his obscene verses and satires, his name was a magnet for a mass of often doubtfully and sometimes erroneously attributed poems in both manuscript and print.' Robinson goes on:

> The textual scholar of Rochester's work can easily find himself drowning in 'doubt's boundless sea.' Vieth attempted to set clear boundaries, Walker and Lyons render them less clear but in so doing they offer a picture of the canon which better represents the dubieties that accompany the man. One example of the texts in question is the verse play *The Farce of Sodom, or The*

Quintessence of Debauchery for which Lyons offers the first reliable text since the inception of modern Rochester scholarship.

After giving a brief overview of textual history of the play, Robinson concludes:

> Probably written in 1672 and addressed to the Declaration of Indulgence *Sodom* is a political satire which uses obscene fantasy to attack the English Court. Charles, for example, becomes Bolloxinion and Buckingham becomes the Buggermaster-general Bortastus. It satirizes those 'who declare their sin as Sodom, and hide it not, that take it upon their shoulders, and bind it to them as a Crown.' These are the words of Isaiah 3:9 as quoted by Parsons in his funeral sermon to picture Rochester's brazen recommendation of sin. If *Sodom* is his, it is as much one of his 'Panegyricks upon Vice' as a satire. It fits with poetry known to be by Rochester which offers pyrotechnic displays of obscene wit, which turn in upon themselves with disgust that sits in uneasy tension with this bravura quality. *Sodom* might seem to show Rochester's hand but it might be another case of his notoriety attracting attributions which lack decisive authority even if they are in their own way informed about his style.[16]

In his 1995 study, *Sexual Freedom in Restoration Literature*, Warren Chernaik was more confident that Rochester had a hand in writing *Sodom*. In analysing the '"scepter" lampoon' Chernaik notes: 'A similar equation of authoritarianism and the tyrannous rule of sexual desire underlies the satire of *Sodom*, too often stigmatized as mere pornography, and informs Rochester's play *Valentinian*, with its sharp criticism of Charles II and his court.' To this he added a footnote, which reads in part:

> Lyons's edition, which accepts *Sodom* as authentic, provides readily accessible texts of *Sodom* and *Valentinian*. The most extensive recent study, J.W. Johnson, 'Did Lord Rochester Write *Sodom*?', *Publications of the Bibliographical Society*, 81 (1987), 119–53, assigns the play to Rochester, as does Larry Carver in 'The Texts and the Text of *Sodom*', *PBSA*, 73 (1979), 19–40. A.S.G. Edwards, in 'The Authorship of *Sodom*', *PBSA*, 71(1977), suggests a hypothesis of multiple authorship, pointing out that the play exists in two widely different versions; on the relationship of the various MSS of *Sodom*, see also Carver, 'Texts'. Edwards and Carver convincingly refute the argument, advanced by Rodney Baine, 'Rochester or Fishbourne: A Question of Authorship', *Review of English Studies*, 22 (1946), 201–6, that the author of the play is the otherwise obscure Christopher Fishbourne. Johnson overstates the case when he claims to have demonstrated 'as fully as is epistemologically possible that John Wilmot was the writer responsible for *Sodom* as it has come down to us' (p. 120), since he treats his evidence with insufficient skepticism. But it seems reasonable to conclude that Rochester is either sole author or principal author of *Sodom*.[17]

Chernaik does not cite Love's critique of Johnson and may not have known about it. Germaine Greer, however, did, but nevertheless in *John Wilmot, Earl of Rochester* published in 2000, she attributes *Sodom* to Rochester: 'It was at this time [1675] that Rochester began writing for the stage; his first effort was a scene for a play by Sir Robert Howard. This was followed by new scenes for Fletcher's tragedy *Valentinian* and the accompanying farce *Sodom*' (Greer, p. 22). Later in her study, Greer goes on to observe:

> *Valentinian* is far more subversive than Rochester's original play *Sodom*, written immediately afterward. Scholars are squeamish about fathering *Sodom* on Rochester, but it does him less discredit than other works that are willingly attributed to him. In many ways *Sodom* is a parody of *Valentinian*; the maids of honour, for example, defend their submission to the king's peculiar sexual demands as the subjects' duty of passive obedience. (Greer, p. 63)

Greer is acute in the parallels she draws between *Sodom* and *Valentinian*, but qualifies her ascription of *Sodom* solely to Rochester, opining:

> *Sodom* is like other works of Rochester's in that it could have been written by an uproarious committee of wits whose imaginations became more outrageous as the levels of in their flagons went down. It is even possible to imagine the paper circulating in a kind of game in which each of the company had to add a speech or couplet capping the last. (Greer, p. 64)

In reviewing Love's 1999 edition Greer would write: '*Sodom*, a grotesque burlesque in which obscenity is the medium rather that the message, functions as a farcical postlude to and commentary on Rochester's dead serious *Valentinian*. It probably contains Rochester's work but is equally probably not the work of Rochester alone.'[18]

In an article on 'Rochester's homoeroticism' (2000), Paul Hammond observes: 'That homosexual sex is supplementary, always a sign of something else, may be seen in the two plays with which Rochester is associated, *Sodom* and *Valentinian*.' He goes on to write: 'However, I offer no opinion as to the authorship of *Sodom*.'[19] That same year Simon Hampton in 'Rochester, *The Man of Mode* and Mrs. Barry', writes: 'That [Rochester] was interested in the theatre is certain. He adapted Fletcher's tragedy *Valentinian* for the stage (performed Monday 11 February 1684) and he is credited with having, a least, a hand in the satirically obscene *Sodom*, which may have been published in 1684.'[20]

While acknowledging that the authorship of *Sodom* is disputed, Christopher Tilmouth in *Passion's Triumph over Reason* (2007) draws a number of parallels between the play, citing Love's text, and Rochester's work, while calling into question part of Love's rationale for doubting Rochester's authorship. In discussing, for example, 'A Satyre against Reason

Appendix: Authorship of Sodom

and Mankind' and the persona's contention that 'reason must "bound" (line 102) man's otherwise boundless desires in order to ensure that, in the long-term, they prove themselves truly satisfying', Tilmouth has this footnote: 'In a striking parallel to this, *Sodom and Gomorah's* Bolloxinian suggests, in Sc. B5, lines 7–14, that "Cunts" no longer "hug" nor therefore "tickle" the "Pintle", because through overuse they have grown "voyd of ... bounds". (References to this play, the authorship of which is disputed, are to Rochester 1999)' (Tilmouth, p. 352).

Later, in discussing *Lucina's Rape*, Tilmouth writes: 'In contrast to her [Marcellina], the Emperor (being like *Sodom*'s Bolloxinian, a slave to "boundless pleasure" (Sc. 1, line 16; Sc. A2, line 85) is addicted to exactly the sorts of irrational libertinism which kill delight with their very extremism' (Tilmouth, p. 363). And then there is this:

> By contrast, the Emperor's understanding of the term is a corrupt, inverted one: to his degenerate mind, only the rapist's 'Force' is 'the most Generous/ For what that gives it freely does bestow' (iv. ii. 202–4). Given the piquancy of these comments at a time when, to judge by Freke's *History of Insipids*, England was at its lowest ebb, it is tempting to put aside Love's cautious judgement that Rochester hints here at York's depravities (because he would never attack Charles 'frontally'), and to suggest that *Lucina's Rape*, like *Sodom*, is precisely a deliberate affront to the King. (Tilmouth, p. 364)

In summing up his account of *Lucina's Rape* Tilmouth writes:

> However, the intuition that behind the composition of this play sits a shared self, passion, and villainy, yoking together Emperor and servant; the intuition, too, that the vigour of the attack upon Vallentinian reflects a protégé's *Oedipal* turn against his monarch-father, and a turn against his own likeness, surely does point to Rochester's relationship with Charles. Just as the Earl seemed to implicate himself in his 'Satyre's' critique of the role played by wits in court society; just as he, too, was sometimes guilty of nurturing the oppressive culture of Hobbism attacked in that poem; so, here, he acknowledges his own shameful part in what he presents as Charles's tragedy. Inevitably, that concession does something to extenuate the potency of his attack. (Tilmouth, p. 367)

And Tilmouth adds this footnote:

> Cf. Burns 1995: 35–6, where Clark points to further 'displaced self-loathing' in 'In the Isle of Britain'. For this same reason one of Love's reasons for questioning Rochester's authorship of *Sodom* must be doubtful. Love claims (Rochester 1999: 498) that Rochester cannot be the author because that play, in satirizing the venality of Charles's courtiers, thereby implicates the Earl himself in that critique. Rochester seems not to be as adverse to such self-laceration as Love supposes. (Tilmouth, p. 367)

Tilmouth clearly thinks Rochester had a hand in writing *Sodom*.

Not so, Nicholas Nace. Accepting Love's argument that *Sodom* in all probability is not by Rochester, that it may date not from the early 1670s but the late 1670s and that it 'does not exhibit the detailed, specific references to events and personalities that we would expect from satire written by a court insider for the entertainment of other insiders (Love edition, 497)', Nace in an exhaustive and hugely valuable article

> examines all the known evidence for *Sodom's* authorship – including that which points to multiple authors – in order to put forth a new candidate whose name is repeatedly linked to the play: Thomas Jordan (*c*.1614–1685), who occupied the position of City Poet of London and was *ex officio* director of the Lord Mayor's pageants from 1671 until his death. Whether or not Jordan himself took part in the writing of *Sodom*, the process of tracing out the association of the farce with 'Jordan' supports a view of the play as originating outside the court, and leaves open the possibility of Fishbourne's involvement. Approaching *Sodom* in the context of Smithfield instead of Whitehall makes sense of the play's obvious send-up of the court, its lack of knowledge about court gossip, and the nonexistence of evidence about its authorship.[21]

Nace brings a great deal of evidence to support Jordan's candidacy and the possibility that Fishbourne too may have contributed in the writing of *Sodom*. And he is right that 'An examination of all the evidence from the Smithfield perspective gives us a new context for the composition of *Sodom* and for its politics' and may well open up future findings. But for now he can conclude only that 'The least that could be said based on this evidence is that *Sodom* has an affinity to Jordan's song-driven pageants and Fishbourne's obscene fragmentary pastiche of ballads and an association with the "vigorous drama outside the theatres"'.[22]

Nace thinks it improbable that Rochester wrote or had a hand in the writing of *Sodom*, 'his candidacy rest[ing] on no more than a general impression of the famously licentious poet he was capable of being', and his may well be the prevailing view in Rochester scholarship at this the third decade of the twenty-first century.[23] Nicholas Fisher in updating and revising Walker's edition in 2010 dropped Walker's reference to *Sodom*, adding a footnote: 'The case for Rochester's authorship of the obscene farce *Sodom* is unconvincing (see Harold Love, 'But Did Rochester *Really* Write *Sodom?*' PBSA, 87 (1993), 319–36)' (Walker and Fisher, p. xviii). In a 2015 article, 'Rochester, the theatre and Restoration theatricality', David Francis Taylor writes: 'With the obscene face *Sodom and Gomorah* now widely believed to be misattributed, Rochester's dramatic output is minimal'.[24] The debate about Rochester's role, if any, in writing *Sodom*, however, goes on.[25]

Notes

1. Rodney M. Baine, 'Rochester or Fishbourne: A Question of Authorship', *Review of English Studies*, 22, 87 (1946), p. 203.
2. John Harold Wilson, *The Court Wits of the Restoration* (Princeton, NJ: Princeton University Press, 1948), pp. 169–70 and 239, n. 39.
3. John Adlard, ed., *The Debt to Pleasure* (Manchester: Fyfield Books, 1974), p. 12.
4. Adlard, *Debt to Pleasure*, pp. 12–13.
5. A.S.G. Edwards, 'The Authorship of *Sodom*', *PBSA*, 71 (1977), pp. 209–10.
6. Edwards, 'Authorship of *Sodom*', p. 210.
7. Nicholas Nace, 'Some New Light on *Sodom*', *The Book Collector*, 63 (2014), pp. 559 and 561–62.
8. Edwards, 'Authorship of *Sodom*', p. 210.
9. Edwards, 'Authorship of *Sodom*', p. 212.
10. J.W. Johnson, 'Did Lord Rochester Write *Sodom?*' *Publications of the Bibliographical Society*, 81 (1987), pp. 119–20.
11. See J.W. Johnson, *A Profane Wit: The Life of John Wilmot Earl of Rochester* (Rochester, NY: University of Rochester Press, 1974), chapter 12, 'Sodom (1673)', pp. 164–81.
12. *Complete Poems*, p. 312.
13. *Complete Works*, p. xiv.
14. Love, 'But Did Rochester Really Write "*Sodom*"?', p. 336.
15. Love, Rev. of *A Profane Wit*, p. 138.
16. Ken Robinson, 'John Wilmot, Earl of Rochester: An Author in Search of a Character', in *The Art of Literary Biography*, ed. John Batchelor (Oxford: Oxford University Press, 1995), pp. 104–5.
17. Warren Chernaik, *Sexual Freedom in Restoration Literature* (Cambridge University Press, 1995), pp. 231–32.
18. Germaine Greer, Rev. of *The Works of John Wilmot, Earl of Rochester*, ed. Harold Love, *London Review of Books*, 16 September 1999, p. 10.
19. Paul Hammond, 'Rochester's Homoeroticism', in *That Second Bottle: Essays on John Wilmot, Earl of Rochester*, ed. Nicholas Fisher (Manchester: Manchester University Press, 2000), pp. 10 and 208, n. 57.
20. Simon Hampton, 'Rochester, *The Man of Mode* and Mrs. Barry', in *That Second Bottle: Essays on John Wilmot, Earl of Rochester*, ed. Nicholas Fisher (Manchester: Manchester University Press, 2000), p. 167.
21. Nicholas Nace, 'The Author of *Sodom* Among the Smithfield Muses', *The Review of English Studies*, New Series, 68, 284 (2016), pp. 297–98.
22. Nace, 'The Author of *Sodom*', p. 321.
23. Nace, 'The Author of *Sodom*', p. 298.
24. David Frances Taylor, 'Rochester, the Theatre and Restoration Theatricality', in *Lord Rochester in the Restoration World*, eds Matthew C. Augustine and Steven N. Zwicker (Cambridge University Press, 2015), p. 121.

25 We know of two early printed editions of *Sodom*, one in 1684 and another in 1689, though no copies now exist. Intriguingly, a copy of a printed edition of the play has come to light, probably printed in the 1720s. The Sotheby's *Cataloguing Preview* of 4 January 2016 lists the title as *Sodom, or The Gentleman Instructed. A Comedy*. Hague [London]: Printed in the Year 1000000. It was sold at Sotheby's in the John Brett-Smith sale and is available as a facsimile reprint. The relationship of this text to the extant manuscripts of *Sodom* or to the earlier printed editions of the play has yet to be worked out.

Bibliography

Adlard, John ed. *The Debt to Pleasure*. Manchester: Fyfield Books, 1974.
Aubrey, John. *Brief Lives*, ed. John Buchanan-Brown. London: Penguin Books, 2000.
Auerbach, Erich. *Mimesis: The Representation of Reality in Western Literature*, trans. Willard Trask. New York: Doubleday Anchor Books, 1957.
Alsop, D.K. '"An Epistolary Essay from M.G. to O.B. upon their Mutual Poem" and the Problem of Persona in Rochester's Poetry', *Restoration Studies in English Literary Culture, 1660–1700*, 12, 2 (1988), pp. 61–68.
Augustine. *On Christian Doctrine*, trans. D.W. Robertson. New York: The Liberal Arts Press, 1958.
Augustine, Matthew C. 'Trading Places: Lord Rochester, the Laureate and the Making of Literary Reputation', in *Lord Rochester in the Restoration World*, eds Matthew C. Augustine and Steven N. Zwicker. Cambridge University Press, 2015, pp. 58–78.
Babcock, Barbara. *The Reversible World: Symbolic Inversion in Art and Society*. Ithaca, NY: Cornell University Press, 1978.
Baine, Rodney M. 'Rochester or Fishbourne: A Question of Authorship', *Review of English Studies*, 22, 87 (1946), pp. 202–06.
Beaumont, Francis and John Fletcher. *Comedies and Tragedies Written by Francis Beaumont And John Fletcher Gentleman. Never printed before, And now published by the Authors Originall Copies*. London, 1647.
Behn, Aphra. *The Works of Aphra Behn*, ed. Montague Summers. New York: Benjamin Blom, 1915; reissued 1967.
Berman, Ronald. 'Rochester and the Defeat of the Senses', *Kenyon Review*, 26 (1964), pp. 354–68.
Blount, Charles. *The Miscellaneous Works of Charles Blount, Esq.* N.P. 1695.
Booth, Wayne. *The Rhetoric of Irony*. Chicago: University of Chicago Press, 1974.
Boyle, Roger. *The Tragedy of Mustapha*. London: 1665.
Braverman, Richard. *Politics and Counterplots: Sexual Politics and the Body Politic in English Literature, 1660–1730*. Cambridge University Press, 1993.
Brooks, David, ed. *Lyrics & Satires of John Wilmot Earl of Rochester*. Sydney, Australia: Hale & Iremonger, 1980.
Bunyan, John. *A Book For Boys and Girls: or, Country Rhimes For Children*. London: Elliot Stock, 1890.
Burke, Kenneth. *A Grammar of Motives*. Prentice-Hall, 1945; Berkeley, CA: University of California Press, 1974.

Burke, Kenneth. *A Rhetoric of Motives*. Englewood Cliffs, NJ: Prentice-Hall; rpt. Berkeley, CA: University of California Press, 1969.
Burke, Kenneth. *Attitudes Toward History*. Editorial Publications, 1937; rpt. Berkeley, CA: University of California Press, 1984.
Burke, Kenneth. *Counter-Statement*. Berkeley, CA: University of California Press, 1968.
Burke, Kenneth. *Language as Symbolic Action: Essays on Life, Literature, and Method*. Berkeley, CA: University of California Press, 1966.
Burke, Kenneth. *Permanence and Change: An Anatomy of Purpose*. Indianapolis, IN: Bobbs-Merrill, 1975.
Burke, Kenneth. *The Philosophy of Literary Form: Studies in Symbolic Action*. Louisiana State University Press, 1941; rpt. Berkeley, CA: University of California Press, 1973.
Burke, Kenneth. *The Rhetoric of Religion*. Boston: Beacon Press, 1961; rpt. Berkeley, CA: University of California Press, 1970.
Burnet, Gilbert. *Some Passages of the Life and Death Of the Right Honorable John Earl of Rochester*. London: Printed for *Richard Chiswel*, 1680.
Burnet, Gilbert. *Some Passages of the Life and Death of Rochester*, in *Rochester: The Critical Heritage*, ed. David Farley-Hills. New York: Barnes & Noble, 1972.
Burrows, John and Harold Love. 'Attribution Tests and the Editing of Seventeenth-Century Poetry', *The Yearbook of English Studies*, 29 (1999), pp. 151–76.
Burrows, John and Harold Love. 'Mulgrave, Dryden, and *An Essay upon Satire*', *Script & Print*, Special Issue, 33 (1–4) (2009), pp. 76–91.
Canfield, J. Douglas. 'The Significance of the Restoration Rhymed Heroic Play', *Eighteenth-Century Studies*, 13 (Fall 1979), pp. 49–62.
Canfield, J. Douglas. *Word as Bond in English Literature from the Middle Ages to the Restoration*. Philadelphia, PA: University of Pennsylvania Press, 1989.
Carver, Larry. 'The Texts and The Text of *Sodom*', *The Papers of the Bibliographical Society of America*, 73, 1 (1979), pp. 19–40.
Carver, Larry. 'Rascal Before the Lord: Rochester's Religious Rhetoric', *Essays in Literature*, 9, 2 (Fall 1992), pp. 155–69; reprinted in *John Wilmot, Earl of Rochester: Critical Essays*, ed. David M. Vieth. New York and London: Garland Publishing, (1988), pp. 89–112.
Carver, Larry. 'Rochester's *Valentinian*', *Restoration and 18th Century Theatre Research*, 2nd series, 4, 1 (Summer 1989), pp. 25–38.
Carver, Larry. 'A Painter, Man of Letters, Novelist, and a Poet: Mary Beale, J. Frank Dobie, and Graham Greene Encounter the Earl of Rochester', *The Library Chronicle of The University of Texas*, 23 (1993), pp. 118–29.
Chantlet, Ashley. 'The Meaning of "Scotch Fiddle" in Rochester's "Tunbridge Wells"', *Restoration*, 26(2) (2002), pp. 81–84.
Chernaik, Warren. *Sexual Freedom in Restoration Literature*. Cambridge University. Press, 1995.
Chernaik, Warren. 'Sex, Tyranny, and the Problem of Allegiance: Political Drama During the Restoration', in *Theatre and Culture in Early Modern England, 1650–1737: From Leviathan to Licensing Act*, ed. Catie Gill. Farnham: Ashgate, 2010, pp. 87–105.
Clark, Sandra. 'Sex and Tyranny Revisited: Waller's "The Maid's Tragedy" and Rochester's 'Valentinian', *Theatre and Culture in Early Modern England,*

1650–1737: From Leviathan to Licensing Act, ed. Catie Gill. Farnham: Ashgate, 2010, pp. 75–86.

Colie, Rosalie L. *Paradoxia Epidemica: The Renaissance Tradition of Paradox*. Hamden, CT: Archon Books, 1976.

Combe, Kirk. *A Martyr for Sin: Rochester's Critique of Polity, Sexuality, and Society*. Newark, NJ: University of Delaware Press, 1998.

Cowley, Abraham. *Poems*, ed. A.R. Waller. Cambridge University Press, 1905.

Crowne, John. *Charles The Eighth Of France. The Dramatic Works of John Crowne*, 1. London: H. Sotheran & Co., 1873.

Crowne, John. *Calisto*. London: Tho: Newcomb, 1675.

Culler, Jonathan. *Structuralist Poetics: Structuralism, Linguistics and the Study of Literature*. Ithaca, NY: Cornell University Press, 1975.

Danielson, Bror and David M. Vieth, eds *The Gyldenstolpe Manuscript Miscellany of Poems by John Wilmot, Earl of Rochester, and Other Restoration Authors*. Stockholm Studies in English 17. Stockholm: Almqvist & Wiksell, 1967.

Davies, C.S.L. 'John Wilmot, Earl of Rochester: His Childhood and Experience at Oxford', *Huntington Library Quarterly*, 81, 2 (2018), pp. 171–89.

Davis, Paul, ed. *Rochester: Selected Poems*. Oxford University Press, 2013.

Davis, Paul, 'Recovering a Restoration Scribal Poet: The Life and Work of Robert Wolseley, with Notes on His Association with Rochester', *Huntington Library Quarterly*, 79, 4 (2016), pp. 677–704.

Diderot, Denis. *Le Neveu De Rameau*, in *Diderot Oeuvres*. Editions Gallimard: 1951.

Doody, Margaret Anne. *The Daring Muse: Augustan Poetry Reconsidered*. Cambridge University Press, 1985.

Dryden, John. *The Works of John Dryden*, eds H.T. Swedenberg, Jr. *et al*. Berkeley, CA: University of California Press, 1956–1984.

Dryden, John. *Aureng-Zebe*, ed. Frederick M. Link. Lincoln, NE: University of Nebraska Press, 1971.

Dryden, John. *Marriage à la Mode*, ed. Mark S. Auburn. Lincoln, NE: University of Nebraska Press: 1981.

Edwards, A.S.G. 'Libertine Literature in Restoration England: Princeton MS.AM 14401', *Book Collector*, 25 (1976), pp. 354–68.

Edwards, A.S.G. 'The Authorship of *Sodom*', *The Papers of the Bibliographical Society of America*, 71 (1977), pp. 208–12.

Ehrenpreis, Irvin. *Literary Meaning and Augustan Values*. Charlottesville, VA: University of Virginia Press, 1974.

Elias, Richard. 'Political Satire in *Sodom*', *Studies in English Literature*, 18 (1978), pp. 423–38.

Ellenzweig, Sarah. 'Hitherto Propertied: Rochester's Aristocratic Alienation and the Paradox of Class Formation in Restoration England', *English Literary History*, 69, 3 (Fall 2002), pp. 703–25.

Ellenzweig, Sarah. 'The Faith of Unbelief: Rochester's *Satrye*, Deism, and Religious Free Thinking in Seventeenth-century England', *Journal of British Studies*, 44 (2005), pp. 27–45.

Ellenzweig, Sarah. *The Fringes of Belief: English Literature, Ancient Heresy, and the Politics of Freethinking, 1660–1760*. Stanford University Press, 2008.

Ellis, Frank H., ed. *John Wilmot, Earl of Rochester: The Complete Works*. London: Penguin Books, 1994.

Ellis, Frank H., ed. 'Wilmot, John, second earl of Rochester', *Oxford Dictionary of National Biography*. https://doiorg.ezproxy.lib.utexas.edu/10.1093/ref:odnb/29623, 3 January 2008.

Empson, William. *Some Versions of Pastoral*. New York, NY: New Directions, 1968.

Etherege, George. *The Poems of Sir George Etherege*, ed. James Thorpe. Princeton, NJ: Princeton University Press, 1963.

Etherege, George. *The Man of Mode, or Sir Fopling Flutter: A Comedy*. London: Printed by J. Macock for *Henry Herringman*, 1676.

Evelyn, John. *The Diary of John Evelyn*, ed. E.S. de Beer. London: Oxford University Press, 1959.

Fabricant, Carole. 'Rochester's World of Imperfect Enjoyment', *Journal of English and Germanic Philology*, 73 (1973), pp. 338–50.

Fane, Francis. *Love in the Dark*. London: Printed by T.N. for *Henry Herringman*, 1675.

Farley-Hill, David, ed. *Rochester: The Critical Heritage*. New York: Barnes & Noble, 1972.

Farley-Hill, David, *Rochester's Poetry*. Totowa, NJ: Rowman & Littlefield, 1978.

Farley-Hill, David, *The Benevolence of Laughter: Comic Poetry of the Commonwealth and Restoration*. London: Macmillan and Rowman & Littlefield, 1974.

Farley-Hill, David, 'Rochester and the Theatre in the Satires', in *That Second Bottle: Essays on John Wilmot, Earl of Rochester*, ed. Nicholas Fisher. Manchester: Manchester University Press, 2000, pp. 151–64.

Ferraro, Julian. 'Pope, Rochester and Horace', in *Lord Rochester in the Restoration World*, eds Matthew C. Augustine and Steven N. Zwicker. Cambridge University Press, 2015, pp. 119–31.

Fisher, Nicholas. 'Love in the Ayre: Rochester's Songs and Their Music', in *That Second Bottle: Essays on John Wilmot, Earl of Rochester*, ed. Nicholas Fisher. Manchester: Manchester University Press, 2000, pp. 63–80.

Fisher, Nicholas. 'Mending What Fletcher Wrote: Rochester's Reworking of Fletcher's *Valentinian*', *Script & Print*, Special Issue, 33, 1–4 (2009), pp. 61–75.

Fisher, Nicholas. 'A New Dating of Rochester's *Artemiza to Chlöe*', *English Manuscript Studies 1100–1700*, 8, *Seventeenth-Century Poetry, Music and Drama*, ed. Peter Beal. London: The British Library, 2000, pp. 300–19.

Fisher, Nicholas. 'Jacob Tonson and the Earl of Rochester', *The Library*, 7th series 6, 2 (June 2005), pp. 133–60.

Fisher, Nicholas. 'Manuscript Miscellanies and the Rochester Canon', *English Manuscript Studies 1100–1700*, 13, *New Texts and Discoveries in Early Modern English Manuscripts*, ed. Peter Beal. London: The British Library, 2007, pp. 293–99.

Fisher, Nicholas. 'Rochester's *An Allusion To Tacitus*', *Notes and Queries* (October 2010), pp. 503–6.

Fisher, Nicholas. '"I abhor what I Soe long lov'd": An Exploration of Rochester's "death bed repentance"', *The Seventeenth Century*, 25, 2 (2010), pp. 323–49.

Fisher, Nicholas. '"Damn'd in the Cup": Faith, Poetry, and the Earl of Rochester', *English: Journal of English Association*, 62, Issue 237 (2013), pp. 166–92.

Fisher, Nicholas. 'The Perspective of Rochester's Letters', in *Lord Rochester in the Restoration World*, eds Matthew C. Augustine and Steven N. Zwicker. Cambridge University Press, 2015, pp. 250–69.

Fisher, Nicholas. 'Isaac Barrow and the Earl of Rochester', *Notes and Queries*, 65, Issue 2 (June 2018), pp. 207–9.
Freud, Sigmund. *Jokes and Their Relationship to the Unconscious*, trans. James Strachey. New York: Norton, 1963.
Geertz, Clifford. *The Interpretation of Cultures*. New York: Basic Books, 1973.
Gibbon, Edward. *The Decline and Fall of the Roman Empire*. London: 1909; rpt. New York: AMS Press, 1974.
Greene, Graham. *Lord Rochester's Monkey: Being the Life of John Wilmot, Second Earl of Rochester*. New York: Viking Press, 1974.
Greer, Germaine. 'Doomed to Sincerity', rev. of *The Works of John Wilmot, Earl of Rochester*, ed. Harold Love. *London Review of Books*, 16 September 1999, pp. 9–11.
Greer, Germaine. *John Wilmot, Earl of Rochester*. Devon: Northcote House Publishers, 2000.
Griffin, Dustin H. *Satires Against Man: The Poems of Rochester*. Berkeley: University of California Press, 1973.
Hamilton, Count Anthony. *Memoirs of the Count De Gramont*, two volumes. London: Vizetelly & Co., 1889.
Hammond, Brean and Paulina Kewes. 'A Satyre Against Reason and Mankind from Page to Stage', in *That Second Bottle: Essays on John Wilmot, Earl of Rochester*, ed. Nicholas Fisher. Manchester: Manchester University Press, 2000, pp. 133–52.
Hammond, Paul, ed. *John Wilmot, Earl of Rochester: Selected Poems*. The School of English, University of Leeds, 1982.
Hammond, Paul, 'Two Echoes of Rochester's *A Satire against Reason and Mankind* in Dryden', *Notes & Queries*, 33 (1988), p. 171.
Hammond, Paul, 'The King's Two Bodies: Representations of Charles II', in *Culture, Politics, and Society in Britain, 1660–1800*, eds Jeremy Black and Jeremy Gregory. Manchester: Manchester University Press, 1991, pp. 13–48.
Hammond, Paul, 'Rochester's Homoeroticism', in *That Second Bottle: Essays on John Wilmot Earl of Rochester*, ed. Nicholas Fisher. Manchester and New York: Manchester University Press, 2000, pp. 47–62.
Hammond, Paul, *The Making of Restoration Poetry*. Cambridge: D.S. Brewer, 2006.
Hampton, Simon. 'Rochester, *The Man of Mode* and Mrs. Barry', in *That Second Bottle: Essays on John Wilmot, Earl of Rochester*, ed. Nicholas Fisher. Manchester and New York: Manchester University Press, 2000, pp. 165–78.
Hawkins, Harriet. *Likeness of Truth in Elizabethan and Restoration Drama*. Oxford: Clarendon Press, 1972.
Hayward, John, ed. *Collected Works of John Wilmot, Earl of Rochester*. London: Nonesuch Press, 1926.
Hill, Christopher. *The Collected Essays of Christopher Hill*, 1. Amherst, MA: University of Massachusetts Press, 1985.
Hill, Christopher. *Puritanism and Revolution: Studies in Interpretation of the English Revolution of the 17th Century*. London: Martin Secker & Warburg, 1958; rpt. London: Panther Books, 1965.
Hill, Christopher. *The World Turned Upside Down: Radical Ideas During the English Revolution*. London: Maurice Temple Smith, 1972; rpt. Harmondsworth: Penguin Books, 1976.
Hobbes, Thomas. *Leviathan*. London: Andrew Crooke, 1651.

Holland, Norman N. *The First Modern Comedies*. Cambridge, MA: Harvard University Press, 1959.

Hook, Lucyle. 'The Publication Date of Rochester's *Valentinian*', *Huntington Library Quarterly*, 19 (1956), pp. 401–7.

Hume, Robert D. *The Rakish Stage: Studies in English Drama, 1660–1800*. Carbondale, IL: Southern Illinois University Press, 1983.

Hume, Robert D. Rev. of *The Letters of John Wilmot Earl of Rochester*, ed. Jeremy Treglown. Eighteenth Century Studies (Spring, 1983), pp. 353–56.

Johnson, James William. 'Lord Rochester and the Tradition of Cyrenaic Hedonism, 1670–1790', *Studies on Voltaire and the Eighteenth Century*, 153 (1976), pp. 151–67.

Johnson, James William. 'Did Lord Rochester Write *Sodom*?' *The Papers of the Bibliographical Society of America*, 81, 2 (1987), pp. 119–53.

Johnson, James William. *A Very Profane Wit: The Life of John Wilmot, Earl of Rochester*. Rochester, NY: University of Rochester Press, 2004.

Johnson, Jos. A. Jr '"An Allusion to Horace": The Poetics of John Wilmot, Earl of Rochester', *The Durham University Journal*, 66, 1 (n.s. 35.1) (December 1973), pp. 52–59.

Johnson, Samuel. *The Lives of the Poets*, ed. John H. Middendorf. New Haven, CT: Yale University Press, 2010, vol. 21.

Johnson, Samuel. *A Dictionary of the English Language*. London: W. Strahan, 1755; facsimile edition, New York: Arno Press, 1979.

La Rochefoucauld, Francois, Duc de. *Oeuvres complètes*. Paris: Éditions Gallimard, 1964.

Leavis, F.R. *Revaluation: Tradition & Development in English Poetry*. New York: George W. Stewart, 1947.

Lee, Nathaniel. *The Tragedy of Nero*. London: Printed by T.R. and N.T., 1675.

Lee, Nathaniel. *The Works of Nathaniel Lee*, ed. Thomas B. Stroup and Arthur L. Cooke. New Brunswick, NJ: Scarecrow Press, 1955.

Lee, Sidney. 'John Wilmot', *Dictionary of National Biography*, eds Sir Leslie Stephen and Sir Sidney Lee. London: Oxford University Press, 1917, 21, pp. 534–38.

Lockwood, Tom. 'Rochester and Rhyme', in *Lord Rochester in the Restoration World*, eds Matthew C. Augustine and Steven N. Zwicker. Cambridge: University Press, 2015, pp. 270–90.

Lord, George deF., ed. *Poems on Affairs of State: Augustan Satirical Verse, 1660–1714*. New Haven, CT: Yale University Press, 1963, vol. 1.

Love, Harold. 'Rochester and the Traditions of Satire', *Restoration Literature: Critical Approaches*. London: Methuen & Co., 1972, pp. 145–75.

Love, Harold. 'Scribal Publication in Seventeenth-Century England', *Transactions of the Cambridge Bibliographical Society*, 9 pt. 2 (1987), pp. 130–54.

Love, Harold. 'Scribal Texts and Literary Communities: The Rochester Circle and Osborn b. 105', *Studies in Bibliography*, 42, ed. Fredson Bowers. Charlottesville, VA: University Press of Virginia, 1989, pp. 219–35.

Love, Harold. 'But Did Rochester *Really* Write "*Sodom*"?' *The Papers of the Bibliographical Society of America*, 87 (1993), pp. 319–36.

Love, Harold. 'The Scribal Transmission of Rochester's Songs', *Bibliographical Society of Australia and New Zealand Bulletin*, 20 (1996), pp. 161–80.

Love, Harold. ed. *The Complete Works of John Wilmot Earl of Rochester*. Oxford: Oxford University Press, 1999.

Love, Harold. 'The Rapes of Lucina', in *Print, Manuscript & Performance: the Changing Relations of Media in Early Modern England*, eds Arthur F. Marotti and Michael D. Bristol. Columbus, OH: Ohio State University Press, 2000, pp. 200–14.
Love, Harold. 'Was Lucina Betrayed at Whitehall?' in *That Second Bottle: Essays on John Wilmot, Earl of Rochester*, ed. Nicholas Fisher. Manchester: Manchester University Press, 2000, pp. 179–90.
Love, Harold. *English Clandestine Satire, 1660–1702*. Oxford University Press, 2004.
Love, Harold. Rev. *A Profane Wit: The Life of John Wilmot, Earl of Rochester*, by James William Johnson. *Seventeenth-Century News*, 63 (2005), pp. 137–41.
Lovejoy, Arthur O. *Essays In The History Of Ideas*. Baltimore, MD: The Johns Hopkins Press, 1948.
Lucretius. *On Nature*, trans. Russel M. Geer. New York: Bobbs-Merrill, 1965.
Lyons, Paddy, ed. *Rochester: Complete Poems and Plays*. London: J.M. Dent, 1993.
Mannheimer, Katherine. 'Poetic Style and the Mind-Body Problem: Sound and Sense, Flesh and Spirit in the Work of John Wilmot, Second Earl of Rochester', *English Literary History*, 83, 2 (Summer 2016), pp. 489–516.
McFadden, George. *Dryden The Public Writer*. Princeton, NJ: Princeton University Press,1978.
McFadden, George. 'Political Satire in *The Rehearsal*', *Yearbook of English Studies*, 4 (1974), pp. 120–28.
McKeon, Michael. *The Origins of the English Novel, 1600–1740*. Baltimore, MD: Johns Hopkins University Press, 1987.
McKeon, Michael. *Politics and Poetry in Restoration England*. Cambridge, MA: Harvard University Press, 1975.
Miller, Henry Knight. 'The Paradoxical Encomium: With Special Reference to its Vogue in England, 1600–1800', *Modern Philology*, 53 (1956), pp. 145–78.
Moehlmann, John Frederick. *A Concordance To The Complete Poems of John Wilmot, Earl of Rochester*. Ann Arbor, MI: University Microfilms International, 1977.
Munns, Jessica. 'Images of Monarchy of the Restoration Stage', *A Companion to Restoration Drama*. London: Blackwell, 2001, pp. 109–25.
Murdock, Kenneth B. *The Sun at Noon: Three Biographical Sketches*. New York: Macmillan, 1939.
Nace, Nicholas. 'Some New Light on *Sodom*', *The Book Collector*, 63 (2014), pp. 557–67.
Nace, Nicholas. 'The Author of *Sodom* Among the Smithfield Muses', *The Review of English Studies*, New Series, 68, 284 (2016), pp. 296–321.
Nicoll, Allardyce. 'Dryden, Howard, and Rochester', *London Times Literary Supplement*, 13 January 1921, p. 27.
Ogg, David. *England in the Reign of Charles II*. Oxford: Oxford University Press, 1934; rpt. Oxford University Press, 1967.
O'Neill, John H. 'Rochester's "Imperfect Enjoyment": "The True Veine of Satyre" in Sexual Poetry', *Tennessee Studies in Literature* 25 (1980); rpt. in *John Wilmot, Earl of Rochester: Critical Essays*, ed. David M. Vieth. New York: Garland Publishing, 1988, p. 135.
Otway, Thomas. *Alcibiades*. London: 1675.

Otway, Thomas. *Titus and Berenice with the Cheats of Scapin*. London: Printed for Richard Tonson, 1677.

Parsons, Robert. *A Sermon Preached At the Funeral of the Rt Honorable John Earl of Rochester, Who died at Woodstock-Park, July 26. 1680, and was buried at Spilsbury in Oxford-shire, Aug. 9*. Oxford: Printed at the Theater for *Richard Davis* and *Tho: Bowman*. 1680.

Pasch, Thomas K. 'Concentricity, Christian Myth, and the Self-Incriminating Narrator in Rochester's *A Ramble in St. James's Park*', *Essays in Literature* (Spring 1979), pp. 21–28; rpt. in *John Wilmot, Earl of Rochester: Critical Essays*, ed. David M. Vieth. New York: Garland Publishing, 1988, pp. 149–61.

Pepys, Samuel. *The Diary of Samuel Pepys*, eds Robert Latham and William Matthews. Berkeley, CA: University of California Press, 1979.

Pinto, Vivian de Sola. *Rochester: Portrait of a Restoration Poet*. London: The Bodley Head, 1935; rpt. as *Enthusiast in Wit*. Lincoln, NE: University of Nebraska Press, 1962.

Pinto, Vivian de Sola. 'Rochester, Dryden, and the Duchess of Portsmouth', *Review of English Studies*, 16 (1940), pp. 177–78.

Pinto, Vivian de Sola. 'John Wilmot, Earl of Rochester, and the Right Veine of Satire', *Essays and Studies* (The English Association) new ser. 6 (1953), pp. 56–70; rpt. *Seventeenth-Century English Poetry: Modern Essays in Criticism*, ed. William R. Keast. New York: Oxford University Press, 1962, pp. 359–74.

Pinto, Vivian de Sola. ed. *Poems By John Wilmot Earl of Rochester*. London: Routledge & Kegan Paul, 1953.

Pinto, Vivian de Sola. *Restoration Carnival*. London: The Folio Society, 1954.

Pinto, Vivian de Sola. 'Rochester and Dryden', *Renaissance and Modern Studies*, 5 (1961), pp. 29–48.

Pinto, Vivian de Sola. ed. *The Famous Pathologist or The Noble Mountebank by Thomas Alcock and John Wilmot, Earl of Rochester*. Nottingham University Miscellany 1. Nottingham: Sisson and Parker for the University of Nottingham, 1961.

Popkin, Richard H. *The History of Scepticism from Erasmus to Descartes*. Netherlands: Van Gorcum & Company, 1960.

Porter, Roy. 'Mixed Feelings: The Enlightenment and Sexuality in Eighteenth-century Britain', in *Sexuality in Eighteenth-century Britain*, ed. Paul Gabriel Boucé. Manchester: Manchester University Press, 1982, pp. 1–27.

Porter, Roy. *English Society in the Eighteenth Century*. Harmondsworth: Penguin Books, 1982; rpt. 1983.

Prinz, Johannes. *John Wilmot Earl of Rochester: His Life and Writings*. Leipzig: Mayer & Muller, 1927.

Pritchard, R.E. 'Rochester's "Postboy" and Buckingham', *Notes & Queries*, 257 of the continuous series [New Series, 59], 2 (June 2012), pp. 185–86.

Righter, Anne. 'William Wycherley', in *Restoration Theatre*, eds John Russell Brown and Bernard Harris. London: Edward Arnold, 1965; paperback 1973, pp. 71–91.

Righter, Anne. 'John Wilmot, Earl of Rochester', *Proceedings of the British Academy*, 13 (1967), pp. 47–69.

Robinson, Ken. 'John Wilmot, Earl of Rochester: An Author in Search of a Character', in *The Art of Literary Biography*, ed. John Batchelor. Oxford: Oxford University Press, 1995, pp. 101–14.

Römer, L.S.A.M. von. *Rochester's Sodom*. Paris: H. Welter, 1904.
Sackville, Charles. *The Poems of Charles Sackville, Sixth Earl of Dorset*, ed. Brice Harris. New York: Garland, 1979.
Sanchez, Melissa E. 'Libertinism and Romance in Rochester's Poetry', *Eighteenth-Century Studies*, 38, 3 (Spring 2005), pp. 441–59.
Sanchez, Melissa E. 'Sex and Sovereignty in Rochester's Writing', in *Lord Rochester in the Restoration World*, eds Mathew C. Augustine and Steven N. Zwicker, Cambridge University Press, 2015, pp. 184–206.
Selden, Raman. *English Verse Satire 1590–1765*. London: George Allen & Unwin, 1978.
Settle, Elkanah. *Cambyses King of Persia*. London: Printed for *William Cademan*, 1671.
Settle, Elkanah. *The Empress of Morocco*. London: Printed for *William Cademan*, 1673.
Settle, Elkanah. *The Conquest of China*. London: Printed for *William Cademan*, 1675.
Shadwell, Thomas. *The Royal Shepherdess*. London: Printed for *Henry Herringman*, 1669.
Shadwell, Thomas. *Epsom Wells*. London: Printed by J.M., 1673.
Sheffield, John, Earl of Mulgrave. *An Essay Upon Poetry*. London: Printed for. *Joseph. Hindmarsh*, 1682.
Sheffield, John, Earl of Mulgrave. *The Works of John Sheffield, Earl of Mulgrave, Marquis of Normandy, and Duke of Buckingham*. London: 1723.
Sheffield, John, Earl of Mulgrave. *The works of John Sheffield, earl of Mulgrave, marquis of Normandy, and duke of Buckingham*. London: Printed for J.B., 1729, 2 vols.
Sitter, John E. 'Rochester's Reader and the Problem of Satiric Audience', *Papers on Language and Literature*, 12 (Summer 1976), pp. 285–98.
Sprague, Arthur Colby. *Beaumont and Fletcher on the Restoration Stage*. New York: 1926; rpt. New York: B. Blom, 1975.
Staves, Susan. *Players' Scepters: Fictions of Authority in the Restoration*. Lincoln, NE: University of Nebraska Press, 1979.
Stone, Lawrence. *The Crisis of the Aristocracy*. Abridged Edition. Oxford: Oxford University Press, 1967.
Summers, Montague. *The Playhouse of Pepys*. London: Kegan Paul, 1935.
Summers, Montague. Letter in *London Times Literary Supplement*, 27 January 1921, p. 60.
Taylor, David Francis. 'Rochester, the Theatre and Restoration Theatricality', in *Lord Rochester in the Restoration World*, eds Matthew C. Augustine and Steven N. Zwicker. Cambridge University Press, 2015, pp. 121–40.
Thormählen, Marianne. *Rochester: The Poems in Context*. Cambridge University Press, 1993.
Thormählen, Marianne. 'Dissolver of Reason: Rochester and the Nature of Love', in *That Second Bottle: Essays on John Wilmot, Earl of Rochester*, ed. Nicholas Fisher. Manchester: Manchester University Press, 2000, pp. 21–33.
Tilmouth, Christopher. *Passion's Triumph over Reason: A History of the Moral Imagination from Spenser to Rochester*. Oxford: Oxford University Press, 2007; paperback 2010.

Tilmouth, Christopher. 'John Wilmot, Second Earl of Rochester', 'Introduction', *Oxford Bibliographies*. www.oxfordbibliographies.com.
Tilmouth, Christopher. 'Rochester and the play of values', in *Lord Rochester in the Restoration World*, eds Matthew C. Augustine and Steven N. Zwicker. Cambridge University Press, 2015, pp. 141–61.
Treglown, Jeremy. 'The Satirical Inversion of Some English Sources in Rochester's Poetry', *Review of English Studies*, n.s. 24 (February 1973), pp. 42–48.
Treglown, Jeremy. 'Rochester and Davenant', *Notes and Queries*, 221 (December 1976), pp. 554–59.
Treglown, Jeremy. 'The Date of Rochester's "Scaen"', *Review of English Studies*, n.s. 30 (1979), pp. 434–36.
Treglown, Jeremy. ed. *The Letters of John Wilmot Earl of Rochester*. Chicago: University of Chicago Press, 1980.
Treglown, Jeremy. ed. *Spirit of Wit: Reconsiderations of Rochester*. Oxford: Basil Blackwell, 1982.
Treglown, Jeremy. '"He knew my style, he swore"', in *Spirit of Wit: Reconsiderations of Rochester*, ed. Jeremy Treglown. Hamden, CT: Archon Books, 1982, pp. 75–91.
Turner, James G. 'The Properties of Libertinism', in *'Tis Nature's Fault: Unauthorized Sexuality during the Enlightenment*, ed. Robert Parks Maccubbin. Cambridge University Press, 1987, pp. 75–87.
Underwood, Dale. *Etherege and the Seventeenth-Century Comedy of Manners*. New Haven, CT: Yale University Press, 1957; rpt. Archon Books, 1969.
Vieth, David M. 'A Textural Paradox: Rochester's "To a Lady in a Letter"', *The Papers of the Bibliographical Society of America*, 54 (1960), pp. 147–62.
Vieth, David M. *Attribution in Restoration Poetry: A Study of Rochester's "Poems" of 1680*. Yale Studies in English 153. New Haven, CT: Yale University Press, 1963.
Vieth, David M. ed. *The Complete Poems of John Wilmot, Earl of Rochester*. New Haven, CT: Yale University Press, 1968.
Vieth, David M. 'Toward an Anti-Aristotelian Poetic: Rochester's *Satyr Against Mankind* and *Artemisia to Chloe*, with Notes on Swift's *Tale of a Tub* and *Gulliver's Travels*', *Language and Style*, 5 (1972), pp. 123–45.
Vieth, David M. 'Sir Charles Sedley and the Ballers Oath', *The Scriblerian*, 12, 1 (Autumn, 1979), pp. 47–49.
Vieth, David M. '"Pleased with the Contradiction and the Sin": The Perverse Artistry of Rochester's Lyrics', *Tennessee Studies in Literature*, 25 (1980), pp. 35–56.
Vieth, David M. *Rochester Studies, 1925–1982: An Annotated Bibliography*. New York: Garland Publishing, 1984.
Vieth, David M. and Dustin Griffin. *Rochester and Court Poetry*. Los Angeles, CA: William Andrews Clark Memorial Library, 1988.
Villiers, George, Second Duke of Buckingham, *Plays, Poems, and Miscellaneous Writings associated with George Villiers, Second Duke of Buckingham*, vol. 1, eds Robert D. Hume and Harold Love. Oxford: Oxford University Press, 2007.
Walker, Keith, ed. *The Compete Poems of John Wilmot Earl of Rochester*. Oxford: Basil Blackwell, 1984.
Walker, Keith, '"Not the Worst part of my wretched life": Three New Letters by Rochester, and How to Read Them', *English Manuscript Studies 1100–1700*,

8, *Seventeenth-Century Poetry, Music and Drama*, ed. Peter Beal. London: The British Library, 2000, pp. 293–99.

Walker, Keith, and Fisher, Nicholas, eds *John Wilmot, Earl of Rochester: The Poems and Lucina's Rape*. Oxford: Wiley-Blackwell, 2010.

Waller, Edmund. *The Poems of Edmund Waller*, ed. G. Thorn Drury. Scribner's, 1893; rpt. New York: Greenwood Press, 1968.

Weber, Harold. *The Restoration Rake-Hero*. Madison, WI: University of Wisconsin Press, 1986.

Webster, Jeremy W. *Performing Libertinism in Charles II's Court: Politics, Drama, and Sexuality*. New York: Palgrave Macmillan, 2005.

Weil, Rachel. 'Sometimes a Scepter is Only a Scepter', in *The Invention of Pornography: Obscenity and the Origins of Modernity, 1500–1800*, ed. Lynn Hunt. New York: Zone Books, 1993, pp. 125–53.

Weinbrot, Howard D. 'The "Allusion to Horace": Rochester's Imitative Mode', *Studies in Philology*, 69 (July 1972), pp. 348–68.

Weinbrot, Howard D. 'The Swelling Volume: The Apocalyptic Satire of Rochester's *Letter from Artemisia in the Town to Chloe in the Country*', *Studies in the Literary Imagination*, 5 (October 1972), pp. 19–38.

Welleck, René and Austin Warren. *Theory of Literature*. 1942; rpt. New York: Harcourt, Brace & World, 1956.

Whibley, Charles. 'The Court Poets', in *The Cambridge History of English Literature*, 8: *The Age of Dryden*. New York: G.P. Putnam's Sons and Cambridge University Press, 1912, pp. 224–52.

Wilcoxon, Reba. 'Rochester's Philosophical Premises: A Case for Consistency', *Eighteenth Century Studies*, 8 (Winter 1974–75), pp. 183–201.

Wilcoxon, Reba. 'The Rhetoric of Sex in Rochester's Burlesque', *Papers on Language and Literature*, 12 (Summer 1976), pp. 273–84.

Williamson, George. *The Proper Wit of Poetry*. Chicago: University of Chicago Press, 1961.

Wilmot, John, Earl of Rochester. *Valentinian: A Tragedy. As 'tis Alter'd by the late Earl of Rochester*. London: 1685.

Wilson, John Harold. 'Rochester's *Valentinian* and Heroic Sentiment', *English Literary History*, 4 (1937), pp. 265–73.

Wilson, John Harold. 'The Dating of Rochester's "Scaen"', *Review of English Studies*, 13 (1937), pp. 455–58.

Wilson, John Harold. 'Satiric Elements in Rochester's *Valentinian*', *Philological Quarterly*, 16 (1937), pp. 41–48.

Wilson, John Harold. ed. *The Rochester-Savile Letters 1671–1680*. Columbus, OH: Ohio State. University Press, 1941.

Wilson, John Harold. *The Court Wits of the Restoration*. Princeton, NJ: Princeton University Press, 1948.

Wilson, John Harold. *Court Satires of the Restoration*. Columbus, OH: Ohio State University Press, 1976.

Winn, James Anderson. *John Dryden and His World*. New Haven, CT: Yale University Press, 1987.

Zwicker, Steven N. 'Lord Rochester: A Life in Gossip', in *Lord Rochester in the Restoration World*, eds Matthew C. Augustine and Steven N. Zwicker. Cambridge University Press, 2015, pp. 79–98.

Index

Note: literary works can be found under authors' names. The note number refers to the page where the actual note occurs.

Adlard, John 73n.34, 235–36
Alsop, D.K. 39
Auerbach, Erich 156n.25
Augustine, Matthew C. 154n.13, 178n.10
Augustine, Saint 62

Baine, Rodney M. 235–36
Barrow, Isaac 43
Barry, Elizabeth 121, 166, 190–91, 194–99, 226
Behn, Aphra 90
Blount, Charles 186
Booth, Wayne 12
Boyle, Roger, 1st Earl of Orrery 88
Brooks, David 39
Buckingham, George Villiers, 2nd Duke of 83, 164
  The Chances 158
  The Rehearsal 85, 87, 89, 113, 114, 118
Bunyan, John 228
Burke, Kenneth 35, 43, 56, 56, 67, 170, 174, 194
Burnet, Gilbert 19, 51, 52, 54, 55, 56, 68, 78, 102, 107, 110, 111, 149, 168, 170–71, 212–19 *passim*, 225, 229–30

Canfield, J. Douglas 70n.11
Catherine of Braganza 80, 81, 82
Catholicism and Catholics 83, 84, 94, 99, 101

Catullus 58, 60
Charles II 49, 52, 55, 80, 83, 93, 95, 100, 163, 169
Chernaik, Warren 57, 73n.33, 187, 239
Chiffinch, William 82, 83
Christian and Christianity 36, 52, 60, 94, 97, 133, 143–46, 184, 186–89, 221, 223–25, 228–30
Churchill, John (future Duke of Marlborough) 83, 98
Clarendon, Edward Hyde, Earl of 52
Cleveland, Barbara (née Villiers) Palmer, Countess of Castlemaine, Duchess of 82, 83, 98, 99, 101
Collie, Rosalie 7, 145–47, 224, 229
Cowley, Abraham
  Davideis 224
Crowne, John
  Calisto 161
  The History of Charles the Eighth of France 113

Diderot, Denis 148
Dorrell, Sir Francis 118
Dryden, John 23–35 *passim*, 86, 87, 88, 89, 118, 119, 122–24, 137, 158–62, 175
  All for Love 160, 175
  The Assignation 159
  Aureng-Zebe 23–27 *passim*

The Conquest of Granada 86, 87, 158
The Indian Emperour 113, 158
Marriage à La Mode 23, 137, 159
A Scaen of Sir Robert Hoard's Play 158
Secret Love 85
Tryannick Love 86, 87, 90, 91

Edwards, A.S.G. 236–37
Ehrenpreis, Irving 37
Elias, Richard 78, 80
Ellenzweig, Sarah 70n.18, 188, 231n.14
Ellis, Frank 39, 187, 234n.47, 237
Empson, William 149, 229
Epicurean 36, 133
Etherege, George 113, 118
   The Man of Mode 147

Fabricant, Carole 72n.30
Fane, Sir Francis
   Love in the Dark 161
Farley-Hills, David 38
Fishbourne, Christopher 235
Fisher, Nicholas 39, 43, 105n.35, 134, 179n.15, 180n.19, 188, 200, 231n.15, 232n.22, 242
Fletcher, John 158–63
   The Island Princess 86
Freud, Sigmund 227

Gertz, Clifford 8
Gildon, Charles 235
Gramont, Philibert, comte de 118
Greene, Graham 46n.17, 186
Greer, Germaine 57, 76, 104n.31, 166, 187–88, 240
Griffin, Dustin 8–15 *passim*, 34–38 *passim*, 57, 60, 125, 174, 186, 200, 235
Gwyn, Nell 90, 91, 101, 172

Hammond, Paul 41, 103n.22, 134, 151n.4, 240
Hampton, Simon 240

Hawkins, Harriet 165
Hayward, John 76
Hill, Christopher 54, 188–89
Hobbes, Thomas 128, 130, 224
Howard, Sir Robert
   The Great Favourite, or the Duke of Lerma 158
Hume, Robert D. 77, 189

Jermyn, Henry 83, 98
Johnson, James William 35, 39, 41, 42, 46n.17, 57, 71n.22, 78, 80, 167, 237–38
Johnson, Samuel 202

Knight, Mary 98, 99

La Rochefoucauld, Francois, Duc de 148–49
Leavis, F.R. 199
Lee, Nathaniel
   Nero 161
Lee, Sidney 76
Livy 164
Lockwood, Tom 122
Lord, George deF. 38
Louis XIV 80, 101
Love, Harold 39, 42, 43, 47n.46, 57, 76, 77, 78, 80, 81, 103n.7, 154n.8, 164, 166–67, 179n.15, 180n.19, 237–38
Lucretius 23, 25, 124, 214
Lyons, Paddy 41, 81, 187, 237

Mannheimer, Katherine 106n.41
Mazarin, Hortense Mancini, Duchess of 101
McKeon, Michael 54
Monmouth, James Scott, Duke of 83, 86
Mulgrave, John Sheffield, Earl of 10, 17, 82, 95, 119, 124, 126
   'An essay on satyr' 20, 29, 30
   '*An Essay Upon Poetry*' 21
   Memoirs 19, 22, 29
   'Ode to Brutus' 22
Murdock, Kenneth B. 186

Nace, Nicolas 77, 78, 236, 242
Otway, Thomas
   Titus and Berenice 161
   Don Carlos 161
Ovid 56, 213

Parker, Samuel 118
Parsons, Robert 68, 225
Pasch, Thomas K. 71n.28
Pepys, Samuel 55, 93, 104n.34
Pierce, Dr Thomas 189, 230
Pinto, Vivian de Sola 10, 76, 157, 173, 186, 200, 235
Pope, Alexander 109
Porter, Roy 55
Portsmouth, Louise de Kéroualle, Duchess of 82, 101, 124, 192–94, 197–99
Prinz, Johannes 76, 102n.2
Pritchard, R.E. 234n.45

Righter, Anne 186
Robinson, Ken 69n.1, 238–39
Rochester, Anne, Dowager Countess of 54, 175n.1, 189–90
Rochester, Charles, 3rd Earl of 53
Rochester, Elizabeth (née Malet), Countess of 52, 168–69, 174, 190–92, 194–99, 201–03, 225–26
Rochester, Henry Wilmot, 1st Earl of 49, 100
Rochester, John Wilmot, 2nd Earl of
   letters 51, 53, 122–24, 149, 189–99
   plays
      Lucina's Rape Or The Tragedy of Vallentinian 100, 157–75 *passim*, 240
      Scaene 1st. Mr. Daynty's chamber 118
      Sodom 19, 76–101 *passim*, 235–42 *passim*
   poems
      'Absent from thee I languish still' 146, 210, 223
      'The advice' 204
      'An Age in her Embraces pas'd' 208
      'An Allusion to Horace' 13, 119–25 *passim*, 163
      'Artemiza to Chloe' 92, 133–47 *passim*, 221
      'As *Chloris* full of harmless thought' 205
      'Could I but make my wishes insolent' 221
      'A Dialogue between Strephon and Daphne' 207
      '*Dialogue L:R.*' 101
      'The Disabled Debauchee' 147–50
      'Epilogue to *Circe*' 68
      'Epilogue to *Love in the Dark*' 125
      'An Epistolary Essay' 10–17 *passim*, 23, 26, 31–34 *passim*, 36
      '*Faire Cloris* in a Pigsty lay' 206
      'The Fall' 132, 146, 207, 223
      'How perfect Cloris, and how free' 204
      'The Imperfect Enjoyment' 73n.34
      'Impromptu on Charles II' 102
      'Impromptu on court personages' 102
      'In the Isle of Brittain' 100
      'Leave this gaudy gilded stage' 9
      'Love and Life' 13, 146, 206, 223–24
      '*Love to a Woman*' 62
      '*My Lord* All-Pride' 20, 29, 126
      'Nestor' 204
      'On *Mrs Willis*' 102
      '*On Poet Ninny*' 102, 126
      'On Rome's *Pardons*' 220
      '*On The Suppos'd Author of A late Poem in Defence of SATYR*' 125
      'The Platonick Lady' 211
      'Quoth the *Dutchess of Cleveland*, to Counsellor *Knight*' 98
      '*A Ramble in St.* James's Park' 56–69 *passim*, 76, 79, 92, 93, 95, 96, 109, 125, 126, 221
      'Rochester extempore' 226–28

'A Satyre against Reason and Mankind' 92, 126–33 *passim*, 146, 173, 220
'Senec. Troas. Act. 2. Chor.' 221
'*Signior Dildo*' 99
'Sternhold and Hopkins had such qualms' 160
'*Timon*' 13, 109–14 *passim*
'To A Lady, in A Letter' 204
'To Corinna' 204
'To His Sacred Majesty' 49
'Too longe the Wise Commons have been in debate' 96, 221
'TO *The Honourable****In the Pall-Mall*' 204, 222–23
'To the Post Boy' 149, 213, 228–29
'To this Moment a Rebell, I throw down my Arms' 204
'Tunbridge Wells' 114–19 *passim*, 220
'Upon Betty Frazer' 102
'*Upon Nothing*' 220, 224
'A very heroical epistle' 10–17 *passim*, 23, 26, 27–31 *passim*, 36
'What vain unnecessary things are men' 220
'Womans Honour' 204
'A Young Lady to her Antient Lover' 208
prose
  Alexander Bendo's brochure 16

Sanchez, Melissa E. 170n.16, 182n.29
Savile, Henry 149, 167, 169, 170–72, 191–94, 198–99, 226
Scroope, Sir Carr
  'In defence of Satyr' 150, 159
  '*Madam./*I cannot chang as others doe' 9
Sedley, Sir Charles
  Antony and Cleopatra 159
Selden, Raman 187
Settle, Elkanah 86, 88, 89, 158
  The Empress of Morocco 113

Shadwell, Thomas
  Epsom-Wells 118
  The Libertine 126
  The Royal Shepherdess 86
  Timon 159
Sprague, Arthur Colby 170
Staves, Susan 54
Stone, Lawrence 52, 54
Summers, Montague 76, 186

Taylor, David Francis 242
Thormählen, Marianne 40, 71n.28, 187, 237
Tilmouth, Christopher 40, 188, 240–42
Tregown, Jeremy 153n.5, 187, 232n.22
Turner, James G. 72n.32

Underwood, Dale 146

Vieth, David 9–16 *passim*, 35–40 *passim*, 42, 56, 94, 95, 113, 114, 126–27, 130, 133, 135, 157, 159, 161, 200, 235

Walker, Keith 39, 42, 149, 237
Waller, Edmund 60
Webster, Jeremy W. 178n.14
Weil, Rachel 103n.22, 179n.16
Weinbrot, Howard 187
Welleck, René and Austin Warren 165
Whitehall, Robert 55
Wilcoxon, Reba 186, 200
Williamson, George 187
Wilson, John Harold 14, 82, 163, 199–200, 235
Winn, James 176n.2
Wolseley, Robert 107, 157, 171

York, James Stuart, Duke of 83, 86
York, Mary of Modena, Duchess of 99, 100

Zwicker, Steven 40, 151n.4

EU authorised representative for GPSR:
Easy Access System Europe, Mustamäe tee 50,
10621 Tallinn, Estonia
gpsr.requests@easproject.com

www.ingramcontent.com/pod-product-compliance
Lightning Source LLC
Chambersburg PA
CBHW051607230426
43668CB00013B/2014